AF573699

Gothic

ART POCKET

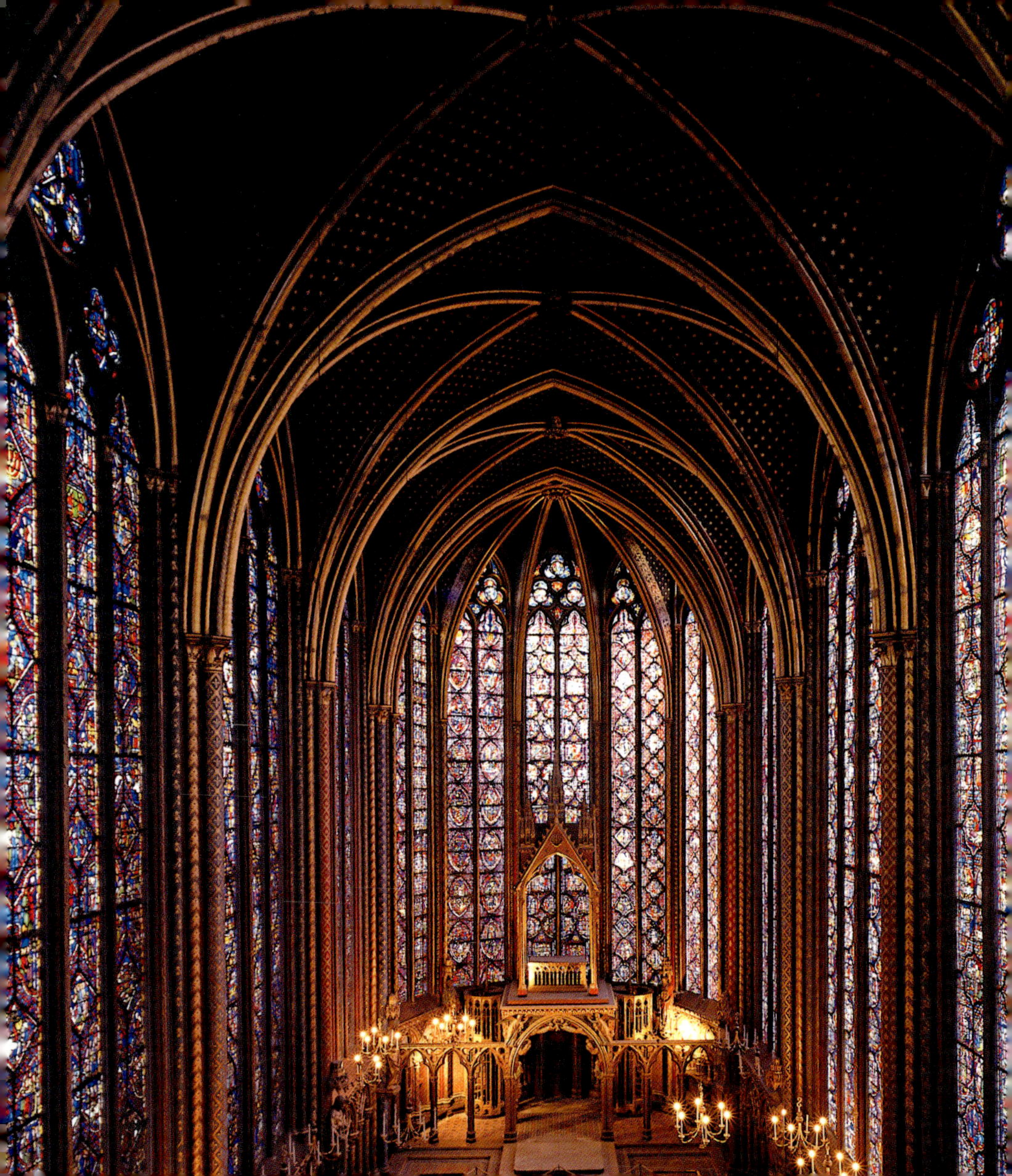

Clemens Schmidlin
Caroline Eva Gerner

Gothic

ART POCKET

h.f.ullmann

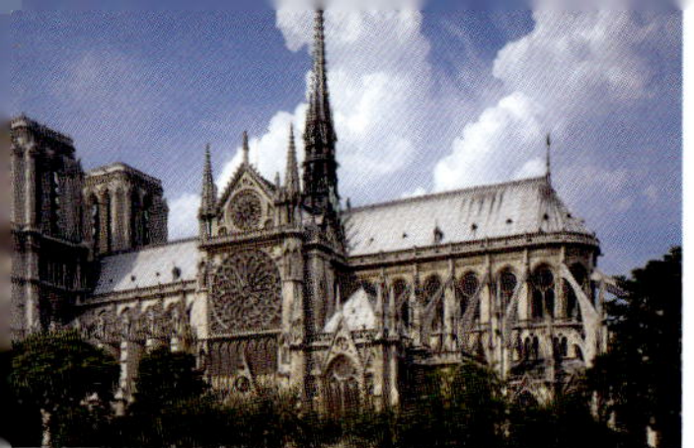
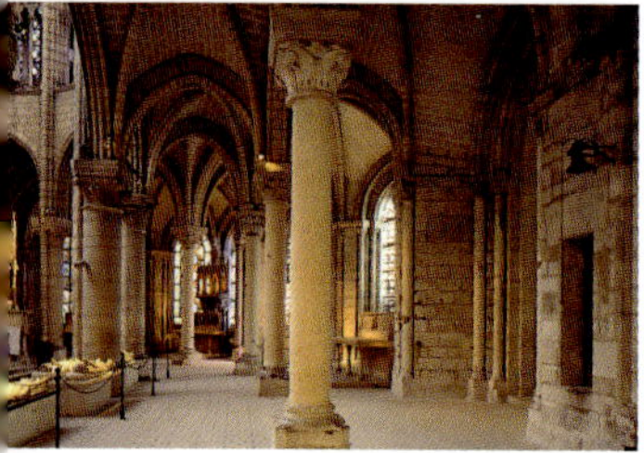
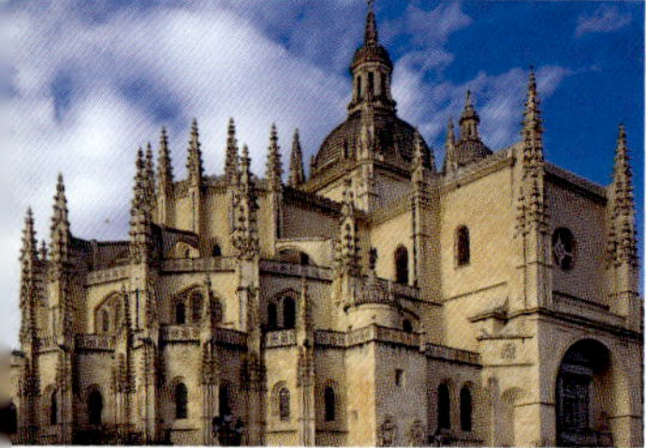
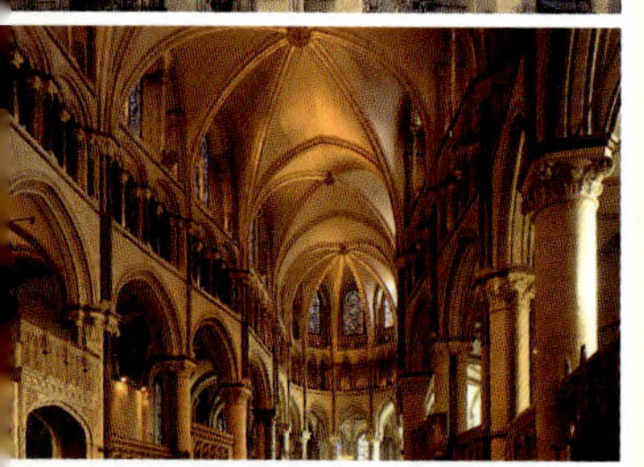
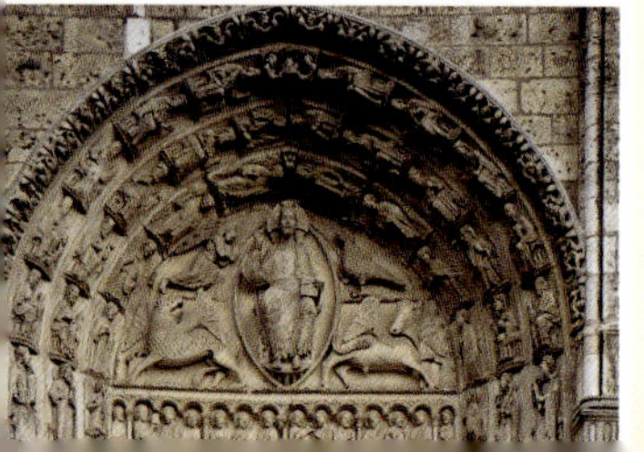

Contents

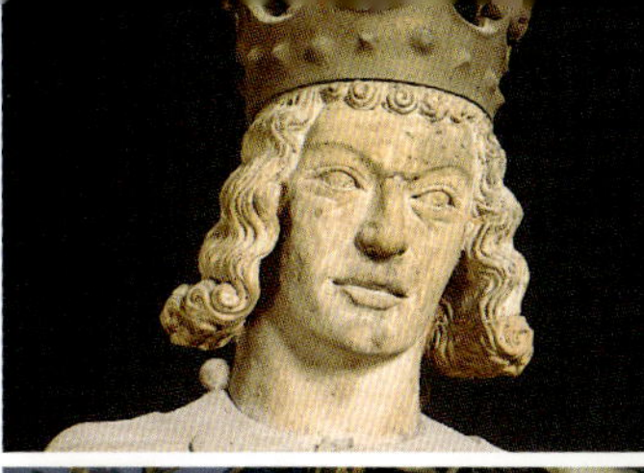

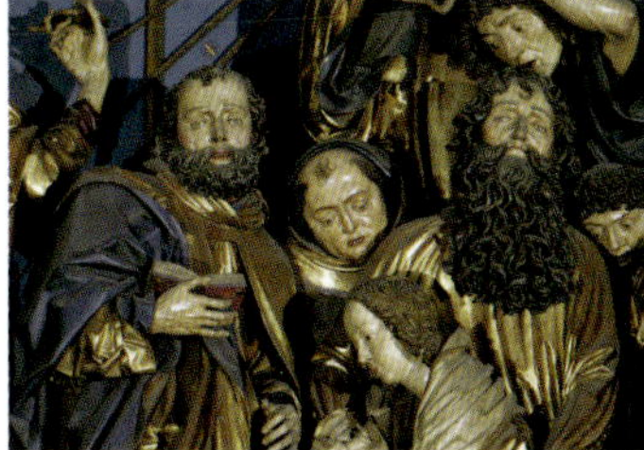

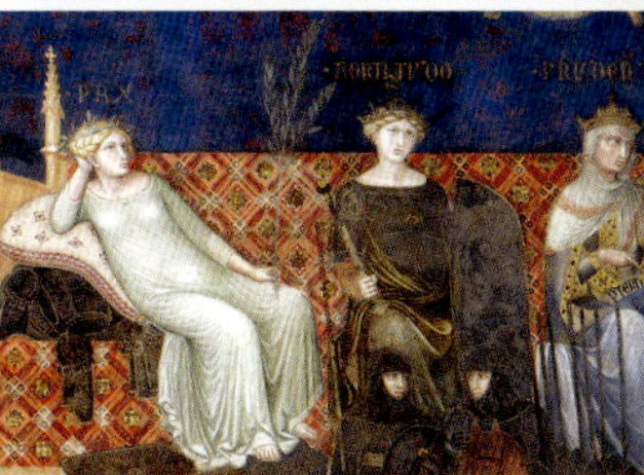

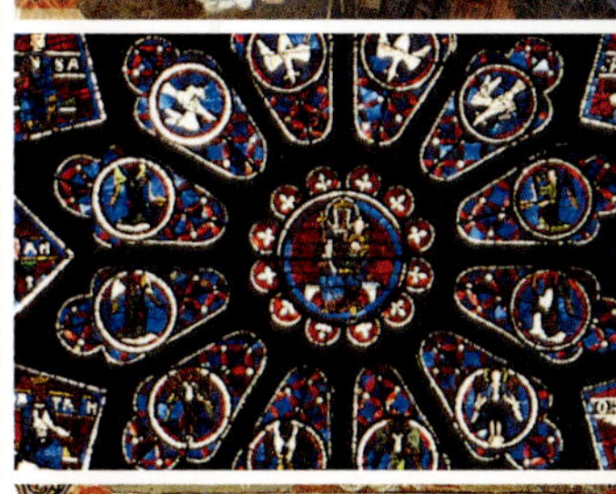

Introduction

An era that ranges from French church architecture of the mid-12th century to oil paintings of the late 15th century: Gothic. An era? While in early 15th-century Italy the Renaissance was already dawning, sculptors in some parts of northern Europe still adhered to the Romanesque style. What we define as a style is characterized by the fact that it can appear at different times in various regions, that it takes on different forms according to the medium employed, and, most importantly, that it remains a formula which later generations superimpose on history in order to categorize and thus better understand the past. What is it that the art of four centuries that is known as "Gothic" has in common?

View of Cologne
with the uncompleted cathedral, copper engraving, 1531

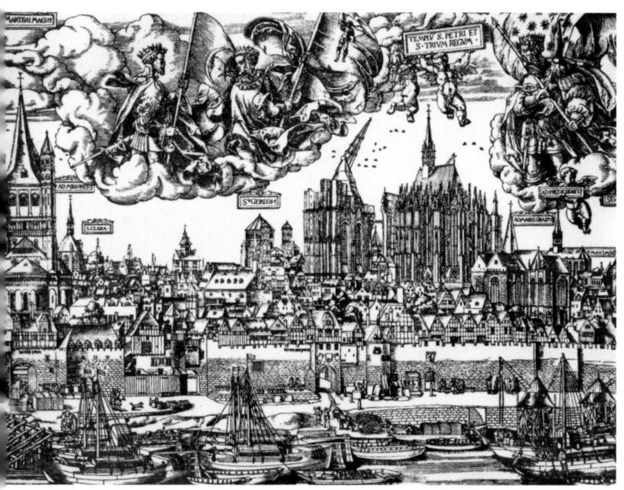

The Gothic Style

What sets Gothic art off from the style that preceded it and the one that followed? Every generation will seek its own answer and find a solution by including some works of art and excluding others. However, over the centuries from the 16th to the 21st, a set canon has evolved. In the chronological order of styles established for European art history, Gothic stands between Romanesque and Renaissance. But that doesn't mean very much.

If, however, we define the Romanesque style as the medieval, at times even fearful striving for perfection in the service of religion and the Renaissance as a phase of intellectual accumulation of knowledge inspired by a return to classical traditions of art and philosophy, then Gothic takes on a decisive role as a phase of transition. Of course, one must consider that every phase is transitional; every yesterday has once been a today. And yet, in retrospect one can define how, in which fields, for what reasons and how fast a given development has taken place. And then one realizes that many things which suddenly seemed possible in the Renaissance, this era which even at the time was already seen as exceptional and heaped with self-praise, turns out to have been prepared well in advance.

Retracing the transitional character of the Gothic era is part of the scope of this book. It is possible to show the transition by studying the works of art. Was it a radical change? Was it defined by content or by form? Who were the clients, which were the driving forces? At first glance, it seems that Gothic art with its predominantly religious topics was indebted to medieval and Byzantine tradition, merely searching for a new expressive form, a more sensual, direct, naturalistic language of images. But when taking into consideration the clients, emerging social changes such as the growing power of the burghers in the flourishing cities are also reflected in the artistic production of the time.

Certain questions concerning the conditions, the motivators of Gothic art and architecture cannot be answered by art history alone. Consider aspects such as logistic efforts, courage and humility, the willingness to face financial risks or even failure – all these are traits necessary to a community of the 12th or 13th century in order to commission a construction workshop with the erection of a cathedral of heretofore unknown dimensions.

Bernhard de Montfaucon/ Antoine Benoît,
column statues from the facade of Saint-Denis, drawing, 1729

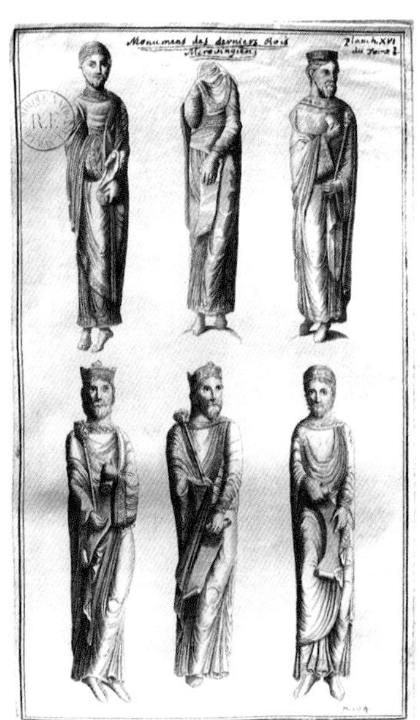

The Rediscovery of Gothic

Step by step, the beauty of Gothic art was rediscovered. For architecture, the new attention brought to Gothic style can be dated relatively exactly: In his treatise "Über die deutsche Baukunst" ("On German Architecture", 1792) the German poet Johann Wolfgang von Goethe formulated his own astonishment about the beauty of medieval architecture. With the term "German architecture," the author made use of a common alternative term for Gothic architecture. In both cases, the term denotes the assumption that this style originated in north-eastern Europe. Giorgio Vasari, the Italian architect and art critic of the 16th century, was the first to name the Goths as responsible for the non-classical works of art which he and his contemporaries considered as barbaric. Today, we know that Gothic art originated in France.

"Like an article in a dictionary, the rubric *Gothic* to me was a collection of all those synonymous misperceptions concerning things indecorous, unnatural, lacking order and beauty, heaped, jumbled and patched, which I had ever come across."

Goethe wrote: "When I first visited the Minster (of Strasbourg), my head was full of general knowledge of good taste. (…) Like an article in a dictionary, the rubric *Gothic* to me was a collection of all those synonymous misperceptions concerning things indecorous, unnatural, lacking order and beauty, heaped, jumbled and patched, which I had ever come across. (…) What unexpected emotional surprise when I suddenly stepped forward and perceived it! An all-encompassing, great impression filled my soul, which, since it consisted of a thousand single elements all in harmony with one another, I could well taste and enjoy, but could not quite realize and explain. (…) The number of times I returned, from various angles, from various distances, in all the many shades of daylight, to perceive its dignity and grandeur. It's hard for human intellect when a fellow human's work is so sublime that one can only bow, and worship."

It is due to Goethe's new view and the aesthetic reappraisal of the Middle Ages in the Romantic era that medieval architecture became increasingly popular. It led, for example, to the readoption of the large construction site of St. Peter and

Mary in **Cologne** (p. 6) in the 19th centurywith the intention of completing the cathedral according to the old surviving building plans. Gothic sculpture had already become the focus of attention in the 18th century, when it was studied amongst others by the Benedictine philologist and art historian **Bernard de Montfaucon** (p. 7). A critical appreciation of the paintings of the Middle Ages took even longer: for example, the **Uffizi in Florence** installed the Sala dei Primitivi (p. 9), a room dedicated to early Italian panel painting, only in the early 20th century. Names of artists widely renowned today such as Cimabue, Duccio and Giotto had then only just been discovered as the forerunners of the Italian art of modern times. But every generation needs to rediscover its past anew and even today there are surprises left for those who interest themselves in Gothic art and architecture.

Room II of the Uffizi Gallery in Florence
Sala dei Primitivi, photography

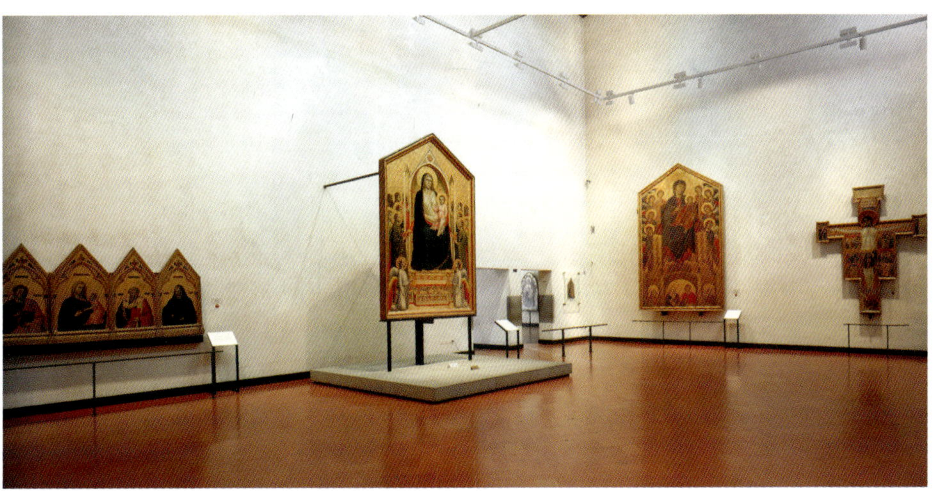

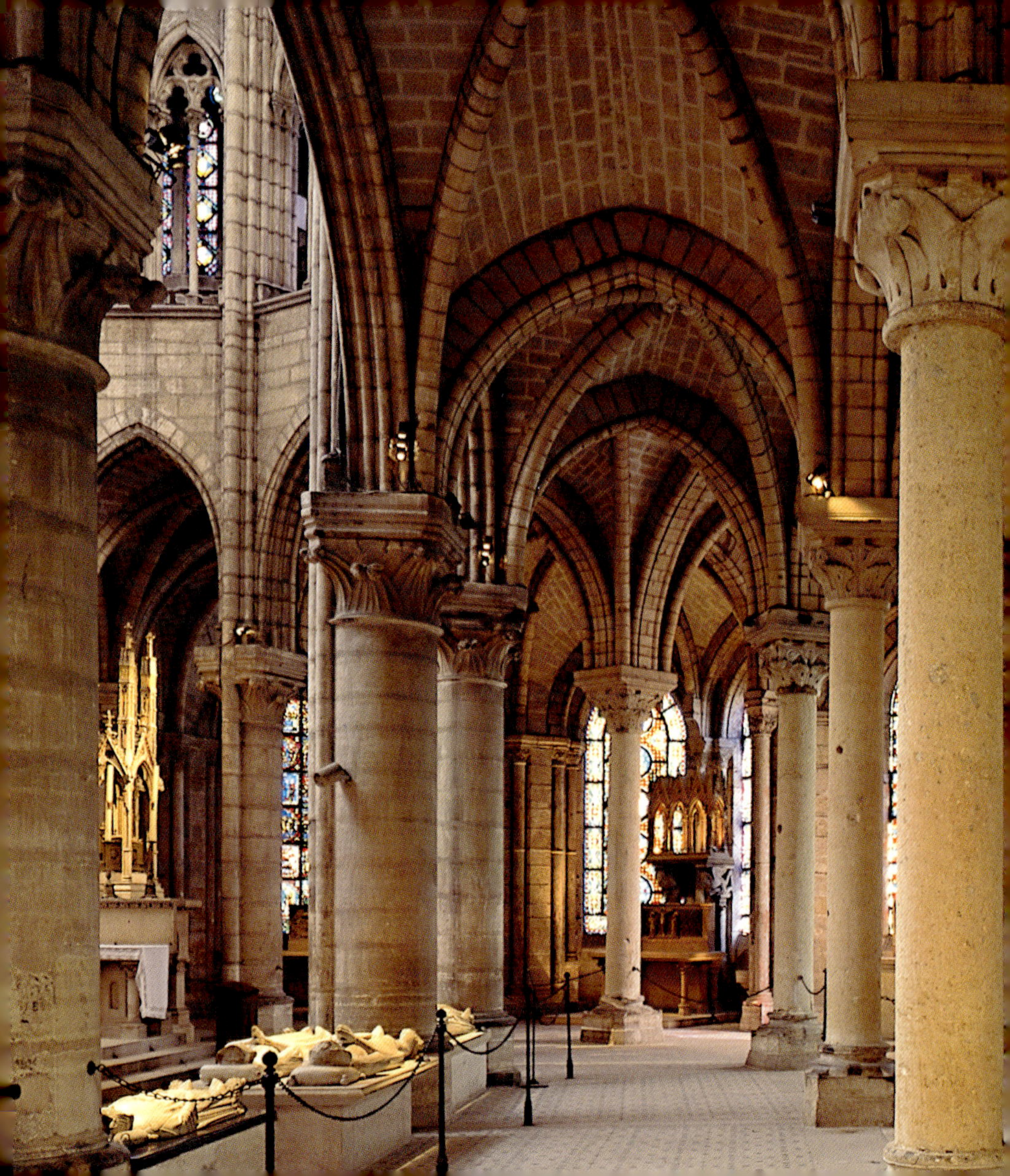

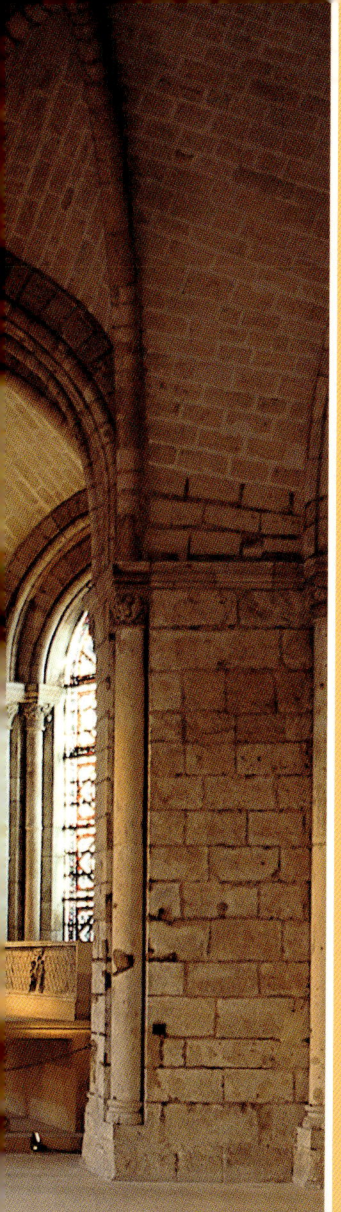

Gothic Architecture

Windows that extend almost from floor to ceiling, an airy network of supporting structures and staves, hardly any walls: this choir aisle historically stands at the beginning of a fundamental change in the appreciation of architecture. The new architectural style evolved from the desire of not just building structures but creating spaces. Walls, pillars and windows are the envelopes which make a sacral space tangible. The technical basis of this innovation is the advanced knowledge of ideal load-bearing techniques – aesthetic desires and technical skills complemented one another. Gothic churches are symbols of the pride and faith of their builders: their site, dimensions and soaring spires ensure that they can be seen from afar and understood as display. In the interiors, however, architecture steps back in favor of light and space, which impress the congregation as earthly reflections of the divine.

Saint-Denis,
former Benedictine
abbey church, choir aisle,
between 1140 and 1144

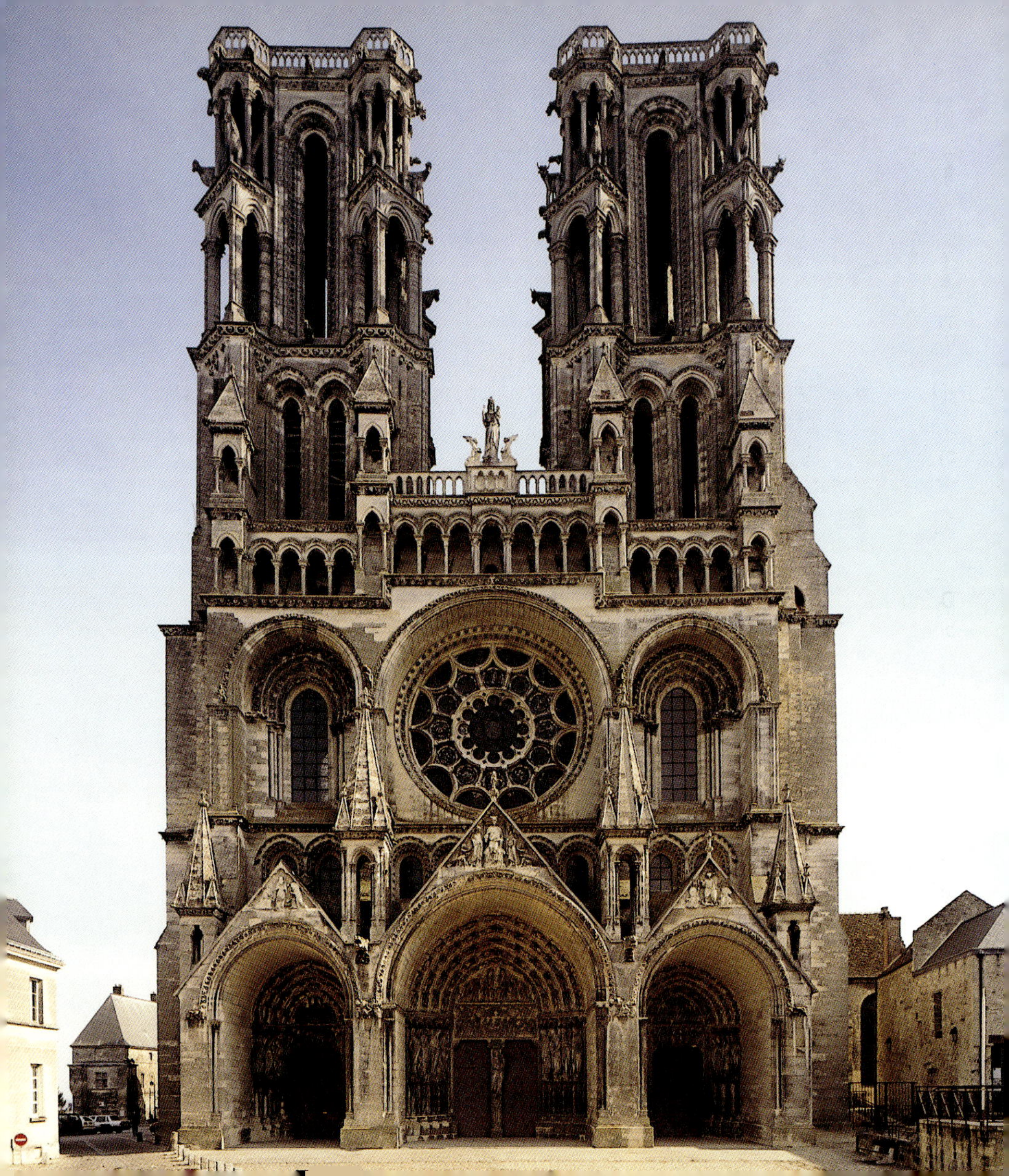

Religious Architecture in France

In the mid-12th century, innovative features of religious architecture developed in France that proved highly influential. The innovations were based on the concept of the church space as an architectural unit. Whereas in the Romanesque style various components had been added to produce an overall effect, the beginning of the Gothic style was marked by taking the space to be shaped as the central feature; the determining framework of walls and pillars, vaults and windows was designed with an eye to the spatial impression.

Laon,
Notre-Dame Cathedral,
facade (left),
begun before 1200,
nave and choir (bottom),
begun *c.* 1160

This development originated not in a city church but in the Benedictine abbey of **Saint-Denis** near **Paris** (pp. 10, 11), the medieval burial place of the French kings. Saint-Denis, begun in 1137 and completed in 1282, was constructed in accordance with the plans of Abbot Suger. Amongst the decisive innovations introduced under Abbot Suger was the presentation of the altars with the saints' relics in the elevated choir. The double choir ambulatory helped channel the flow of pilgrims. The perception of space was mainly influenced through a new technique of shifting weight from the walls themselves through alternative supporting systems. These conveyed the weight of the roofs and vaults via buttresses inside the walls and on their exterior so that the walls could be opened for large windows instead. The new possibilities of lighting which this entailed were also inter-

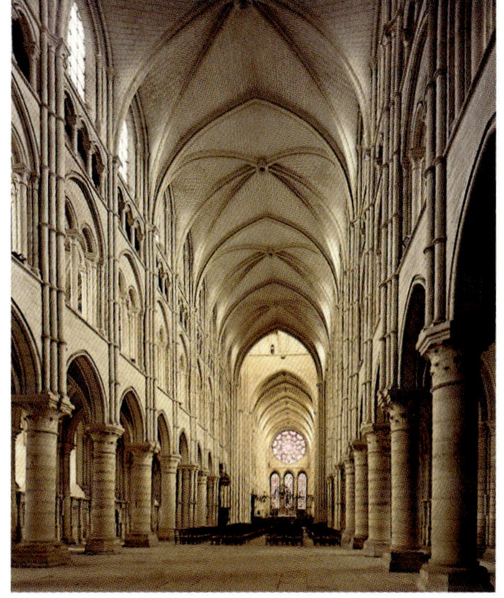

preted symbolically: the brilliant light flooding the choir of Saint-Denis underlines the aspect of the church as a house of God. These huge, majestic openings in the walls, filled by glass windows, are one of the reasons why Gothic cathedrals to this day have an overwhelming effect. Alongside the precious altar furnishings, the colorful stained-glass windows were meant to illustrate the meaning of the church as the Heavenly Jerusalem. The belief in salvation through the return of Christ is so deeply rooted in the Christian faith that the material church, the community of the faithful *(ecclesia)*, saw itself in relation to a heavenly church. A Gothic church interior offered the ideal framework for this. The new architectural style spread in the 12th and 13th centuries from Saint-Denis to the entire Île-de-France region, which more or less corresponds to a 150-km radius around Paris. At the time, this region was the domain of the French kings, whose power was consolidated and enhanced under Louis VI (1108–1137). The cathedrals were a means of expressing secular and spiritual power, because in the Middle Ages the king was understood to be God's representative on earth. The choir and chancel were reserved for the clergy; the laity were only allowed into the nave. A further division between the clergy and the laity was introduced in the form of choir screens, wall-like constructions to partition off the choir area, with doors which were usually closed and seldom allowed a glimpse of the sacred area. The sermon, which in the late Middle Ages became an increasingly important part of the church service, was preached from an elevated

Paris,
Notre-Dame Cathedral,
choir,
begun *c.* 1163

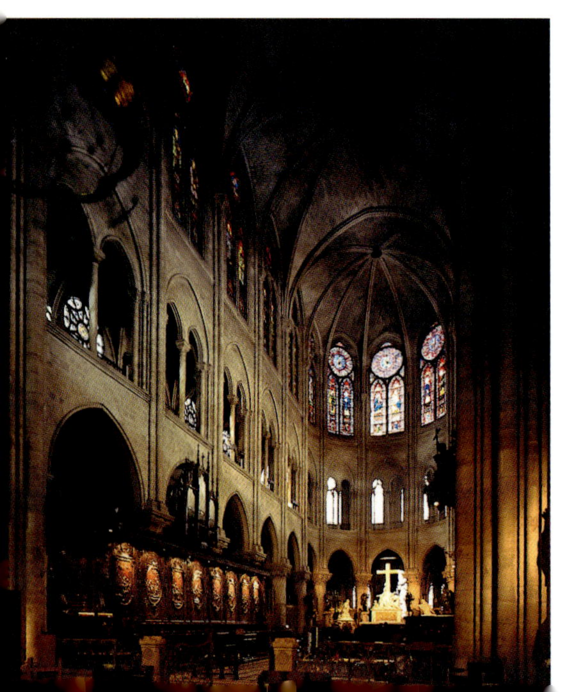

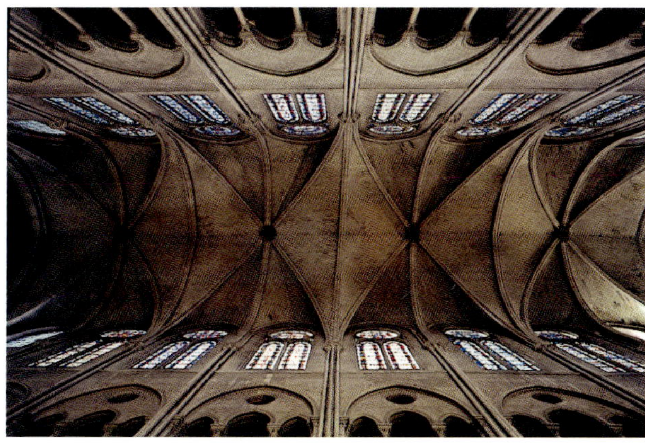

Paris,
Notre-Dame Cathedral,
nave vault,
begun *c.* 1163

pulpit. The nave also served as a place to sleep, for example for pilgrims. The narthex and cloister were open for everybody, which meant that these were busy places where people would eat and drink, hold courts of law and do business. The church regularly took sanctions against excesses, but since it also profited from the revenues, for example from wine sales, it seems that in many places the rules were not adhered to consistently. The growing desire for private prayer was met by erecting chapels for families, guilds and other social groups. In times characterized by plagues, war and famines, people worried greatly about the salvation of their souls. The church not only profited from all kinds of donations: from the 13th century on, it introduced the selling of indulgences, which reduced purchasers' future punishment in purgatory.

Another of the earliest examples of French Gothic architecture is **Laon Cathedral,** constructed from *c.* 1160 (pp. 12, 13). The church is a three-aisled basilica with five towers, although initially seven were planned. The west front was completed in *c.* 1205 and is decorated with a large variety of sculptures as well as an impressive stained-glass rose window. The 13th-century windows, whose light floods the transept and choir, are an exceptional feature of this church. Alongside Saint-Denis, Chartres and Notre Dame in Paris, this building is one of the most important early Gothic cathedrals. Laon strongly influenced major German church buildings such as the cathedrals of Bamberg and Naumburg.

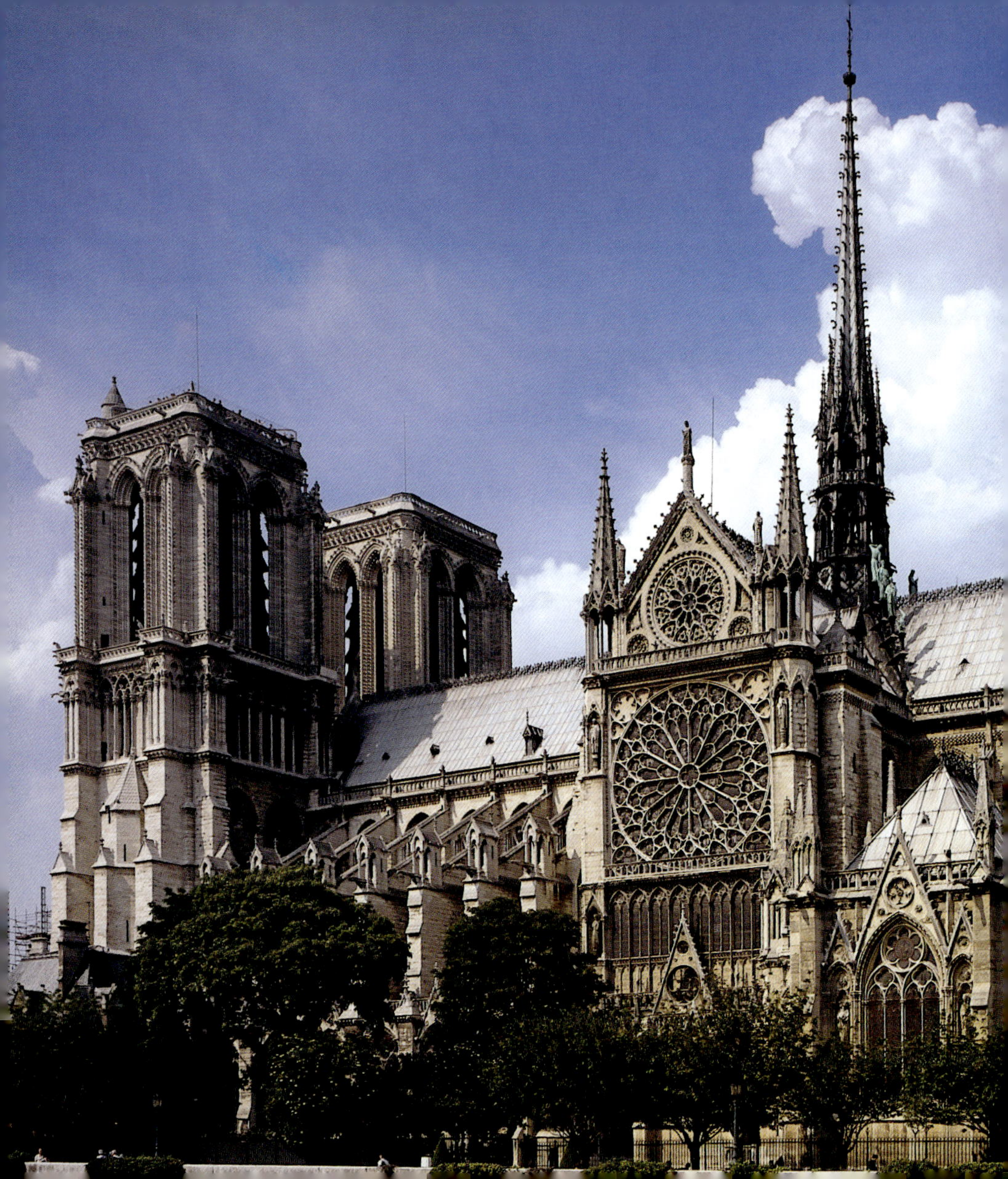

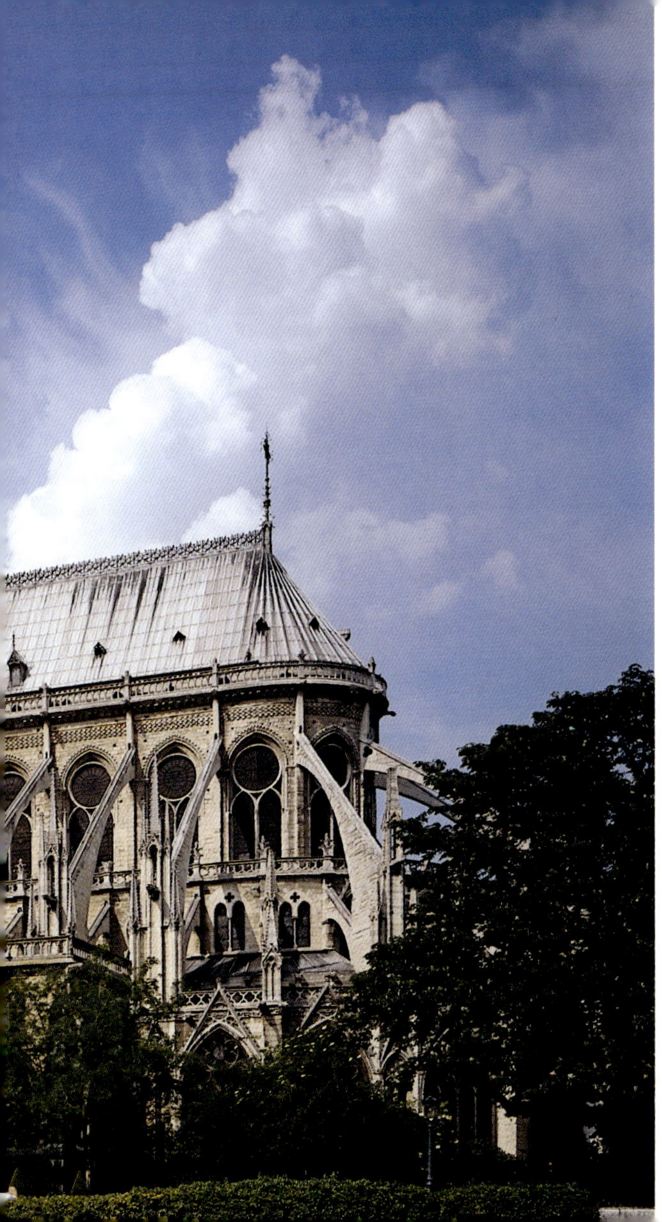

The dimensions of Notre-Dame Cathedral in Paris surpassed all previous buildings. This enhanced the competition among cities for the largest church.

Paris,
Notre-Dame Cathedral,
south side,
begun *c.* 1163

Notre Dame in **Paris,** begun *c.* 1163 (pp. 14, 15, 16, 17) was the church of the French kings in the capital of their realm, and the cathedral was to be exceedingly influential. The choir was consecrated in 1182; west front and transept date from the 13th century; the choir ambulatory followed in the 14th century. Extremely slender shafts and the height of the triforium underline the vertical character; the wall decoration integrates the large rose windows and the lancet windows directly underneath. The exterior of the north facade displays the whole range of Gothic architectural ornamentation: gables, dwarf galleries, crockets and finials. With its interior length of 130 meters and a vault height of 35 meters, this structure surpassed all previous buildings. In the decades to follow, cities began to compete with each other for the mightiest cathedral. As in Saint-Denis and Laon, these new dimensions were made possible through the consistent application of a building technique consisting of the use of a system of reinforced parts – pillars, shafts and ribbed vaults – which allowed the pressure to be diverted downward and outward and made it possible to reduce the massive masonry and open up the walls.

By diverting the weight of the structure towards the outside, the compact masonry of the walls could be opened up, as in Chartres Cathedral. This meant that the interior was flooded with daylight.

Reims with its **Cathedral of Notre-Dame** (p. 21) is also close to the Île-de-France region. The city was closely associated with Saint Remi (*c.* 436–533), its bishop, who is said to have anointed Clovis, king of the Franks, with an oil of heavenly origin. The oil flask was indispensable for the ritual anointing of the French kings is one of its treasures. As the archdiocese of Reims was very wealthy, the archbishop took the initiative of having the cathedral restructured one year after it caught fire in 1210. The prefabrication of various building elements such as pillars in the cathedral workshop was a novelty. Reims tracery, which made detailed ornamentation of the windows possible, developed into an architectural feature in its own right. This cathedral came to great renown because of the artistic sculptural decoration both inside the church and on the facades. This includes the gallery of the kings on the west facade, various sculpted figures, sculpted masks on the corbels as well as the carved ornamentation, which comes to full effect in the capitals, each one fashioned individually. The technical and artistic effort of the stonemasons, who carved each capital in a unique way, is remarkable. The exterior of the cathedral offers another novelty compared to previous buildings: technical innovation led to the buttresses being less massive, since they could now be better integrated into the architectural structure.

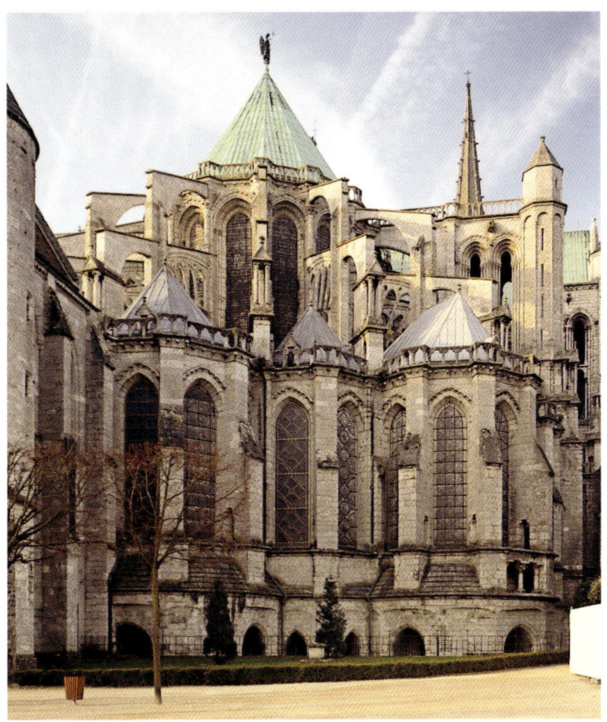

Chartres,
Notre-Dame Cathedral,
exterior view of the choir,
begun in the early 12th century,
reconstructed after
a fire in 1194

During the reign of Philip Augustus (1180–1223), cathedral building yet again reached another dimension. The **Cathedral of Notre-Dame** in **Chartres,** an important destination for pilgrims on the Way of St. James, is an illuminating example. In order to cope with the large number of pilgrims, Chartres has a double choir ambulatory – similar to the one of Saint-Denis. The building was reconstructed after a fire in 1194. The crypt and west portal with a depiction of Christ Enthroned had remained from the mid-12th century and were incorporated into the new design. Chartres is noted for its stained-glass windows, which are almost entirely intact and radiate in vivid hues of blue and red. The rose windows,

Reims,
Notre-Dame Cathedral,
facade,
begun 1210,
facade after 1254

Following double spread:
Albi,
Ste. Cécile Cathedral,
exterior view (left),
nave and choir (right),
begun *c.* 1280

faceted circular windows on the west front and transept facades, are extraordinary (see pp. 254, 255, 256, 257). The wall elevations are divided into three levels. Between the arcades and the clerestory windows, which are of the same height – an unusual feature – runs the triforium, which resembles a small arcade. Four arches of the triforium correspond to one in the lower arcade. From a technical point of view, the height of the clerestory, which is much greater here than in previous buildings, was made possible by reinforcing the system of buttresses. The triple flying buttresses above the aisles ensured stability even in the upper parts of the building, which were exposed to the winds and thus especially vulnerable. The vaults are no less than 37 meters high. Compared with Notre Dame Cathedral in Paris (see pp. 14, 15, 16, 17), where the buttresses were still arranged in double arches, this construction represents technical progress. However, constructional compromises were necessary in the choir area of Chartres, since the crypt of the previous structure had to be incorporated. The pillars in the high nave have a different design: an octagonal nucleus with round colonnettes alternates with a round nucleus with octagonal colonettes. The pillars in the nave, being alternately octogonal and round have different designs in that they form an overall visual harmony with the shafts.

Ste. Cécile Cathedral in **Albi** (pp. 22, 23) is an

Reims and Joan of Arc

Traditionally, Reims Cathedral was the church where the French kings were crowned. During the Hundred Years' War between France and England, the French side faced increasing troubles until in early **1429** a young woman demanded to speak to the French heir to the throne, Dauphin Charles. Jeanne d'Arc – Joan of Arc – told him that she was following instructions by the archangel Michael and not only promised to chase the English out of France but to have the rightful king of France crowned in Reims. Joan managed to convince Charles and was allowed to fight. After she had succeeded in liberating Orleans on **7 April 1429**, the French position became so strong that on 17 July the Dauphin was in fact crowned King Charles VII in the cathedral of Reims. Joan stood next to him, holding the banner of victory. However, in the course of the following year, Joan fell from the king's favor. She was imprisoned in May **1430** and handed over to the Inquisition. Joan of Arc was tried twice and burned at the stake in **1431**.

excellent example of the Gothic architecture of southern France. It was begun in 1280 and completed in the 14th century. This is a single-nave brick building, much in the type of a fortified church. Viewed from the exterior, the massive buttresses and the imposing west tower, which has Gothic features only on the upper stories, predominate. The defensive character of the structure is understandable in the light of the religious and political situation in southern France at the time, where the Catholic Church was fighting against the religious movement of the Cathars, supposed heretics who were also named Albigensians, after the town of Albi. As this lay movement was threatening the Church's claim to secular power, in the early 13th century it was fought and ultimately destroyed, for example during the Albigensian Crusade.

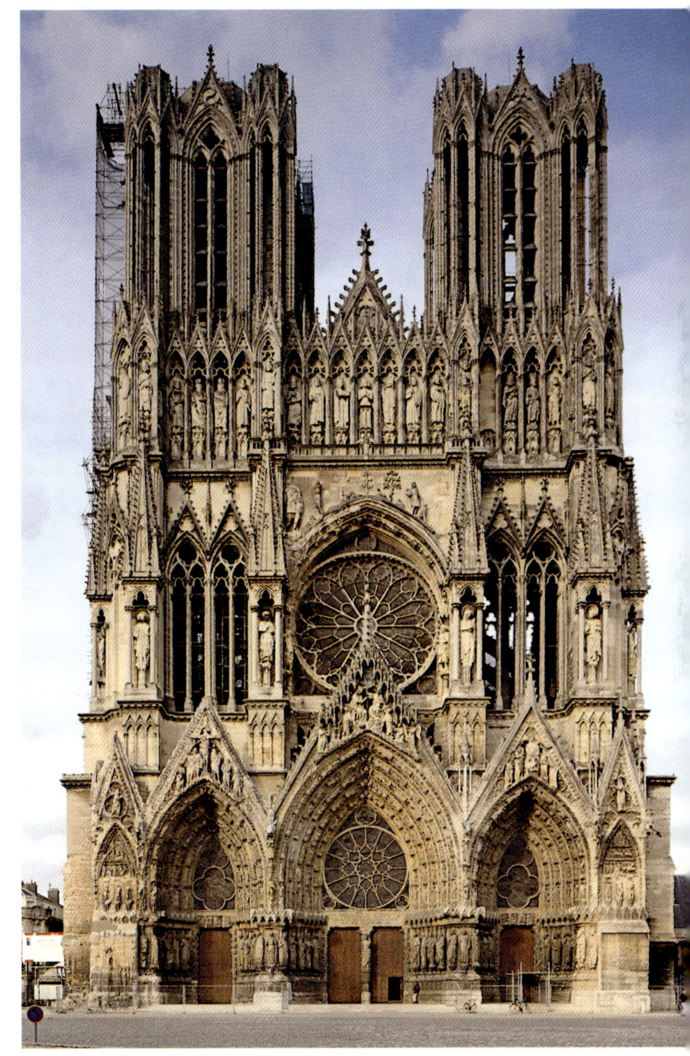

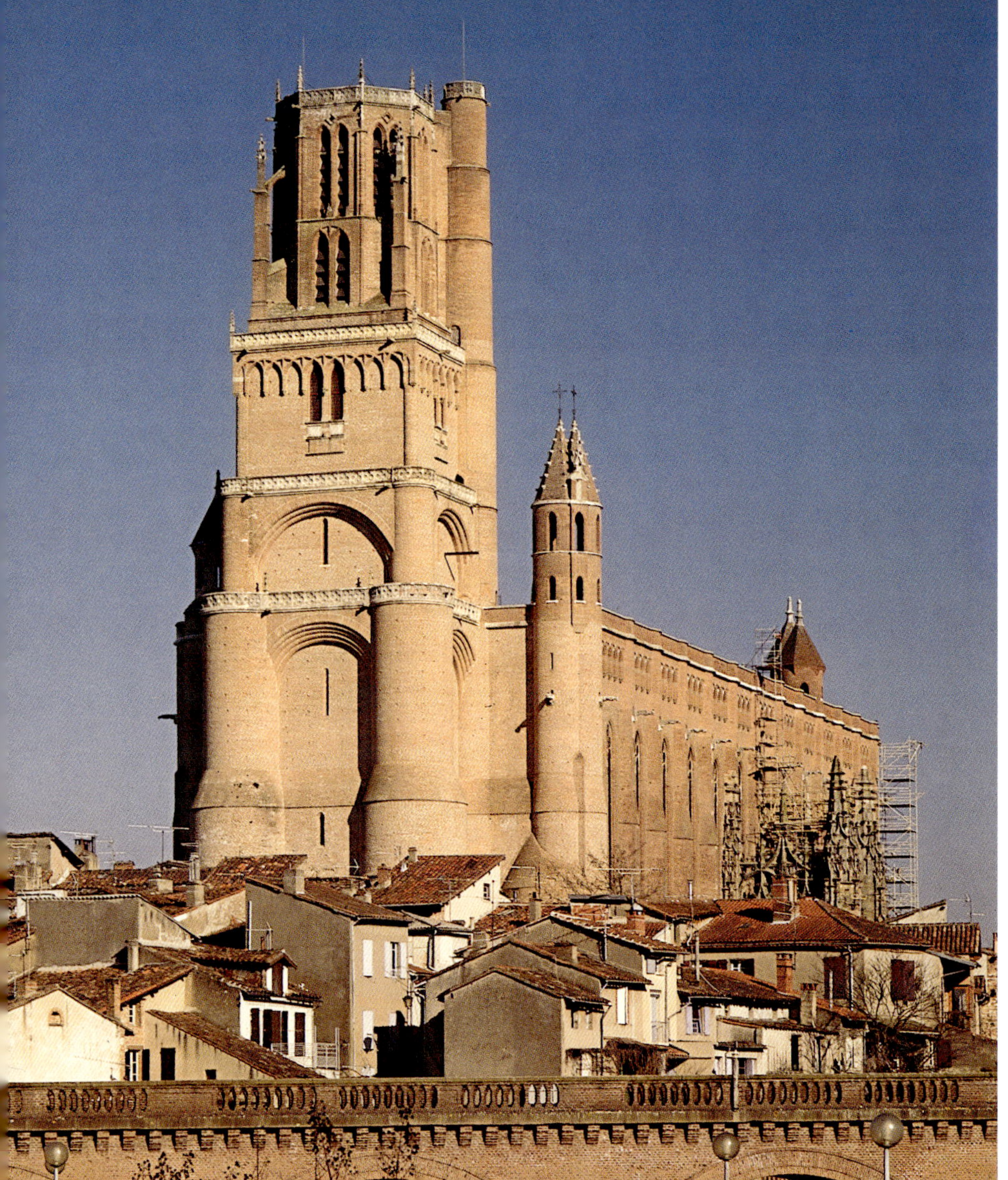

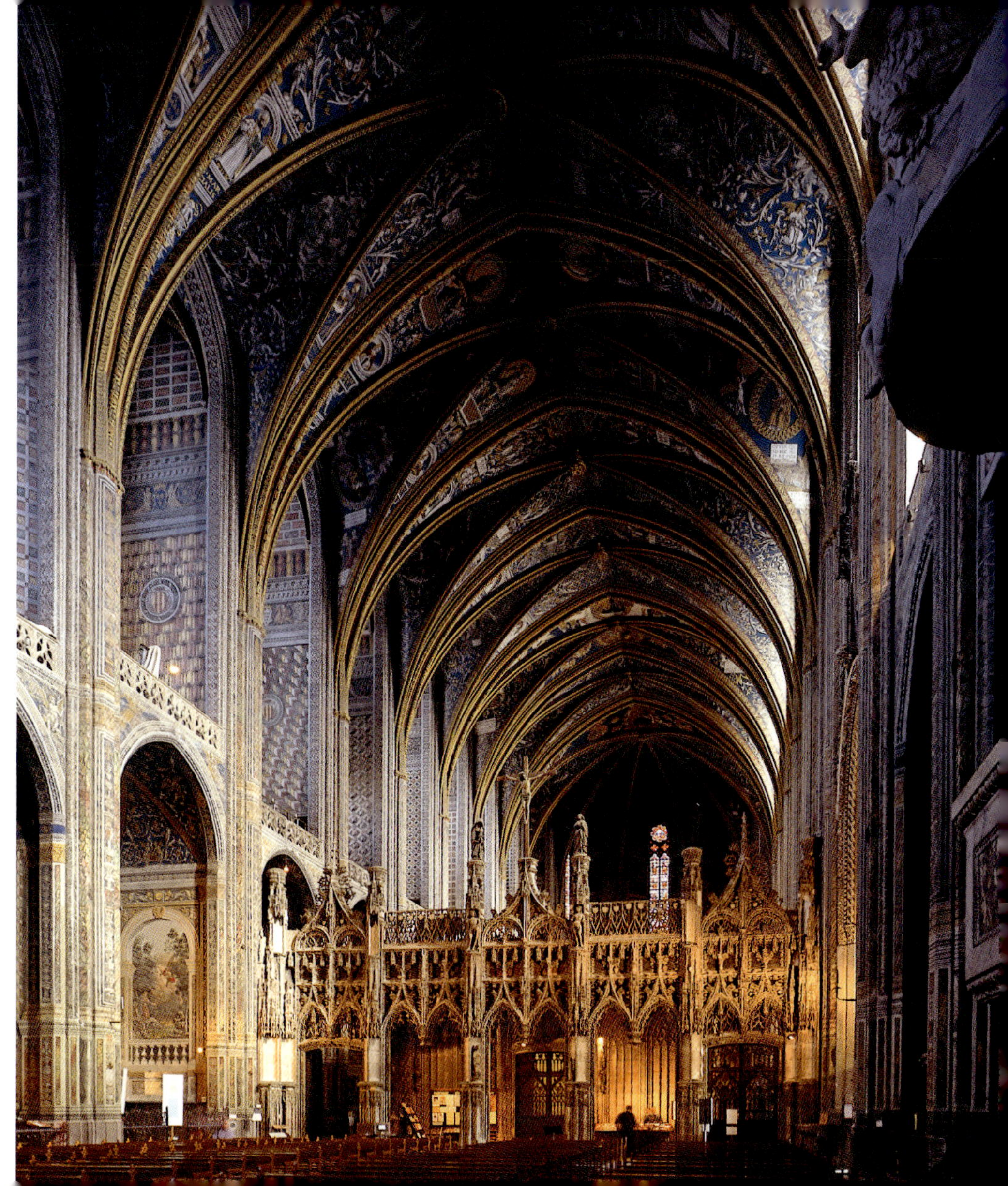

Of Master Masons and Guild Craftsmen – Late Medieval Builders' Workshops

Jean Fouquet,
The Building of Solomon's Temple, illustration of *The Antiquities of the Jews,* illumination, 15th century, Bibliothèque nationale, Paris

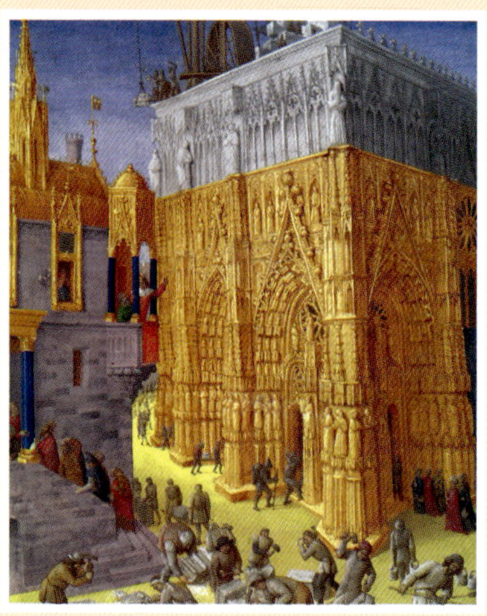

Nowadays, we stand in front of medieval churches and ask ourselves, stunned, how the architects managed to build these structures; how technical, organizational, economical, social, religious and aesthetic talents merged in order to build these houses of God. One explanation lies in the development of what today is referred to as the system of builders' workshops. Whereas in Romanesque times the citizens teamed up with the clergy to design and build their own churches with admirable dedication bordering on self-sacrifice, towards the Late Middle Ages the organization of large building projects changed. The church, being a wealthy client, began to employ an increasing number of professional itinerant craftsmen: stonemasons for the structure; sculptors for the ornamental and figurative decoration; carpenters for the scaffolds and roofs. Project management and finances as well as technical management lay in the care of the master mason, a modern-day managing director, so to speak. He recruited the specialist craftspeople such as glaziers, scaffolders, carpenters, masons and metal workers. A variety of notes and bills have survived documenting the organization of builders' workshops. Initially, these workshops were simple wooden sheds where tools and building materials were kept. But after a while they became larger and were built to offer space and cover for components of stonemasonry to be pre-fabricated during the cold season or when it rained. Whenever we speak of builders' workshops today, we mean this in an allegorical sense, actually referring to the development of a professionally structured organization of independent work processes.

The painter and miniaturist **Jean Fouquet** (*c.* 1420–*c.* 1480) made illustrations for *The Antiquities of the Jews,* a text by first-century Roman author Flavius Josephus. Some of the illustrations allow us a glimpse of everyday work in builders' workshops. The treatise by the historian Josephus, written in Greek, recounts the history of the Jewish people from Genesis to his time. In the Middle Ages, a Latin translation of this text was in circulation; the miniaturist's French translation is based on this. It features an illustration of the Building of the Temple of Jerusalem as described in the Old Testament: At the beginning of the 1st century BC, King Solomon built the first stone temple. Flavius Josephus even gives the measurements of the temple. Jean Fouquet orients himself on the text, on the given measurements of the temple and on the knowledge that the entire building was gilded: the gray part of the miniature in the upper zone of the building refers to the fact that the gilding was not quite completed here. In spite of being true to the source, Fouquet knowingly illustrates this temple as a Gothic cathedral, and a very specific one at that. Some of the details of the facade orna-

The Building of a City, illustration of a novel by Girart de Roussillon, illumination, mid-14th century, Nationalbibliothek, Vienna

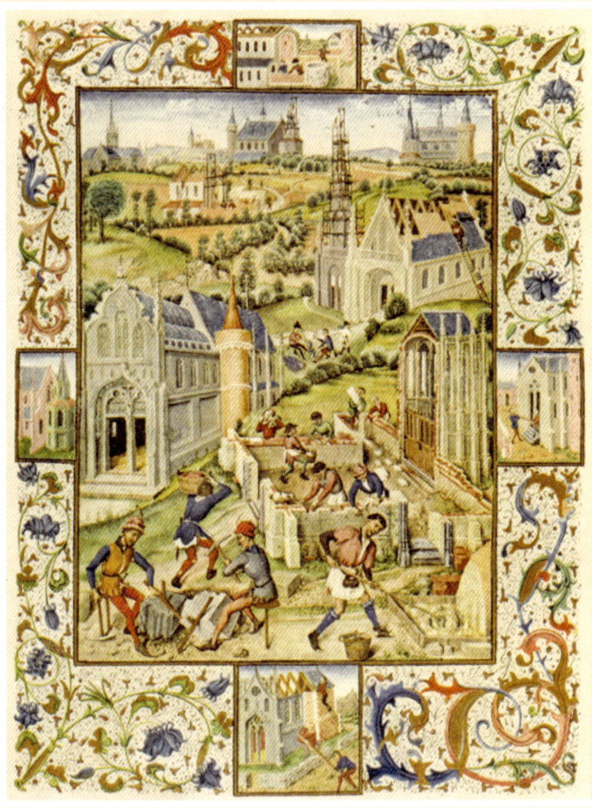

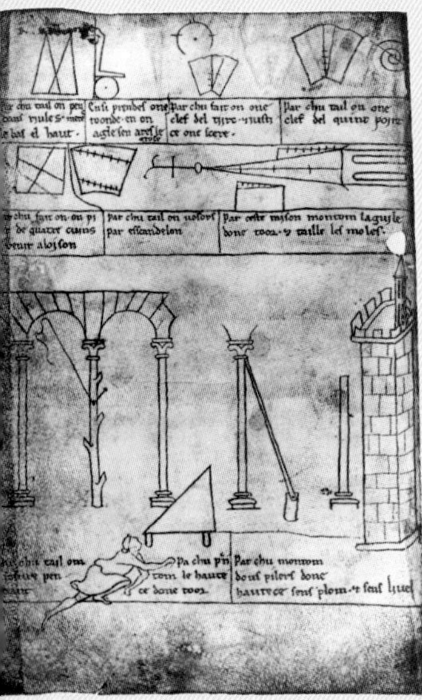

Villard de Honnecourt, technical drawings, portfolio, *c.* 1230, Bibliothèque nationale, Paris

mentation prove that Fouquet was thinking of the cathedral of his hometown Tours, which at the time lacked a spire. He may not have portrayed an accurate likeness, but on closer observation the viewer can indeed detect parallels. The miniaturist also gives us details on the various phases of a building project: in a bay of his palace, Solomon is seen in discussion with an architect. Masons are working the stone blocks, carrying them to the half-completed building and pulling them onto the roof with winches. The dark-skinned surveyor in the foreground, wearing a white headscarf, could be read as an allusion to the cosmopolitan character of the teams of contractors. Another miniature, taken from a novel by **Girart de Roussillon** (p. 25), illustrated in the 14th century, shows an idealized version of the various activities involved in a construction.

A first-hand source for the technical realization of late medieval building projects consists in the surviving portfolio of the architect **Villard de Honnecourt** (active *c.* 1220–1240). The book includes simple drawings and exemplary construction plans, odd designs as well as elaborate architectural drawings. The collection, of which only fragments have survived intact, is flanked with valuable notes by Honnecourt's assistants. It is one of the earliest documents to contain numerous precise accounts of how a building project was realized and as such is a rich source of information for today's scholars of building and architecture in the Middle Ages. Alongside models, elevations and ground plans, it also holds a collection of sketches of sculptures and anatomical drawings of humans and animals based on geometric forms. One of the architectural drawings shows the system of flying buttresses on the exterior, which was fundamental for the spatial effect of Gothic cathedrals, namely the shifting of the weight of the vaults. By diverting this thrust to the outside, high and light interiors could be created, which was the fundamental scope of every Gothic architect. Another drawing (p. 26) shows the deployment of technical instruments such as the plumb line; how to obtain a right angle, measure a pointed arch or design the construction of the Archimedean spiral for the volutes of capitals, as well as patterns for pinnacles. The lower two thirds of this parchment are dedicated to measuring the angles of suspended arches: all of the joints need to be fitted so that the weight of the stones is spread evenly, each of them supporting the other. As shown here to the center left of the parchment, this can be done by positioning a nail in the middle. All of the joints have to end here, forming a star shape, and can be controlled with the help of a string held tight. The second example featured here is an elevation of Reims Cathedral, namely the side aisles seen from the exterior (left) and interior (right). Only at a second glance does one recognize the horizontal shading to the left as the roof of the side aisle. Honnecourt experimented with the growing possibilities of technical drawings, shifting between architectural accuracy and picturesque tableaux. For example, in the exterior view, he lets the slender, high pinnacles end at the height of the barely suggested gargoyles, because otherwise they would have obstructed the depiction of the upper story in this elevation. The flanking text also gives tips for adding passageways for the building phase and as escape routes in case of fire.

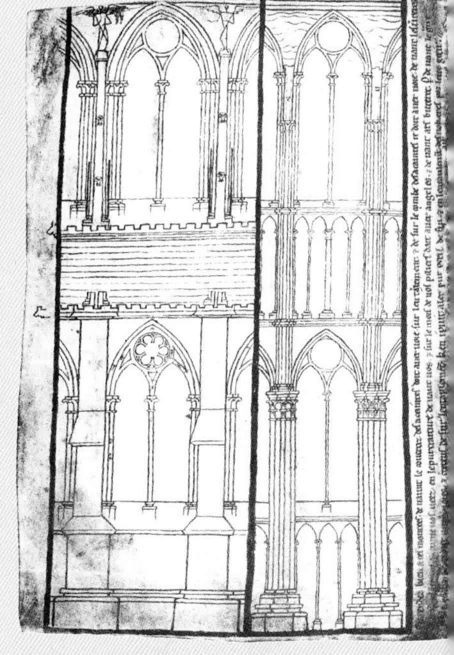

Villard de Honnecourt, interior and exterior view of Reims Cathedral, portfolio, *c.* 1230, Bibliothèque nationale, Paris

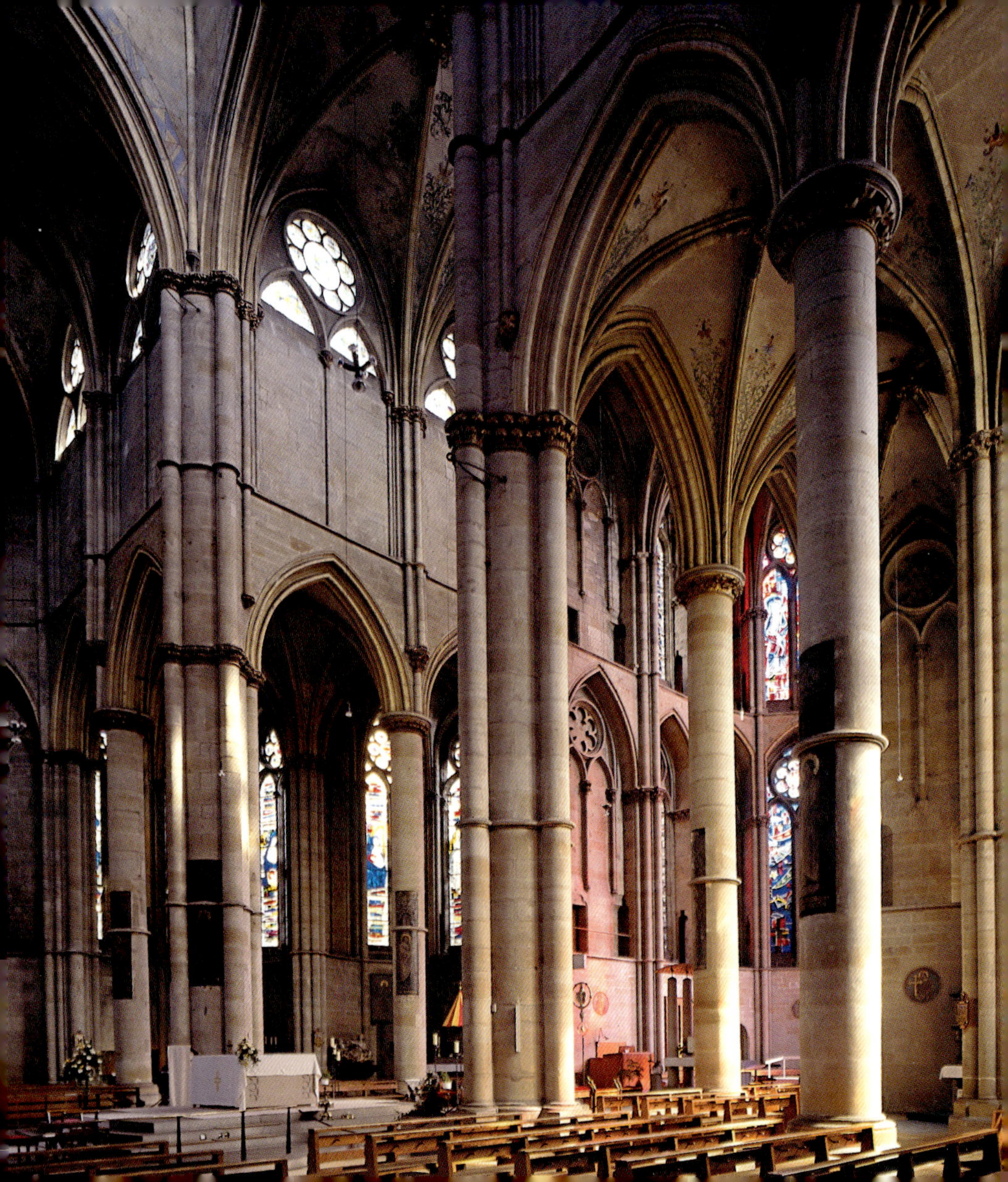

Religious Architecture of the "German Lands"

Determining the exact nature of the "German Lands" was already an issue for the people of the Middle Ages. After all, the term denotes tribes as well as geographic or juridical areas and dominions. This wealth of meanings reflects the patchwork of territories which remained in the northern part of the Holy Roman Empire after the dissolution of the Frankish Kingdom.

From 1200 onwards, these areas were influenced by a manifold range of cultural styles, especially those of Byzantium and France. Gothic art reached the German territories a good 100 years after it had originated in France. Among the first Gothic buildings are St. Elizabeth's Church in Marburg and the **Church of Our Lady** in **Trier.** The latter, a cathedral and abbey church begun in 1227, dates from an Early Christian church. Its extraordinary ground plan follows the previous construction: it is a cruciform central-plan building with lower radiating chapels between the transept arms, and stands in the tradition of the Pantheon in Rome, a Roman temple which in AD 610 was converted into the church of Santa Maria Rotonda. The structure in Trier was designed after the form of a Greek cross, with the choir functioning as an elongation of the eastern arm of the cross. Above the crossing looms a tower. The division of the interior into a high ground floor and a low upper floor is equally uncommon and does not

Church of Our Lady, Trier,
View from the nave into the transept (left), exterior view of the choir (below),
begun 1227

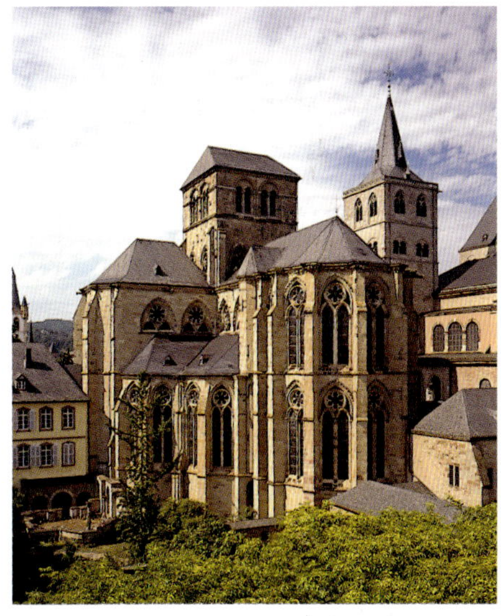

accord with the style of French cathedral architecture. And yet, the various decorative elements are undoubtedly inspired by the examples from the cradle of Gothic architecture. One of the most outstanding features is the window tracery, which shows close parallels to the tracery of Reims Cathedral.

Unlike Trier, **St. Stephen's** in **Vienna** with its ground plan consisting of nave and aisles and the west front adorned with two towers stands in the tradition of medieval church architecture. Construction took more than 300 years. Some parts of the westwork trace back to the former Romanesque church, as does the impressive stepped portal richly decorated with sculptures. The hall choir with aisles followed in the 13th century, as did the nave with side aisles, whose Late Gothic reticulated vaulting in accurate proportions dating from 1450 is especially impressive. The pillars are decorated with canopied Late Gothic sculptures showing the Twelve Apostles, the symbols of Christian faith. The baldachins are ornamented with finials. The exterior of the cathedral is characterized by the steep roof with its geometrically aligned pantiles glazed in various colors. Pantiles like these can also be found in the French region of Burgundy. The richly decorated south tower, 136 meters high, was generously financed by Duke Rudolf IV (1339–1365), the son-in-law of Emperor Charles IV.

The Habsburg Dynasty

From the 14th century onwards, Vienna was one of the main seats of the Habsburgs. This feudal dynasty originated from the Swiss Canton of Aargau, home of Habsburg castle, the family's ancestral seat. At first, the family's dominion was limited to this region. However, in **1273** Rudolph of Habsburg was crowned Rudolph I, King of the Romans and King of Germany. His sons were given the duchies of Austria and Styria. In **1438**, Albert II of Habsburg became Holy Roman Emperor. From that time, every emperor was a member of the Habsburg dynasty, with the exception of the short reign of Charles VII of the House of Wittelsbach (**1742–1745**). The Habsburg monarchs secured Burgundy, the kingdoms of Bohemia, Croatia, Hungary and Spain as well as colonies overseas. After the death of Emperor Charles V the dynasty was split into a Spanish and an Austrian branch. The House of Habsburg lost the Spanish dominions after the War of the Spanish Succession (**1701–1714**). When the Holy Roman Empire of the German Nation was dissolved in **1806**, the House of Habsburg retained the title of Emperor of Austria until 1918.

During this time, the former collegiate church was elevated to a cathedral. 300 years later, Vienna was elevated to an archbishopric.

The construction of **Cologne Cathedral** (pp. 32, 33, 34) takes up a unique position in the history of the architecture of the "German Lands." Construction was begun in 1248 and in 1322 the church was consecrated, but was only completed in the 19th century, thanks to the amazing efforts of the citizens of Cologne. The structure closely follows French examples, which not only can be seen in the division into three zones, but also in the window tracery and the overall ornamentation. Only the west front makes an exception as it lacks the typical rose window, instead featuring two soaring towers. The building project was based on the plans drawn up by master mason Gerhard (died between 1260 and 1271). The plan, which measured more than four meters, was also used when the building was completed in the 19th century. From the very beginning, this construction, a nave with double aisles, impressed with its sheer magnificence. Undoubtedly, this was in part due to the archbishop of Cologne's ambitions to enhance his prestige: he played a prominent role in politics,

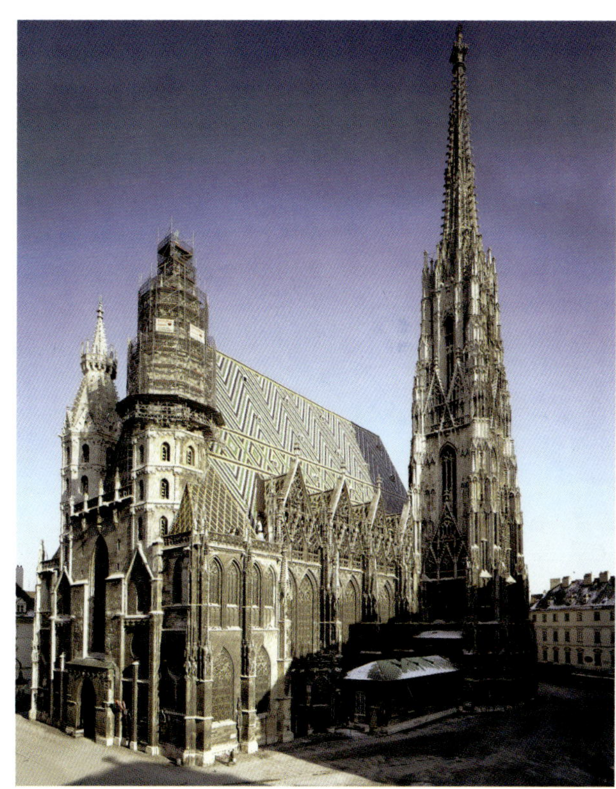

St. Stephen's Cathedral,
Vienna,
begun 1137

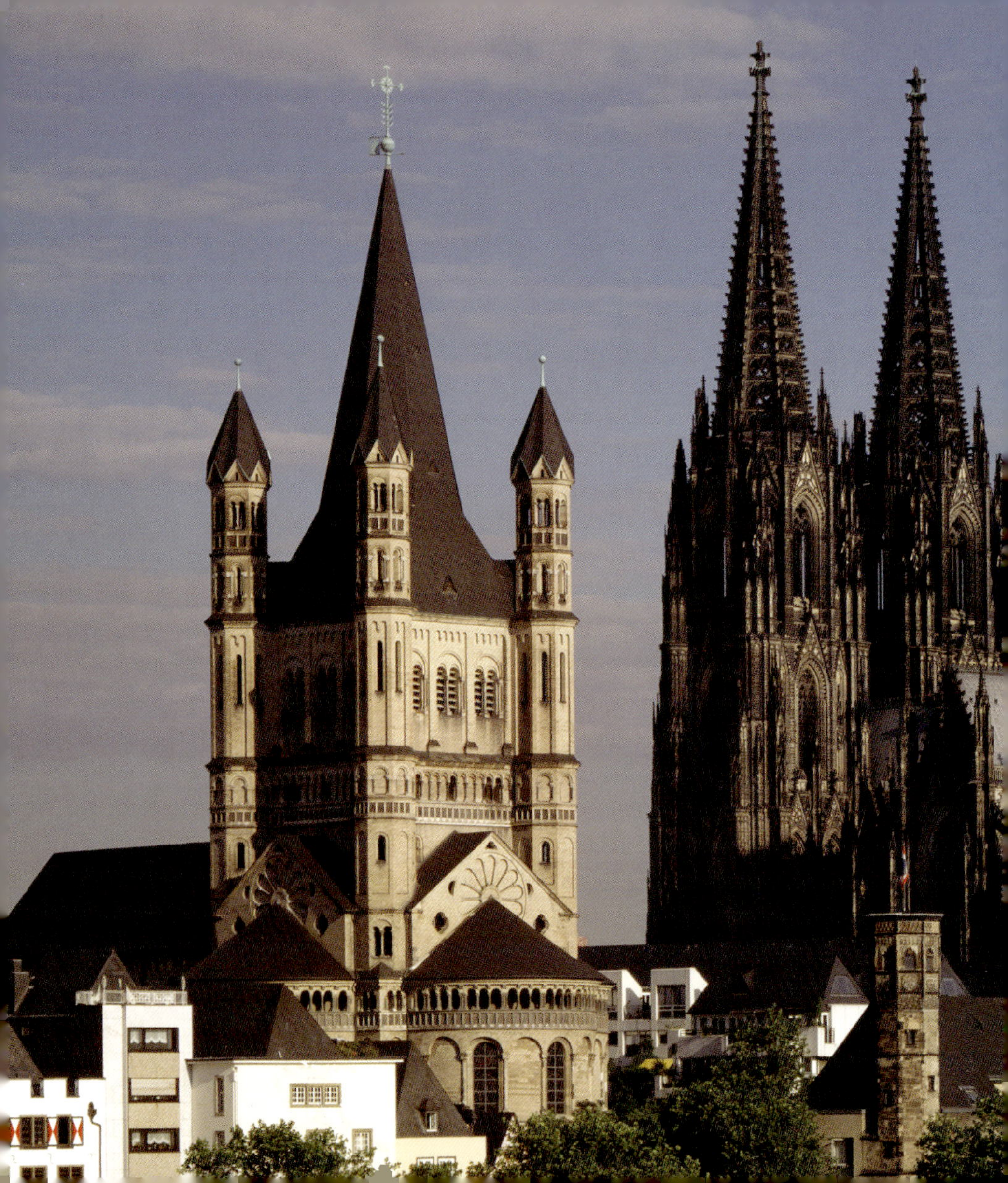

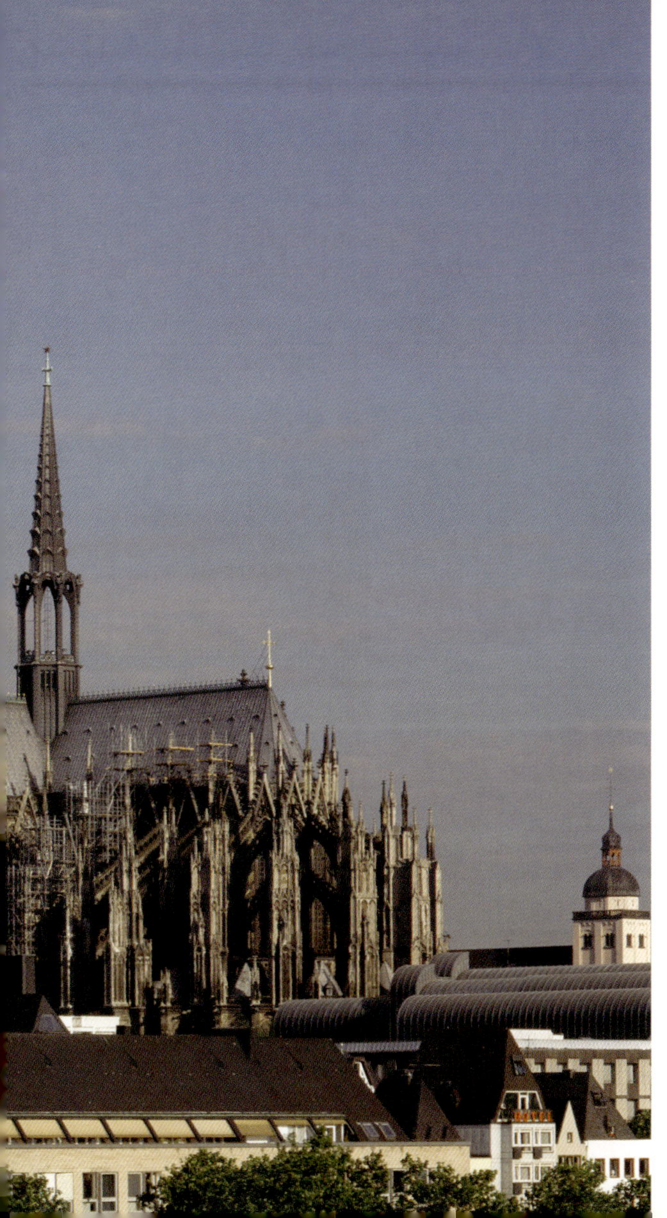

Cologne Cathedral, which from afar can be recognized as a monument of Gothic architecture, was in fact only completed in the 19th century, in accordance with the medieval construction plans.

Cologne Cathedral (High Church of St. Peter and Mary),
begun 1248,
choir consecrated in 1322,
completed in the 19th century

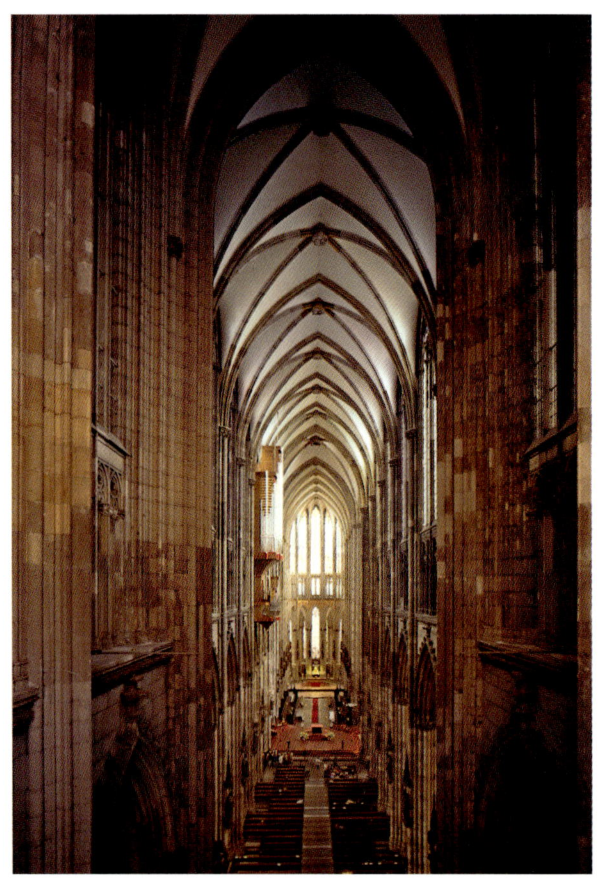

Cologne Cathedral,
choir,
begun 1248,
choir consecrated in 1322

for example in the election of the emperor. But there was another, more pragmatic reason for the cathedral's impressive size: the need to handle the increasing number of pilgrims. The faithful flocked to Cologne to see the Shrine of the Magi, whose relics had been brought to Cologne from Milan in 1164.

In the Middle Ages, the new confidence of the burghers became an important motivation for donations. Numerous churches built in the flourishing trade centers are witness both to the ever-present worries about the salvation of one's soul and to the wish of displaying a new, more prestigious social status in the face of aristocracy. One example is the **Minster of Our Lady** in **Freiburg,** southern Germany. The parish church was begun thanks to the initiative of the Duke of Zähringen, and only became the seat of an archbishop – and thus a cathedral – in 1827. In about 1200, construction commenced with the building of the transept in the Late Romanesque style. Approximately thirty years later, a decisive turn took place when the Romanesque Minster of Basle was no longer used as a model, but instead the Gothic Strasbourg Cathedral. The spire was begun in the mid-13th century and is renowned as one of the most beautiful medieval church spires. Consisting entirely of airy filigree ribs and tracery, it is a masterpiece of engineering. Another technical work of art is the spiral staircase inside the tower, leading up to the spire. The minster was completed in 1536 with the help of extensive donations given by the citizens of Freiburg. The narrative scheme of the stained-glass windows refers to these burgher donors, such as the baker's window, characterized by the beautifully curved pretzel.

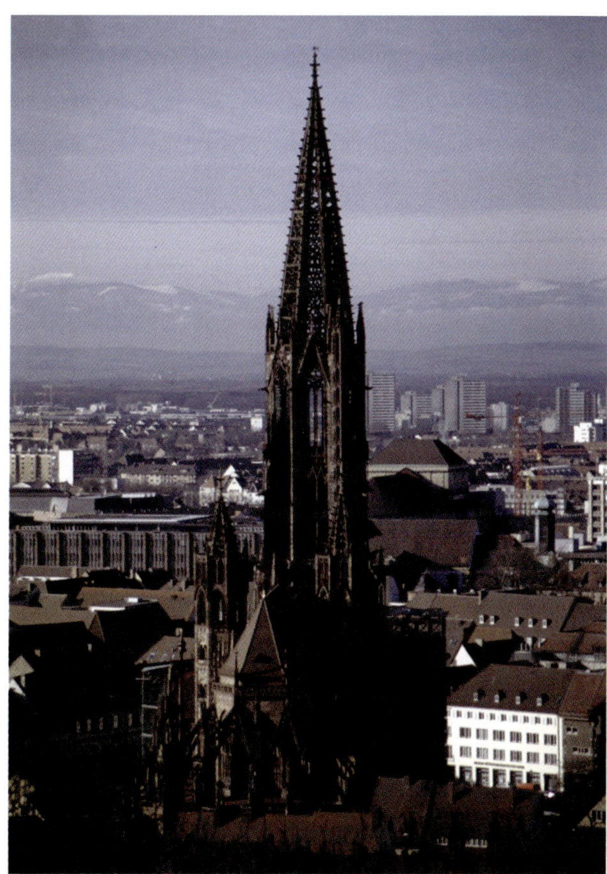

Freiburg Minster, begun 1200, tower mid-13th century

St. Catherine's Church in **Oppenheim** (p. 36) was also planned as a parish church when construction began in the late 13th century. Situated on a plateau hovering over the small winegrowing town in the Rhineland-Palatinate, it presents to the beholder a view of the south front with its unique artistic ornamentation. It was begun in 1317 and inspired by the Late Gothic churches of Cologne, Strasbourg and Freiburg. The reason for the imposing decoration lies in the fact that the parish church was elevated to the status of collegiate church. The facade is divided into

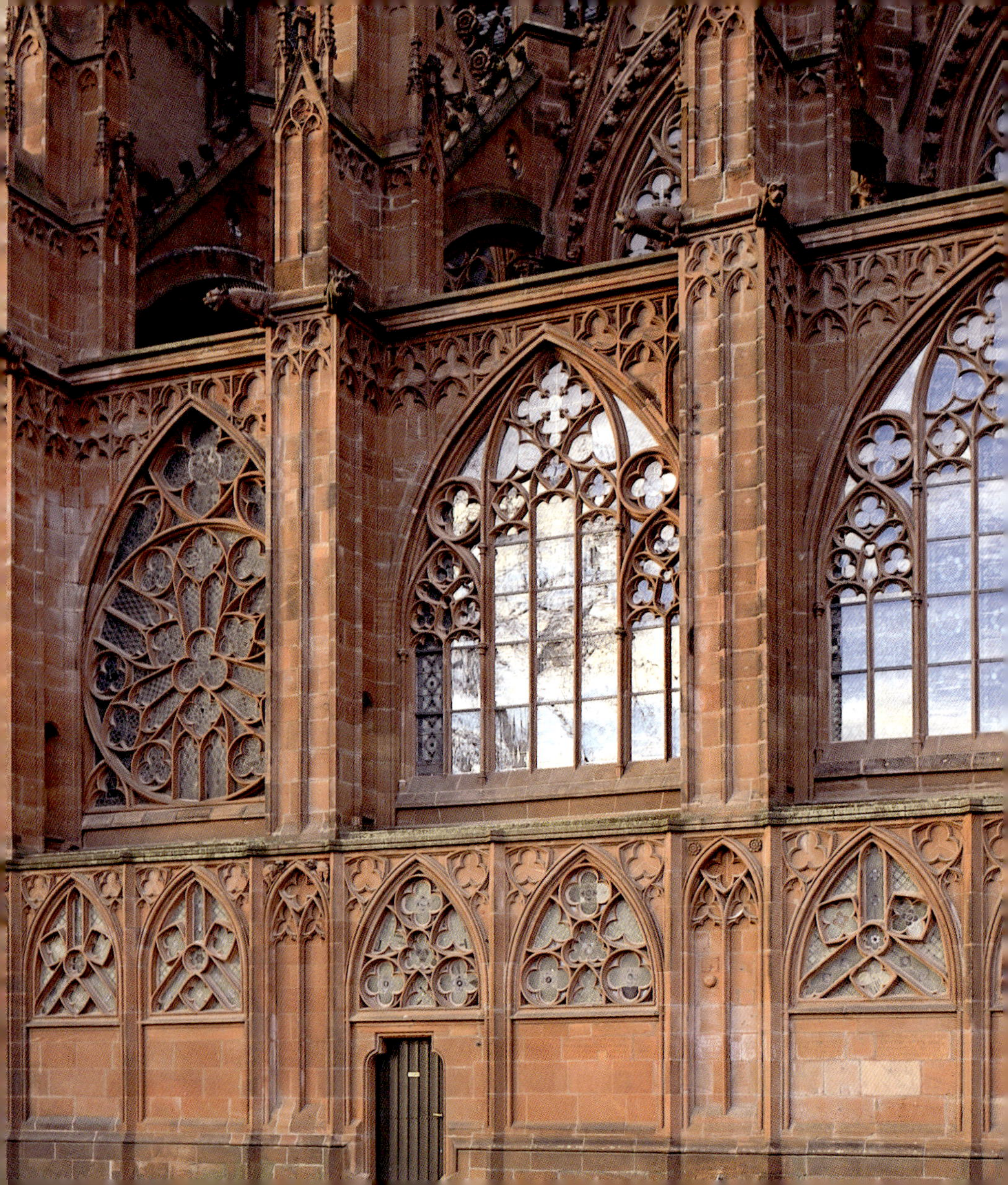

three areas, each of which is set slightly further back than the one below. The lower area consists of the exterior of the aisle chapels, whose windows are adorned with trefoils and quatrefoils. Above these can be seen the wide traceried windows of the aisle. The two rose windows on the far sides are unusual since such windows were usually placed in a central position, i.e. beneath a gable. But the windows feature another innovation: the use of the mouchette motif in the spandrels. The tracery windows of the clerestory are crowned by gables. Small finials decorate the flying buttresses, which also sport the leaf-like crockets, typical features of Gothic ornamentation.

Similar in character is the Late Gothic **Frauenkirche (Cathedral of Our Blessed Lady)** in **Munich** (pp. 38, 39). It is the hallmark of the city in southern Germany, which was founded by Henry the Lion in 1158, and served the Wittelsbach dynasty as their capital for 700 years. The brick building was constructed from 1468 to 1488. With a length of 109 meters, it is among the largest hall churches in southern Germany. The towers, topped by the famous onion-shaped domes, were not built until the 16th century. The church exterior is dominated by high lancet windows inserted into the otherwise bare masonry. The impression of compact wholeness is also caused by the fact that the buttresses here do not extend to the outside. Instead, the interior of the church is a high-vaulted space with the chapels the same height as the nave, which gives the entire space a monumental effect. This is Gothic architecture lacking all ornamentation – the focus on the spatial effect has created an outstanding work of architecture. With its simple geometrical design, the ribbed net vault once more underlines the clarity of the space.

Oppenheim,
Church of St. Catherine,
view of south side,
begun 1317

Following double spread:
Munich, Church of Our Blessed Lady,
exterior view from the
south-east (left),
nave and choir (right),
constructed 1468–1488

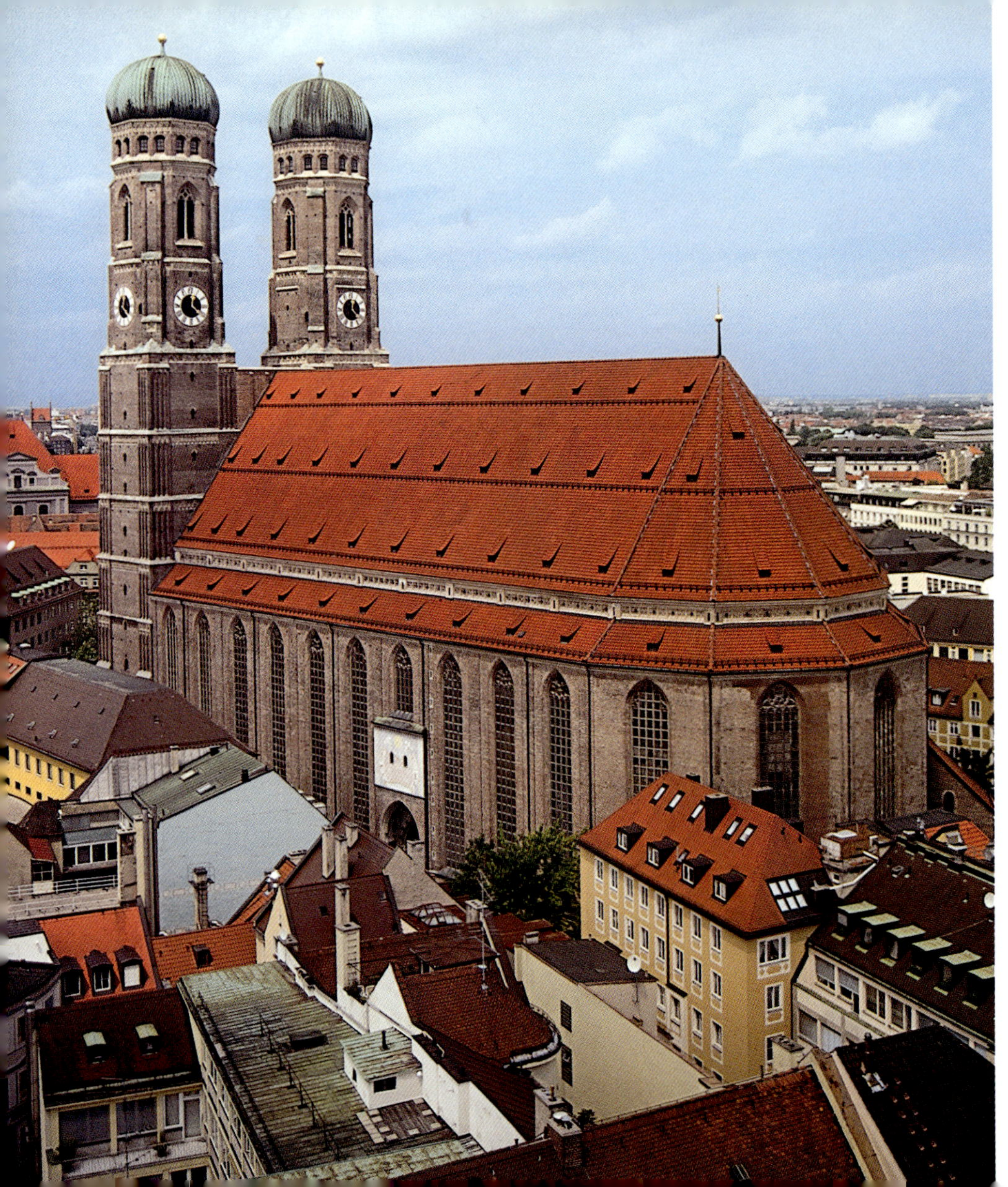

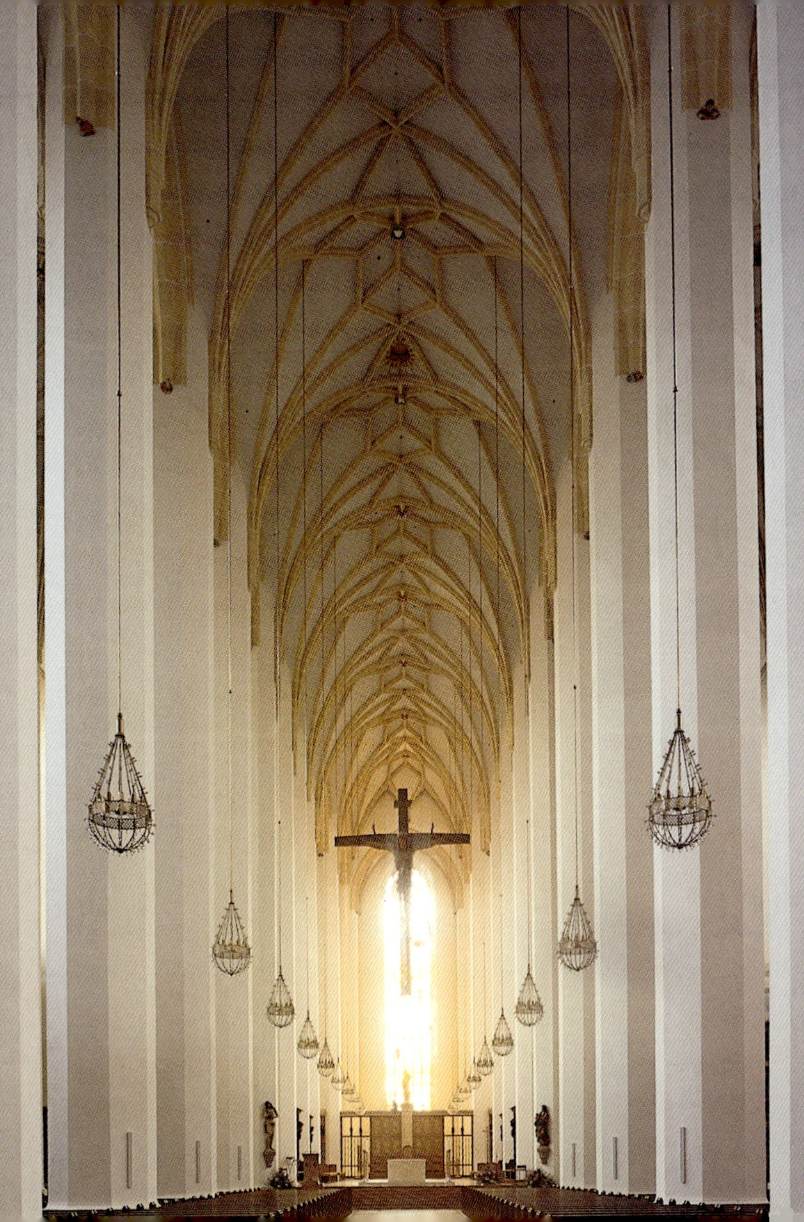

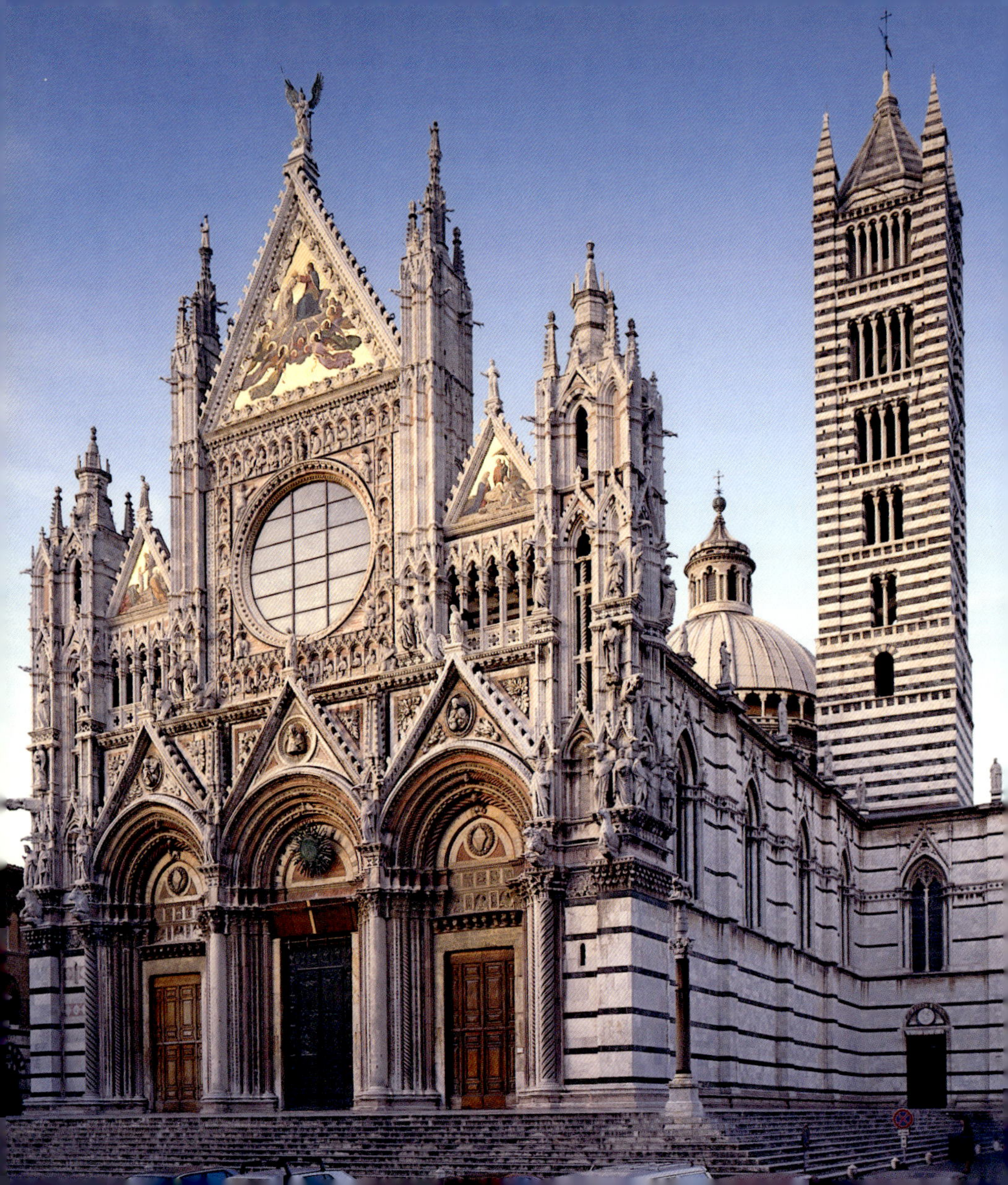

Religious Architecture in Italy

Our perception of Italian architecture is very much influenced by the famous structures of the Renaissance. But several extraordinary buildings were constructed in the Gothic style south of the Alps, too. Italian religious architecture of the 13th and 14th centuries does not, however, have a uniform style. Rather, it shows regional characteristics.

This may be explained by the political situation of the time and the large variety of different claims to power. For example, autonomous city states such as Florence and Siena were situated within the dominion of the Holy Roman Empire, which in turn bordered on the lands ruled by the Papacy in Rome. A multitude of influences and traditions resulted in various cultural developments. 13th-century southern Italy, which was ruled by Emperor Frederick II (1194–1250), was characterized by a specific stylistic mixture of Arabic, Byzantine, Norman and Classical elements, whereas church buildings of central and northern Italy already featured first traces of Gothic architecture. The mendicant orders played a vital role in this development. A good example of this is the Basilica of San Francesco, which, thanks to a gift from Pope Gregory IX, was erected in Assisi from 1230 to 1250. It is the burial place of the founder of the Franciscan Order (see pp. 180, 181).

Siena, Santa Maria Assunta,
facade (left),
nave (below),
reconstruction of the former Norman building commenced in the first half of the 13th century

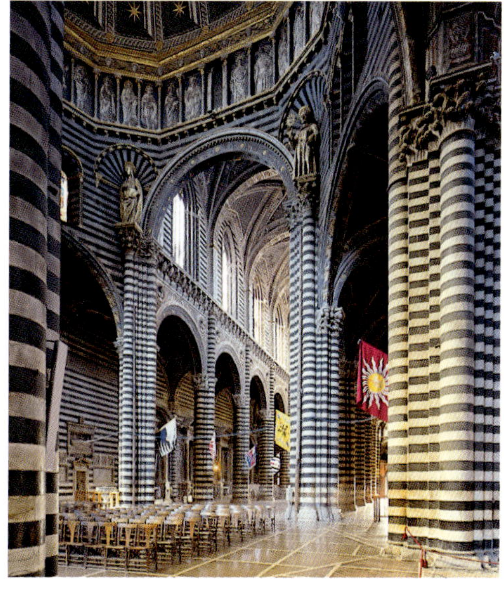

A typical central Italian church in the Gothic style is **Siena** Cathedral, **Santa Maria Assunta** (pp. 40, 41). The exceptional building, begun in the 13th century, was erected to replace a Romanesque church on the site. The construction phase, which extended well into the 14th century, coincides with the boom years of this important city state which had come to great wealth through trading and banking. The construction plans were adapted several times because the new cathedral was to integrate the former church as its transept. Due to static problems and the outbreak of the plague in 1348, all work on the building came to a halt. Today, the interior of the church leaves the impression of a harmonious unity, though the focus on verticality might not be as outspoken as in French churches. Unlike Gothic churches north of the Alps, the wall here remains the main supporting element, there is no use of pointed arches and buttresses to allow more windows. Another feature typical of the region is the polychrome black-and-white marble facade, which can also be seen on the neighboring campanile, the bell tower built in the 13th century. There, the marble's graphic effect is contrasted with arcades which increase in number towards the top. This arrangement in the form of an inverted triangle mitigates the monumentality of the tower, making it seem airy and elegant. The richly sculpted west front of the cathedral was designed by Giovanni Pisano (*c.* 1250–*c.* 1328) and also features mosaics and polychrome marble incrustations.

Florence,
Santa Maria del Fiore, (below) and Campanile (right), begun 1294 and 1334, respectively

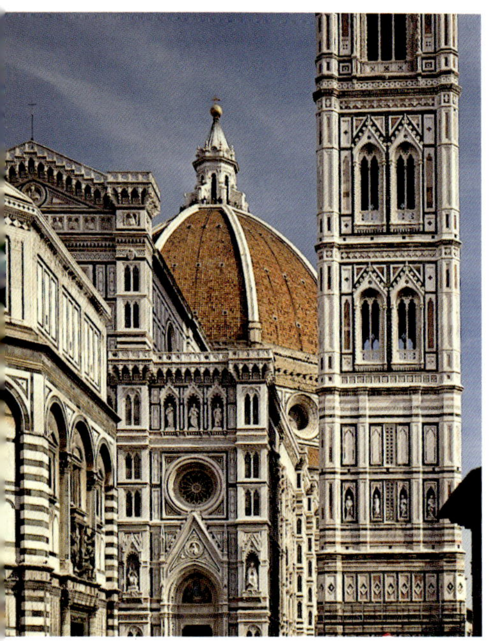

The city of **Florence** perpetually rivaled with Siena, which explains why the **Basilica di Santa Maria del Fiore** was expected to be at least as magnificent as that possessed by its Tuscan neighbor, to say the least. Construction began in 1294 on the site of an Early Christian church. After the death of the architect Arnolfo di Cambio (*c.* 1240/45–1302/1310), Giotto di Bondone continued the building works in 1334. However, his main attention lay on the campanile. Even though the facing of the bell tower, arranged in panels of white and polychrome marble with niches and ornamental statues, stands in clear relation to the cathedral facade, there is an architectural peculiarity here: the various stories of the tower, which is 82 meters high, increase in height towards the top. Although it is a different means than with the Siena campanile, the result is similar in that, seen from afar and taking into consideration the optical foreshortening of the upper stories, the tower seems less massive while at the same time exuding an air of monumentality. Giotto died in 1337 and construction of the cathedral was stalled until Francesco Talenti (*c.* 1300–1369) took over in 1357. As was the case in Siena, the construction plans for Florence Cathedral were also altered. Finally, the decision was made to build a rib-vaulted nave topped by a dome that would be much larger than originally planned. Filippo Brunelleschi (1377–1446) drew up the revolutionary plans and construction was begun in around 1425. The octagonal dome was constructed with double walls. At 91 meters in height it ranks as one of the most outstanding works of art in architecture. In 1436, a good 150 years after the onset of construction, the cathedral was finally consecrated.

The Basilica of **Saint Anthony, "Il Santo"** in **Padua** (pp. 44, 45), was begun in around 1230. It has an entirely different aspect than the basilicas of Siena and Florence. With its brick masonry, accentuated with friezes in a lighter shade and delicate arches, it is more reminiscent of models from Lombardy. San Antonio derives its name from St. Anthony, in whose honor the church was built during a time when Padua was an autonomous and very wealthy city. One of the first universities was founded here in 1222. Amongst the scholars

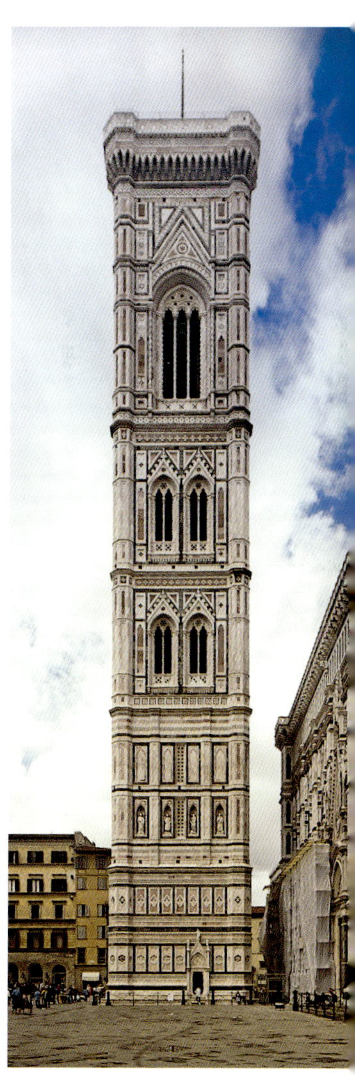

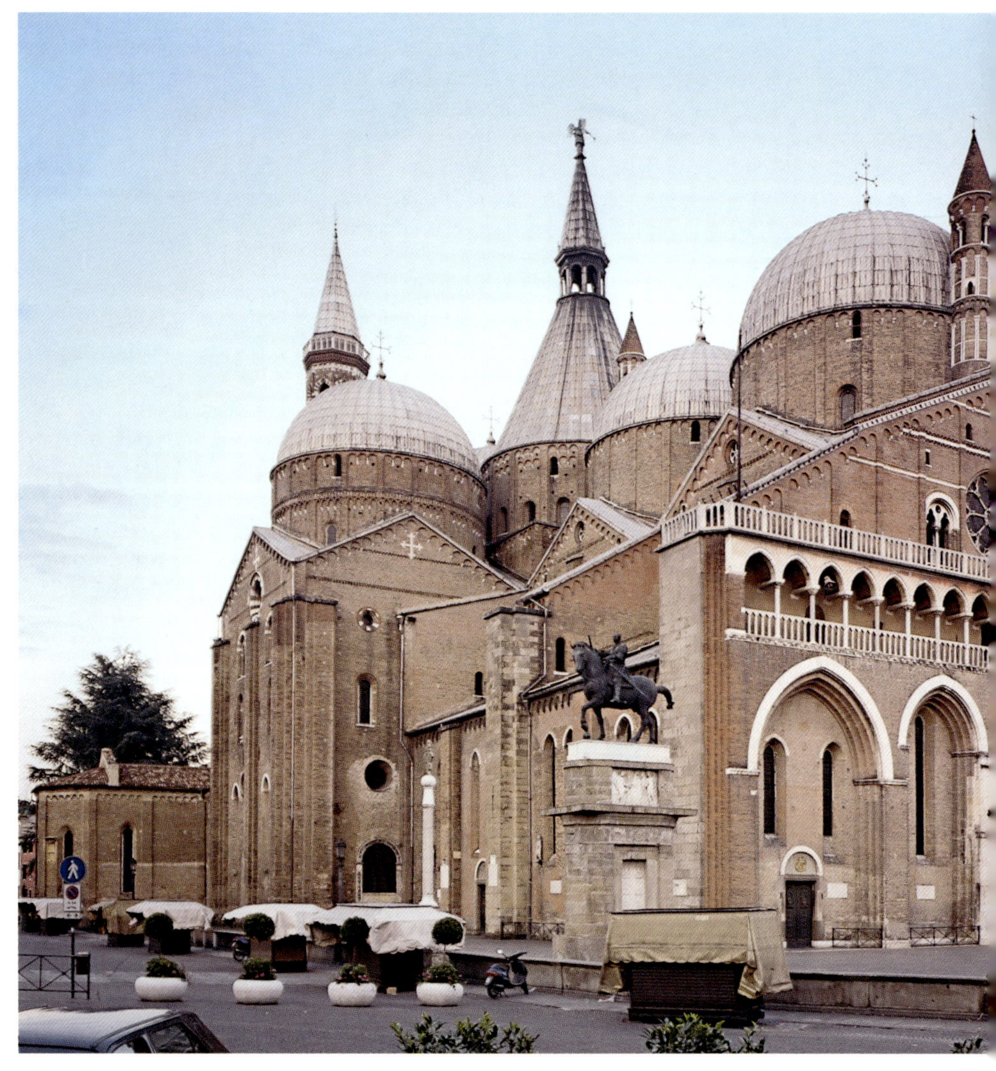

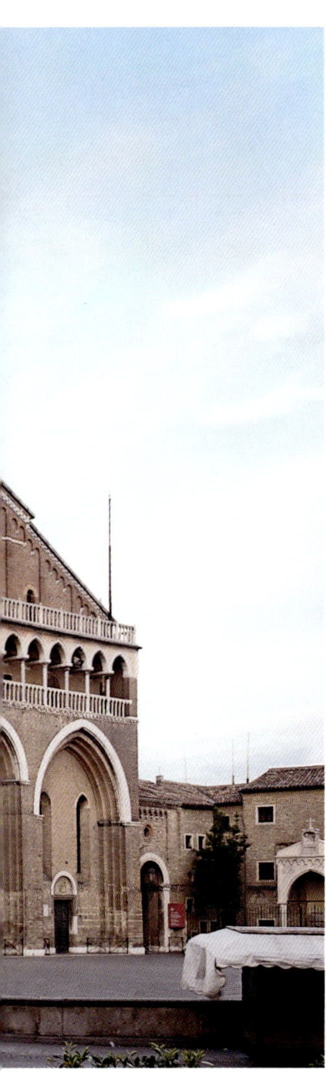

teaching there were Galileo Galilei, and the students included illustrious personages such as the astronomer Nicolaus Copernicus. This church differs from the other two mentioned above not only through its exterior features, but also in its remarkable ground plan: nave and transept are roofed with six domes. Slender spires finish off the overall complex. San Antonio combines features of Romanesque, Byzantine and Gothic architecture. The latter include the recesses and arcaded gallery of the west front.

The large range of styles in Italian Gothic architecture has already been mentioned. A further example is **Milan Cathedral, Santa Maria Nascente** (pp. 46, 47), erected from 1386 onward. Construction was stalled time and again because of the immense challenge in engineering posed by this structure. Experts were called in several times before the cathedral was finally completed in 1572. With a length of 158 meters, it ranks among the largest Gothic church buildings. Of all the Italian churches, this one comes closest to the style of cathedrals built north of the Alps. S. Maria Nascente features a nave with double aisles and a double transept. The facade is clad in light marble and replete with about 2300 sculptures and ornamental decoration – an overwhelming appearance. The monumentality and artistic mastery of the building was also intended to be read as a political statement, since in the 14th century Milan was ruled by Gian Galeazzo of the house of Visconti.

Padua,
San Antonio,
begun *c.* 1230

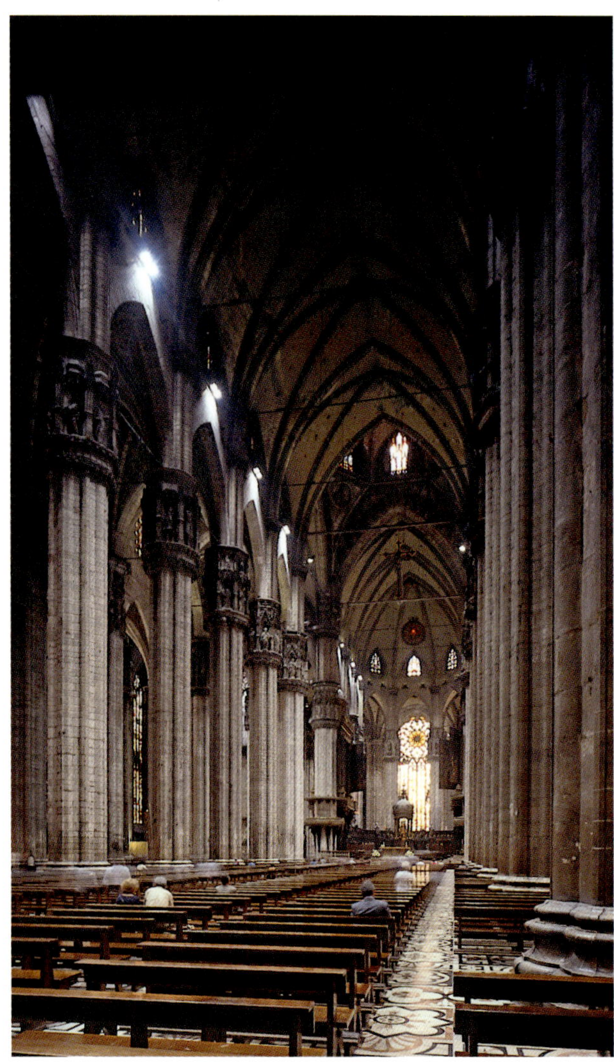

Milan,
Santa Maria Nascente,
nave and choir (left),
exterior view of transept
and choir (right),
begun 1386

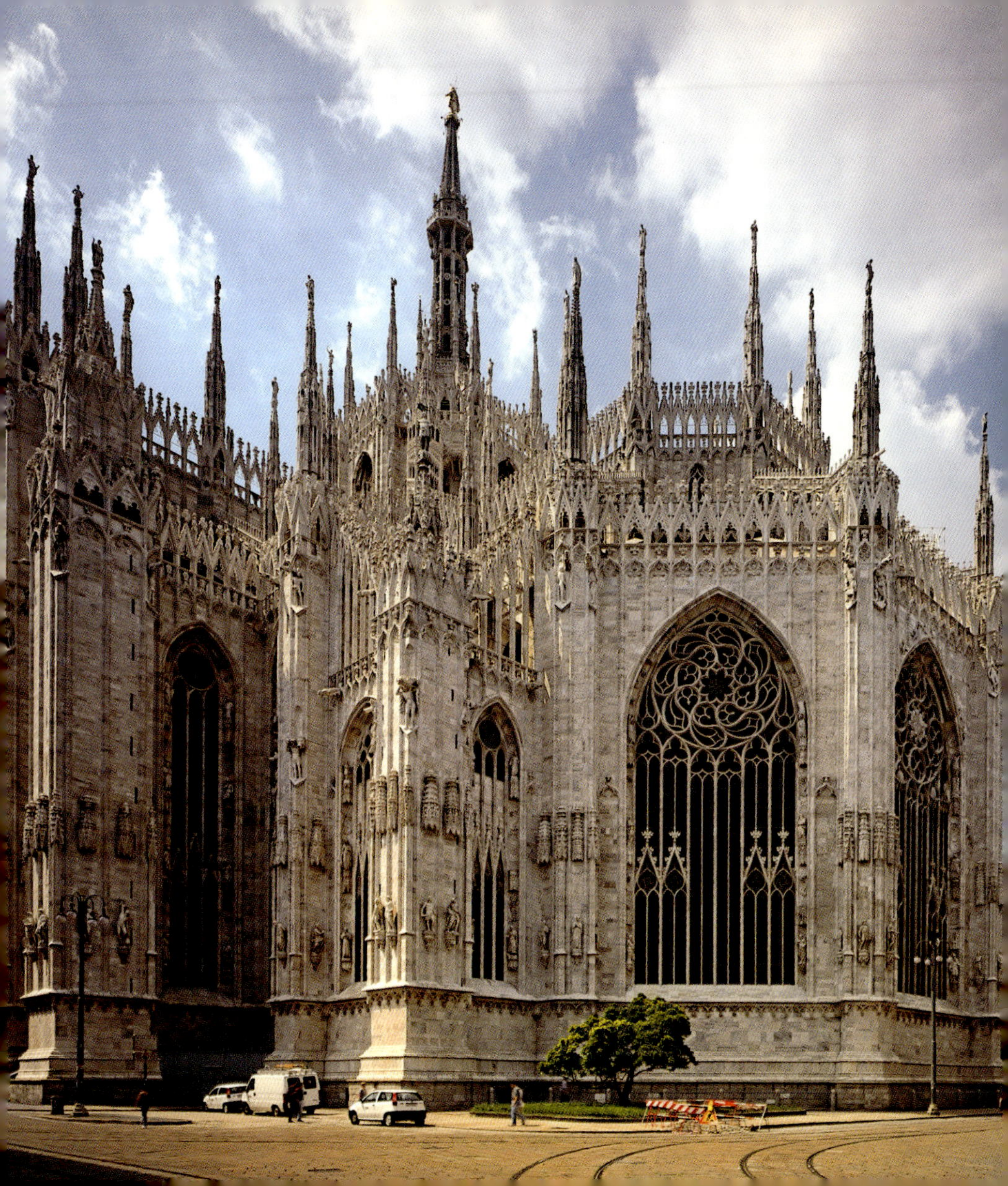

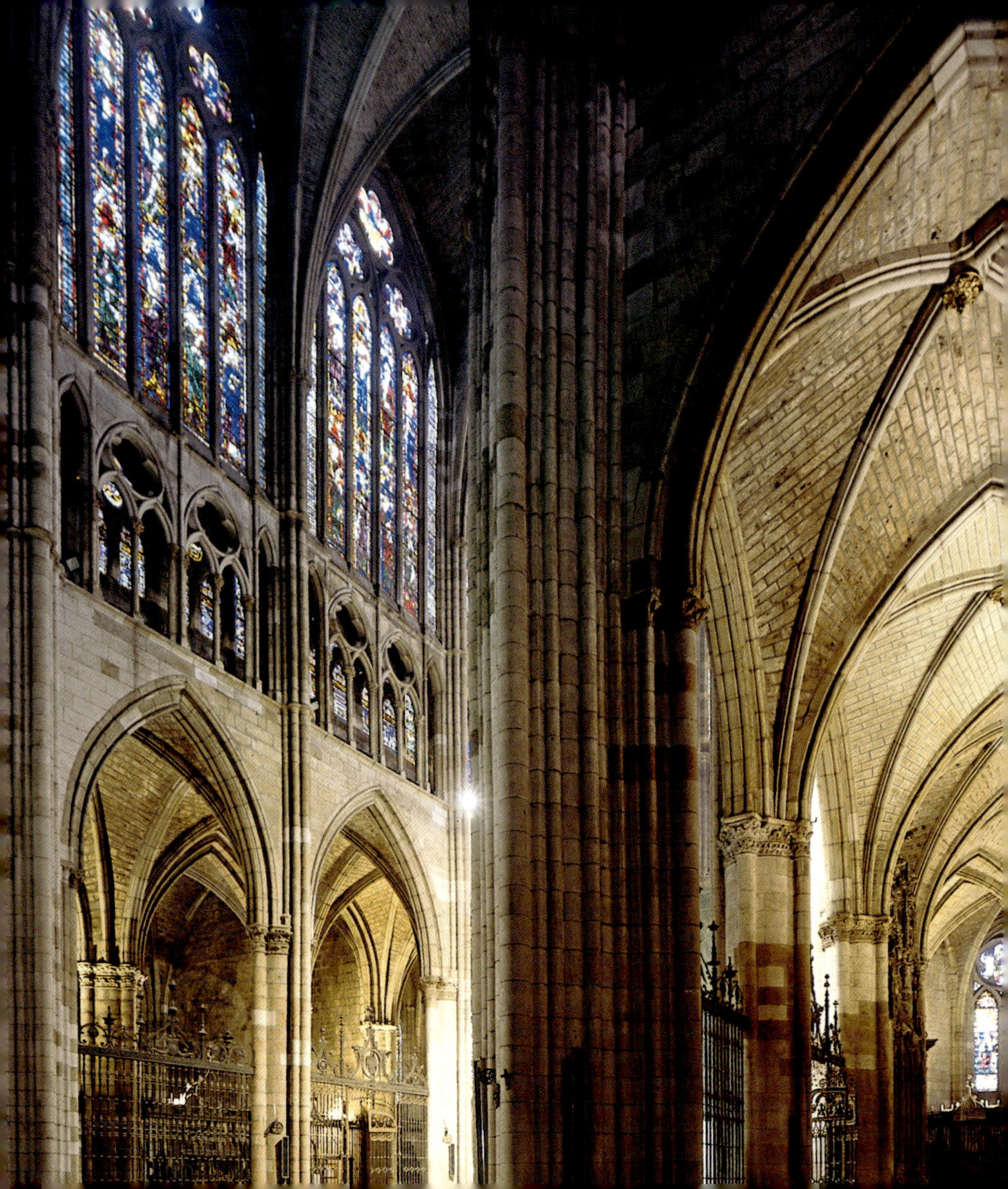

Religious Architecture in Spain and Portugal

Religious Architecture in Spain

The art and culture of Spain were largely influenced by the Moors, who had conquered the Iberian peninsula from 711 onward. But, in the Middle Ages, the Christian monarchs set about recapturing the land and the *Reconquista* successfully ended in 1492, with the victory over the last Islamic stronghold, Granada. The victory of the Christian party, and the power of the Catholic Church, were made manifest in numerous buildings. For example, in the 16th century a cathedral was integrated into the existing mosque of Córdoba. The churches and cathedrals built from the 13th century on were oriented on the Gothic examples of France. French Romanesque architecture of the two preceding centuries had already left its traces in Spain, due to the vivid cultural exchange that took place all along the Way of St. James, which ended in Santiago de Compostela in Spain. The pioneering role of French architecture thus also paved the way for the innovations presented by the Gothic style. Typical of Spanish Gothic, however, are reminiscences of Moorish art. During the Late Gothic, Spain even produced its own idiosyncratic style, the Plateresque. It derives its name from the exuberantly decorated works of art created by the silversmiths and generally features

Left:
León,
interior view, begun in the mid-13th century

Toledo,
Catedral de Santa María, constructed between the 13th and 15th centuries

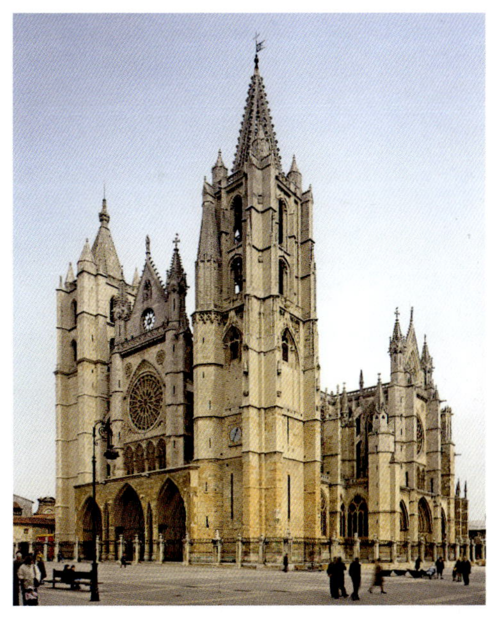

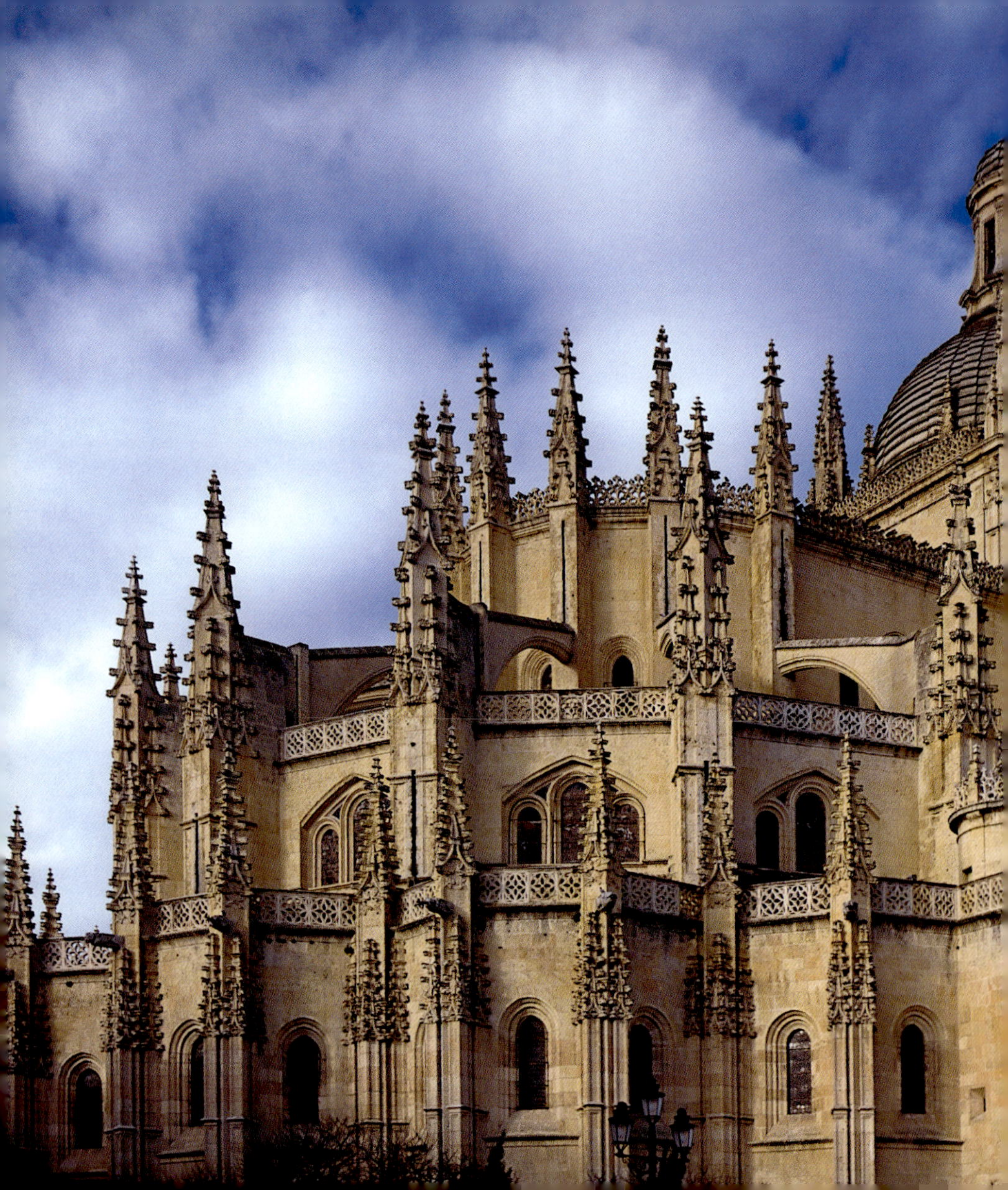

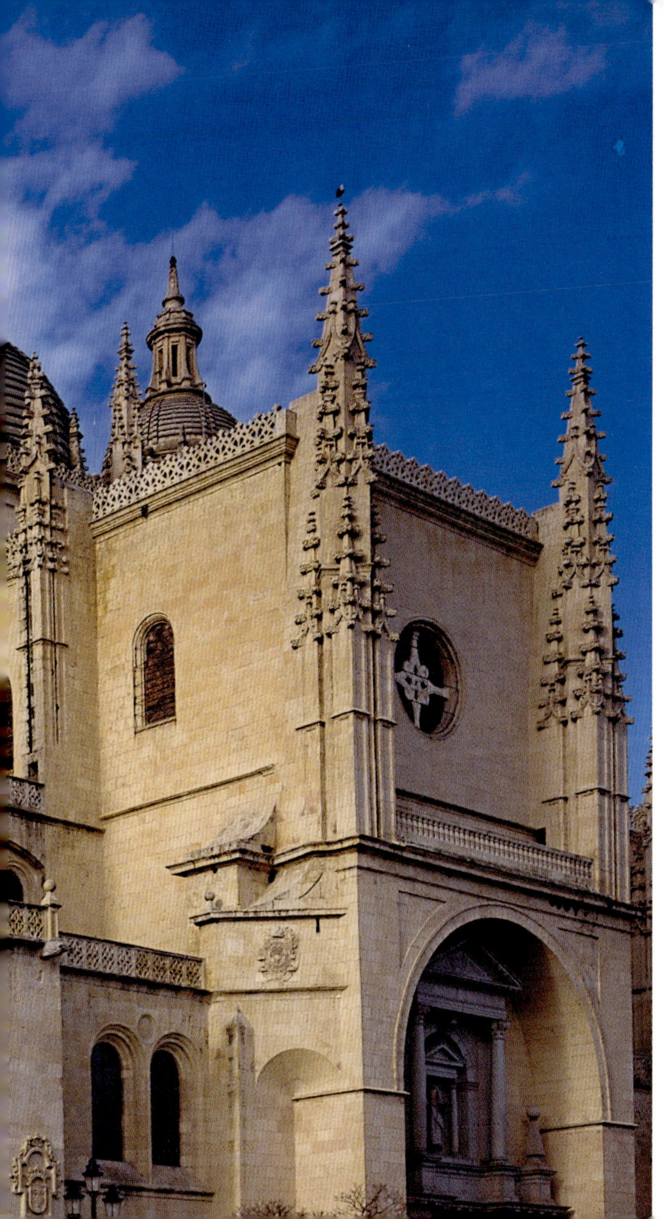

The exterior of Segovia Cathedral would look rather massive if it weren't for the spiny pinnacles, which were inspired by Moorish ornamentation.

Segovia,
Catedral de Nuestra Señora de la Asunción y de San Frutos, exterior view of the choir, begun 1525

the adaptation of Moorish forms and patterns. The greater part of the large cathedrals were built in Castile, where the *Reconquista* had been foremost, and in cities that lay along the Way of St. James. **León** is one such city. In the Middle Ages, it was the capital of the kingdom of Léon and was situated on an important trade route. The towers of the early Gothic cathedral of **Santa María Regla** (p. 48), situated in the heart of the old city, are over 60 meters high and can be seen from afar. Construction was begun in the 13th century. The master masons were evidently inspired by French models, since the impressive stained-glass windows and the rich sculptural ornamentation are reminiscent of Amiens and Reims Cathedrals (see p. 21). Well-worth visiting are the Late Gothic cloisters and the staircase in the Plateresque style.

60 kilometers to the south-west of Madrid lies **Toledo,** over which towers the fortress of Alcázar. Both the spectacular situation atop a cliff and the history of the town dating back centuries lend Toledo, the former capital of Castile, a magnificent air. When the Christian warriors reconquered it in the 11th century, the city looked back on 300 years under Moorish rule. The Christian population at first lived in close communion with the Muslims and Jews, but later the Inquisition drove out all heretics. The **Catedral de Santa María** (p. 49) is situated in the

Portugal as Colonial Power

In **1385**, after the Battle of Aljubarrota, Portugal finally secured its independence from Spain. The nearby Batalha Monastery was founded in commemoration of this occasion. Prince Henry the Navigator, the fourth son of Portuguese King John I, was born in **1394** and in **1415** conquered Ceuta in north Africa. Henry laid the foundations of Portugal's rise to a colonial power by instigating several voyages of discovery. He also founded a school of navigation in Sagres, where the knowledge which Portuguese navigators had increasingly acquired during their voyages across the Atlantic was passed on. It is thanks to Henry's initiatives that Madeira and the Azores were discovered by the Portuguese, who then settled there. In **1498**, Vasco da Gama rounded the African continent and, in the course, discovered the sea route to India. In the years that followed, Portugal established colonies in Brazil, Africa, India, China and Southeast Asia. The empire suffered financial crises in the **15TH** and **16TH CENTURIES**, which led to national bankruptcy. At the same time, other European colonial powers extended their territories and began to rival Portugal. Nonetheless, Portugal remained a colonial power until the **20TH CENTURY**.

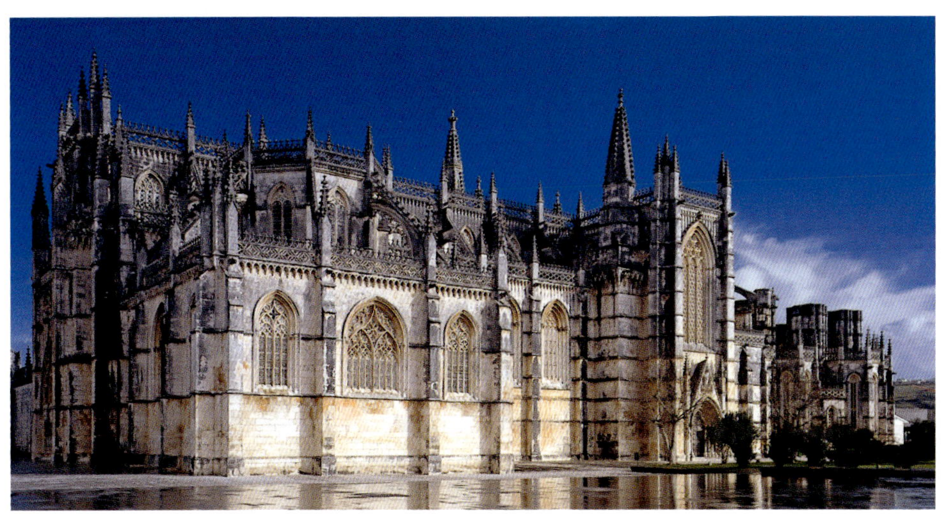

Batalha,
Mosteiro de Santa María da Vitória,
constructed 1388–1533

heart of the old city center, which is steeped in tradition. Built between the 13th and 15th centuries, it is an architectural symbol of Christian power. The impressively large structure has double aisles, a double choir ambulatory, and sports a variety of styles, including some Renaissance elements. The vault is in the Mudéjar style and as such pays homage to the influence left after centuries of Moorish rule. Mudéjar style is the term for works of art done by Muslim artists for Christian clients and typically integrates elements of Arab art into the works.

Segovia is also situated in the vicinity of Madrid. It may not be as impressive as Toledo, but it certainly is equally picturesque. Here as there, the cityscape is characterized by a fortification and a Gothic **cathedral** (pp. 50, 51). The **Catedral de Nuestra Señora de la Asunción y de San Frutos** was built in the 16th and 17th centuries on the site of a former church which had been destroyed in large parts. The cloister dating

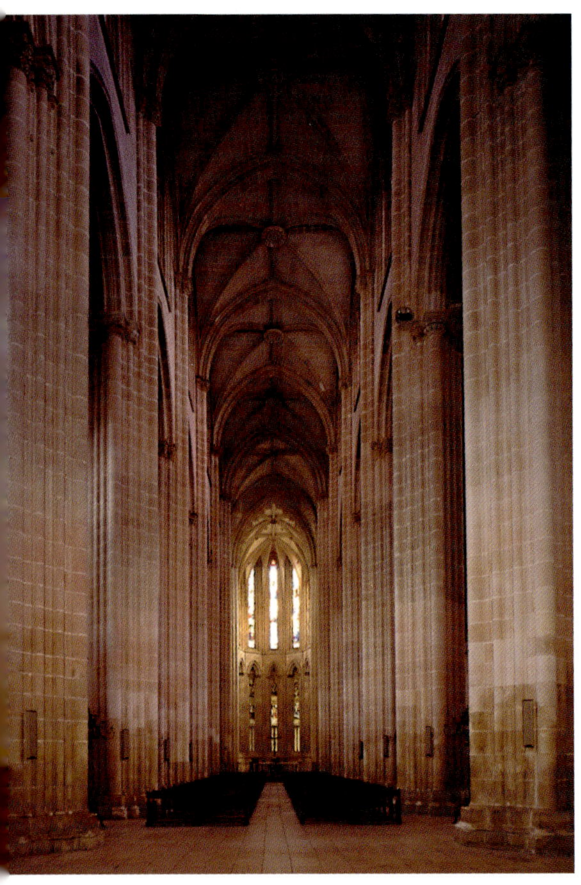

Batalha,
Mosteiro de Santa María da Vitória,
nave and choir,
constructed 1388–1533

from the 15th century was integrated beautifully into the construction.

Religious Architecture in Portugal
Gothic architecture in Portugal was largely influenced by the Cistercian order. A unique feature of Portuguese art is the Manueline style, named after King Manuel I (1495–1521). During his reign, Portugal experienced an economic and cultural heyday which also shows in the architecture of the time. The repertoire of forms is characterized by exuberant ornamentation inspired by maritime motifs and similar to the Plateresque style of Spain. The more naturalistic forms of this style combine elements from the Late Gothic, the Early Renaissance and Moorish art. One of the foremost examples of Manueline style is the **Monastery of Jerome (Mosteiro dos Jerónimos)** in the **Belém** district of Lisbon (pp. 56, 57). It was built in 1502 and survived the disastrous earthquake of 1755. The monastery was built during Portugal's Golden Age, which lasted from 1385 to 1580 and was influenced by numerous voyages of discovery and conquests. Its idiosyncratic, almost austere architectural structure is set into effective contrast with the overbounding imaginative ornamentation. Mention must be made of the cloister with its abundance of sculptural elements, but the elaborate reticulated vaulting of the church is equally worthy of attention. The **monastery of Batalha (Mosteiro**

de Santa María da Vitória) dating from the 14th century is a remarkable work of art (p. 53, 54, 55). The Dominican church was built on the occasion of the victory of Portuguese King John I over the Castilian army in 1385. At 90 meters length, this spacious cathedral ranks among the longest churches in Europe. The magnificent west portal, which served both as main portal and the king's entry, is decorated with a multitude of sculpted figures. The richly ornamented cloister next to the church is a favorite place to rest awhile. The pointed arches and tracery are typical of the Manueline style in as much as the imaginative and exuberant forms transgress the boundaries between ornamentation and figural elements. Batalha Monastery was declared a national heritage in 1840 and is one of the most outstanding Gothic structures of the Iberian peninsula.

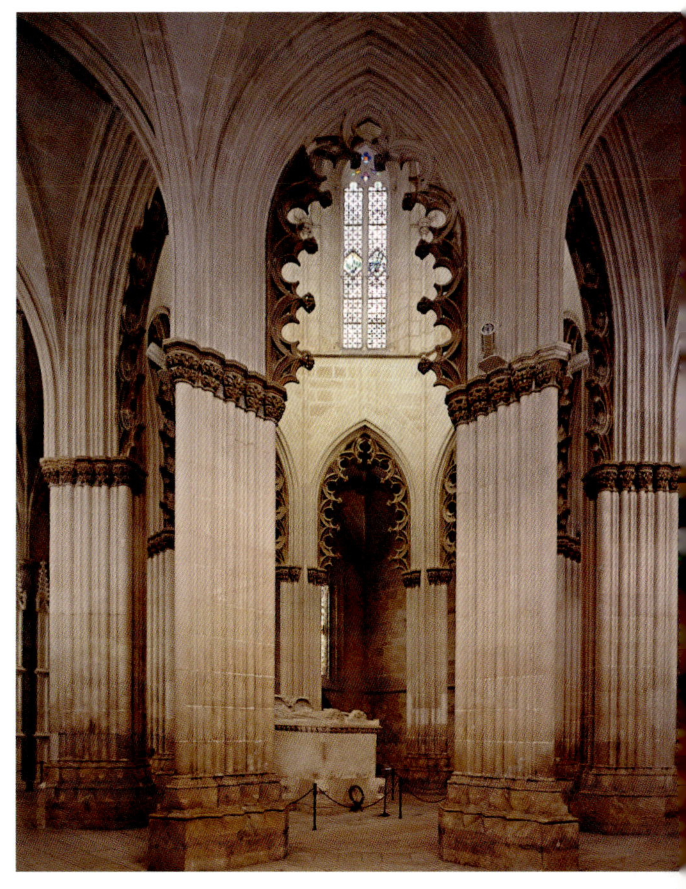

Batalha,
Mosteiro de Santa María da Vitória, Capela do Fundador, chapel constructed 1426–1434

Following double spread:
Belém,
Mosteiro dos Jerónimos, cloister, *c.* 1517

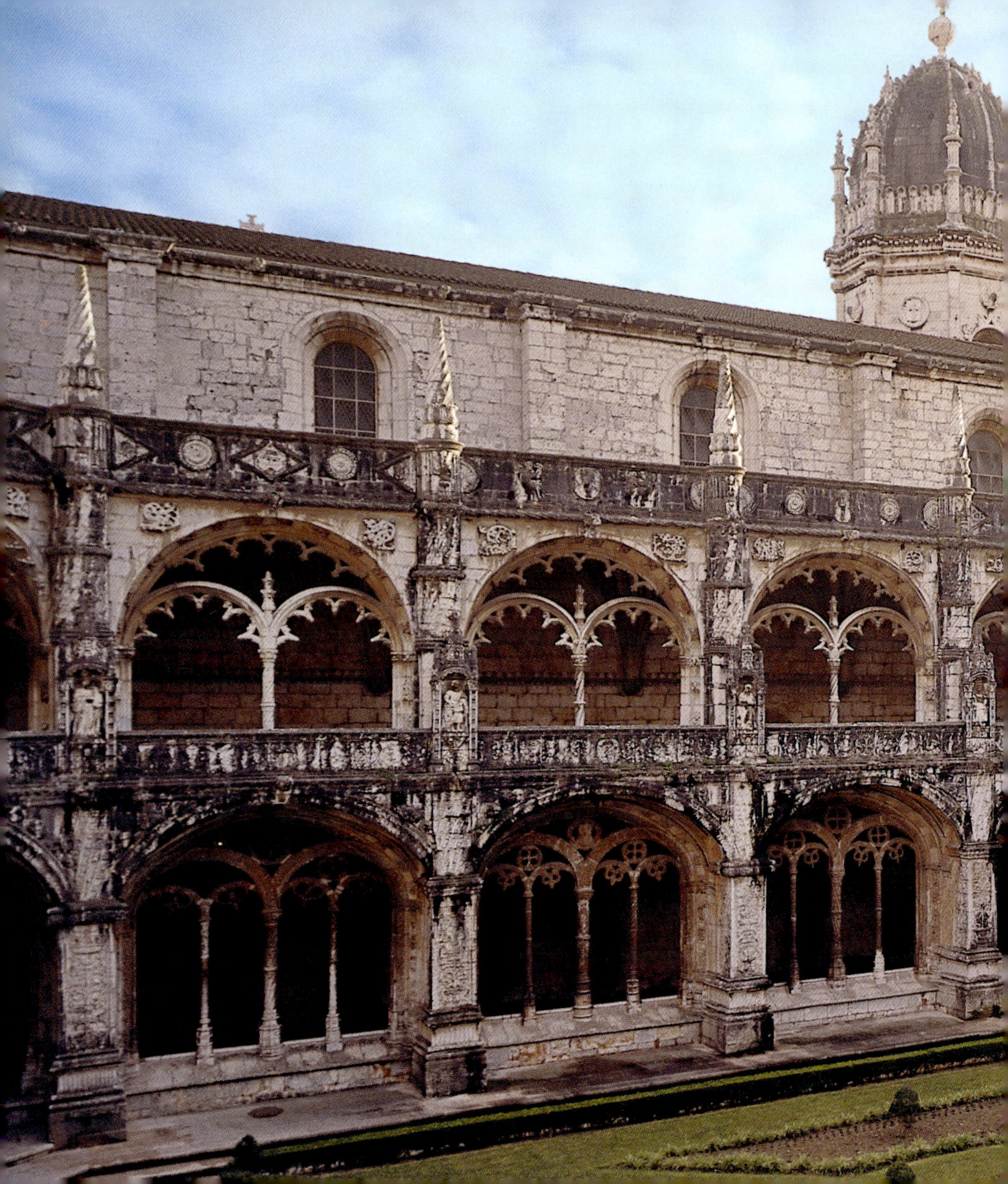

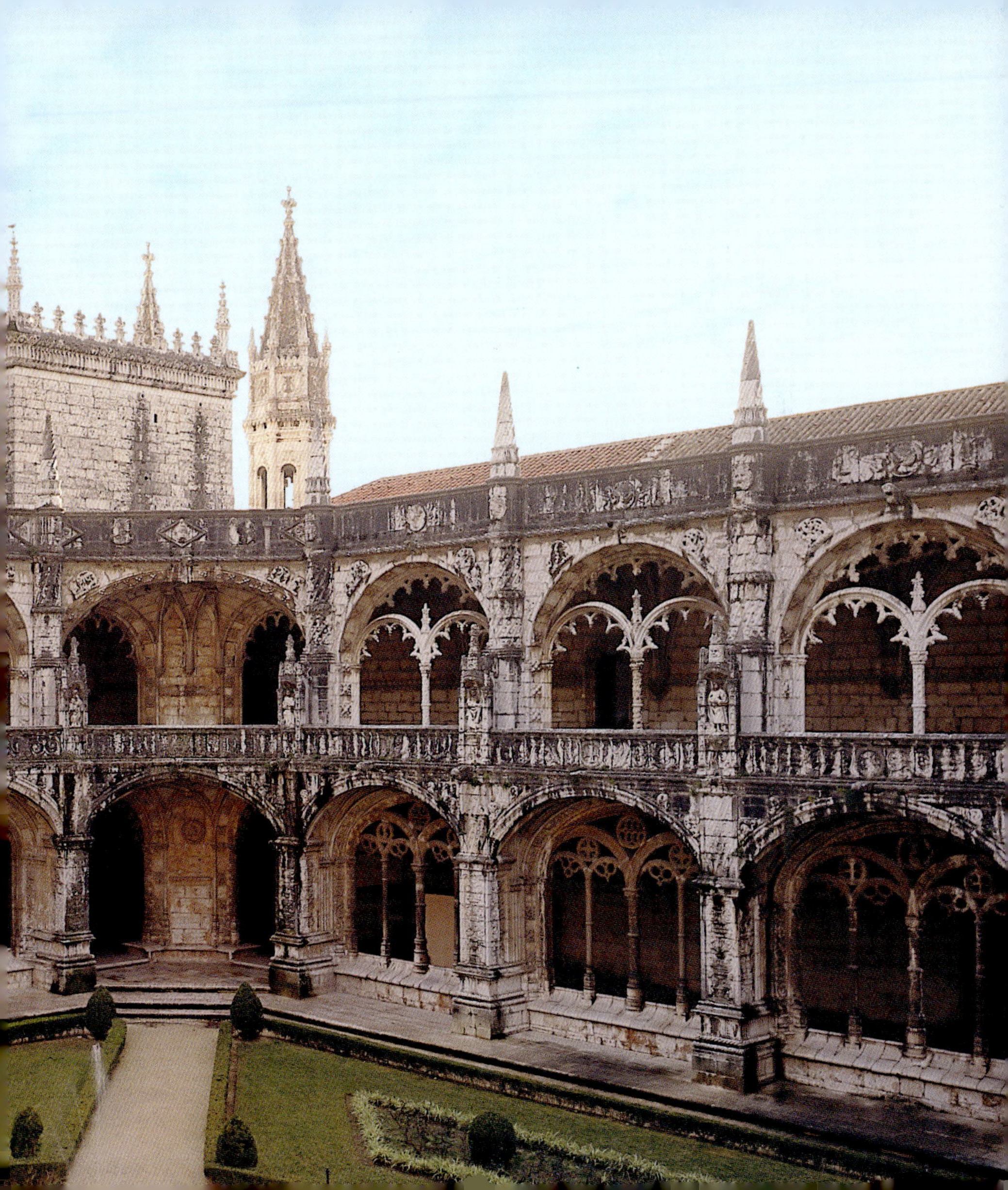

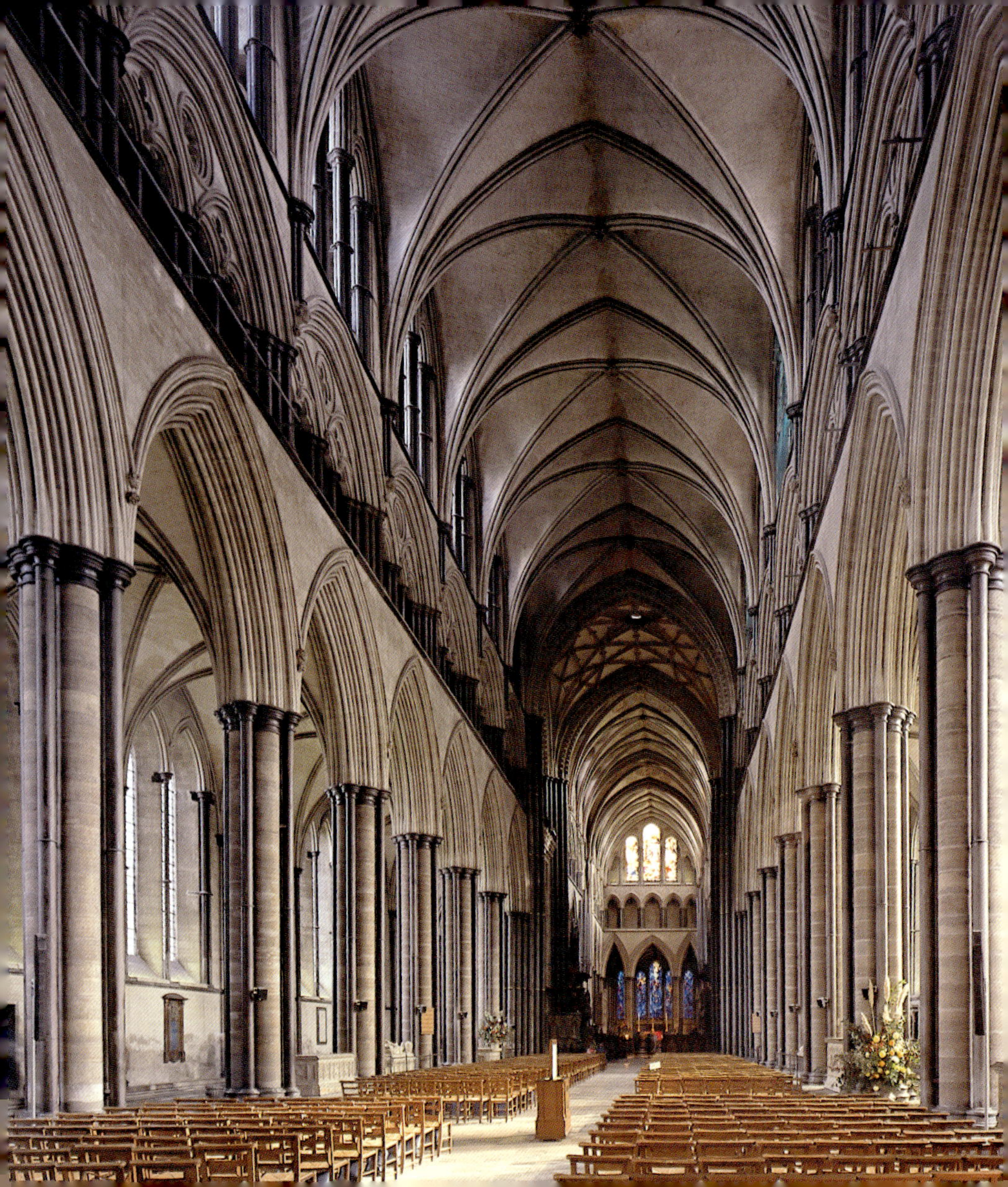

Religious Architecture in England

Ever since the Battle of Hastings in 1066, when William the Conqueror gained a decisive victory over the Anglo-Saxons, England had been closely related to France. Over the centuries, these connections were consolidated through a policy of well-placed marriages. In 1154, the dominion of Henry II extended from England via northern France right down to Aquitaine in southern France. Henry was a scion of the House of Anjou-Plantagenet, which until 1399 would play a major role in English history. The connections between England and the French territories encompassed economic as well as cultural spheres. The works of art and architecture which were created in the regions bordering on the Channel bear vivid witness to this. For example, medieval ivory reliefs have been found in northern France and southern England that cannot be allocated to a specific regional style or artist. On the contrary, busy trade and the fact that most artisans were itinerant craftspeople led to the development of a supraregional style. In comparison to prior centuries, in which the monasteries' own workshops had mostly been responsible for the craftwork, there is an increasing tendency in the 12th and 13th centuries for craftspeople to be contracted for church buildings who were not listed as members of the specific community. This social development was determined by the increasing population of

Salisbury Cathedral,
nave and choir (left), exterior view from north-east (below), constructed 1220–1266

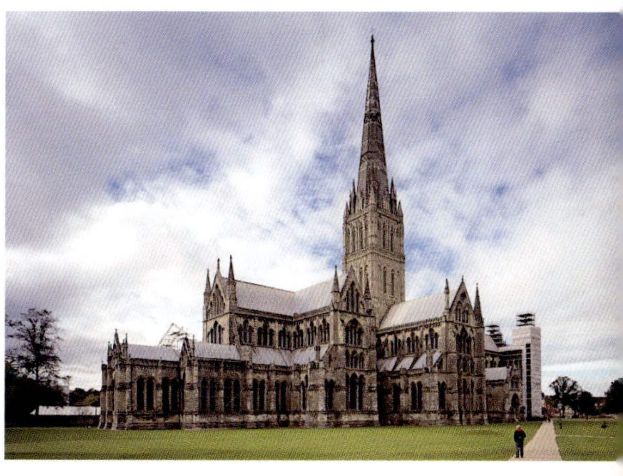

the cities. Wealthy citizens began to act as donors and there was a growing demand in religious art. This led to the emergence of specialist workshops whose members – unlike friars, who were only exceptionally allowed to travel – could travel about and thus increase their knowledge. This phenomenon can be traced when studying the development of the major late medieval builders' workshops (see pp. 24 ff.).

London,
Westminster Abbey,
choir and transept,
interior view towards the
east end,
begun *c.* 1245

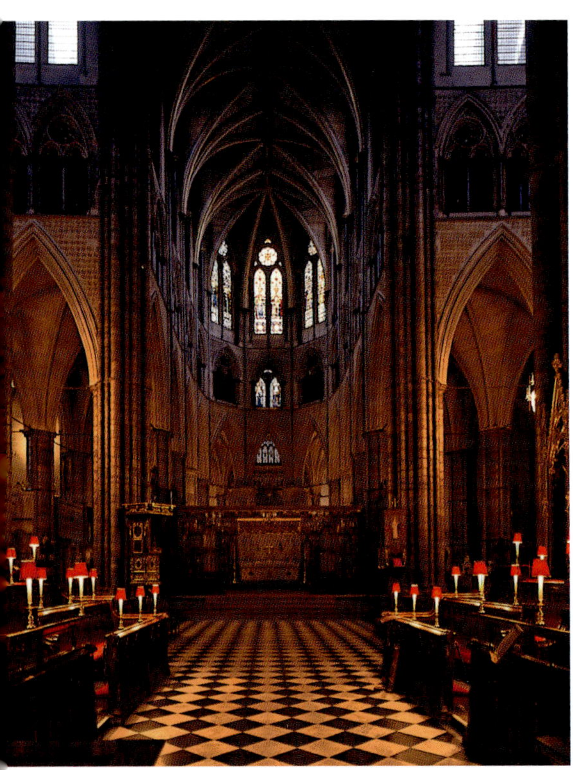

The rise of Gothic architecture in England was instigated through the Cistercian order, although only ruins have remained of their buildings. **Canterbury Cathedral** is the first Gothic cathedral, built in the Early English style (pp. 62, 63, 64). Canterbury had been an archdiocese since the 7th century. The renovation of the choir, which had been destroyed during a fire in 1174, was at first directed by Frenchman William of Sens, and later completed by English architects. Reconstruction of the church developed into an ambitious building project during the course of which the choir was prolonged towards the east end. It was elaborately ornamented to meet the flourishing cult of Saint Thomas Becket, Archbishop of Canterbury, who was murdered in the church in 1170. The shrine containing his relics was presented on an elevated spot in Trinity Chapel, specially constructed for this purpose. Stained-glass windows depict the martyrdom of St. Thomas Becket. The ambulatory was designed to allow a large number of pilgrims, coming to venerate the martyr's shrine. The architects of Canterbury Cathedral's choir ambulatory had thus found a technical solution for an organizational problem; this solution served as a model for many other church buildings.

English Gothic architecture was widely influenced by French cathedrals but soon developed individual solutions. English Gothic is subdivided into three periods with characteristic stylistic features: Early English style, Decorated style and Perpendicular style, in chronological order. Apart from the Norman building style, which originated in 1066, when the Normans under William the Conqueror invaded England, English churches were characterized by sprawling facades and a ground plan which differed exceedingly from that of French cathedrals. Whereas in the cradle of Gothic architecture steps would often lead up from the crossing to the choir, English churches usually stressed the shape of the Latin cross, as in **Salisbury** (pp. 58, 59). **Salisbury Cathedral,** built in light grey limestone, was begun in 1220 and consecrated in 1258. Extensive renovation work followed in the 18th and 19th centuries. The tower at the crossing with its 14th-century spire is 123 meters high. The cathedral was completed within an unusually short space of time.

London,
Westminster Abbey,
nave,
nave completed in 1375

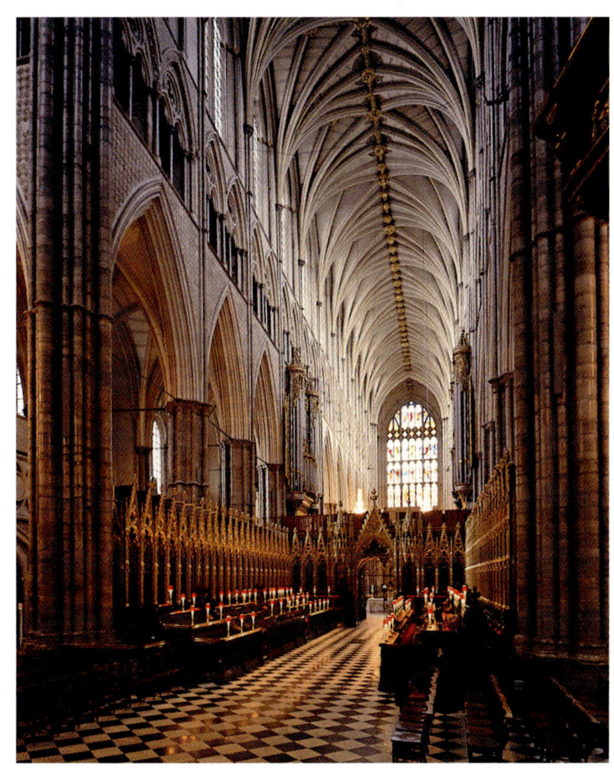

This was made possible by the support of King Henry III and by the fact that it was erected on grounds free of any previous structures, so that there were no architectural elements to be integrated into the plans. Generally, the completion of a cathedral would take centuries. Salisbury, however, was drafted and completed in a very short period. The entire complex is an exceptional example of the Early English style. The harmonious overall impression of the building is underlined by the well-balanced ground plan: two pairs of transepts, the second narrower than the first, lead to the choir while towards the east end the presbytery extends to Trinity Chapel. The evenly structured nave is flooded in light and characterized by a three-storied elevation, fashioned after the example of Lincoln Cathedral (begun 1192). However, the vaulting differs exceedingly: whereas in Lincoln an extravagant design of asymmetrically arranged ribs predominates, Salisbury has a cross-ribbed vault typical of Gothic architecture. The chapel has a generously spacious atmosphere; slender grey marble pillars stand off from the walls and slightly lighter vault. The contrast between the shiny dark Purbeck marble and the light-colored, slightly dull masonry also features in the nave. In the late 13th century, a remarkable cloister with stellar vault was added to the south side. Next to this stands the chapter house for members of the cathedral chapter. Bishop Roger Poore (bishop 1107–1139) initiated the construction. Its delicately worked sculptural ornamentation is in accordance with the high rank of the cathedral building.

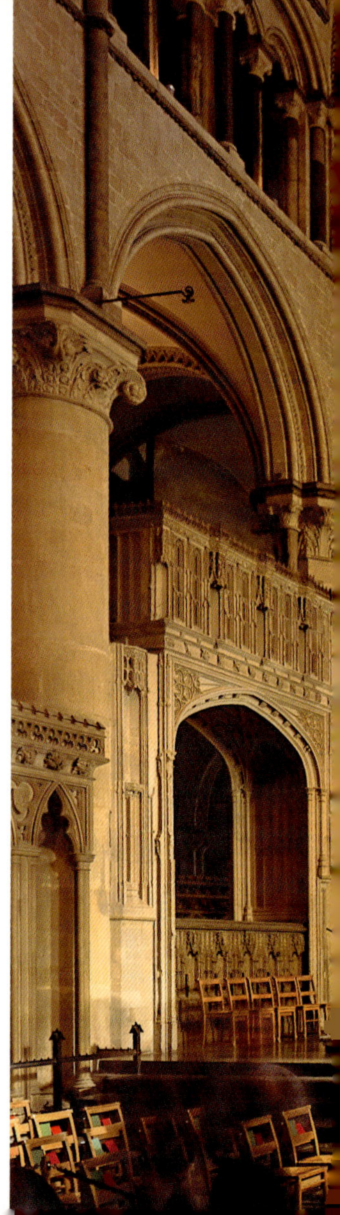

Canterbury Cathedral,
nave and choir,
reconstructed after 1174

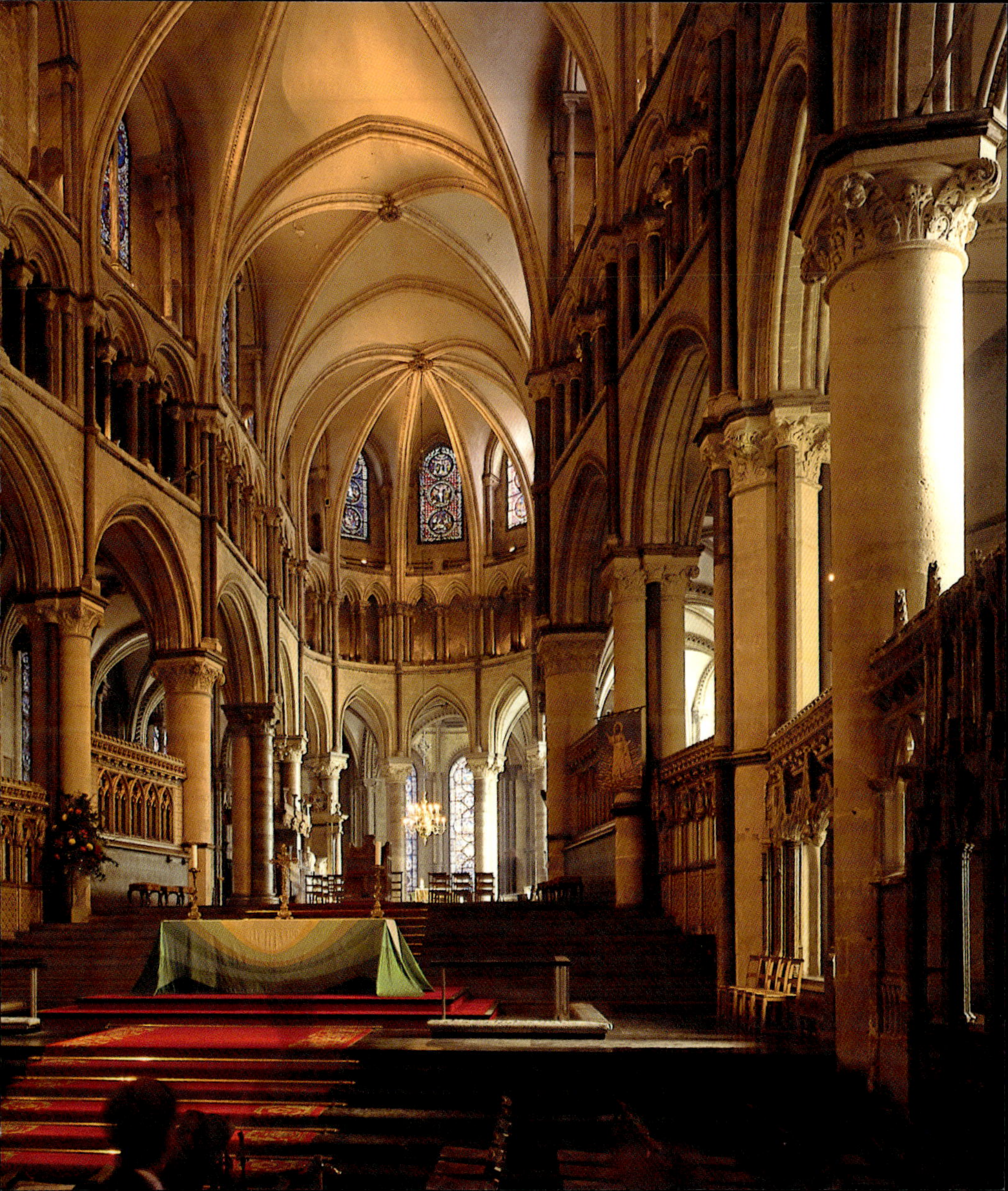

The most important church construction of the 13th century was **Westminster Abbey** in **London** (pp. 60, 61), begun in *c.* 1245 on commission of the king. Led by pragmatic political motivations, Henry III wished the abbey church to be superior to any other in size and grandeur. By building a new burial place for St. Edward the Confessor, Henry's renowned predecessor, he planned to consolidate English power over France. During a time when the king was understood to be God's representative on Earth, presenting a saint as predecessor in office was an argument hard to ignore. The new house of God in Westminster was to set the standards for numerous succeeding buildings. The ornamentation, such as the rich tracery, marks the beginning of a new architectural style, namely the exuberant Decorated style. Amongst the characteristic features of this style are small chiselled rosettes, which were gilded and overpainted. The magnificent interior features were also inspired by the cathedral of Sainte-Chapelle in Paris, which the French King Louis IX had commissioned in *c.* 1241 to hold the relics of the Crown of Thorns (see pp. 140, 141). Westminster Abbey integrates elements typical of French cathedral architecture, such as the rose windows in the transept, but adds individual stylistic elements, such as the construction of a gallery instead of a triforium. The result is a synthesis of the various architectural innovations introduced in Europe. The king did not live to see the completion of his church. When Henry III died in 1272, construction was stalled. The nave was completed after 1375 while the west towers were only completed in the 18th century. In the early 16th century, King Henry VII ordered some restructuring to be done. He chose Westminster Abbey as his future burial place

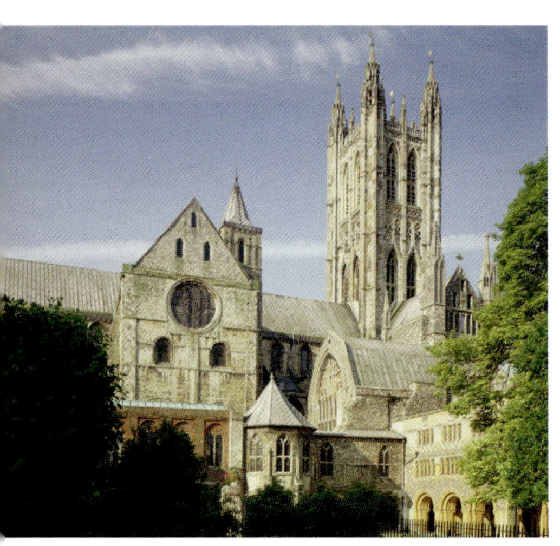

Canterbury Cathedral, reconstructed after 1174

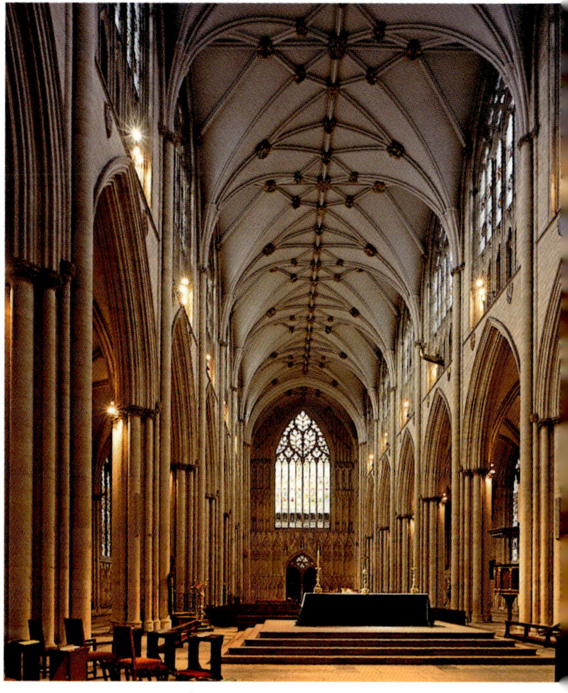

and for this reason had radiating chapels added to the choir aisles. The walls and windows of his chapel are decorated with the typical slender, vertical mullions which gave the Perpendicular style of the Late Gothic period its name. Another typical feature of this style is the wall ornamentation, often consisting of a slender rectangle surmounted by a pointed arch.

York Minster, built between 1361 and 1405 (pp. 65, 66, 67), shows the geometric ornamentation of the Perpendicular style in a more subtle variant. Nave and choir, however, were begun in the 13th century and are an impressive example of the Decorated style, which was heavily influenced by French models, as can be seen in the high pointed arcades and the gabled triforium. The window tracery in the west facade features elaborately sculpted mouchette tracery in the Decorated style. York was an exceedingly important city in England's history, as can be seen from the Late Gothic rood screen decorated with statues of the kings of England. Apart from the cathedral proper, the medieval town center also bears witness to the importance which York traditionally held.

York,
Minster,
view from the choir into the nave, construction of nave 1291–*c.* 1340

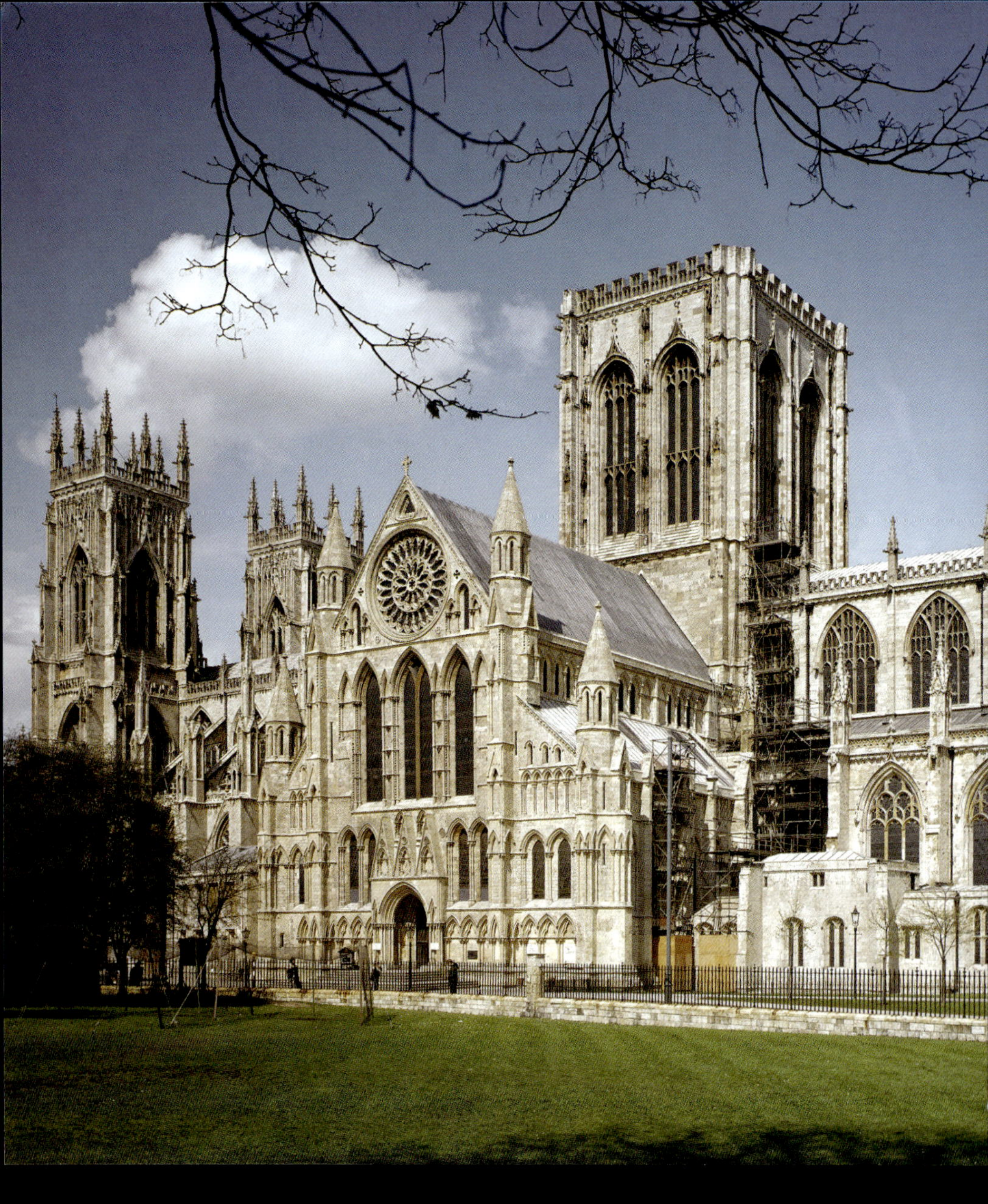

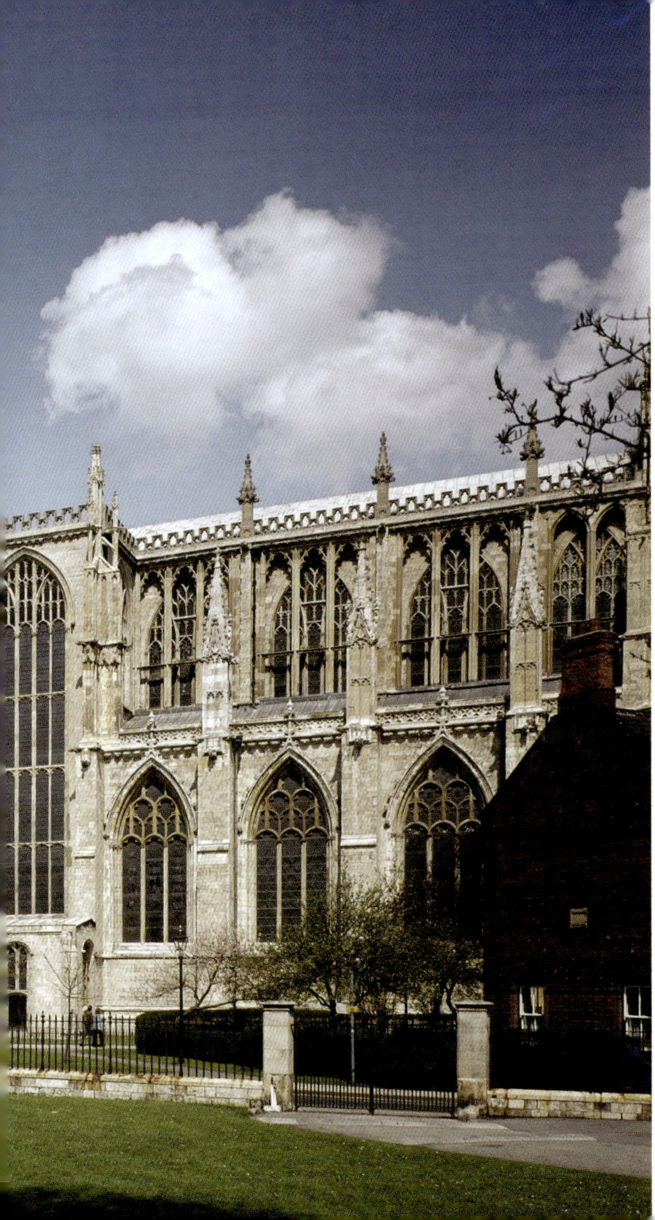

Even though English architects were widely inspired by French Gothic cathedrals, English Gothic soon developed into an individual style. English churches are very long, sprawling and feature more ornamentation of the overall masonry.

York,
Minster,
begun 1291,
choir constructed 1361–1405

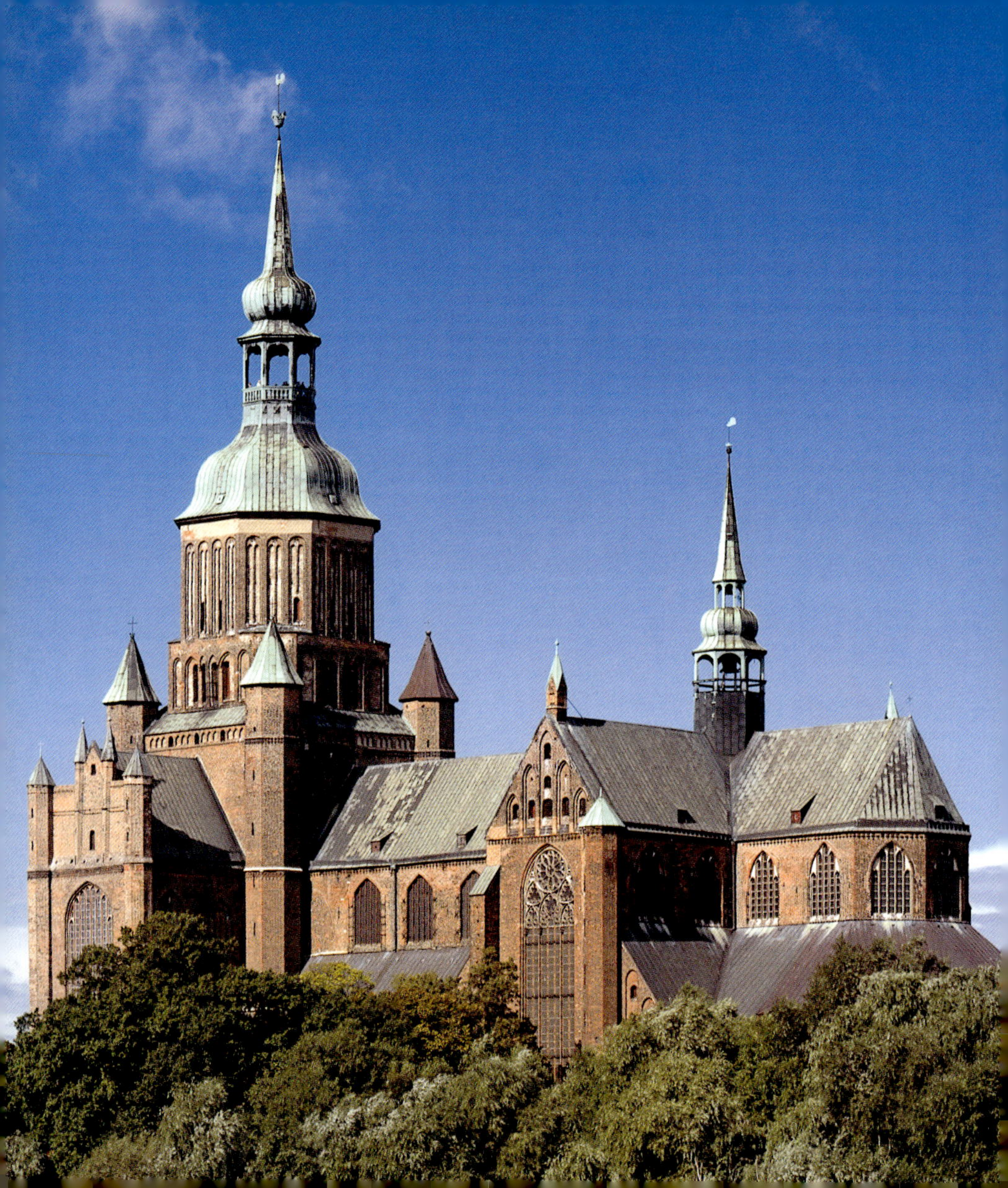

Religious Architecture in Northern and Eastern Europe

Stralsund,
St. Mary's,
exterior view from the
south-east,
c. 1384–1440,
spire 1708 (left),
vaulting of the narthex,
begun after 1380 (below)

North-eastern Europe's Brick Gothic

Brick Gothic is a phenomenon of north-eastern Europe. It refers to buildings constructed out of glazed and decorated red clay bricks, since natural stone was lacking in these regions. Hence the use of bricks for churches in the new, Gothic style. The production technique of making bricks had spread to northern Europe from northern Italy in the 12th century. Clay being a material that could be formed in a variety of shapes, there was no limit to the imagination. Clay also was a rather affordable construction material that offered many possibilities from the engineering point of view. Brick building, which had been known even in Antiquity, is characteristic of many cities of the Baltic region, some of which were founded by the Hanseatic League, an alliance of trading guilds in northern Europe. In Germany, the Hanseatic League emerged in the 14th century and was thenceforth led by the city of Lübeck. Lübeck, founded in 1143, controlled all trade along the Baltic coast until the 16th century. But the Hanseatic League not only imported and exported trading goods, they also introduced technical and aesthetic innovations, in particular the art of brick building. In northern Germany, churches founded by the nobility were already constructed in this technique in the 12th century. They were inspired by buildings made of hewn stone. Due to this new engineering technique, architectural details such as gables were changed. These mountings, much like pinnacles, were realized in a simpler form in brick and mounted in the Gothic churches. Furthermore, charming dec-

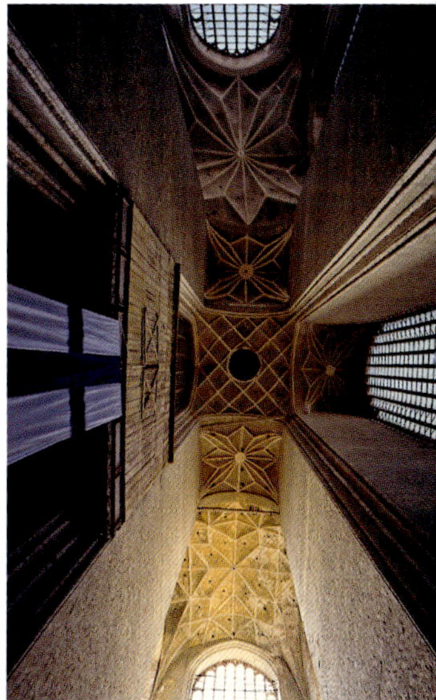

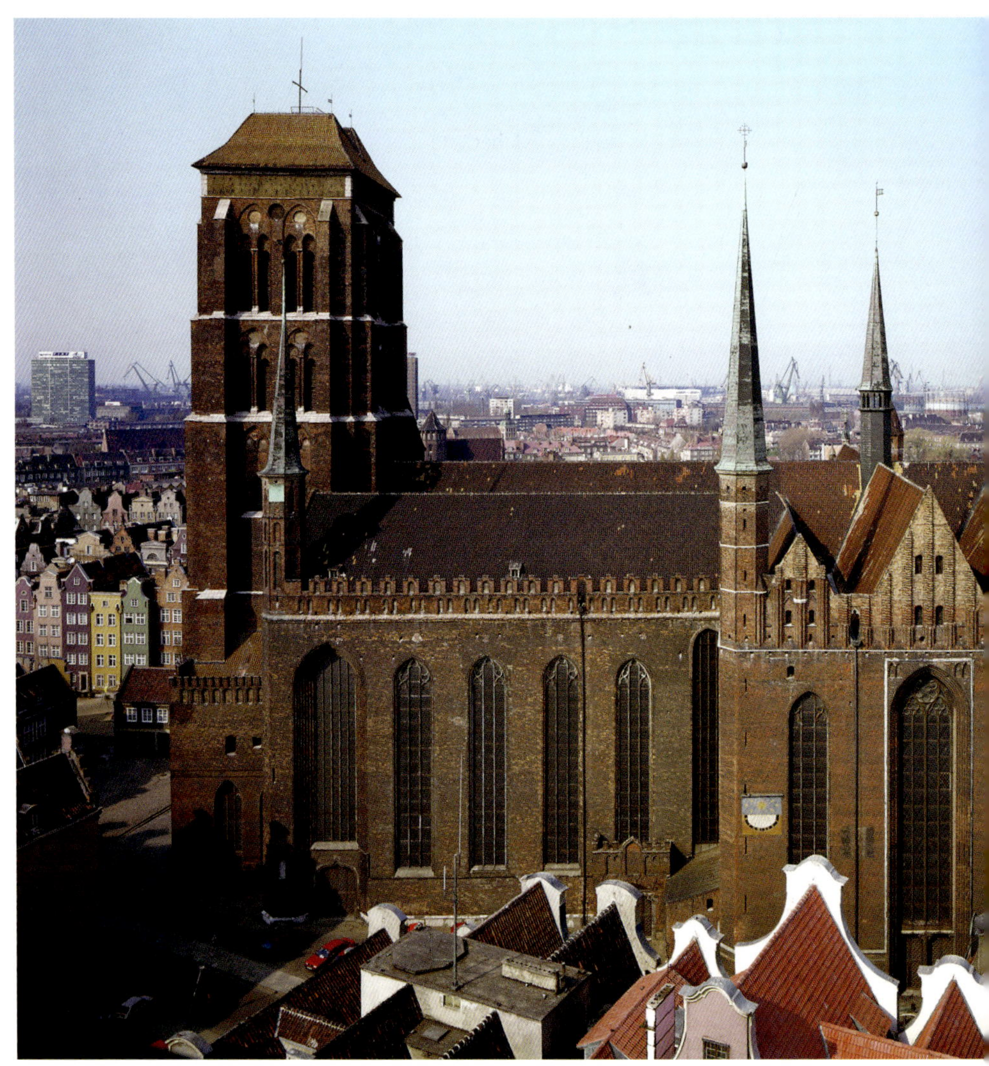

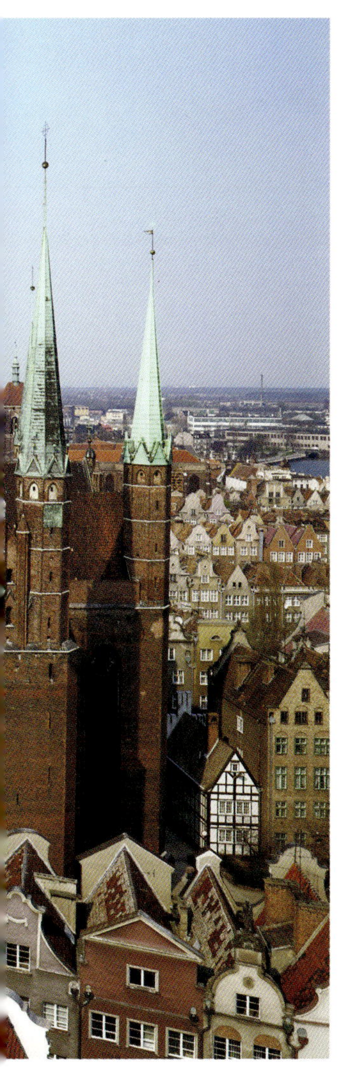

orative solutions were devised, such as the alternating use of colorful glazed and unglazed bricks. The combination of bricks with hewn stones was equally effective. Blind arcades made of bricks could be visually enhanced. Criss cross and stepped ornaments became highly popular, while the shapes of the arches were underlined with friezes and decorative bands. A sheer limitless repertoire of decorations was introduced with the technique of branding the clay brick before it was placed in the kiln. These reliefs or depressions could be both figurative or abstract. The technique of building in brick spread from Lübeck through northern Europe, mainly through the workshops of the Cistercian order.

Numerous churches, city walls, burghers' houses and warehouses throughout northern and eastern Europe bear witness to the power and influence of the Hanseatic League. In Germany, good examples can be found in the Hanseatic cities of Lübeck, Hamburg and Bremen, but also in Wismar, Rostock, Stralsund and Greifswald. The new confidence of the wealthy burghers also led to the foundations of numerous churches. One of these is St. Mary's in Lübeck, built between 1315 and 1317, a pioneering example of Brick Gothic. It was the model for **St. Mary's Church** in **Stralsund,** constructed in 1380 (pp. 68, 69), though this Hanseatic city church has much greater dimensions. The imposing building with its cubic compactness can be seen from afar. Among its remarkable features are the windows ending in half-length lancets and the lack of flying buttresses. The interior has a fascinating and elaborately designed Late Gothic net vault above the basilica-style nave. The west tower, dating from the 15th century, was destroyed by lightning in 1647. In 1708, it was capped with the baroque dome discernible from afar.

Gdansk,
St. Mary's,
constructed 1343–1502

Visitors to St. Mary's Church in Gdansk should let their gaze rise up in order to perceive a finely structured cell vault, a variant of net vaulting with filled borders.

The technique of brick building was soon adopted throughout the Baltic region. In Poland, which had converted to the Christian faith in 966, under King Miezsko I, several medieval monasteries and churches were built in the Romanesque style. In around 1200, a change can be noted in cities of northern Poland towards the Brick Gothic, for example in Szczecin and Stargard. Further towards the south, masons continued to construct with local stones such as gneiss and granite. At times, both styles were incorporated into one building, such as in **Cracow** and Wroclaw. The history of Cracow is more than 1000 years old; it is a city teeming with traditions and historical heritage. To this day, the city center with the old market square is dominated by the soaring **St. Mary's Church** (p. 74). The facade of the basilica, begun in *c.* 1221, makes a compact impression because it lacks the flying buttresses. It is adorned with two different towers, which adds a charming contrast to the rather sober exterior, that largely does without any ornamentation. The higher of the two towers is surmounted by a spire with pyramid-shaped pinnacles, the middle one being decorated with a golden crown. This is an allusion to the "regal" history of Cracow.

The city of **Gdansk** (Danzig) was a member of the Hanseatic League. Its heyday unfolded from the 15th to the 18th centuries, as can be seen to this day when visiting the magnificent buildings of the old city. In its center stands **St. Mary's Church** (pp. 70, 71, 73), begun in 1343 and one of the largest Gothic church buildings throughout Europe. Slender spires, pinnacles and gables give the silhouette an exceedingly picturesque look and detract from the fact that the rest of the exterior lacks ornamentation. Being a reconstruction of a former church, it was designed as a hall church, with nave and aisles of the same height. What remains unusual, however, is the fact that each has its own roof. The church interior is a generously conceived space – an effect further enhanced by the spacious double transept. The vault is done in

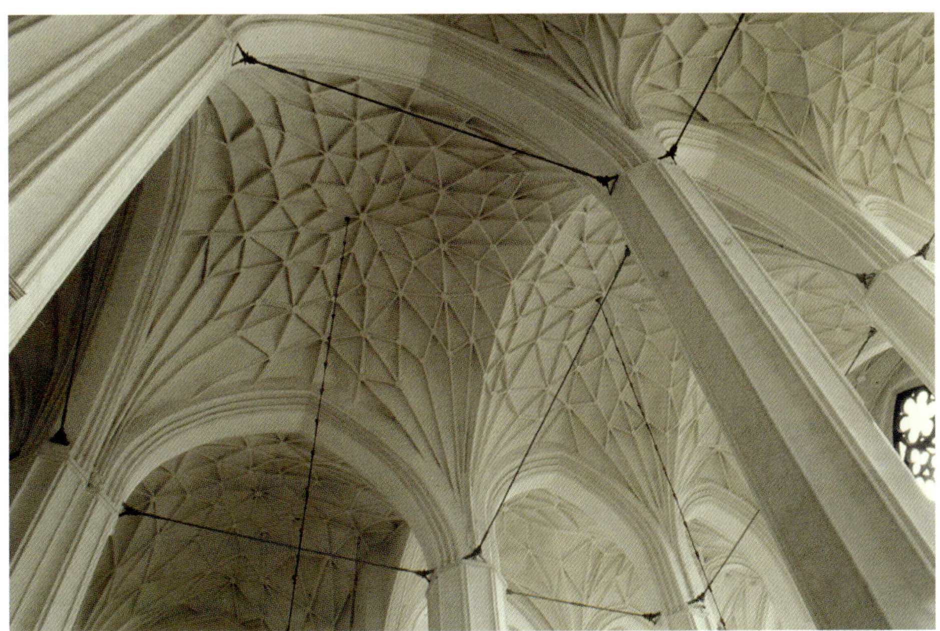

Gdansk,
St. Mary's,
cell vault,
constructed 1343–1502

an exquisitely structured net pattern, a style which can traditionally be traced to Bohemian and Saxon architecture.

Poznán boasts an impressive cathedral island. In lieu of a basilica from the 10th century, which was destroyed, a Gothic cathedral was built here in the 14th and 15th centuries. During that time, Poland had widely expanded under the dominion of the Jagiellon dynasty (1386–1572). It was they who in 1466 finally managed to defeat the Teutonic Knights, who, in 1309, had settled in Malbork. Another church in Brick Gothic is the **Church of St Anne** in **Vilnius,** the capital of Lithuania on the Baltic Sea (p. 75). It was begun in *c.* 1500. A unique work of art is the facade with its combination of powerful profiling and the interior design of the facade, which has

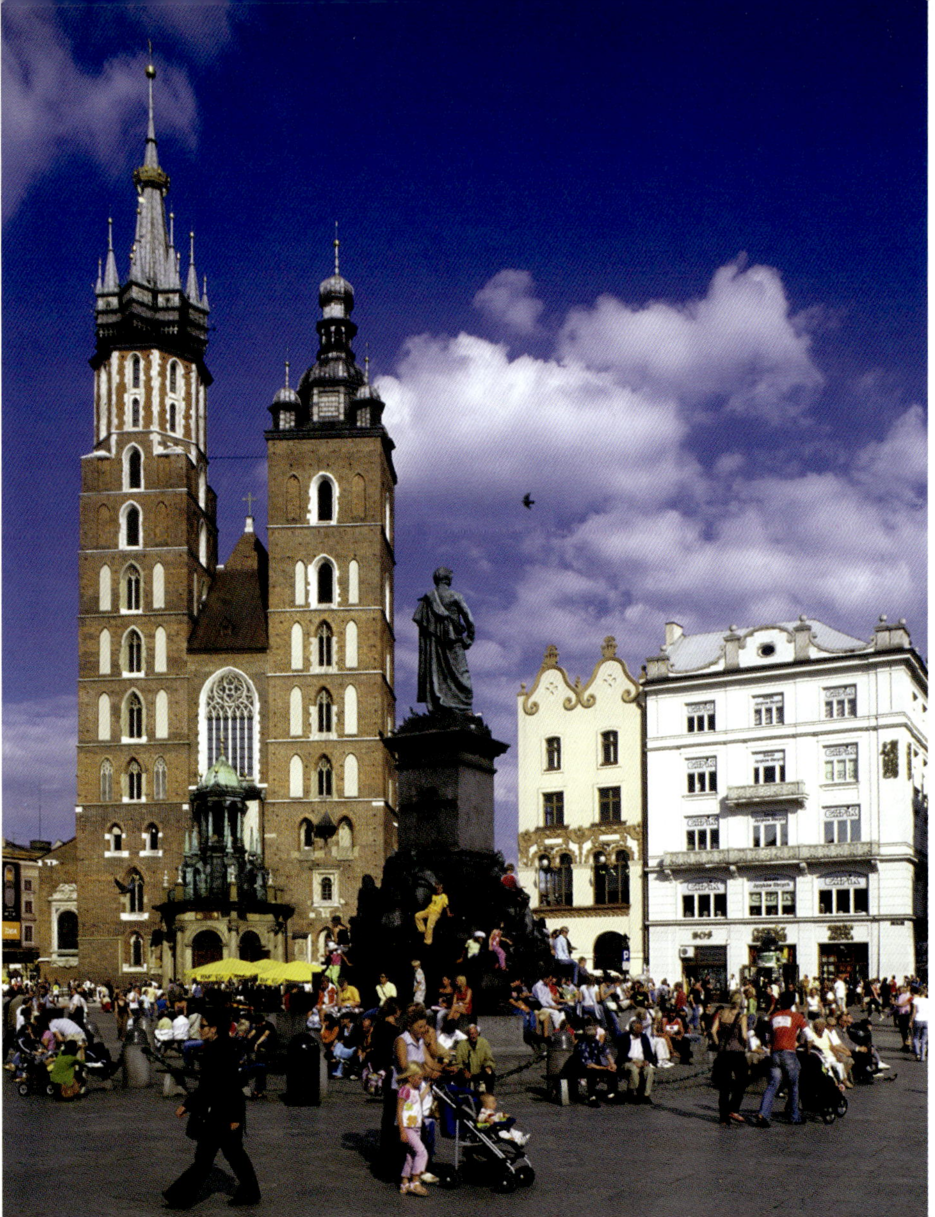

ogee-shaped window arches. The three towers are ornamented with gables and crockets, characteristic of Gothic design. The interior of the church has a very sober lower wall part, which vividly contrasts with the finely nuanced decorations of the windows and vault.

Riga, the capital of Latvia, also has a medieval center worth visiting. It is marked by the cathedral which dates from the 13th century and was commissioned by the founder of the city, Bishop Albert of Bremen (*c.* 1165–1229). The capital of Estonia, Tallinn (formerly known as Reval), also flourished during the Middle Ages. Narrow alleys are flanked by houses that are centuries old and guarded by a fortified city wall with massive towers. Until the 19th century, upper and lower town were divided – both virtually, through two administrations, and literally, through the city walls. The cathedral, constructed in the 13th century and completed later, is one of the landmarks of the upper town.

Left page:
Cracow,
St. Mary's,
begun *c.* 1320

Vilnius,
St. Anne,
facade,
c. 1500

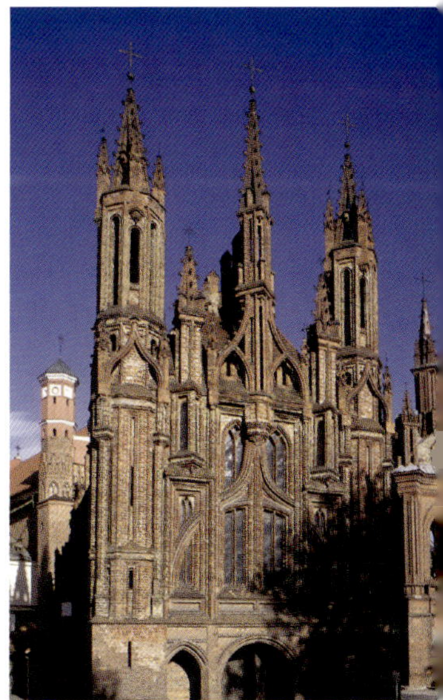

Other Northern European Church Buildings

Brick Gothic was more popular in north-eastern Euope than in the far north. In Denmark, for example, the majority of churches were built in the Romanesque style whereas Sweden experienced the import of French Gothic and German Brick Gothic features. This was due to the fact that master masons from abroad were contracted. Mention must be made of Uppsala Cathedral, consecrated in 1435 and largely influenced by French Gothic. In the Late Middle Ages, the Hanseatic League founded important trading posts in Sweden. One of the most outstanding of these was Visby on Gotland. The charming town is characterized by several Gothic churches which loom above the well-preserved city walls and can be seen from afar.

Norway converted to Christianity around 1000; the first Brick Gothic churches were built from 1160 on. However, French and English architecture were equally influential.

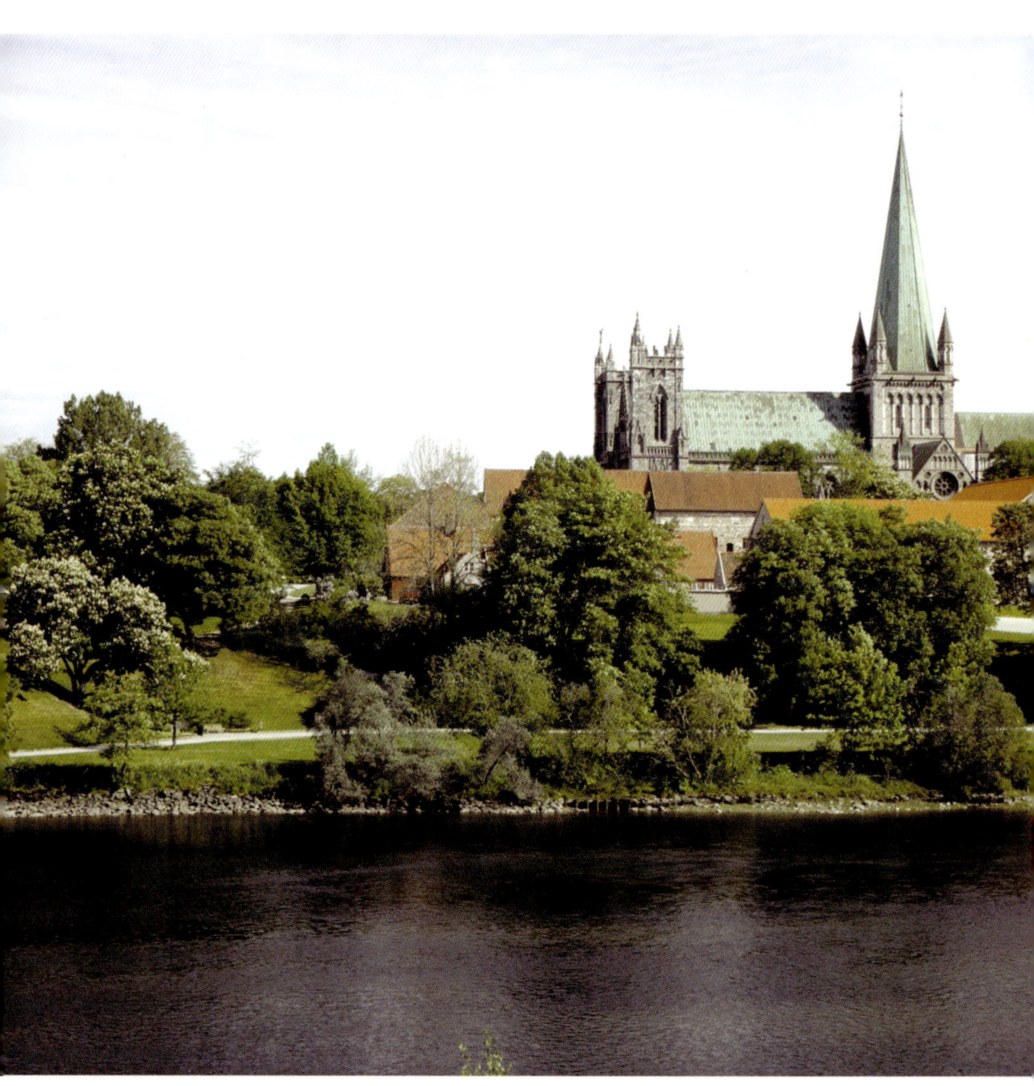

Nidaros Cathedral in **Trondheim** was built over the grave of St. Olav. It exemplifies the economic and artistic role of the city in the Middle Ages. Built on commission of King Olav Kyrre (1050–1093), the church was extended in 1151 after the archdiocese of Nidaros had been established, which comprised all of Norway. Pilgrims flocked here to see the grave of the saint; as a result, the economic and religious power of the city expanded. Since 1814, this is the place where the Kings of Norway have been crowned. Because the construction phase spanned more than two centuries, there is an overlayering of various styles: while the transept shows Late Romanesque and Norman features, the nave and high choir were designed in the Gothic style.

In Finland, the first churches were built in the 12th century. Since they were usually made of timber, a perishable material, hardly any of the original churches have survived. However, those that were made of stone, generally unhewn, are still extant. They usually have a high gabled roof. Traces of Brick Gothic can be found, for example in brick-laid tympanums. Turku, which until 1812 was the capital of Finland, is home to the national sanctuary, a cathedral in Brick Gothic, consecrated in 1300. It is the mother church of the Lutheran Church of Finland.

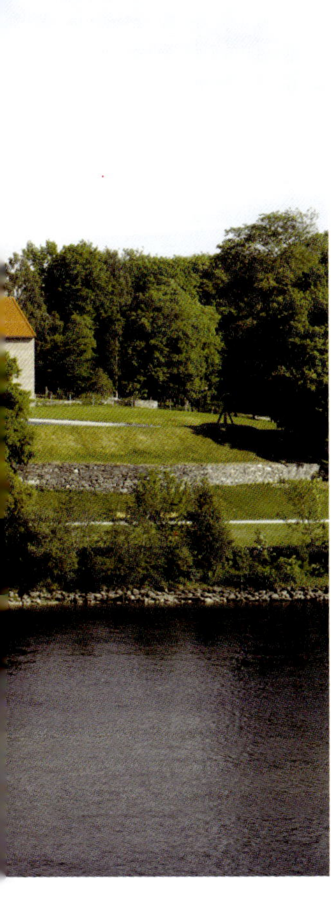

Trondheim,
Nidaros Cathedral,
begun second half of the
11th century,
extended 1151

Of Monks, Friars and Laymen – Life in a Medieval Monastery

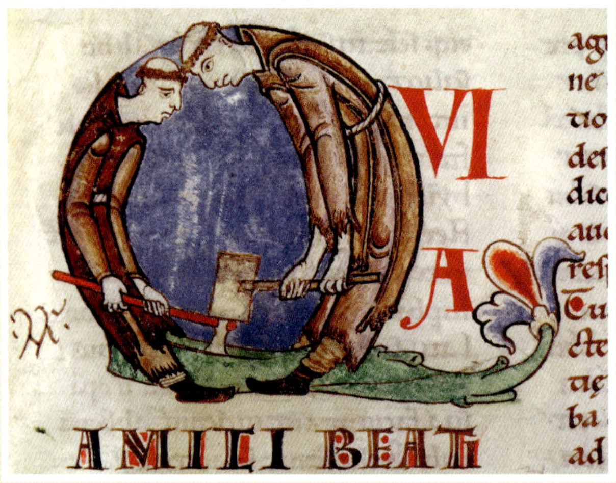

Initial letter Q,
from an illustration of the *Moralia* by Pope Gregory the Great, illumination, 12th century, Bibliothèque municipale, Dijon

Ora et labora – Pray and Work! This was the basic rule for monastic life which Benedict of Nursia (c. 480–547/60) laid down for his confraternity. Apart from the Bible, the Rule of St. Benedict, in which he put down his precepts for monastic life, was the most-copied text of the Middle Ages. The scholar took rules that were already in use and summarized them in a total of sixty-six chapters.

St. Benedict founded Monte Cassino Monastery in central Italy, between Rome and Naples. When the monastery was destroyed by Langobards in the 6th century, the fleeing monks took the *Regula Benedicti* with them to Rome. The work was returned to Monte Cassino in the 8th century, first having been copied at the request of Charlemagne. This first copy is the basis of all successive transcripts, as the original manuscript was destroyed during a fire in the 9th century. Today, only few parts of the 8th-century rebuilding have remained in Monte Cassino. The greater part of the complex was extended several times. Having suffered greatly through wars and looting troops, the complex was rebuilt yet again to monumental grandeur in the second half of the 20th century.

The history of the *Regula Benedicti* and of the monastery founded by St. Benedict is here used as an exemplary case, being the first important central European religious order in a series of many, all of which experienced a checkered history. The most important orders founded in the Middle Ages were the Cistercians, Franciscans and Dominicans. The first of these was the Order of Cistercians, founded in the 11th century. **Bernard of Clairvaux** (c. 1090–1153) (p. 80) is associated with the rising popularity of the order in the 12th century, while the mendicant orders of the Dominicans and Franciscans already became popular during the lifetimes of their founders, St. Dominic (c. 1170–1221) and St. Francis of Assisi (1181/82–1226), respectively. Parallel to these orders, there were also important convents, such as those of the Benedictine Sisters, Cistercians and Claretian Sisters, which exist to this day. During the Crusades, military orders were founded, such as the Teutonic Knights, the Knights of St. John and the Knights Templar. Any confraternity that did not remain strictly loyal to the Pope and the Catholic Church was in danger of being accused of heresy. In other words, it was vital for any order and its rules to be acknowledged by the pope. In the early 13th century, for example, the Dominicans had to cope with re-

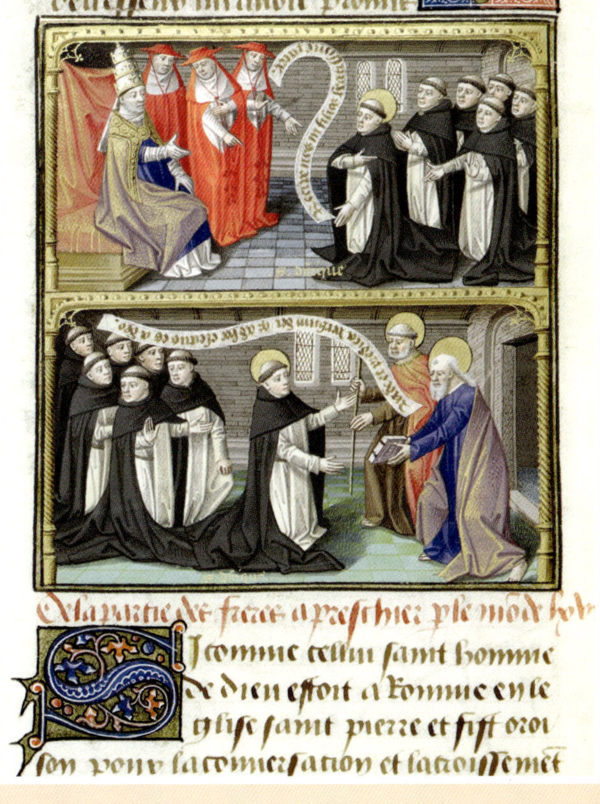

Approbation of the Dominican Rule Given by Pope Innocent III (above),
illustration of the *Speculum Maius* of Vincent de Beauvais, illumination, 15th century, Musée Condé, Chantilly

Jean Fouquet,
St. Bernard Teaching,
from the *Livre d'heures d'Étienne Chevalier,* illumination, *c.* 1455,
Musée Condé, Chantilly

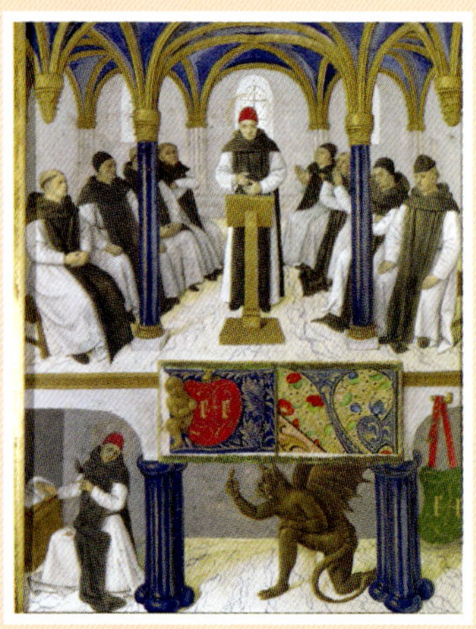

sistance from parish priests and bishops because they claimed the right to deliver sermons.

Most of the other orders evolved from lay fraternities whose friars took on the rank and role of preachers only in the course of time. There were three major rules, the counsels of perfection, to which every confraternity adhered with more or less strictness: poverty, chastity and obedience. Even though on entering monastic life a monk left behind his accustomed social life, the monasteries remained closely connected to medieval society. Monasteries were institutions for education; monks administered all of the sacraments from christening to death; and in times of crisis the walled-in monastery complex could offer shelter for the population. Mendicant orders such as the Franciscans and Dominicans usually depended on donations, in recompense for which they would teach, tend the sick and fulfil pastoral duties. Since monks were accustomed to exertions, the Church would often send them to missions in overseas. The acceptance and renown of monasteries in society was ambiguous. Corruption and decadence within the orders were issues that tended to appear now and then, the immediate reaction to which were new foundations and splinter groups. For example, the male successors to the Order of St. Francis today can be subdivided into three autonomous congregations: Franciscans, Minorites and Capuchins.

What was a day in the life of a monk like? The day was mainly organized around the two canonical hours Laudes and Vespers, morning prayer service (around 6 a.m.) and evening prayer (around 6 p.m.). The rest of the day was spent working, studying religious scripts and dining with the community. Everyday life in such a community required specific spaces, which is the reason why the ground plan and floor plan of most monasteries are similar. Usually, the entire complex was organized around a cloister.

This would be a rectangular courtyard to the south side of the monastery church, with a garden in the middle, enclosed by arcaded corridors. All the important spaces of a monastery had access to the cloister: the church, refectory, dormitory and the library. The enclosed garden in the courtyard usually had a well at its center, which served the monks for washing themselves. The arcaded cloister offered shelter against sun, rain and snow. Whereas in most spaces of the monastery speaking was strictly prohibited, the cloister corridors could be described as the center of communication. Apart from the central complex organized around the cloister, there would be another walled-in, rectangular complex comprizing farm buildings, workshops, a kitchen garden and cattle sheds. The goal of any monastery was to be an autonomous and self-sufficient entity. **Spiritual work and physical labor** (p. 78), which might include anything up to chopping firewood, was to be done by the members of the confraternity themselves. Specialization in certain professions was only accepted as long as it did not lead to overt pride. In the ideal case, a monk should not be distracted by life beyond the convent walls, but a monastery often included diversified holdings and estates.

In England, the monastic estates were dissolved by Henry VIII; on the European mainland, this process of secularization took place in the 18th and 19th centuries.

Mont Saint-Michel,
cloister,
completed 1228

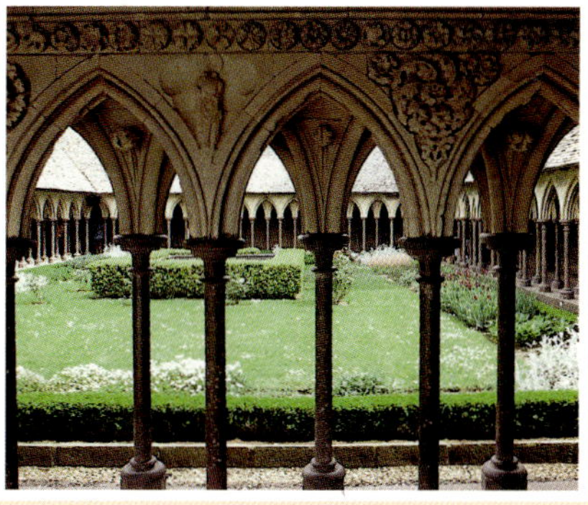

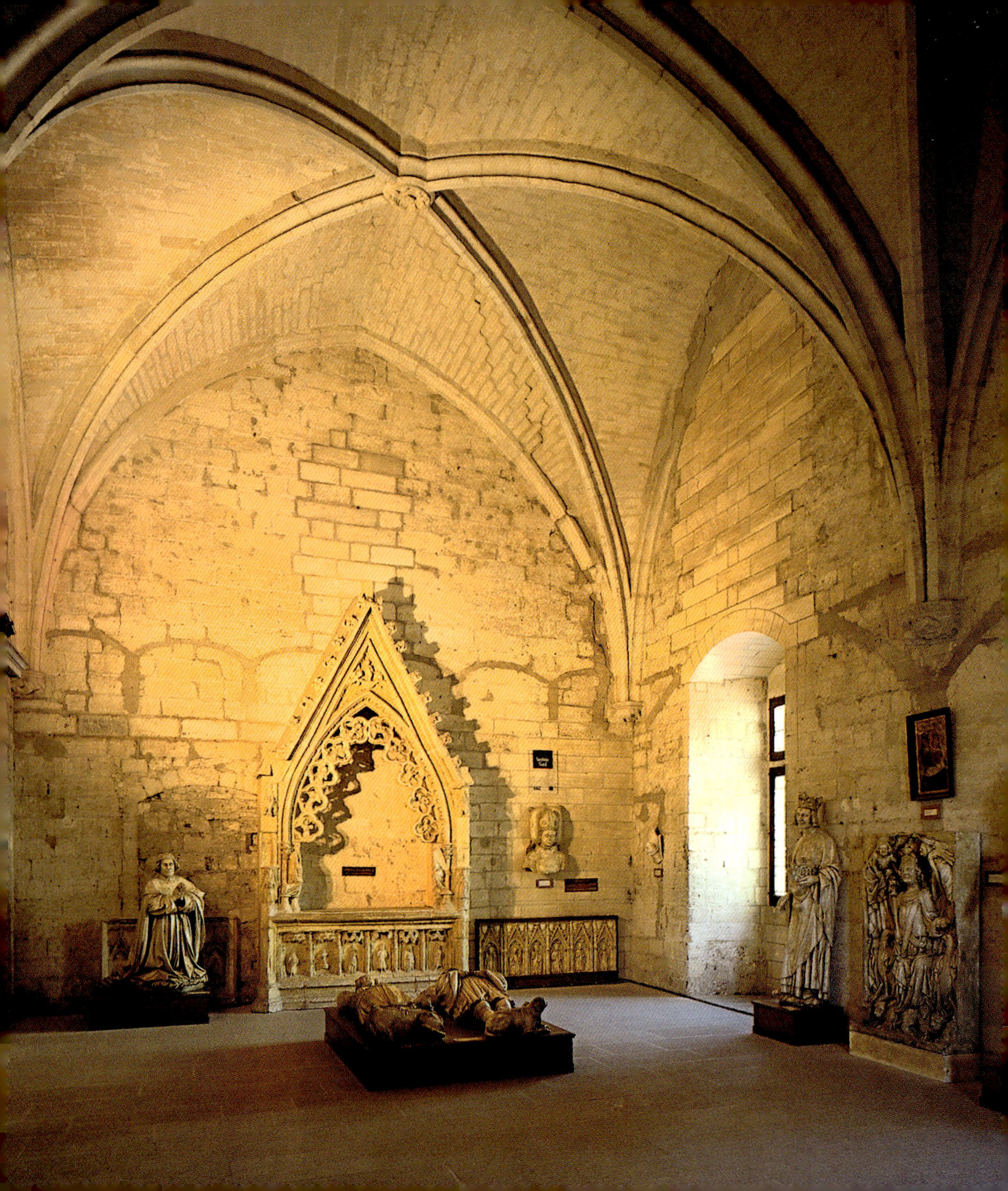

Secular Architecture in France

So far, we have focused on Gothic church architecture. But the innovations of the Gothic period were also used for new conceptions of secular constructions: city fortifications and town halls, market halls and hospitals were erected on commission by city councils, which grew increasingly wealthy. The country estates of the aristocracy also experienced profound changes: former fortresses or multipurpose structures were now separated into pure castles here and prestige palaces there. One of the reasons for this transformation lay in the invention of firearms, which were increasingly put to use. In response to this, the fortification of a castle had to be adapted. The walls of the ground level had to be enforced to become more solid. At the same time, the height of an enclosing wall lost its importance. The country estates of the landed nobility became increasingly luxurious and comfortable; this was in part due to the fact that the feudal lords transformed into more or less autonomous princes. The royal court was no longer itinerant – traveling from one castle to the next – but instead settled in one imposing residence. The itinerant court had been restricted to certain types of furniture that could be moved without coming to harm, such as seats, chests and tapestry to decorate the walls. Once the court settled, the entire architectural space was

Avignon,
Papal Palace,
north sacristy of the Great Chapel (left),
cathedral and Notre-Dame de Dome (below),
constructed mid-14th century

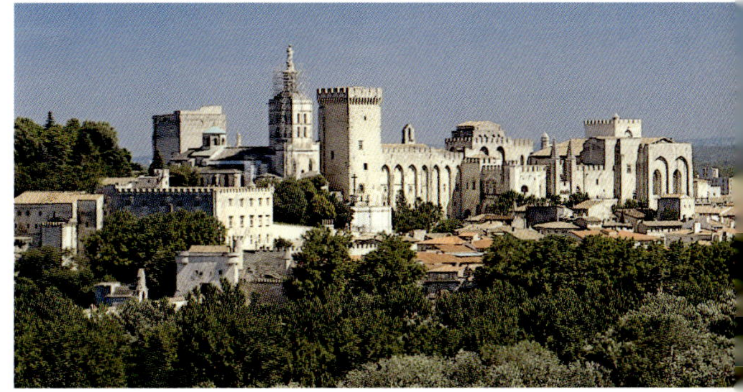

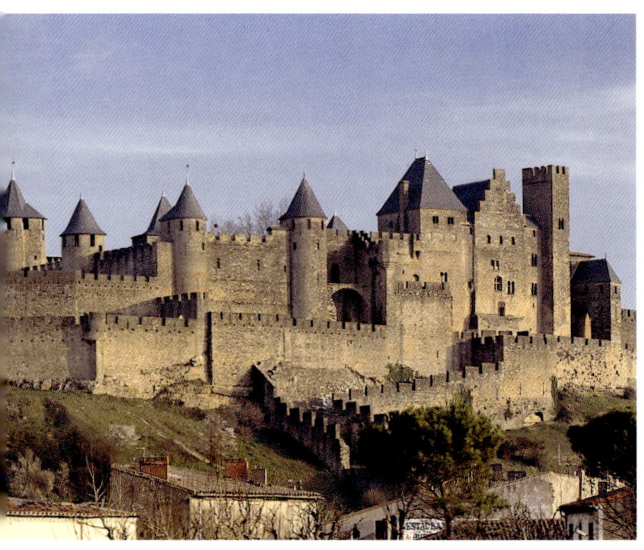

Carcassonne,
La Cité,
begun 1228,
restructured in the 19th century

integrated into the design. Exquisite wood paneling, often with ornamental intarsia, bear witness to this new culture of living.

The innovations in civic architecture are correlated with urban growth and prosperity. Suddenly, municipal administrative bodies commissioned constructions that looked like palaces – a new self-confidence of the townspeople evolved. But the princes also relied on an administration that functioned well: with the growth of monetary economy feudal territories were reformed, and a growing number of officials were employed to keep control of the estates' businesses. Between 1285 and 1314, Philip IV of France reformed his country's fiscal policy by introducing the *Chambre de comptes* (audit court). He also reorganized his defense system. Whereas up to then it had been the feudal lord's duty to follow his king in war, a fact that often had devastating effects for the dependants at home, now fealty could be compounded through payment. In consequence, mercenaries replaced the noblemen, who used their freedom to expand trade and economy in their territories.

During the 14th century, conflicts between the worldly leaders and the spiritual leader, the pope, increased dramatically. On commission from Philip IV, who in 1309 had forced the papal curia to leave Rome and settle in **Avignon** in southern France, one of the most magnificent secular buildings was erected, the **Palais des Papes** (pp. 82, 83). This palace,

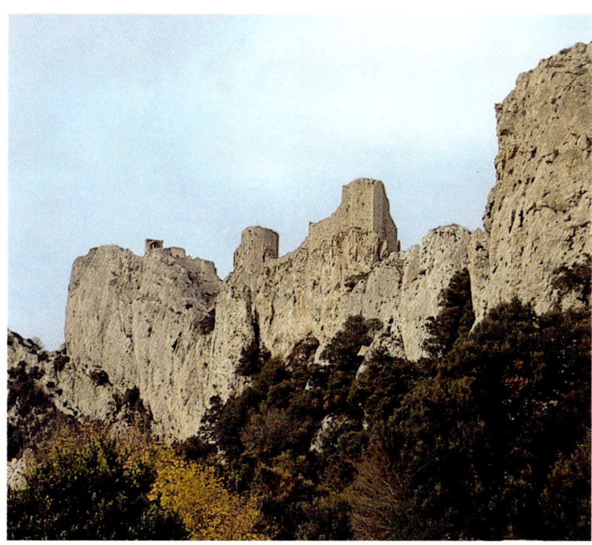

Château de Peyrepertuse (Aude),
constructed in the early 12th century, expanded in the late 13th century

which was begun under Pope Benedict XII in 1335 and has the forbidding outer appearance of a military structure, is one of the world's architectural masterpieces. The complex consists of four wings organized around a central arcaded courtyard. Pope Clement VI had another courtyard, the *Grand Cour,* attached to the south of the older palace. He knew of the importance of imposing ornamentation as a worthy background for papal ceremonies. Clement VI would meet his visitors in the great audience chamber, a generous double-span hall with cross-ribbed vaulting. Among the most impressive works of art to have remained intact are the magnificent mural paintings by Matteo Giovanetti, or Matteo di Giovanetto, from Viterbo, who worked in the Papal Palace from 1343 on. His depictions in the *Chambre du Cerf* (chamber of the hart) are especially vivid and versatile. Painted in bright colors, it depicts detailed hunting scenes as well as other topics such as fishing techniques. The architecture of the Papal Palace of Avignon, which managed to combine functional elements with display features, was to influence all further constructions built in Italy once the papal curia had returned to its traditional home in Rome.

Whereas the Avignon Palais des Papes was a city within a city, the fortification of **La Cité** in **Carcassonne,** on the banks of the Aude River, was intended to shelter the citizens. The double circular walls with numerous watchtowers were constructed in the early 13th century, at a time when the Cathars, or Albigensians, were classified as a heretic sect and persecuted. Further conflicts in southern France were caused by the barons of the region, who were striving for autonomy but ruled over fertile lands much coveted by the king and the nobility of northern France. And so the alleged heretic movement of the Cathars in southern France, who lived according to the example given by Christ himself and would not accept the authority of the Catholic Church, led to an alliance between the pope, the king of the French crown lands and the barons of northern France. An alliance which entailed the fatal destruction of the Cathars: the pope called a formal crusade, the Albigensian Crusade, which was directed against all Cathari supporters, even the aristocrats of southern France. It was the only crusade ever led against fellow countrymen. The many fortifications in the Languedoc, of which Carcassonne is the most imposing, bear witness to these war-ridden times. The monument that towers over the *Ville Basse* (lower city), which was only built later, was thoroughly restructured in the 19th century, according to plans by Eugène Viollet-le-Duc (1814–1879). The old parts of the city had been laid out in a grid pattern in the 14th century; they make an impressive contrast to La Cité itself.

The Conciergerie on Île de la Cité in the heart of Paris looks like a fortress. Today, the former home to the palace guards and chatelain is part of the Palace of Justice.

The **Château de Peyrepertuse** (p. 85), expanded in the 12th and 13th centuries, is an impressive Cathar fortification. It looms 800 meters high above the village of **Duilhac.** The ragged cliffs it was erected on once more underline the necessary military characteristic of castles set in a war-zone countryside. In spite of the feudal lords' close contacts to rulers in northern Spain and Catalonia, and in spite of bitterly fought battles, many castles fell into the hands of the French king, such as Peyrepertuse in 1240. Other fortifications worth mentioning are Quéribus, Puivert and Montségur, all situated in the remote south-east of France.

The **Conciergerie** in **Paris,** built in the 14th century, leaves an entirely different impression. This is also due to the

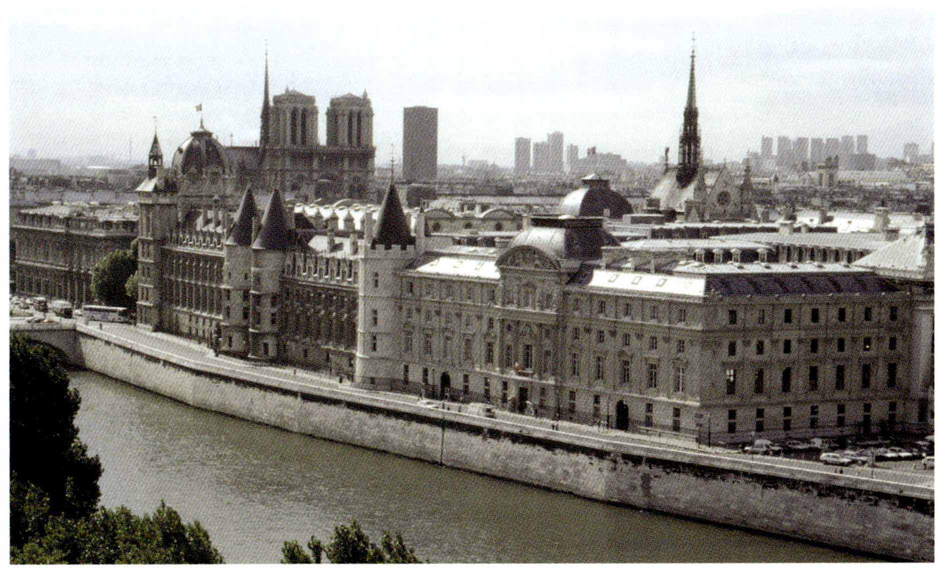

fact that it is situated in the heart of the city. Today it is part of the complex of the former Palais de la Cité, the town hall in the core of medieval Paris, the *Île de la Cité.* The fortified Conciergerie, situated on the *Quai de l'Horloge,* was built during the reign of Philip IV. It housed the palace guards *(Gens d'armes)* and the chatelain *(Concierge),* hence the name. The *Conciergerie* was thoroughly reconstructed during the 19th century. Its two towers can be seen from the opposite river bank as well as from the Seine River itself (for a historic view see p. 264). The clock tower is remarkable. The first public clock of Paris was mounted here in the last third of the 14th century. The high walls of the *Conciergerie* call to mind the times when the king of France had to be able to defend himself against attackers even in his own territory.

Paris,
Conciergerie on Île de la Cité, reconstructed 1302–1313

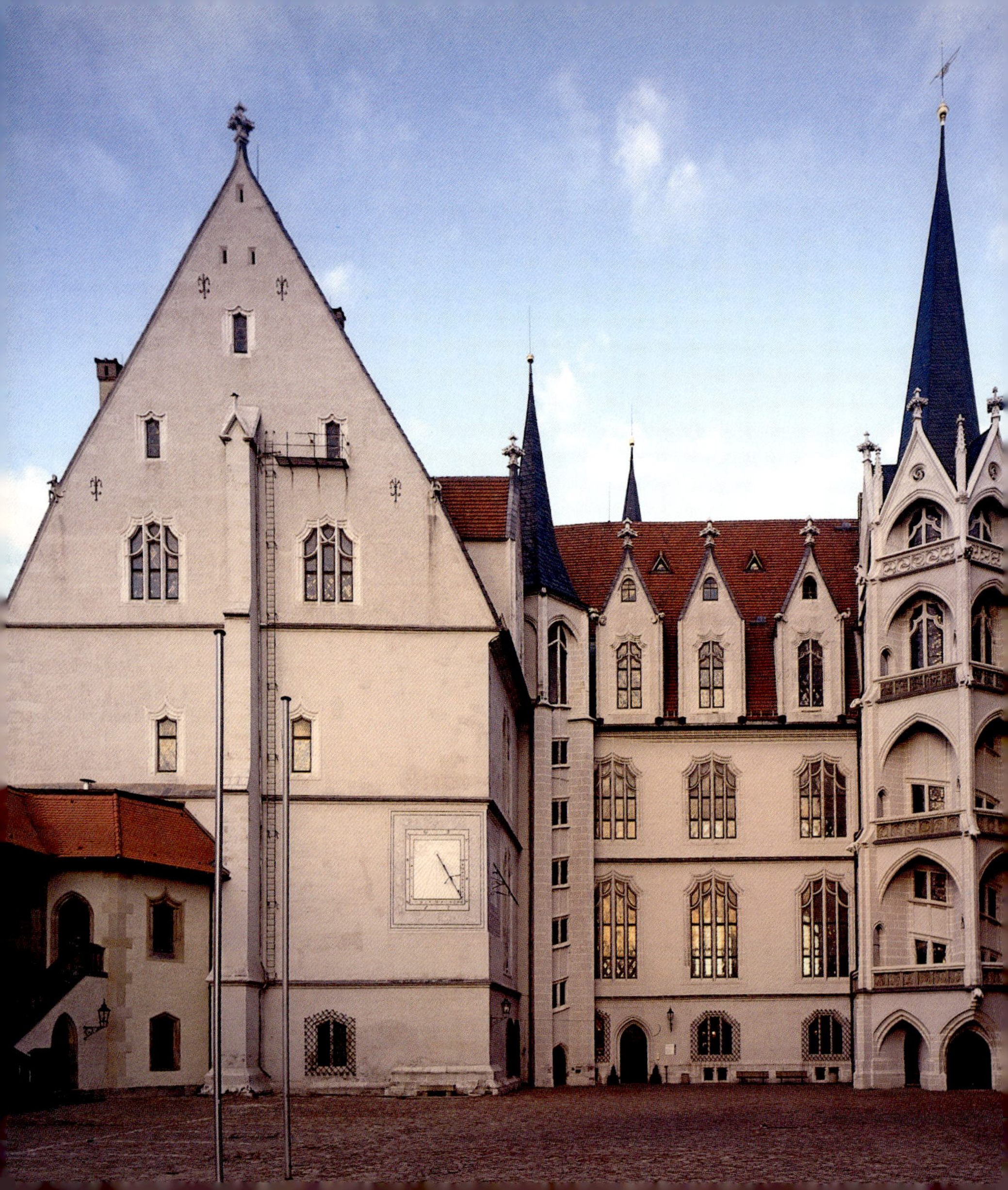

Secular architecture of the "German Lands"

In the 14th and 15th centuries the German lands were dominated by political conflicts. In the Late Middle Ages, those parts of the Holy Roman Empire lying north of the Alps were no longer a centralized political unity but had splintered into a patchwork of cities and duchies of varied and varying dependencies. The Habsburg dynasty tried to defend the dominion of the Holy Roman Empire, which extended from upper Italy through to the North and Baltic seas, against external pressures. At the same time, though, cities and duchies gaining in power weakened the empire from within. This multitude of territories with its specific geographical and political characteristics is also reflected in the various artistic developments of the individual regions. Whereas southern Germany showed a tendency to be influenced by northern Italian styles, artists in northern Germany developed a unique style known as Brick Gothic (see pp. 28ff).

The first palatial residence in Germany, and a fascinating example of courtly life in the Late Middle Ages, is **Albrechtsburg castle** in **Meissen.** It was begun in 1471 under architect Arnold von Westfalen (*c.* 1425/30–1482), who also participated in the construction of Meissen Cathedral. Compared with the former military castles that were principally intended as fortifications, Albrechtsburg, which was conceived as the residence of the Elector of Saxony, features pioneering innovations such as the size of the windows. Windows as large as this would never be used in a fortification and were in fact modeled on the estates of the nobility of the Duchy of Burgundy, which at the time was the leading cultural center north of the Alps. The courtyard is famous for its hexagonal Wendel-

Meissen,
Albrechtsburg,
courtyard facade (left),
interior view of the hexagonal staircase Großer Wendelstein (below), begun *c.* 1470

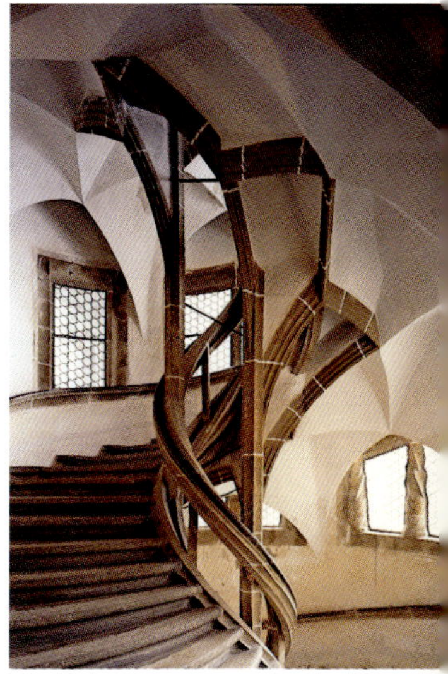

stein, an enclosed spiral staircase with a polygonal cell vault. But the "innards" of the staircase are equally interesting: it merely consists of three slender columns. To bring this unique construction to full effect, distinctive elements such as ribs, pillars and window embrasures were made of brick. The reddish hue of the bricks contrasts beautifully with the natural stone of the masonry and underlines the idiosyncratic character of the staircase. Similar representative staircases were subsequently built in Bamberg, Saxony and Berlin. Another remarkable feature of the staircase is the openwork, arcaded facade, probably modeled on Italian examples. The Late Gothic high gables and steep spires make an impressive contrast to the lower facade. A further highlight of engineering is the double-span ballroom on the first floor, which is 28 meters long and sports a vault with ingenious details. The upper windows with their curtain-style design are equally unusual. The ceiling of another state room, the Elector's chamber, is positively bizarre, with very steeply mounted elements, allowing interesting effects of light and shade.

Apart from residential palaces, the construction of city fortifications also changed dramatically during the 15th century. The new designs showed a decreasing attention to military features in favor of representative

The Powerful Hanseatic League

1143 Lübeck founded. The city enables north German merchants to trade also in the Baltic region, which up until now has been dominated by merchants from the island of Gotland.

1161 The Artlenburg Privilege grants the citizens of Lübeck the same rights as those of Gotland. Subsequently, merchants found groups (Hansa) to better represent their interests.

From *c.* **1250** League of Hanseatic Cities: Cities are established as commercial centers and designed to safeguard the trade routes.

1356 first Hanseatic Diet: the cities are officially united under the leadership of Lübeck. From then on, the Hansa dominates trade in the Baltic region, which leads to a series of armed conflicts with rivals.

1494 The Hansa trade post in Novgorod is closed. Trade in Russian goods shifts to Baltic towns. Subsequently, the Hansa's importance and membership decreases.

16TH CENTURY Overseas trade becomes increasingly important, the Hanseatic League diminishes further.

19TH CENTURY The remaining Hanseatic posts in London and Antwerp are sold.

functions. This development can best be seen when studying the **Holstentor Gate** of **Lübeck,** a brick construction erected from 1464 to 1478. Originally, this defensive gate house, flanked by two solid round towers, was only one of four gates built in a row that were designed for the defense of the city. The corbie gable is not at all characteristic of a defensive structure; in fact, it is purely representational. The gate is a symbol of the self-confidence of the Hanseatic city of Lübeck, which in the Middle Ages ranked among the most important cities of Europe. Founded in 1143, Lübeck experienced its economic heyday in the 14th and 15th centuries. The painstakingly restored facades of the civic houses and the numerous churches of this delightful old town reflect an era of wealthy merchants and proud burghers. The Brick Gothic style of architecture spread from Lübeck to the entire Baltic region.

In the course of the Middle Ages, supraregional trading increased. Trade routes were expanded and monetary economy began to dominate in lieu of the former direct exchange of goods. Banking became more professional, so that the agreed purchasing power of the currency could be relied on. Trade also increased because the citizens grew increasingly wealthy and consequently showed a growing interest in spending money on luxury goods. Nobility and burghers wanted to live in imposing homes and sur-

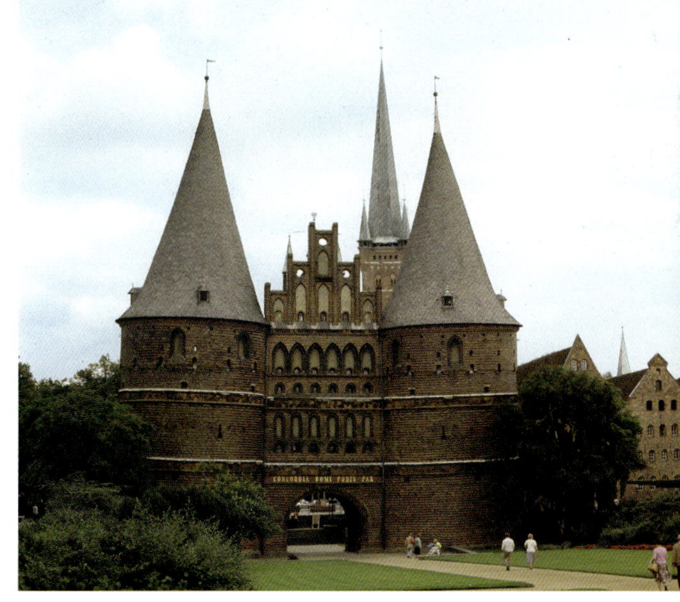

Lübeck,
Holstentor gate,
constructed 1464–1478

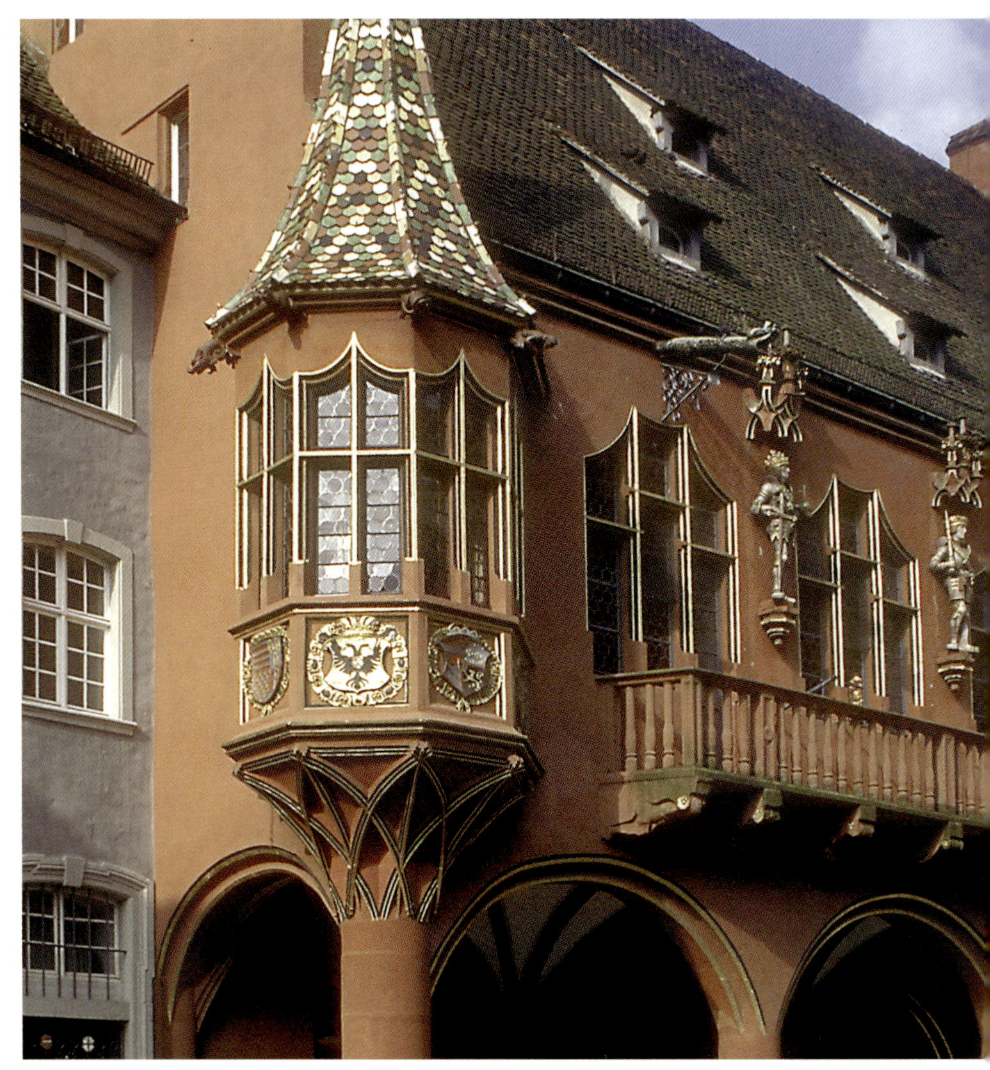

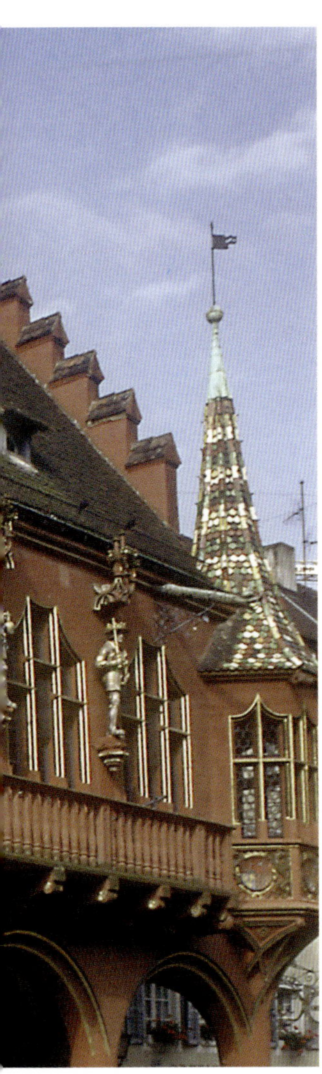

round themselves with exquisite pieces of furniture, precious fabrics and select artworks. A more sophisticated lifestyle also brought about new rituals concerning social behavior, a fact that is reflected in the larger range of silverware. Other branches of economy such as coal mining were alternative sources of increasing wealth. The new prosperity of cities and their inhabitants is illustrated by the architecture, for example the **historic store house (Historisches Kaufhaus) Freiburg im Breisgau** in southern Germany, built in 1532. It is located on the city's main square, Münsterplatz. The red facade is an eyecatcher, as are the turreted alcoves on the corners of the building and the arcades that call to mind Italian structures. The corbie gable, profuse in sculpted ornaments, enhances the picturesque effect of this traditional monument, a trading post where national and international goods changed hands. Trading was liable to duty and overseen by municipal clerks and thus furnished the basis of urban prosperity.

Freiburg,
historic store, reconstruction completed in 1532, further alterations from 1555, restored in 1988

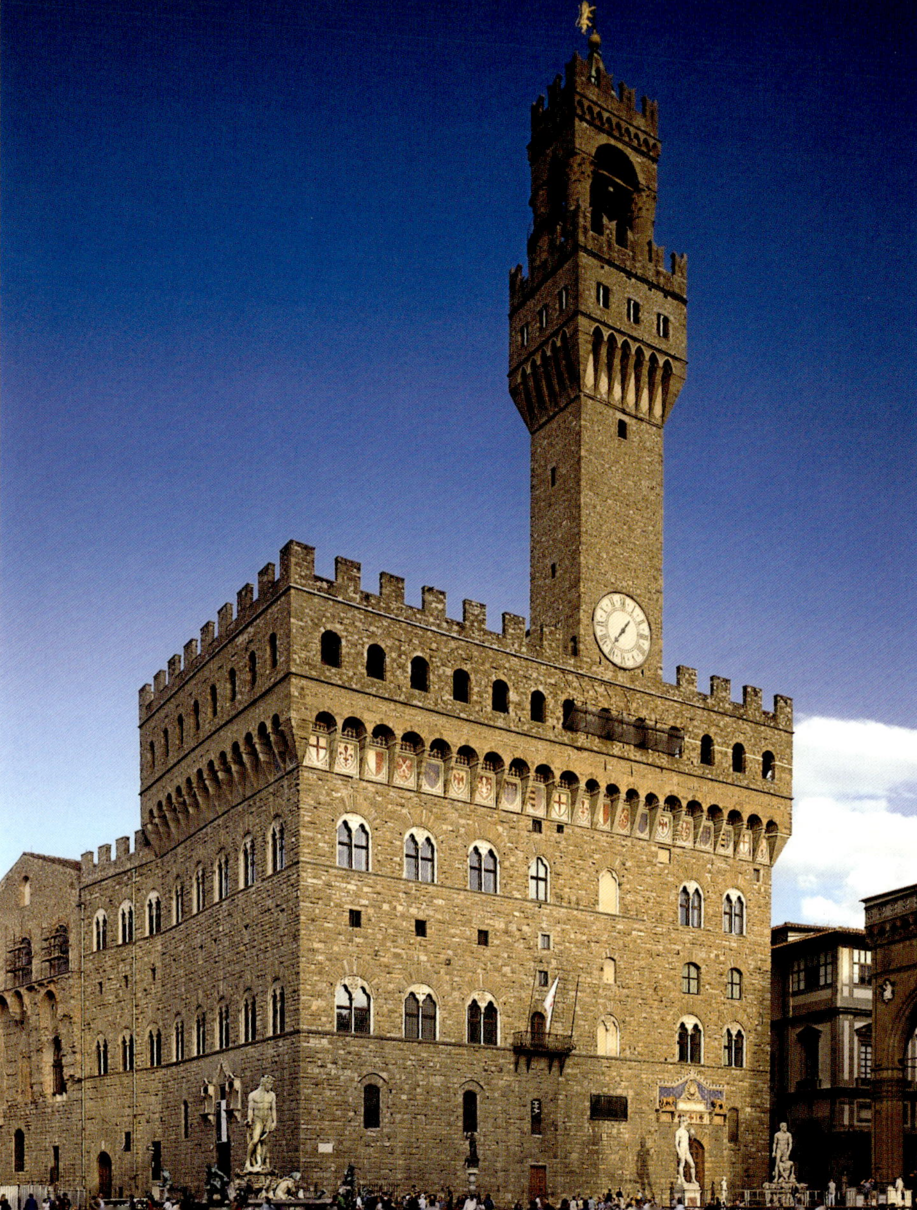

Secular Architecture in Italy

Since the 10th century, northern Italy had been part of the Holy Roman Empire, which had evolved out of the East Frankish Kingdom. Political life in Italy during the Middle Ages was determined by conflicts between the supporters of the emperor, the Ghibbellines, and the Guelphs, who supported the pope. These conflicts even affected autonomous city states such as Florence, Siena, Perugia and Venice. Profiting from the increase of trade and industry, these city states began to flourish from the 11th century onward. But the successful merchants and master craftsmen did not settle for economic progress, they increasingly demanded political power, as well. Their growing influence is reflected in the imposing civic palaces of the autonomous city republics. Both pope and emperor tried to win these states over and afforded them privileges that enhanced their economic prosperity. However, the cities were shaken by unending disputes between the leading families as to which power was to be supported; disputes that often ended in brutal battles.

In the course of the Middle Ages, **Florence,** which since the 13th century had been mostly supporting the pope, evolved into an important economic center, also offering ideal conditions for scholars and artists. In the heart of the city, on the *Piazza della Signoria,* the **Palazzo Vecchio** was constructed in around 1300, the new town hall where

Florence,
Palazzo Vecchio,
constructed *c.* 1300–1320/30

Siena,
Il Campo with Palazzo Pubblico,
square designed post-1280

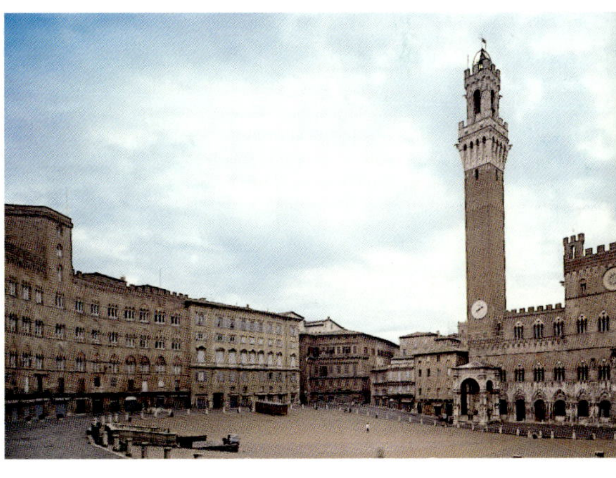

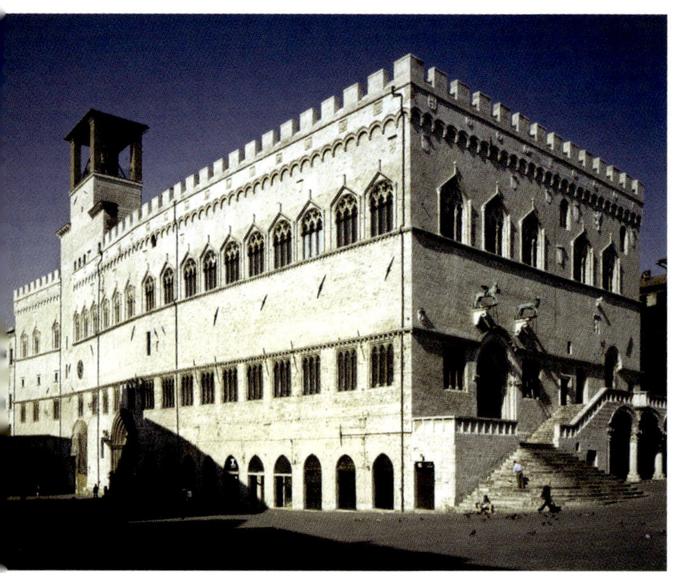

Perugia,
Palazzo dei Priori,
begun 1293

the city council convened. The crenelation and the imposing tower still recall the original function of the building as a fortification. However, the compact effect of the architecture is softened up by windows with double and triple arches and by the added balcony.

Siena, the traditional antagonist to Florence, usually supported the emperor, a fact that further enhanced the rivalry between the two cities. The city center of Siena consists of an equally fascinating large square, the **Piazza del Campo** (p. 95). Semicircular in form, it dramatically focuses on the town hall, the *Palazzo Pubblico* (*c.* 1280 to early 14th century). The city council decided to have their town hall built in the style of an urban palace and, to ensure an harmonious overall impression, decreed that the neighboring edifices should not have any balconies, but arcaded windows. The harmonious proportions of *Piazza del Campo* and the adjoining *Palazzo Pubblico* have an extraordinary effect. An innovation in contrast to Florence is the ground floor arcades, which now have been opened. High above the palace looms the tower, overlooking the surrounding countryside and rounding off the theatrical impression of the slightly sloping square.

Perugia also has a communal palace that served as seat for administration and government. The **Palazzo dei Priori** in the city center was constructed between *c.* 1293 and 1297 by two local master builders; the building was extended in the first half of the 14th century. Perugia had a civic government from the 11th century on, its heyday lay in the 13th and 14th centuries. As in Siena, here too the austere facade is broken up by filigree windows and arcades on the ground floor. The sheer size of the building and the impressive portal are symbols of the growing civic confidence.

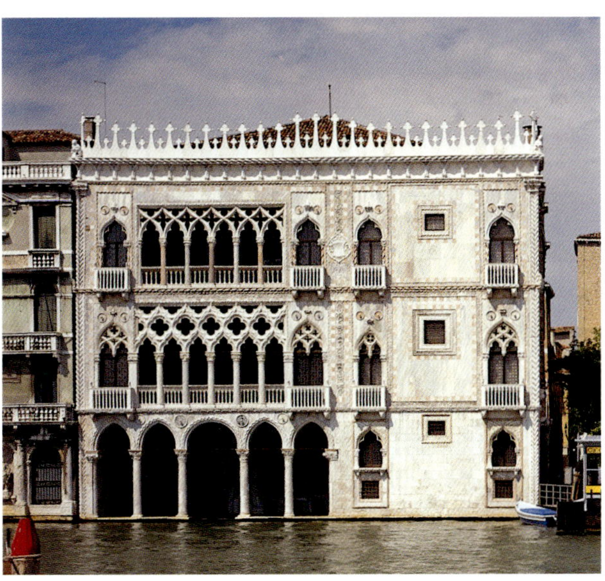

Venice,
Ca 'd'Oro,
front facing Canal Grande,
constructed 1421–1440

Due to its exceptional situation on the lagoon, the secular structures of the Late Gothic period in **Venice** were oriented toward the canals. Venice, which is built on over 100 single islets, until the 15th century ruled over the Mediterranean Sea, rivaled only by Genoa. Among the many magnificent Palazzi, mention must be made of the **Ca 'd'Oro,** the "golden house". It was built between 1421 and 1440 on the city's main waterway, the *Canal Grande.* The multifaceted facade is dominated by two loggias richly ornamented with tracery, behind each of which a great hall is situated. The ground floor consists of arcades. The finely nuanced ornamentation bears witness to the influence of Byzantine art. During the Crusades, numerous works of art imported from the Middle East were brought back to Venice and integrated into the building of nearby St. Mark's Cathedral. *Ca 'd'Oro* offers an exceptional mixture of styles, combining various periods and regional features.

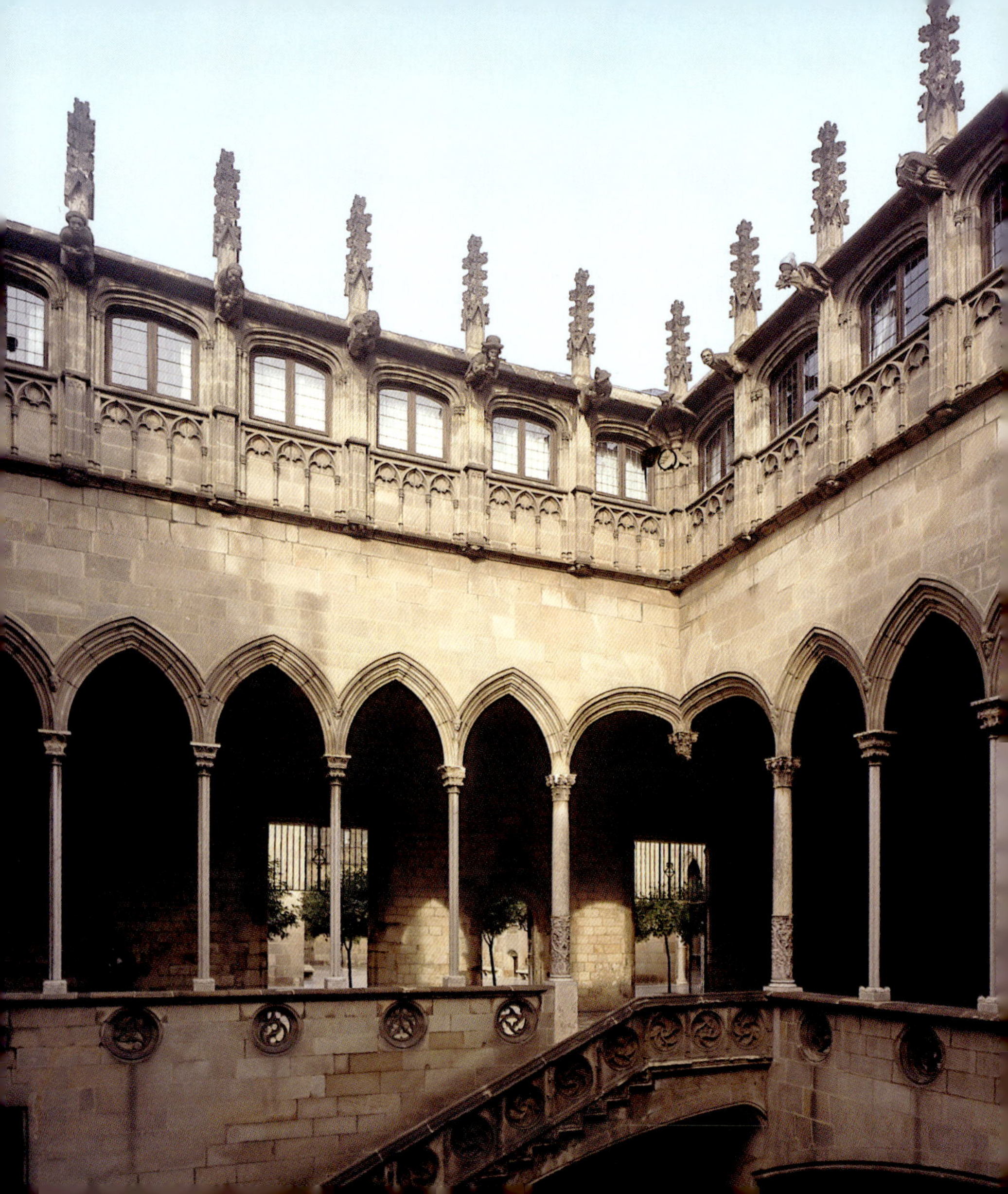

Secular Architecture in Spain and Portugal

Secular Architecture in Spain

The history of the Middle Ages on the Iberian Peninsula was largely dominated by the *Reconquista,* a time stretching from the 10th to the 15th centuries, when Christian rulers set about reconquering those territories which in the 8th century had been invaded by the Moors. The marriage of Isabella of Castile and Ferdinand II of Aragon in the 15th century finally led to the formation of the Spanish state as we know it. The arts flourished, even though – or because – Spain in the Late Middle Ages was highly influenced by conquests overseas and a Catholicism verging on hysteria. During the Middle Ages, **Barcelona,** at the time belonging to the Kingdom of Aragon and Catalonia, and today the capital of Catalonia province, was one of the most important Spanish cities. Picturesque houses line the Gothic district, the *Barri Gòtic,* including the imposing governmental palace, the **Palau de la Generalitat.** It was built in the 15th century to house the council, which comprised representatives of the nobility, the church and burghers. Two portals lead into it, one in the style of the Renaissance, the other Gothic. The latter is crowned with a relief of St. George, the patron saint of Barcelona. A large staircase leads from the inner Gothic courtyard to a gallery. The palace chapel boasts a richly ornamented facade in the exuberant Flamboyant style.

Apart from urban palaces, magnificent country estates were also erected on the Iberian Peninsula. One of these is **Castillo de**

Barcelona,
Palau de la Generalitat,
Pati Gòtic,
1425

Castillo de Manzanares el Real,
begun 1435

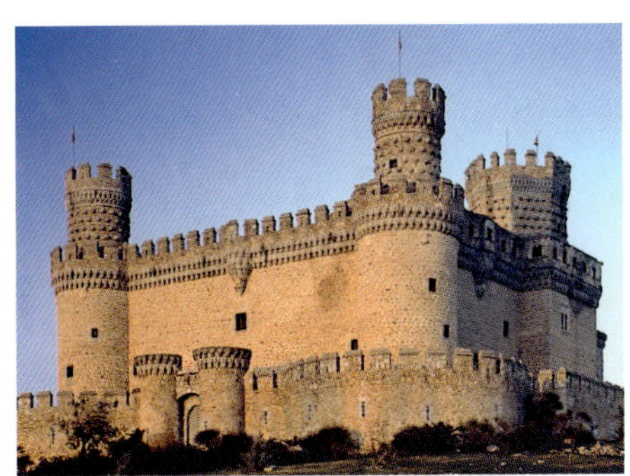

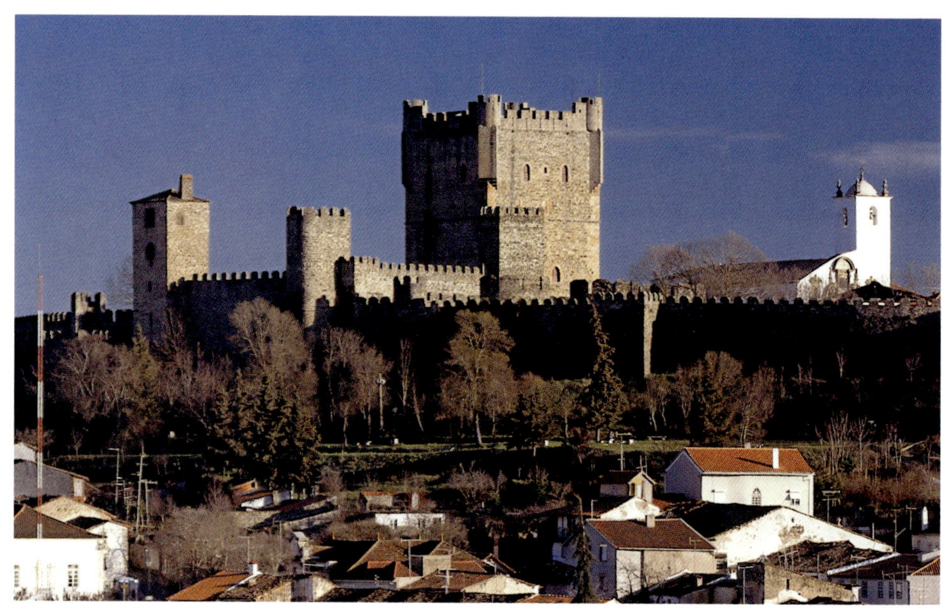

Bragança,
fortification,
constructed between the 12th and 16th centuries

Manzanares el Real (p. 99), situated in the *Sierra de Guadarrama,* to the north-west of Madrid, in the very heart of Spain. Part castle, part palace, this building was constructed in the 15th century in the typically Spanish Mudéjar style, using Gothic architectural innovations and profuse Moorish ornamentation. Crenelations, pinnacles and massive towers lend it the air of a fortress.

Secular Architecture in Portugal

Portugal came to fame as a seafaring nation. Between the late 14th and the late 16th centuries, colonies in Africa, Asia and America guaranteed an economic and cultural golden age. Toward the end of this period, a specific architectural style was developed, the Manueline style, named after the reign of King

Manuel I (1495–1521). This sumptuous architectural ornamentation can best be traced in **Belém,** the western quarter of Lisbon. It was largely left unharmed by the earthquake of 1755 and thus is a fascinating document of the glorious past of the Portuguese Empire. Commissioned by Manuel I, a watchtower was erected on the mouth of the Tejo River, the **Torre de Belém** (1515–1521), in honor of the glorious navigator Vasco da Gama. Its flat cupolas and finely nuanced ornamentation call to mind Moorish examples. This is the spot where the seafarers took leave, trusting in God's grace and hoping for a bright future. The name "Belém" alludes to Bethlehem, the birthplace of Jesus Christ.

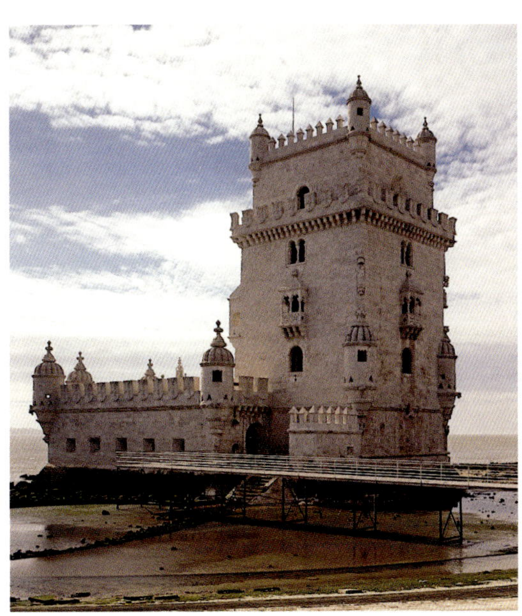

Belém,
Torre de Belém,
constructed 1515–1521

The fortification defending the city **Bragança** on the border with Spain, to the north-east of Portugal, features an architectural style entirely different from that of the profusely decorated *Torre de Belém.* This was the seat of the Bragança dynasty, Portugal's royal family from the 17th to the early 20th century. The **fortress,** *Fortaleza,* is enclosed by double walls and dates from the twelfth century. It was extended in the early 15th century under John I.

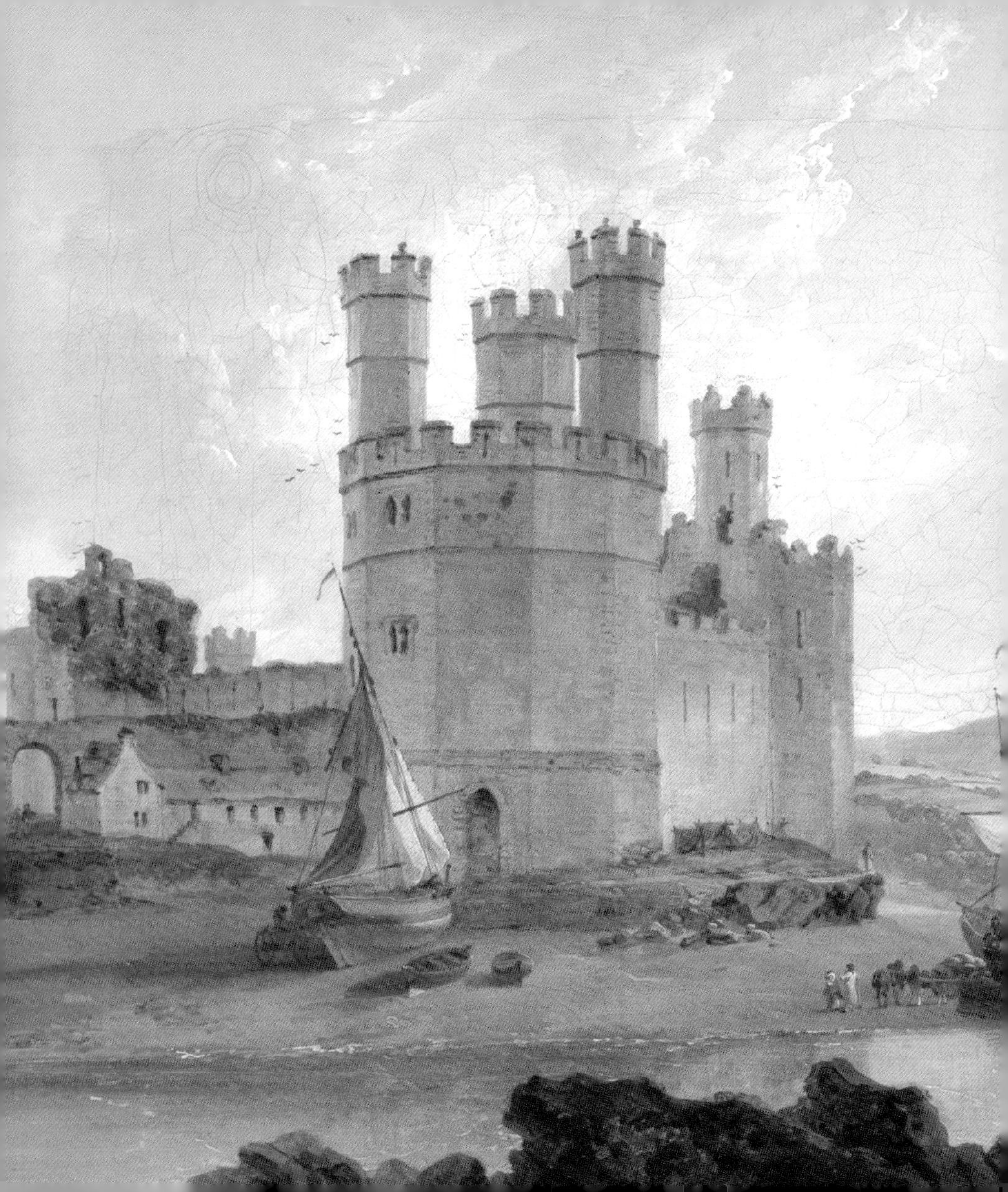

Secular Architecture in England and Wales

The history of England in the Middle Ages was dominated by internal and external conflicts, much like that of other European kingdoms. In the late 13th century, King Edward I (ruled 1272–1307) managed to consolidate the power of the crown by promoting trade and reorganizing the administration. In 1290, however, he expelled all Jews from England. Edward I successfully conquered Wales and thereafter had several fortresses erected there. The most imposing of these is **Caernarfon Castle,** begun in 1283. The fortress is built on the shoreline, to the north-west of the little town of Gwynedd. The crenelated fortification, constructed according to plans by royal architect Master James of St. George, has thirteen polygonal towers of varying size. Some of the larger towers are surmounted by slender watchtowers. Three of these crown the so-called Eagle Tower facing the sea, which was intended as the last refuge in the case of an attack. The castle was also fitted out with loopholes and hatches through which hot pitch would be poured over the enemy. The gate leading to the city was adorned with a statue of the king. The masonry, light-colored limestone, is decorated with horizontal bands of sandstone. 11th-century Norman remains were integrated into the courtyard in order to justify the annexation of Wales. A decade after Caernarfon Castle, Beaumaris Castle was constructed on Anglesey, an island off the Welsh coast (begun 1295). Another early example of the series of royal fortresses is Flint Castle (begun 1277).

Julius Caesar Ibbetson,
Caernarfon Castle,
oil painting, 1792,
National Museum and Gallery of Wales, Cardiff

Caernarfon Castle,
expansion begun 1283

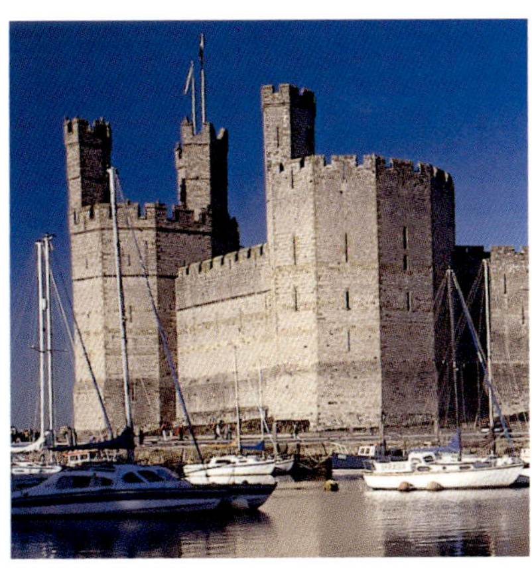

Life in a castle centered on a large rectangular hall. This is where the ruling dynasty's social life took place. A vivid example of court life is given by **Westminster Hall** (constructed 1394–1401) in **London.** It is the oldest surviving part of Westminster Palace (now part of the Parliament complex) and a truly magnificent building. Westminster became a prestigious district under William II Rufus, the son of William the Conqueror, who used Westminster Hall for festivities, representational events and to house the Court of Justice. Notable trials were held here, amongst others those of the Gunpowder Plot conspirators (1606) and King Charles I (1649). Today, Westminster Hall is the magnificent stage for important state ceremonies such as the Golden Jubilee of Queen Elizabeth II. Westminster Hall was built in the 14th century, commissioned by King Richard II. The architects integrated the walls of the previous Norman structure dating from the 11th century and introduced a spectacular hammer-beam oak roof, a construction made of wooden pointed arches, which spans the entire hall. The horizontal beams are decorated with figures of angels and support the arched segments that lead up towards the center of the roof. This feat of engineering allowed for even large spaces such as Westminster Hall to dispense with supporting pillars. The hammer-beam technique is one of the features of the Perpendicular style (see pp 58 ff.) of the Late Gothic period. This style is characterized by

London,
Westminster Hall,
reconstructed 1394–1401

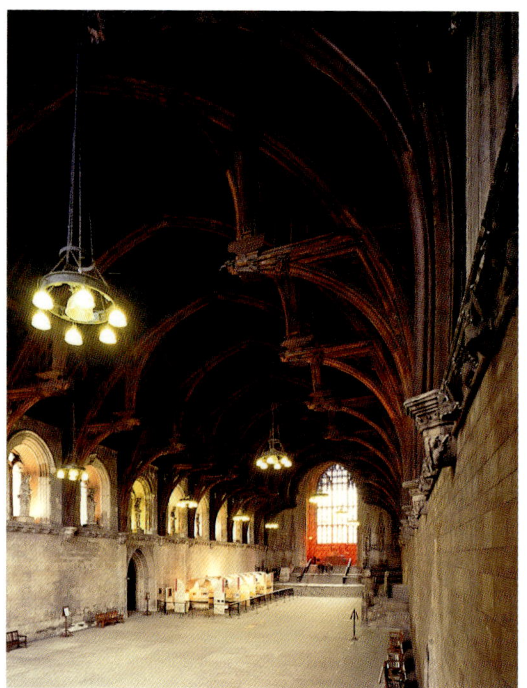

elaborate ornamental structures focusing on the verticality of a space. But beams and arches were not simply reduced to their technical functions, they were understood as sculptural parts of an imposing building and decorated accordingly: carved, painted and gilded.

The new technical possibilities of vaulting a large space had been handed down by the Gothic church architects. In Norfolk, several examples have remained of churches with hammer-beam roof constructions. A unique example is St Wendreda's Church in March, Cambridgeshire. This was begun in the 14th century and restructured in the 16th century. The spectacular double hammer-beam roof decorated with carved angels dates from this period. The wooden vault leaves a filigree and elegant impression. It shows how well the architects at the time knew about the ideal distribution of a vault's weight.

Thomas Rowlandson,
Westminster Hall,
colored ink drawing,
published 1809,
original held in a private collection

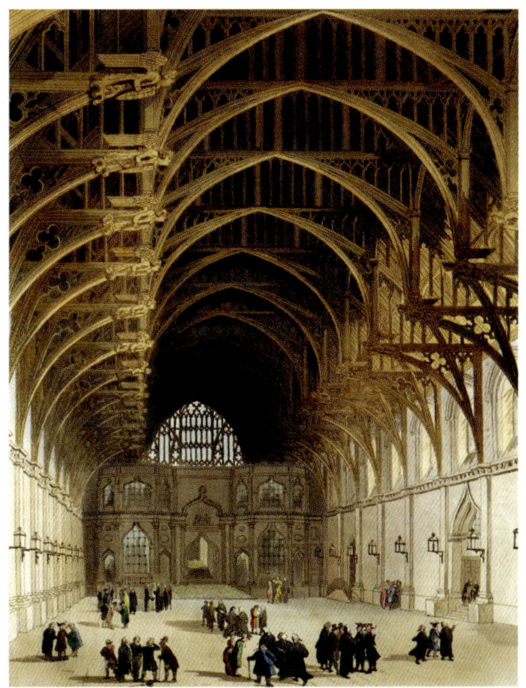

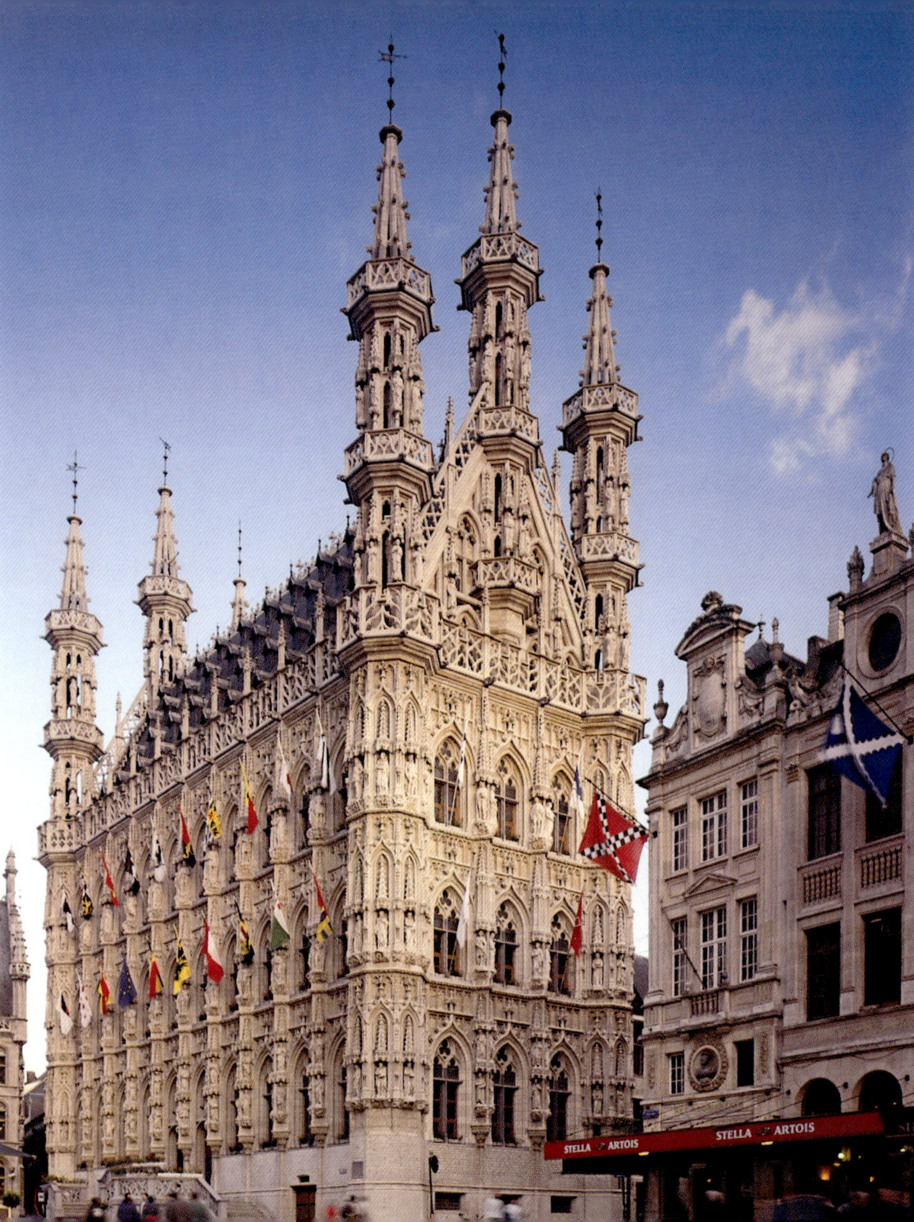
STELLA ARTOIS
STELLA ARTOIS

Secular Architecture in the Duchy of Burgundy

For more than a century (1363–1477), the Duchy of Burgundy, occupying what is now north-eastern France, Belgium, and the Netherlands, was an important territory. Through acquisitions and heritages, the dukes of Burgundy constantly expanded their feudal territory, which comprized economically important regions such as Flanders, Artois and Brabant. These were the basis for a century of wealth and courtly magnificence. Palatial administrative seats were constructed in the medieval centers of the towns, which were relatively autonomous. The secular architecture of the Late Gothic period used the technical and artistic innovations of the previous generations to devise a new type of building: the town hall. These town halls can be read as symbols of the new confidence of the middle class, which consisted of master craftsmen and merchants – citizens who desired to have some political influence. Craftsmen and tradespeople organized themselves in guilds that had a growing impact in everyday municipal politics. This social development is reflected in the elaborately designed town halls, which often also are surmounted by a soaring tower, an acknowledged symbol of political power.

We will take a closer look now at three exemplary towns. The first is **Leuven** in the Belgian province of Brabant. Founded in the 9th century as a Carolingian fortification, Leuven steadily grew to become an important center of the medieval cloth trade. The renowned university was founded as early as 1425. In the very center lies the market square, *Grote Markt.* The **town hall** was constructed between 1447 and 1469 by master builder Matheus de Layens (died 1483), who also built St. Peter's Church and the transept of St. James's as

Leuven,
town hall,
constructed 1447–1469

Brussels,
town hall,
begun 1401

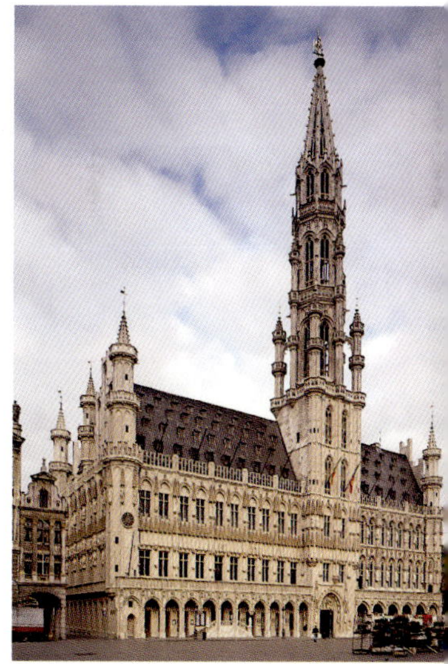

well as some buildings in Mons. The town hall's three facades are covered with elaborately worked sculptures that recall the finely nuanced wrought silver decorations on Late Gothic shrines.

Another impressive **town hall** is that of **Brussels** (p. 107). It was begun in 1401 in the Lower Town and completed a good fifty years later. The facade was restored in the 19th century. The Late Gothic structure is situated on the central *Grote Markt* and flanked by an impressive ensemble of buildings from the Gothic and Gothic Revival periods. The ground floor arcades open up the facade and call to mind Italian town houses. At 96 meters height, the centrally placed tower with soaring spire draws all the attention. It is elaborately decorated with oriel pinnacles, finials and delicate tracery.

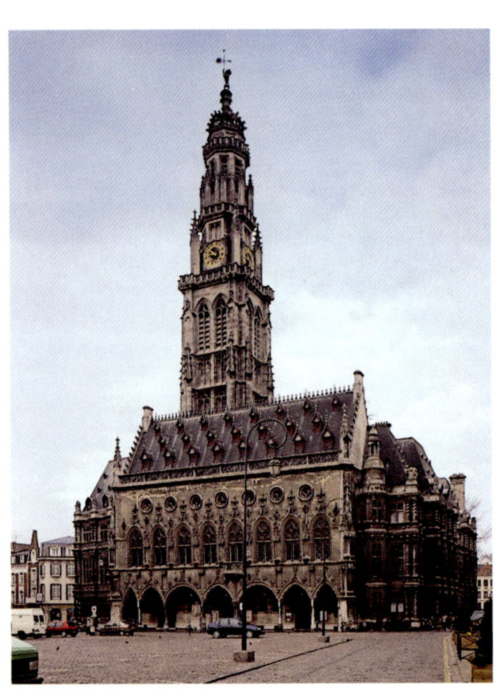

Arras,
town hall,
c. 1450–1572

With its gabled houses and arcades, **Arras** in northern France even today looks explicitly Flemish. Arras came to prosperity in the 11th century as a renowned center of the cloth and wool industry. From the 14th century, famous large-format tapestries were made here. The **town hall** was built between 1450 and 1572. Similar to the one in Brussels, it has arcades on the ground floor. The large assembly hall on the first floor can be discerned from the outside by a row of large lancet windows. Rich tracery, crockets and finials add to the overall precious effect. These ornaments were also applied to the soaring tower which has an octagonal structure and tapers toward the tip, ending in a crown shape.

Another remarkable example of Late Gothic secular architecture is found in **Bruges (Brugge):** the cloth halls. In the 14th and 15th centuries, until the harbor was silted up, the capital of Flanders was one of the leading trade centers of Europe. The medieval old town with its numerous ecclesiastical and secular structures bears witness to this golden age. The *Grote Markt,* the centrally situated market square, is a magnificent panorama of medieval architecture. The square is surrounded by gabled houses and dominated by the imposing **cloth halls.** These halls, built in the 13th and 14th centuries, were not only the location where goods were traded but also functioned as assembly halls. They are overtowered by the belfry, which is 83 meters high and was completed in 1486. The belfry had various important functions. It served to store important documents and for transmitting important bell signals, for example in case of fire. Bruges also has a Gothic town hall. Compared with the town hall of Leuven (p. 106), which was built 100 years later, the one in Bruges has a much more sober facade. The increase of ornamentation in Leuven signifies the growing confidence of the citizens at that period.

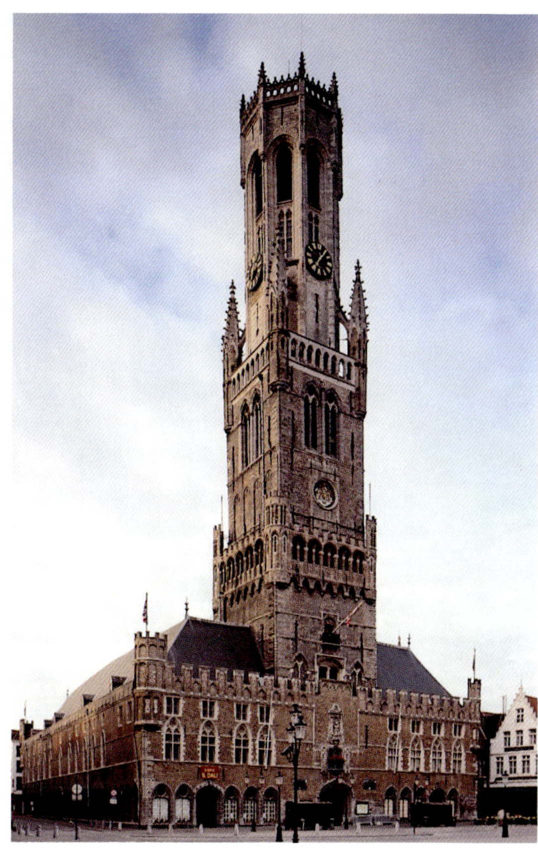

Bruges,
cloth hall with belfry,
constructed in the 13th century,
belfry completed 1486

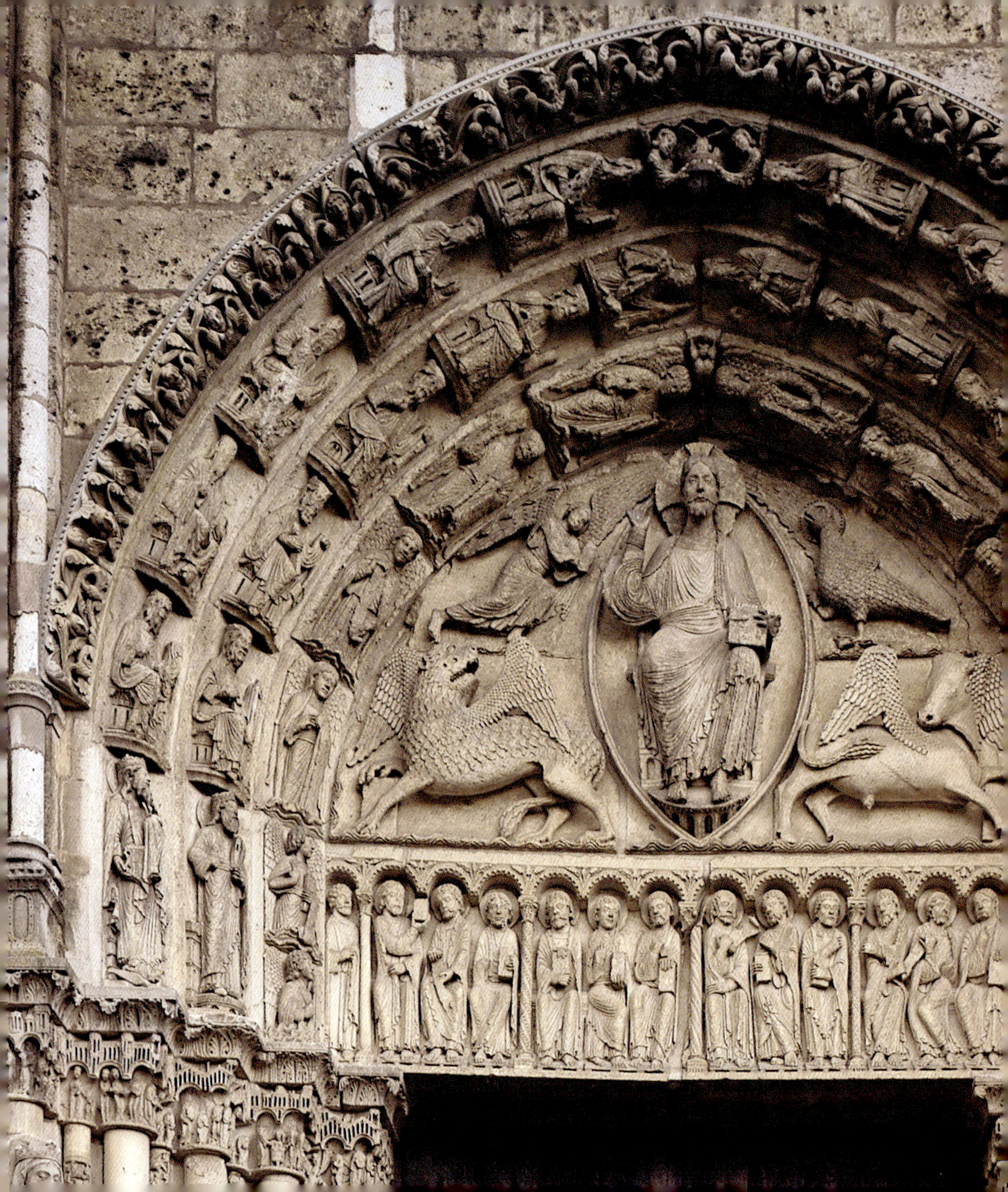

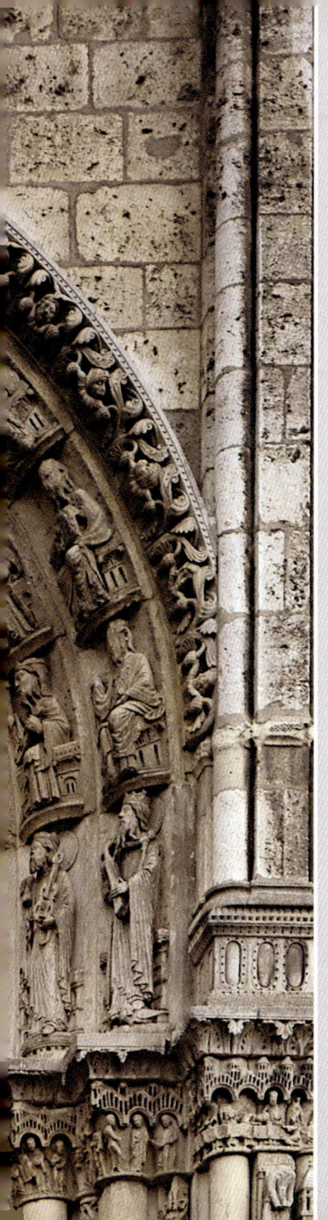

Gothic Sculpture

Every Christian enters through this portal in the knowledge of his or her sins: The antedated Last Judgment is led by the enthroned Son of God, Christ the Judge. The Four Evangelists of the New Testament, Matthew, Mark, Luke and John, sit by his side, they are symbolically represented as angel, lion, bull and eagle. The church's interpretation of religious texts guaranteed the correct faith for its followers. Fear of God's punishment but also confidence in the afterlife determined everyday Christian life. Gothic sculptors endeavored to give sensory expression to Christian belief, thus making their sculptures more secular. It is a fascinating voyage from the portal sculptures whose backbones form this godly structure to the free-standing figures with no religious meaning.

Chartres,
Notre-Dame Cathedral,
Christ the Judge, the tympanum of the middle entrance of the west portal,
c. 1145–1155

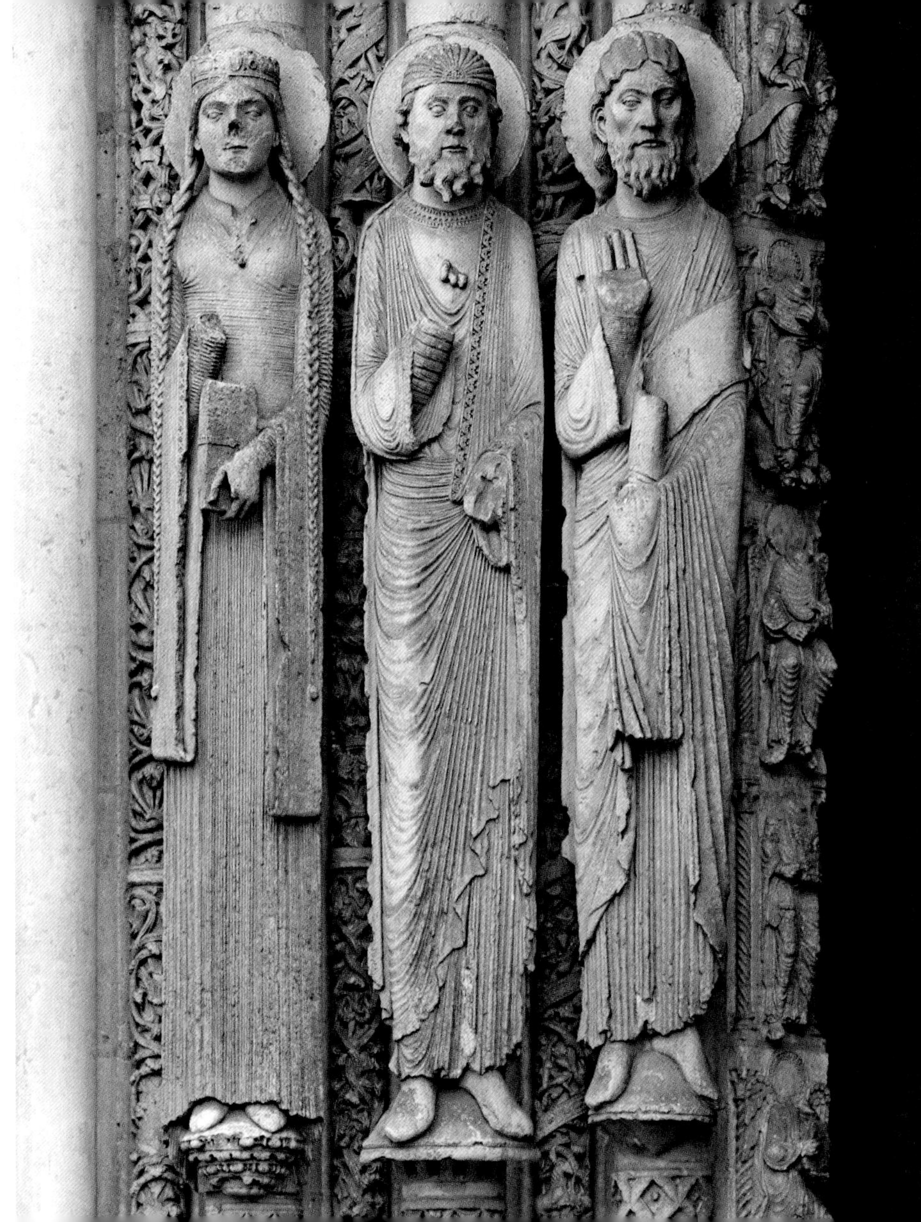

The Portal Sculpture

Some find it strange that Christian sculpture ever developed. Early Christians, fighting against the ancient heathen religion, objected to the human depictions of the gods. The God of the Old Testament forbade his followers to make likenesses of him and early Christians interpreted this as a ban on all physical depictions of God. Only symbols such as the fish, whose Greek letters were the same as the first letters of "Jesus Christ, Son of God," were allowed. Soon enough though the people started rebelling against this interdiction and arguments arose as to whether religious imagery should or should not be allowed. In the 8th and 9th centuries this developed into a major dispute, the *Iconoclastic controversy.* This serious and fiercely disputed argument was not only about religious imagery, it focused also on the whole question of Christian worship. The devout Christian laity yearned for a visual and tangible sign of their faith, but the theologians of the day wrote treatises against this, considering this form of visual religiosity too superficial. During the Middle Ages this view changed and, for pragmatic and political reasons, Christian imagery was eventually approved. At that time no one could have possibly dreamed of the magnificence that the following centuries of religious art would produce.

In this chapter we will look at the sculpture of the early French portals and those of the neighboring "German lands" from the mid-twelfth century to the second half of the 13th century. The following chapter is devoted to the secular and religious works of Gothic statuary,

Chartres,
Notre-Dame Cathedral,
Portal figures left of the middle entrance of the west portal (left), middle entrance of the west portal (right),
c. 1145–1155

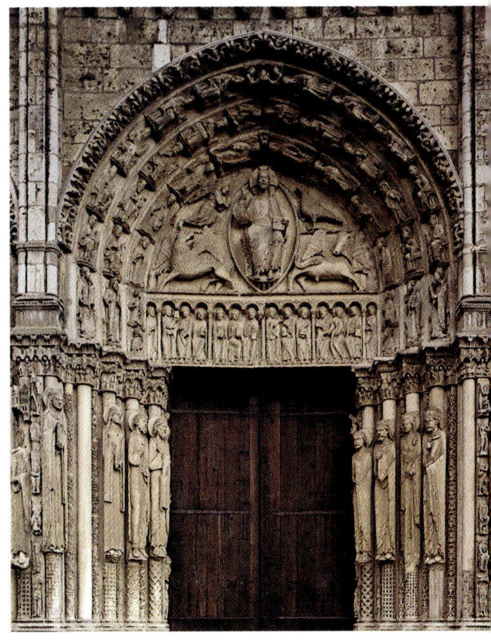

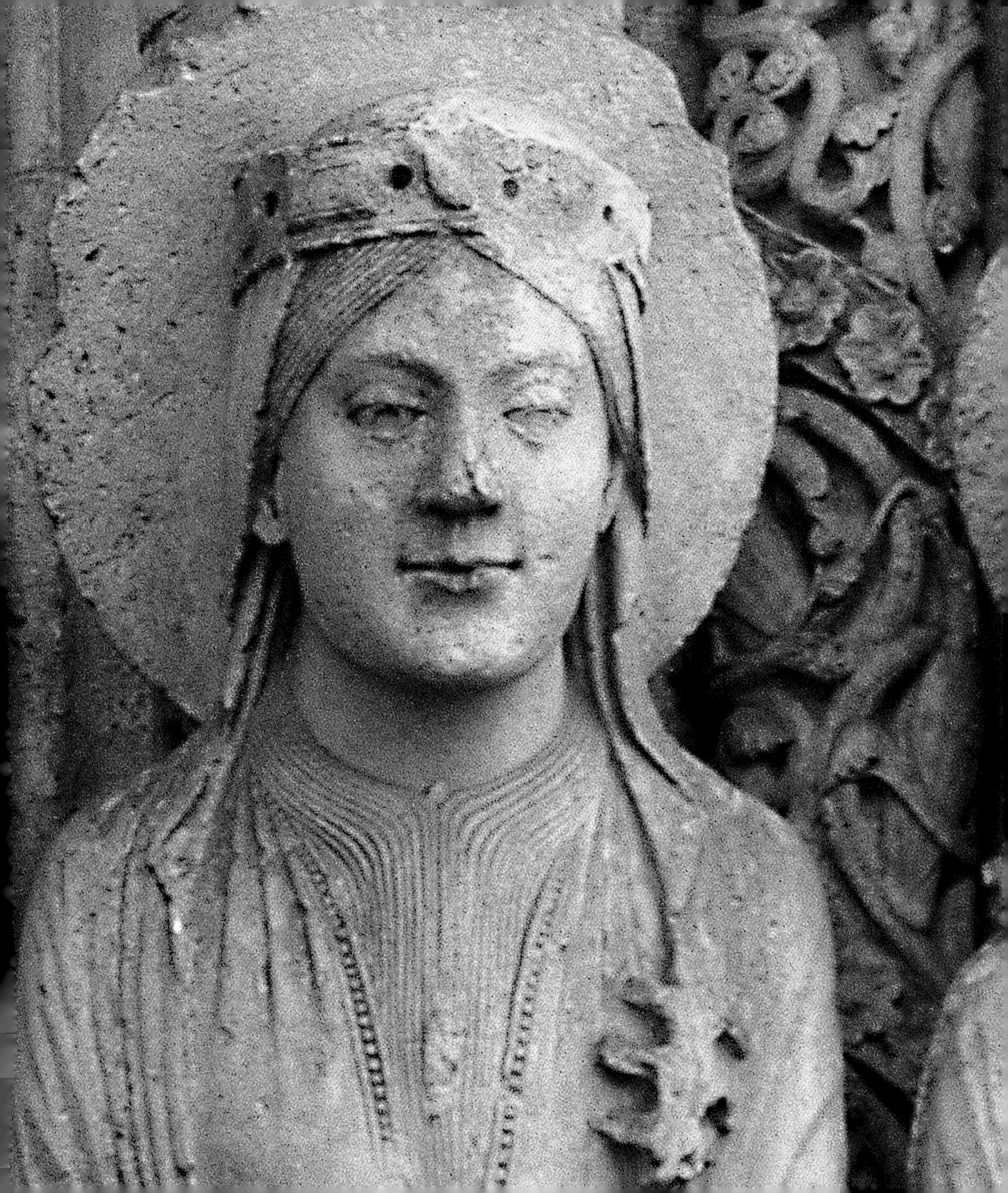

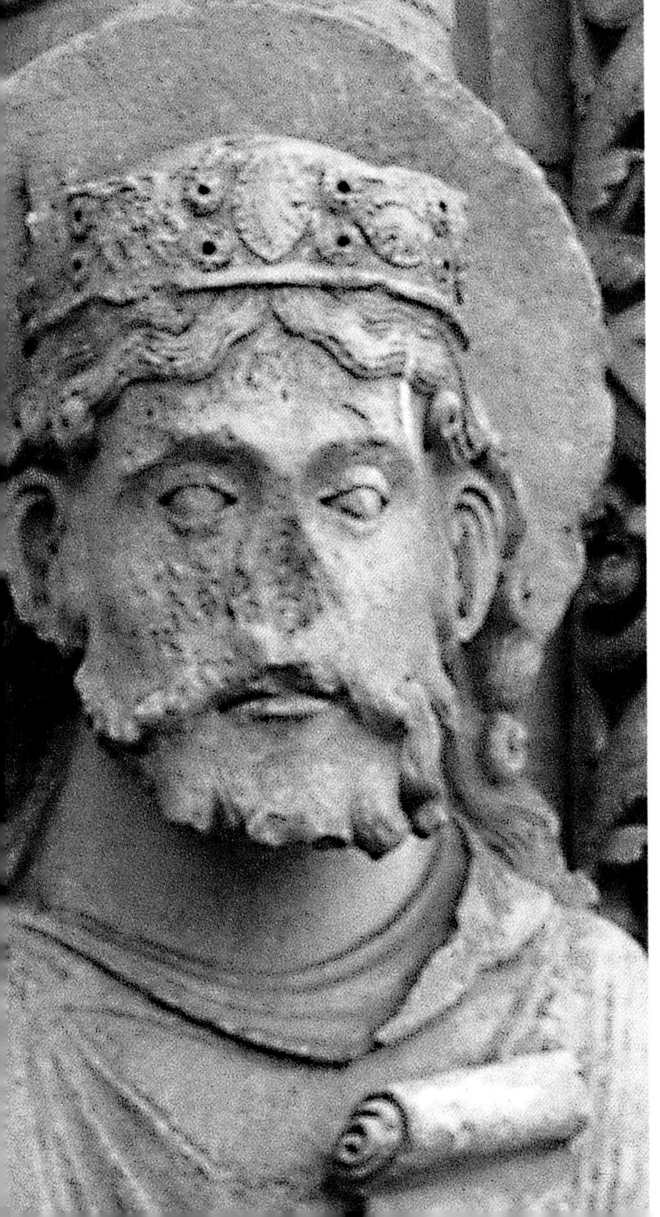

King Solomon is crowned and holds a scroll with both hands. The Queen of Sheba indicates an ethereal smile with her taut lips.

Chartres,
Notre-Dame Cathedral,
Portal figure to the right of the middle entrance of the west portal, *c.* 1145–1155

which are free-standing and created without any particular supporting architectural context. In the third and final chapter we will show the different regional trends, using examples of outstanding works from different European countries.

Primarily in France and in the areas influenced by French architecture a new dynamic in the genre of portal sculpture developed as a result of the need to design the facades of new cathedrals. The former Romanesque church entrances were also often adorned with figures. Now, however, the artists responded to the new style of architecture, which on its part supported an elaborate artistic program, including projections and recesses of facades, accentuating different zones and hierarchical levels, working in thematic references and accents. One of the earlier examples of this is the three-doored **west portal of Chartres Cathedral** (pp. 110, 111, 112, 113, 114, 115). The entrance, which dates from the mid-twelfth century, carries the oldest architectural sculptures of the building. Unfortunately the complete ensemble does not remain and the original color has faded. Of the twenty-four original clad figures presented on the columns of the second lowest wall area only nineteen have remained. In addition, some of them have been changed and extended through various restorations. These **robed figures** (pp. 112, 114, 115) are generally held to mark the beginning

Notre-Dame Cathedral as the Temple of Reason

Not only were the sculptures of this Parisian cathedral subject to change. The building itself also looks back on a turbulent history: most notably in the French Revolution of **1789** it was not spared. In the context of the increasing radicalization not only was a break with the previous political regime to be implemented. The spiritual and moral basis of society was also to be rebuilt. Religion was denounced as irrational, the means used by the previous rulers to oppress the people. As a result, in **1792**, the cathedral was closed, paintings and statues were destroyed, and liturgical implements made from precious metals were melted down. The cathedral was declared a "Temple of Reason" along with all other ecclesiastical buildings; in November **1793** a "Festival of Reason" was celebrated there. After the French Revolution the building was used, among other things, as a wine cellar. In **1802** the cathedral was re-consecrated. In **1805** Napoleon was crowned emperor here.

of Gothic sculpture. They represent a new demeanor, a new style: in spite of the extreme lengthening of the bodies and the summary conception of the materiality the figures appear organic, their gestures are softer and more natural than earlier sculptures, the tension in their faces brings them to life. The use of minimal technical tricks introduces a new interaction among the figures and also sets them in relation to their architectural context. For example, the figures leading to the doors gradually increase in size. The names of these robed figures are, however, largely unexplained. Are they repetitions of the

Paris,
Notre-Dame Cathedral,
Enthroned Madonna,
detail from the tympanum of the St. Anne Portal,
c. 1210

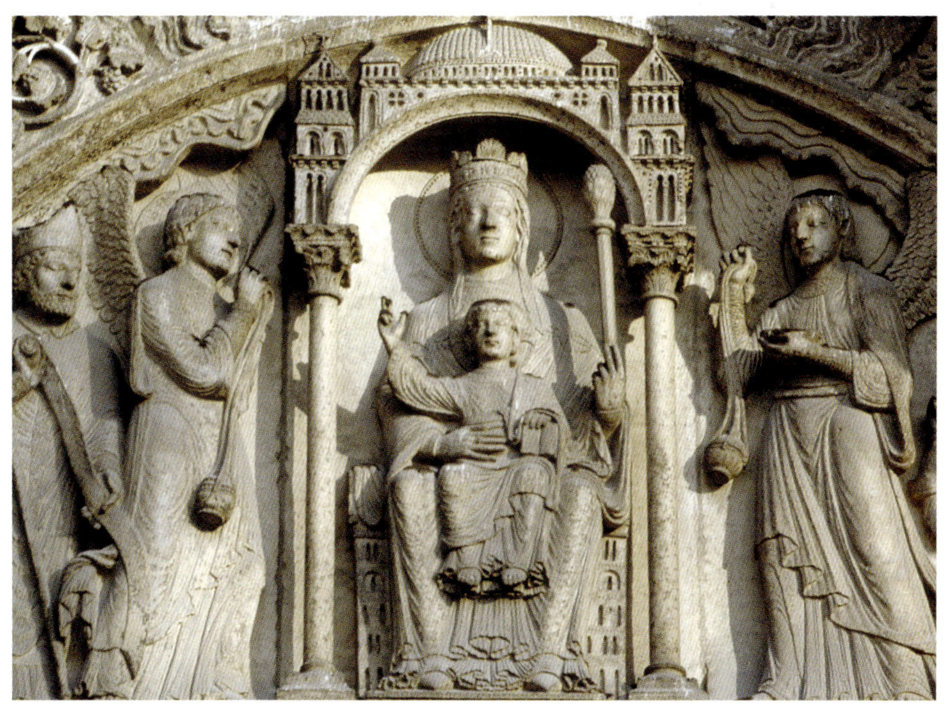

Apostle figures, which are already represented on the lintel of the middle portal? Are the prophets of the Old Testament among them? Which locally important saints could have found their place here? At least two of the robed statues (p. 114, 115) are believed to have been named; according to this interpretation King Solomon and the Queen of Sheba stood, for the incoming churchgoers, to the right of the main entrance. The legendary king of the golden age of Israel is crowned and holds a scroll in both hands. His neighbor, with elegant high cheekbones and half-closed eyelids, hints at an ethereal smile with her taut lips.

Christ's Ascension into heaven is represented in the tympanum of the left entrance of the west portal of Chartres Cathedral; the right arch panel is dedicated to Mary and the early childhood of Jesus. The tympanum of the **main entrance** (p. 113) shows the **Enthroned Christ** (pp. 110, 111). The theme of Christ the Judge at the portal entrance is not new, it was also used in church entrances by the Romanesque sculptors. What is new – as research has so accurately put it – is the coolness and the worldly-wise solemnity of the figure of Christ, the serenity and detachment that speaks from the depth of the eyes through the half-closed eyelids. Never before had such involvement been seen in a complex figural conception. An abundance of narratives and figures can be found across the individual archivolts, lintels, and on the capitals: stories from the New Testament are set beside personifications of the seven

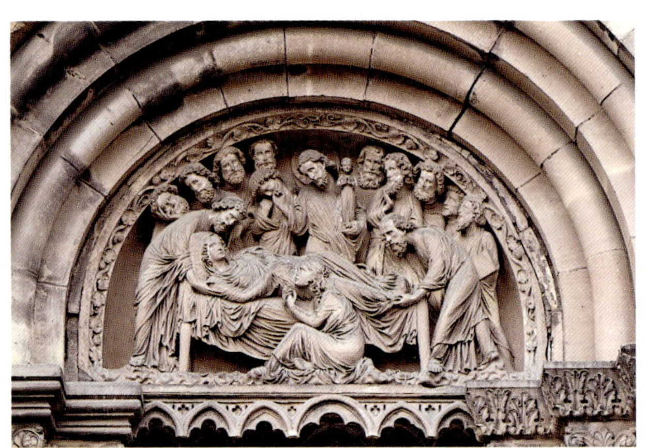

Strasbourg Cathedral,
Left portal tympanum of the south transept,
c. 1235

liberal arts, labors of the month next to the signs of the zodiac. At the same time, one can feel already here with some of the earliest examples of Gothic portal sculpture, that this conception of church entrances would set the new standard. The portals of the following decades are ultimately similar, and so are less imaginative and appropriate than they were in the Romanesque period.

The development of the west portal of Chartres Cathedral has been dated to virtually the same time as the arch panel on the **right entrance of the west facade of Notre-Dame** in **Paris.** The tympanum of the St. Anne Portal (p. 117) from the mid-twelfth century was reused in the rebuilding, which was carried out in the 13th century. This type of recycling may seem unusual but the reuse of building elements, knwn as *spolia,* was standard in Antiquity and the Middle Ages. Numerous columns, capitals and cornices from heathen temples found themselves new homes in church buildings. And so, the conversion of a barely fifty-year-old tympanum, which was a small change, led to decades of confusion for researchers. In the meantime it has been deduced that the arch panel with the enthroned

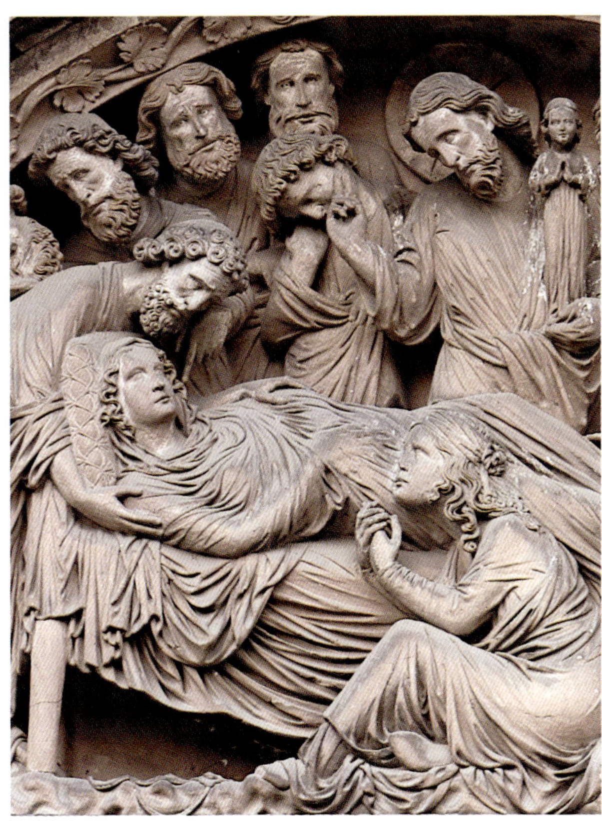

Strasbourg Cathedral,
The death of Mary,
detail from the left portal tympanum,
c. 1235

Madonna and Child in severe frontality was given a new thematic concept: the portrayal stemming from a Marian portal is now set in the context of St. Anne, the mother of Mary, hence the name St. Anne Portal. The first frieze underneath the enthroned Mary shows us the events of the birth of Jesus. This sculpture work is from the mid-twelfth century, but the frieze on the lintel dates from the early 13th century and deals with scenes from the life of St. Anne. These relief figures are vividly executed and strongly detached from the background. Nevertheless, the attempt was made, through the repetition of the art of the upper relief, to adapt these new representations to the older sections of the work.

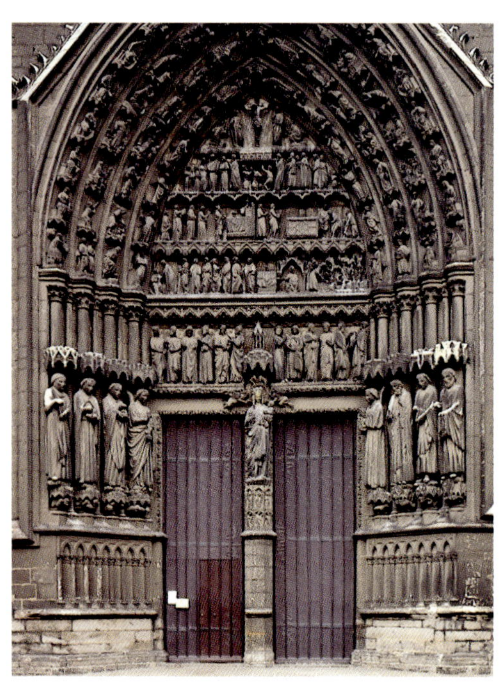

Amiens,
Notre-Dame Cathedral,
south transept tympanum,
c. 1240–1245

Another tympanum with the Marian theme can be found on the left entrance of the **double portal of the south transept in Strasbourg Minster.** This portrays the death of Mary (pp. 118,119). Dated circa 1235, and therefore crafted many generations later than the arch panel we have just examined, the great freedom of the figures here impresses us in comparison to the surrounding architecture. This is not only in the sense that these figures are more vividly portrayed but they are also distributed appropriately across the area without seeming measured. In the given semicircle the mourning Apostles stand around the dying Mary who appears almost to float on her bed. The two standing on the outer right and left bend slightly forward, thus adapting naturally to the architectural limitations. The heads of those standing overlap with the meander, the collective outcome gives the impression of a snapshot. By the subtle foreshortening of the body parts and the slight lift of the bed and the body of the Mother of Christ the composition is perfectly aligned to meet the eye of the beholder who is about to enter through the portal.

This technique, which is based on including the view of the beholder and consciously steering their impression, would become more polished in the following years. In this way the **portal of the south transept in Notre-Dame Cathedral in Amiens** (pp. 120,121) is cleverly focused entirely on one figure which stands between the two doors and whose head reaches over the lintel and into the arch panel: Mary (p.121). The tympanum friezes increase in plasticity towards the bottom, until they reach the practically lifelike figure of the Madonna. Three angels hold Mary's halo, an idiosyncratic concretion of this religious symbol. Her right hand has been replaced, but presumably it originally pointed to the Son of God whom she supports with her left hand: a little bundle of joy who holds the globe in his baby hands. The *Vierge*

Amiens,
Notre-Dame Cathedral, Madonna and Child, so-called *Vierge Dorée,* section of the portal of the south transept, c. 1240–1245

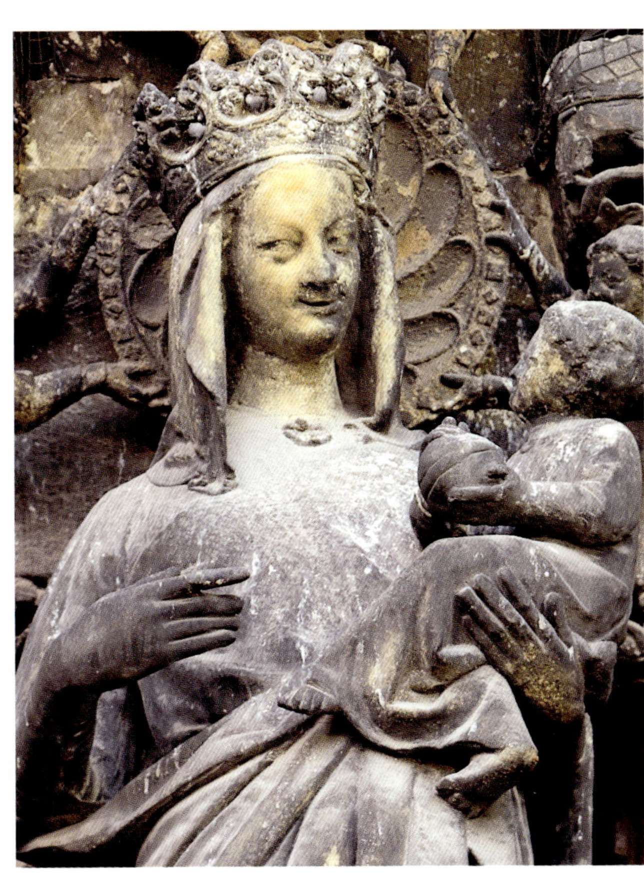

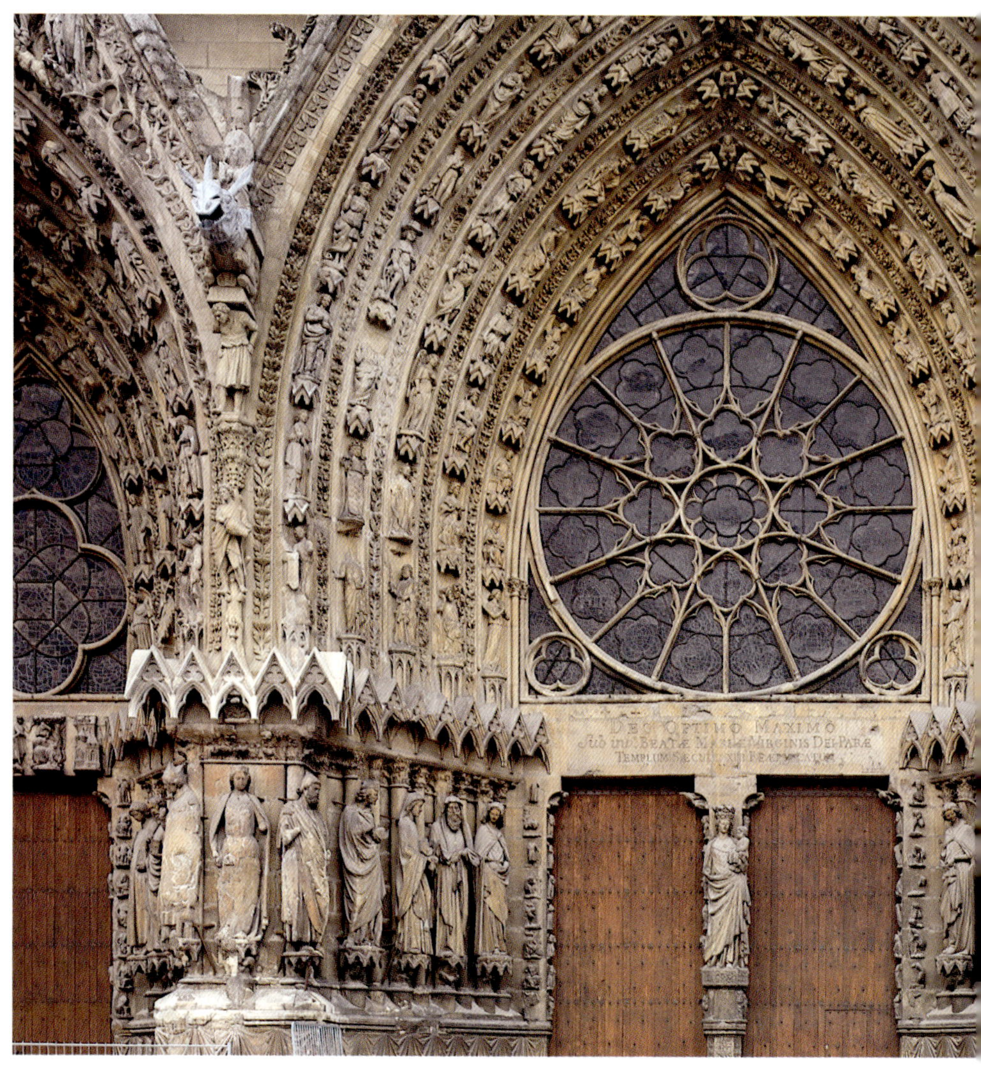
DEO OPTIMO MAXIMO
BEATÆ VIRGINIS DEI-PARÆ
TEMPLUM

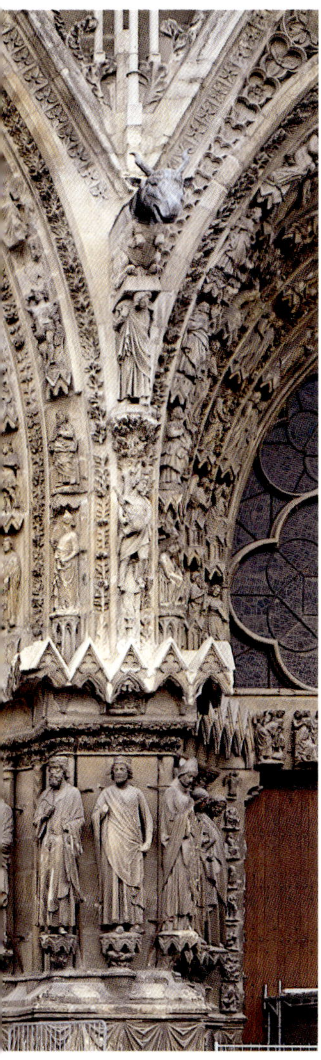

Dorée, the Gilded Virgin, still has some remains of her precious coloration on her face; which originally must have increased the focusing effect. She is kept within the church these days, on an equally elevated position, so that the original perspective of the churchgoer from a downward angle remains. Her slight inclination to the side, to balance out the weight of the boy, indicates the more naturalistic representation of High Gothic art; her smile, which can be interpreted as benign and motherly, is often drawn on as evidence of the greater humanness of the sculpture of this phase. The portal was built in the 1240s. Like many other portals from the first half of the 13th century, the upper area of the gradually recessing pointed arch is bordered with rows of small, overlapping figures. Their attributes and faces cannot be seen clearly from the ground, but they are very elaborate: a technique used in classical art to give the impression of overwhelming abundance.

Reims,
Notre-Dame Cathedral,
central west portal,
c. 1252–1275

A similar concept, but with a completely different implementation, can be seen in the middle **west portal in Notre-Dame Cathedral in Reims** (pp. 122, 123, 124, 125) from the years 1252 to 1275: here also, in the archivolts on the monumental graduated pointed arch, the little figures are ancillary to the entirety of the architecture. However, the area that is normally used for the tympanum is perforated with rose windows. The lower zone is again comparable with the existing examples of early Gothic portal design: robed figures stand in rows along the protruding wall between the entrances, the area between the double doors at the entrance is, as in Amiens, filled with a raised Madonna and Child. The **robed figures** (pp.124, 125) on the lower wall area depict various Old Testament characters, Apostles and saints. On the basis of misalignment scars carved into the backs of some figures it has been determined that in the intervening time some of them have been swapped around. The original placement can no longer be deduced. Stylistically, they draw on classical elements such as the attention to texture in the working of the folds of the fabrics. Furthermore, their backs are more or less independent of the supporting columns; apparently free enough for them to turn to one another. Some remains of the original coloration are to be seen, reinforcing the obvious intention of the sculptors: to accentuate the vitality of the statues.

Reims,
Notre-Dame Cathedral,
portal figures to the left of the central west portal,
c. 1252–1275

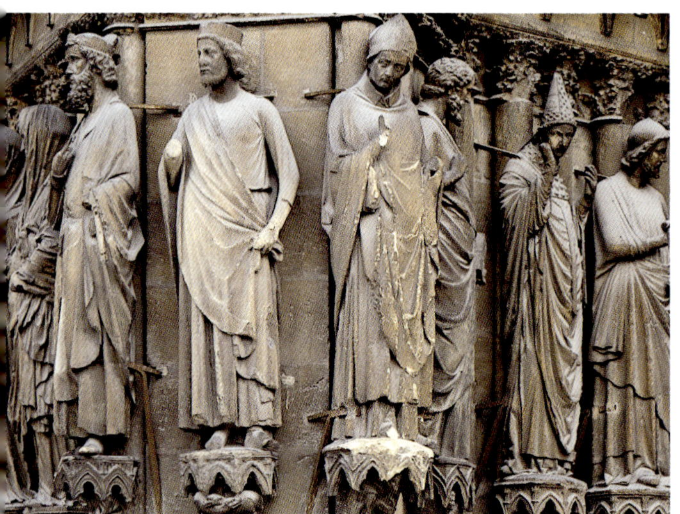

The west facade of

Reims Cathedral, constructed in second half of the 13th century, was erected several meters in front of the existing facade, with the intention of enlarging the church. This was to increase the size of the church interior and thus render it more appropriate for its status as cathedral and chosen place of coronation. Within the chronology of Gothic architecture, this facade plays a special role: it is the only one which was created after the complete dissociation of Gothic facade construction from its Romanesque precursors, and completed before the over-extravagant show facades of the 14th century. Here as with the later examples we are confronted with sculptures on portals rather than portal sculpture in the original sense: the statues no longer depend on the support of the architecture.

Reims,
Notre-Dame Cathedral,
portal figures to the right of the central west portal,
c. 1252–1275

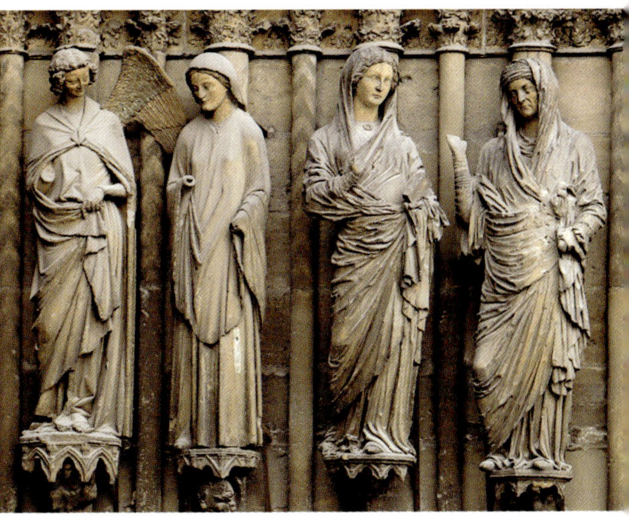

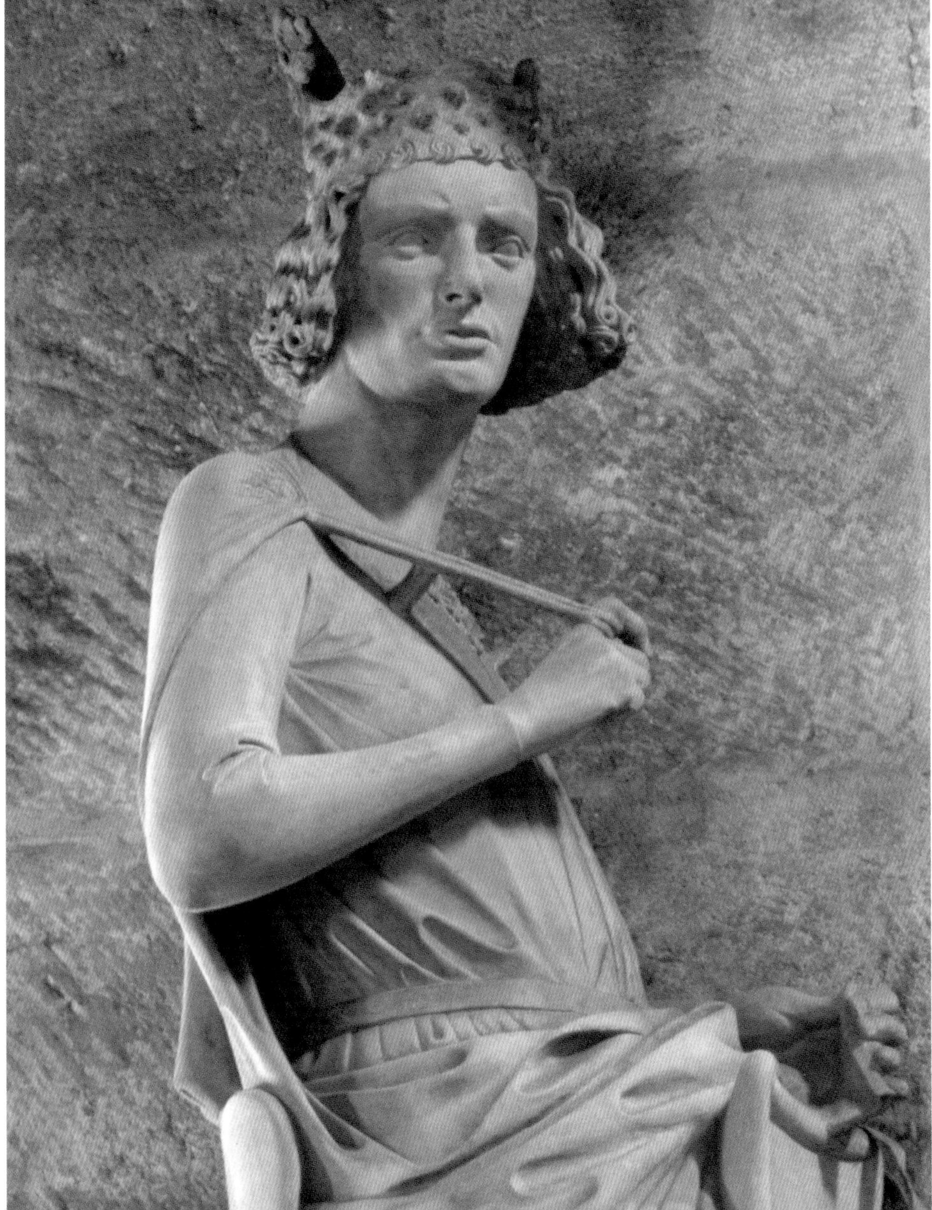

The Emergence of Free-Standing Sculpture

In the last chapter we pursued the separation of portal sculpture from its architectural backbone. Now we will look at secular and religious works of Gothic sculpture that are free standing and manage without supporting architecture. The function and style of these works developed in parallel, mutually enriching one another: just as the sculptures freed themselves from the architectural structure the themes stepped out of the shadows of the religious canons and it was possible to portray secular people. The earliest three-dimensional Gothic sculptures do not portray saints but more likely rulers. Admittedly: these new secular effigies were most often to be found in churches.

Bamberg Horseman, height *c.* 230 cm, sandstone, *c.* 1225–1235, Bamberg Cathedral

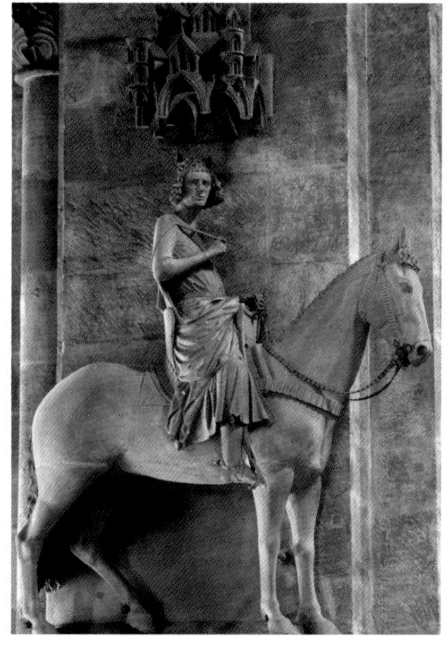

The Equestrian Statues of Bamberg and Magdeburg

Among the first known free-standing stone statues of the Middle Ages are two equestrian statues: the Bamberg Horseman from around 1230 and the Magdeburg Horseman in the Old Market (pp. 128,129) from the 1240s. In both cases it is not known who is portrayed. We cannot assume, based on the composition of facial expression or the hair, that this is not a religious portrayal. Adapting Old Testament prophets, Apostles and saints to appear more contemporary was common. We will examine the statues more closely: the Magdeburg Horseman is slightly larger than life, the head with its wavy hair is crowned, and he is wearing a traveling

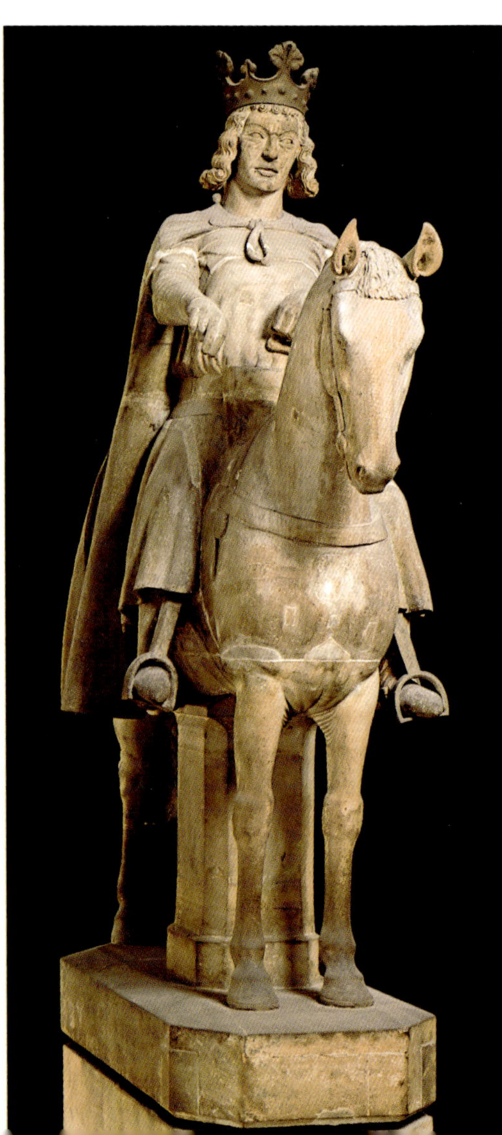

cloak. The left hand hold the reins close to his body, the right hand is stretched out and appears to point to something. Originally he was accompanied by two female figures. He stood on a column in the Old Market square and was protected by a baldachin. He is facing the facade of the town hall and the Court of Justice, as if he had just arrived there. The larger than life Bamberg Horseman also wears a cloak; the belt of which is wrapped around his right index finger, as if he is about to take it off. His left hand, in the original version, holds the reins tight as if he is just stopping. His head is also crowned, he is also sheltered by a baldachin. Horseman and horse stand on a console, which was designed for them. Apart from stylized leaves, similar to those of a capital, this console displays a demonic face on its preserved right side, the meaning of which is unexplained. Overall the Bamberg Horseman is more finely designed; the horse is not so bulky as the one from a group in Bamberg which is several years younger. The Magdeburg Horseman cannot have been made without knowledge of the Bamberg Horseman or that of a missing example on which both are based. In both cases it is impossible to name who is being portrayed, though they are most probably interpretations of secular people. There are no Christian comparisons for equestrian statues, whereas equestrian statues of rulers of Antiquity still exist. Here, at this early stage of the Gothic period, free-standing sculpture and secular representation are found together.

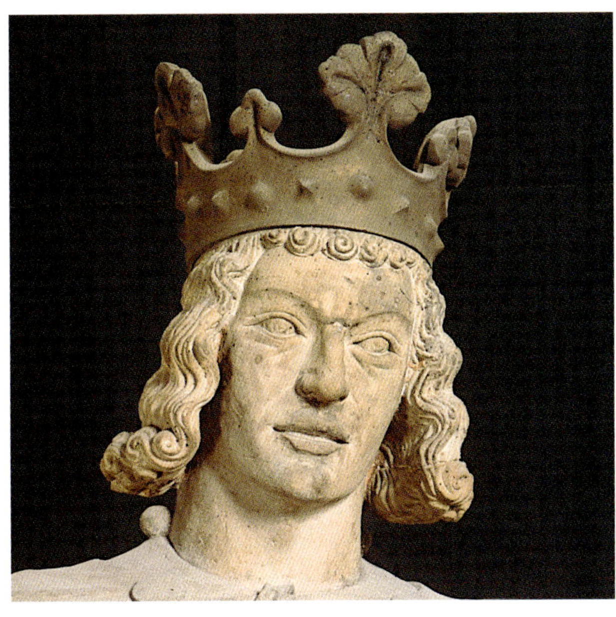

The Magdeburg Horseman, Old Market, Magdeburg, height *c.* 240cm, sandstone, *c.* 1245–1250, Kunsthistorisches Museum, Magdeburg

The Donor Statues in Naumburg and Meissen

A total of twelve life-size sculptures stand raised in the **west chancel of Naumburg Cathedral.** The two most famous of the **donor figures** are the **Margrave Ekkehard II of Meissen** and his wife **Uta von Ballenstedt** (p. 131). The margrave came from the noble Ekkehardiner dynasty, of which he was the last in the line; the dynasty died with him in the year 1046. During his rule the bishop's see was moved from Zeitz to Naumburg, justifying his presence in the ensemble of benefactors. The sculptor of these works from the mid-13th century is unknown, scholars use the designation: Master of Naumburg. The beholder gazes on humans with individual facial expressions and physiques, accentuated with polychrome coloration. Admittedly, here – as in the case of the equestrian statues – we are not dealing with portraits in the modern sense but with successful free creations of physiognomy. The Master of Naumburg, or at least his workshop, also operated in **Meissen.** Many of the sacred figures in the cathedral there exhibit a very similar artistic signature; especially the over-

Benefactor figures Ekkehard and Uta,
limestone, *c.* 1250
Naumburg Cathedral of St. Peter and St. Paul

dimensioned highly expressive **figures of the benefactor couple Otto I and his wife Adelheid** (p. 132), created in the years 1255 to 1260. The figures stand on consoles under a baldachin in front of the smooth exposed masonry of the north wall. Both are crowned and the polychrome coloration reinforces the magnificence of their robes. The situational gestures and facial traits may seem unusual to us: Otto, with drooping corners of the mouth, wide-open eyes and wrinkled forehead, appears horrified, annoyed or unsure. Adelheid, on the other hand, turns to him with an amused smirk. But we are dealing with statues of benefactors in a 13th-century cathedral. The sculptor's reasoning must have been other than to damage the authority of those portrayed. Here, again, we are not dealing with contemporaries of the Master of Naumburg: Emperor Otto I died in 973, his wife Adelheid, for whom this was her third marriage, in the year 999. They were allocated a statue to honor the fact that they founded the diocese of Meissen in the year 968. Apart from a possible consultation of a 200-year-old illumination containing a portrait of Otto I, the sculptor was given free hand in the realization of the imperial couple. The bottom line is that the sculptor decided on a human depiction. Not accuracy – Adelheid was twenty years younger than Otto – nor boring exaggeration – Otto

The Late Career of Uta von Naumburg

Today, the best-known of the benefactor figures in Naumburg Cathedral is Uta. But for centuries no one paid her much attention. Keen art travelers did not visit the cathedral at all. Or, like Goethe, they found the medieval figures unusual but not particularly noteworthy.

Uta can thank the photographs by Walter Hege from the **1920s** for her fame. These seemed to inspire life in the figure. Very quickly Uta became a representative of German art and culture. She was considered the ideal of charm and dignity, but also of aloofness and purity.

Copies of the Naumburg figure abounded, as did theatrical pieces about her life – a telling proof of her popularity.

During the Third Reich, from **1933** to **1945**, the adoration of the statue reached its tragic peak: the sculpture was taken as the purest expression of German art and at the same time as the ideal embodiment of German women.

holds the insignia of his command casually in his right hand – but rather, the vibrancy of expression was the main objective.

Three-Dimensional Sacral Sculptures

The rediscovery of the possibilities of free-standing sculptures was not limited to portrayals of secular people. Rather, we must assume that for sculptors of the twelfth and 13th centuries the church was practically the only employer they could have. Their contracts with itinerant artists, sculptors' and builders' workshops became the first basis for artistic exchange and with that advanced the stylistic development of the works. The benefactor figures we have just seen are also church fittings. Nonetheless, the joy of innovation in free-standing sculpture and its individual portrayal seems to have been triggered more by memorial statues such as the equestrian statues and benefactor figures. The portal program of the cathedrals was too standardized for this. But here, also, new room for free-standing sculpture was sought. In the south transept of Strasbourg Cathedral stands the so-called Pillar of Angels (pp. 134, 135). The octagonal pillar from the years 1225 to

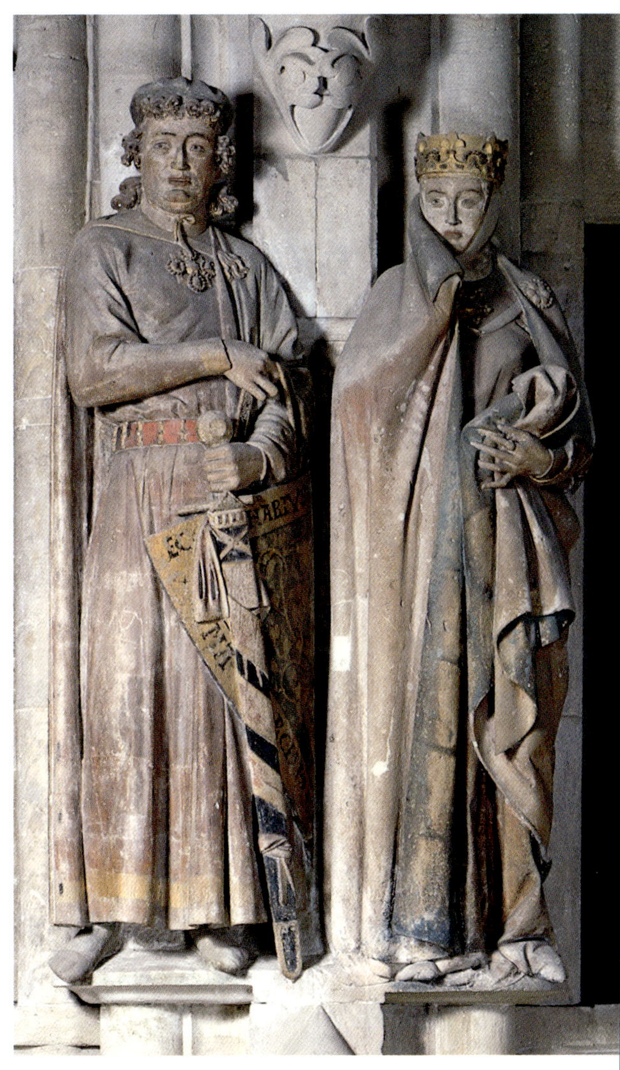

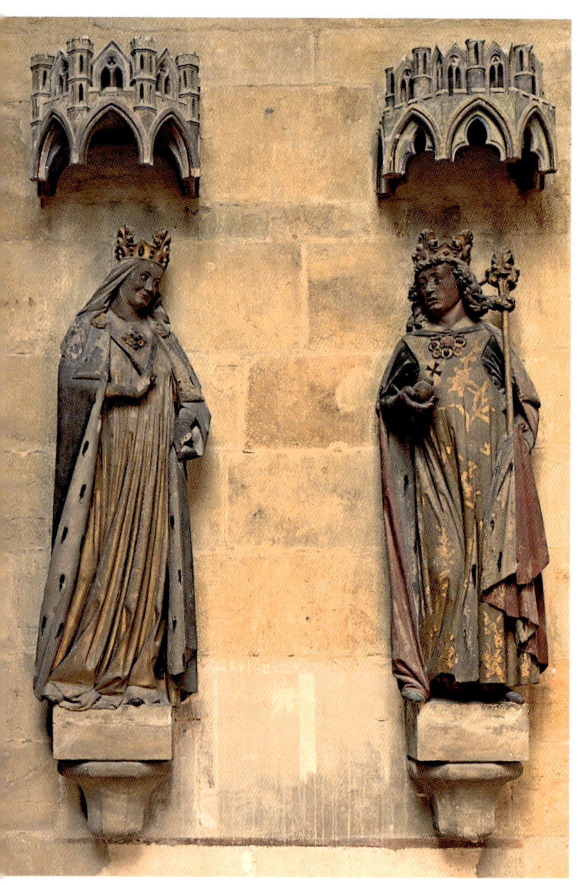

1230 is separated into three zones each of which is adorned with four figures, which themselves are separated with unadorned shafts. The lowest row shows the Four Evangelists as overlong, bearded, robed figures with scrolls. Above it follow four angels with trumpets announcing the Last Judgment. In the uppermost zone the Enthroned Christ sits somewhat uncomfortably in a tight space surrounded by three angels. His function is World Judge; the entire pillar is part of an iconographic concept which starts with the portal of the south transept (see pp. 118, 119). Most of the statues from this entrance are lost, but we can reconstruct the theme: between the portals sat King Solomon, the wise judge of the Old Testament. In the Middle Ages, at this portal, justice was dispensed under his gaze. Entering the cathedral, the faithful were reminded by the Pillar of Angels of the vastly more important Last Judgment. The figures, while standing on column drums or capitals set deep between the shafts, are virtually free-standing. The Four Evangelists show their independence from the architecture in the way they turn their bodies; Christ through his lateral posture. At the same time the entire conception is aligned with the location. The columnar elongation of the figures is not only in line with the Gothic aesthetic, but is also appropriate to their location between the shafts.

Emperor Otto I and Adelheid,
sandstone,
c. 1255–1260,
Meissen Cathedral

The Wise and the Foolish Virgins of **Magdeburg Cathedral** (pp. 136, 137) from around 1245 are even more independent of their location than the Pillar of Angels. This is shown by the fact that they did not originally belong to the north entrance of the cathedral, known as the Paradise Portal. They were created for placement on a wall and therefore designed to be looked upon frontally. With that, they are well placed in the niches of the narthex although their original location is unknown. Maybe they belong to the church's lost rood screen. In swaying robes and with flowing bodies, sometimes leaning to one another, the virgins stand on small consoles, the wise ones are excited about paradise, and the foolish ones cry and mourn. The viewer's involvement in the event is increased by the developed variants of individual joy and mourning. The emotional portrayal of the New Testament parable of the virgins, of which half have only thought of their lamps and not of the oil for their nocturnal wedding, was to prompt people to show more clear-sightedness in their own lives.

Following double spread:
Strasbourg Cathedral,
Pillar of Angels,
(left) Christ,
(center) angel with trumpet,
(right) Evangelists,
c. 1225–1230

Perspective: A Portal from around 1400

All the representations of secular people we have seen – with the exception of the Magdeburg Horseman – were benefactor figures displayed in a church context and those portrayed were long dead or even canonized. Also our last example in this series is a case of sacred sculpture: we will take a look at the over-extravagant, seemingly baroque portal sculpture of the Late Gothic period. **Claus Sluter** (*c.* 1355–1406) – the fact that we can name the artist testifies to the changes – created the **portal sculpture for the Duke of Burgundy's Church of the Holy Sepulchre in Dijon** in the last years of the 14th century (pp. 138, 139). Here, also, we see a Madonna and Child between the doors, comparable with the portals in Amiens (see p.120) and Reims (see p.122). But what a change: she is not only fully three-dimensionally executed, her body in a flowing s-form, but her entire body turns from the wall, there

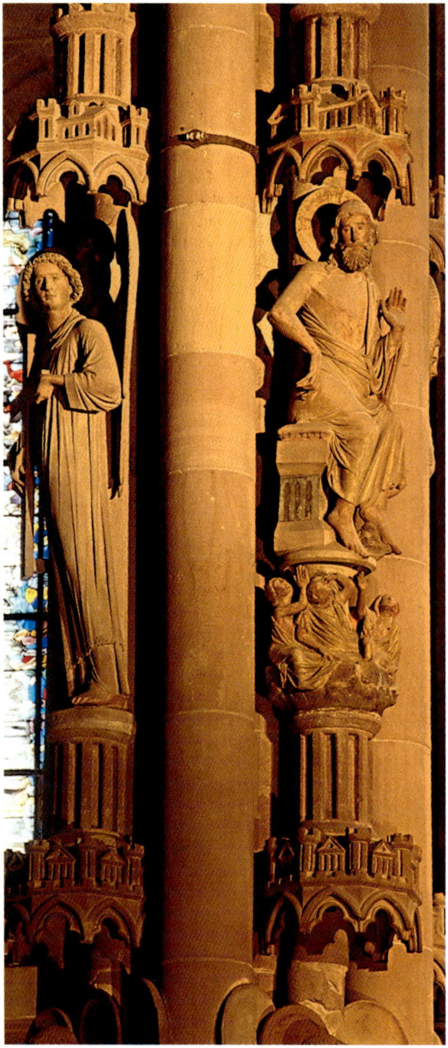

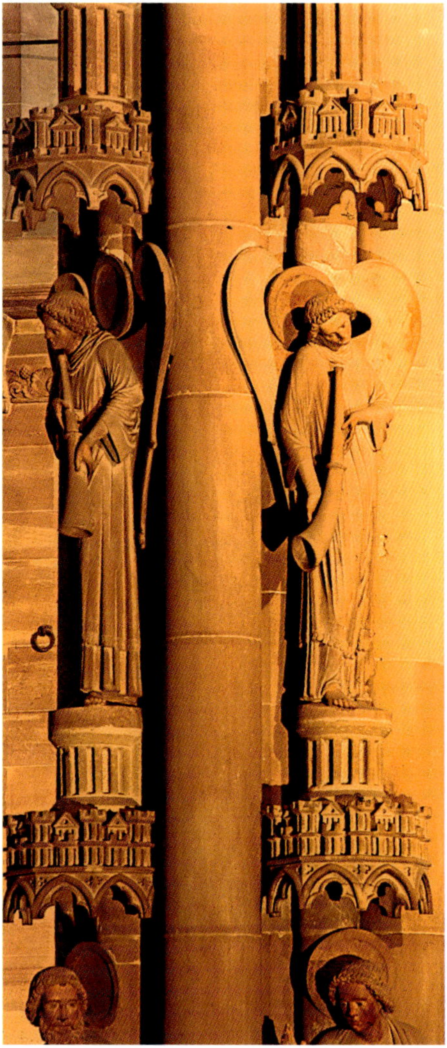

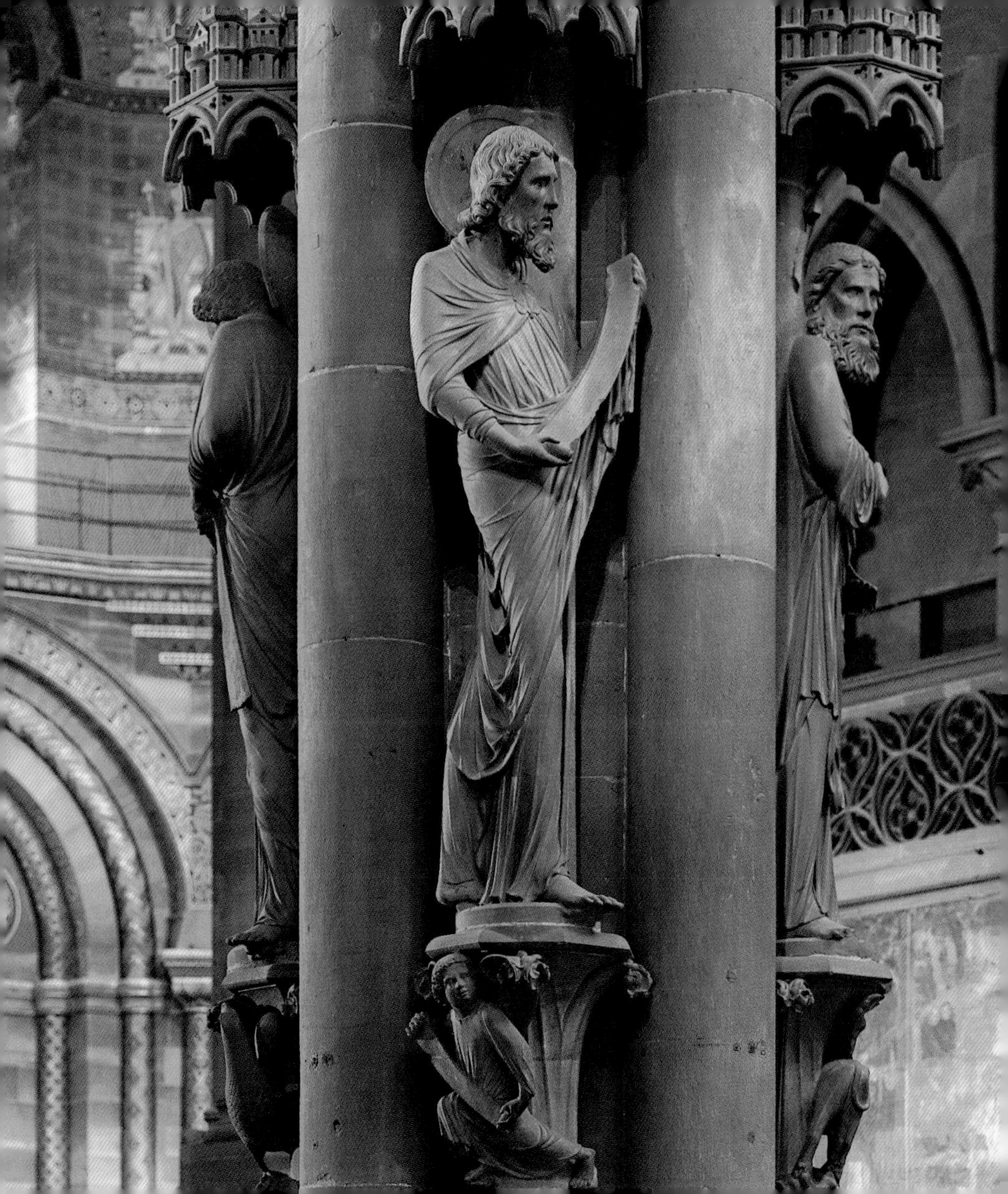

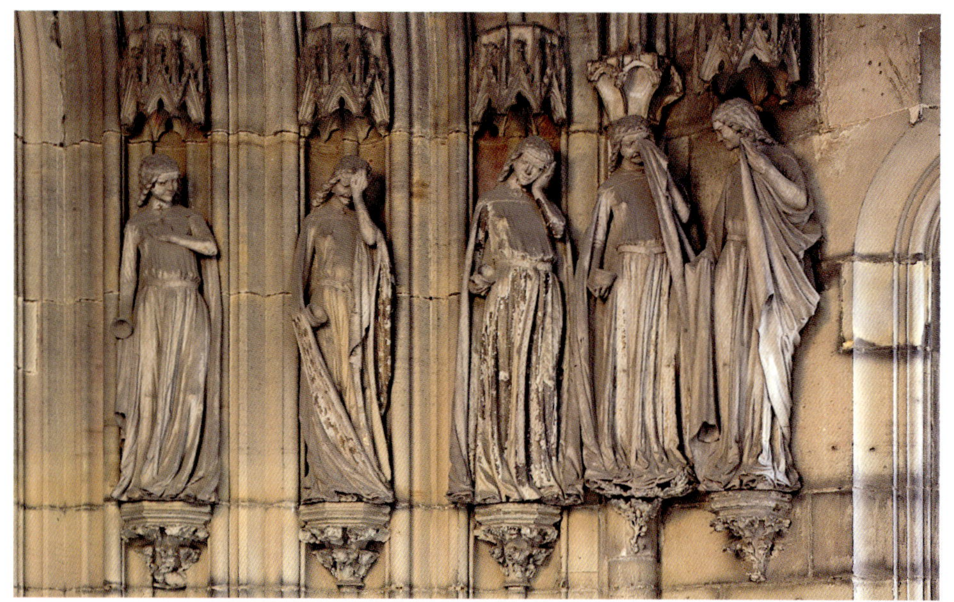

Magdeburg Cathedral, foolish virgins as robed figures on the Paradise Portal, c. 1245

is no column to be seen behind the figure. The baldachin reminds us of the earlier compositions but it is no longer part of the architecture, but presented before the smooth masonry. The style and iconography remind one of wooden sculptures of the beautiful Madonna, also created at the time, and the panel paintings of the devotional altars in the Soft style (see p.238). Alongside these stylistic changes, to which also the wind-torn robes belong, there is another major development in the iconography: the robed figures flanking the portal are neither Old Testament prophets nor Apostles. In fact here we find the kneeling and praying Duke of Burgundy, Philip the Bold, alongside his wife Margaret; St. John and St. Catherine accompany them as their mentors. Indeed, the duke and his wife are portrayed clearly smaller than the accompanying saints, but here

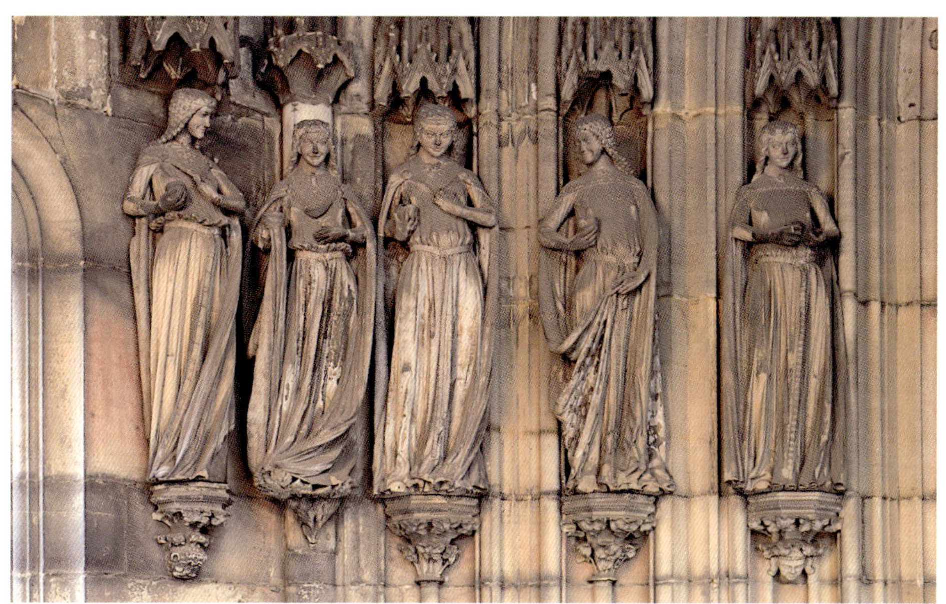

we are dealing with the portrayal of contemporary mortals – a break with centuries-old tradition. It was not just the style that became more sensuous during the Gothic period. Sculpture now begins to treat secular topics, to the point where, as here, it becomes a demonstration of secular power and religious humility. The effigy of a living mortal finds space in the heart of religious architecture.

Magdeburg Cathedral,
wise virgins as robed figures on the Paradise Portal,
c. 1245

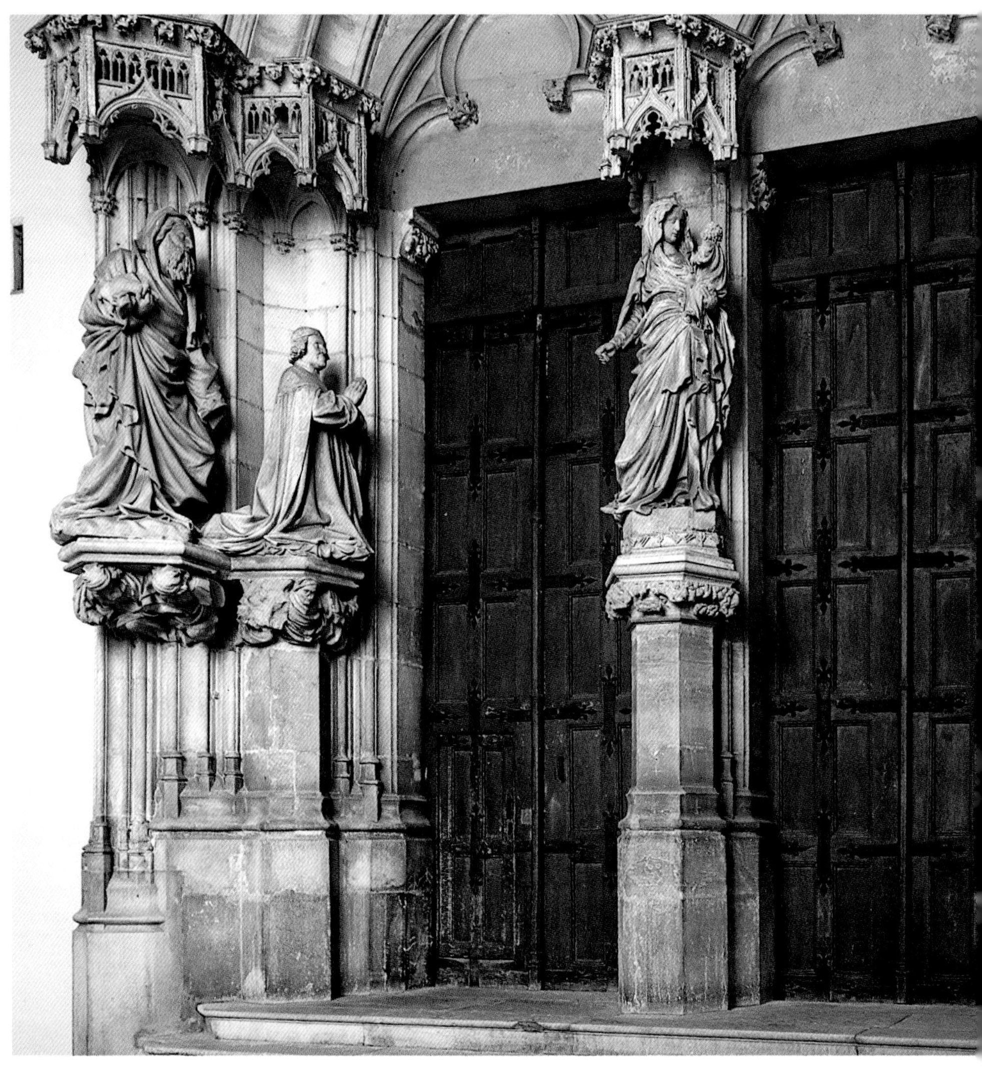

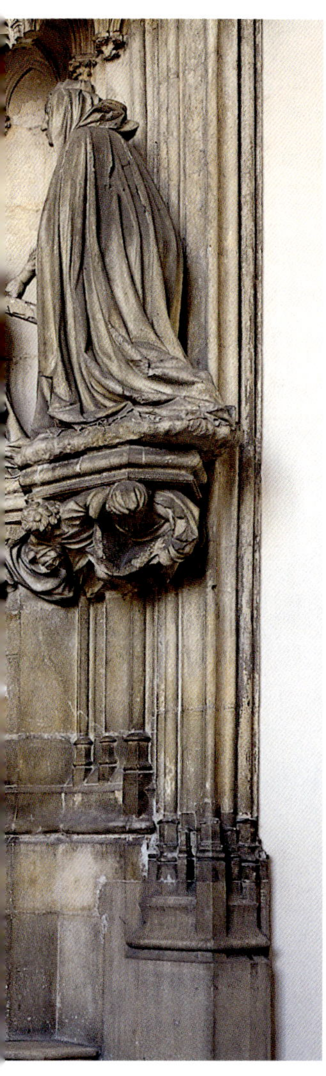

Dijon,
portal of the Church of the Holy Sepulchre,
sculptures by Claus Sluter,
c. 1389–1406

Ultramarine and Powdered Gold – The Colors of Gothic Architecture and Sculpture

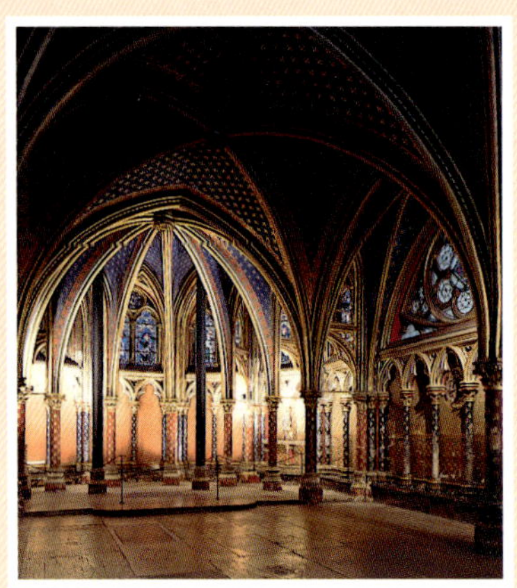

Paris,
Sainte-Chapelle, Lower Church,
consecrated 1246,
restored in the 19th century

For his more than ten-meter-high Marian altar (see pp. 158, 159, 161) Veit Stoss received payment of 2000 guilders. This was to cover his years of work, as well as that of his helpers, his tools, maintenance of his workshop, and also the carefully selected wood pieces for his work. One of the highest outgoings was probably the cost of painting the figures. In comparison: Tilman Riemenschneider's workshop received approximately one tenth of this sum for a normal-sized altarpiece with uncolored figures. But it wasn't just the liberal use of gold by the Gothic artists assigned to coloring the sculptures that hit the accounts so hard. Some of the pigments made from organic and inorganic materials were also very expensive. The ground semi-precious stone, lapis lazuli, was balanced with gold in some places: its ultramarine color is therefore mostly only used over small areas, for accentuation. At the same time the expenditure on coloring for sculptures shows us the relevance color had for the contemporary viewer. Complete rooms were also painted, with figural murals as in Italy (see pp. 172 f.), or with detailed ornamentation like the Upper and Lower Churches of Sainte-Chapelle in Paris.

The sheer unbelievable height of **Sainte-Chapelle,** within the *Palais de la Cité* in Paris, leaves visitors gasping with admiration. Entering the Lower Church one sees the low vaults and supporting columns, profusely decorated with patterns. Further through the narrow stairway, one steps into the Upper Church. Here, at last, the architecture of this grand building opens up: a 16-meter-high space whose boundaries are practically completely composed of windows, columns and shafts. The aisle-less church was the private devotional church of the French kings as well as the home of two important relics: the Crown of Thorns and part of the True Cross. The windows are predominantly in red and blue tones. The ceiling is painted with golden stars on a dark blue ground, the columns, arches and capitals are decorated or gilded, likewise the buttresses and the ribs of the vault. The colored decorations are ornamentally conceived in a specific pattern of repetition and placement. The sculptures on the protruding cornices on the intersection between the lower wall area and the incipient lancet windows are painted. The harmonic unity of the abundantly covered areas and the dark colors is surprising. All in all, the Upper and Lower Churches of Sainte-Chapelle are a wonderful example of the colorfulness of Gothic spaces, because here the architecture and the furnishings relate to one another as a single entity.

The frequent cleaning of earlier restorations, as well as the development of patina, in the form of bleached and broken coloring, has often altered the authentic look of the original sculpture. Gothic panel painters even give the impression that

Paris,
Sainte-Chapelle, Upper Church,
consecrated 1246,
restored in the 19th century

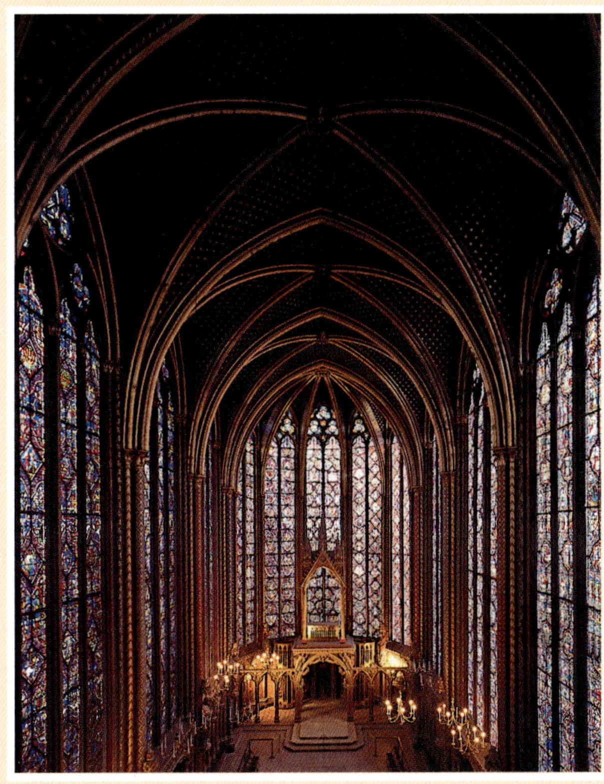

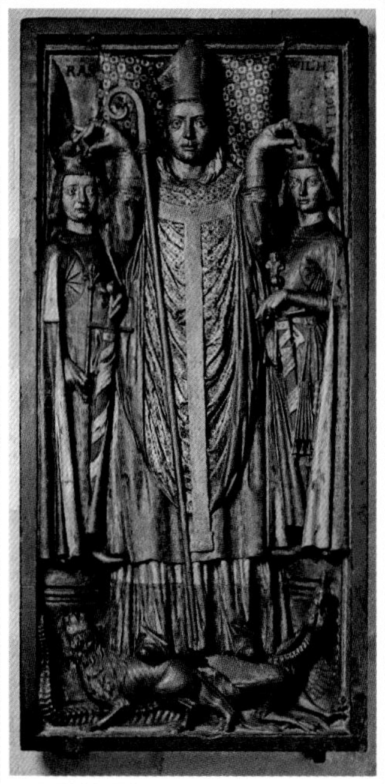

Tomb Slab of Archbishop Siegfried III,
Cathedral of St. Martin and St. Stephen, Mainz,
Painted sandstone,
post 1249

statues were never colored by painting statues in tones of grey, the *grisaille* technique. This was to show that they were not portraying a human being (see p. 223). In fact, though, enough medieval sculptures have survived that were not whitewashed or robbed of their coloring over the years, and these give us a, perhaps faded, first impression of how expressive these painted sculptures could be. A particularly beautiful example is the **tomb slab of Archbishop Siegfried III von Epstein,** in Mainz Cathedral. Here, too, the effect of the coloration is to underline the portrayed motifs: although we are dealing with a tomb slab, the likeness is exceedingly vivid. The eyes are open and the hands are in movement. The head lies on a burial cushion, which is typical of tomb portraits, but the feet stand on two fantasy creatures. The color not only manages to make the physicality of the robes and the different materials more precise and sensuous, it is also responsible for the impression of alertness in the archbishop's eyes. His resolute look, in combination with his red cheeks, underscores the episcopal claim to continue to conduct the coronation of German kings.

The visibility of materials was something to be played with in Gothic; as a result, the surface of the materials themselves became a topic. The fact that greater workmanship is required for uncolored statues may have also played a role in this, as here you cannot hide attachments, discoloring or mistakes under the coloration. In the early 16th century, Tilman Riemenschneider made an exciting breakthrough in uncolored wooden figures, but his stone works were always colored. We thus recognize the Gothic period as a phase of change and of scrutiny of old habits, where artistic development was not a one-way street. Uncovered stone sculptures had been possible centuries before; we have many examples of them from Italy. A Madonna and Child from around 1342 has been attributed to **Andrea Pisano:** the noble white marble is only gilded on the hair and the borders of the robes, although restoration tests have still to decide whether other body parts once had a coloration or if the gold was added later. For such gilding a mixture of powdered gold and copper was used. This was not only because gold was so expensive but also because it is difficult to handle. On some of the abrasions we can see that the powdered gold alloy is placed on top of a middle layer that helps the gold stick better. This binding agent could have been paste that was mixed with a dark reddish or greenish pigment that could disguise tiny defects in the gilding.

Andrea Pisano (attributed)
Madonna and Child,
marble and gilt coloration,
c. 1342, 92cm,
Museo Nazionale di San Matteo,
Pisa

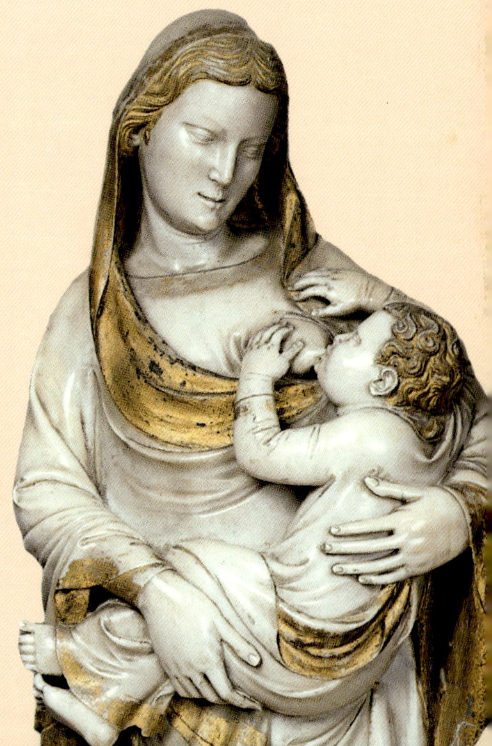

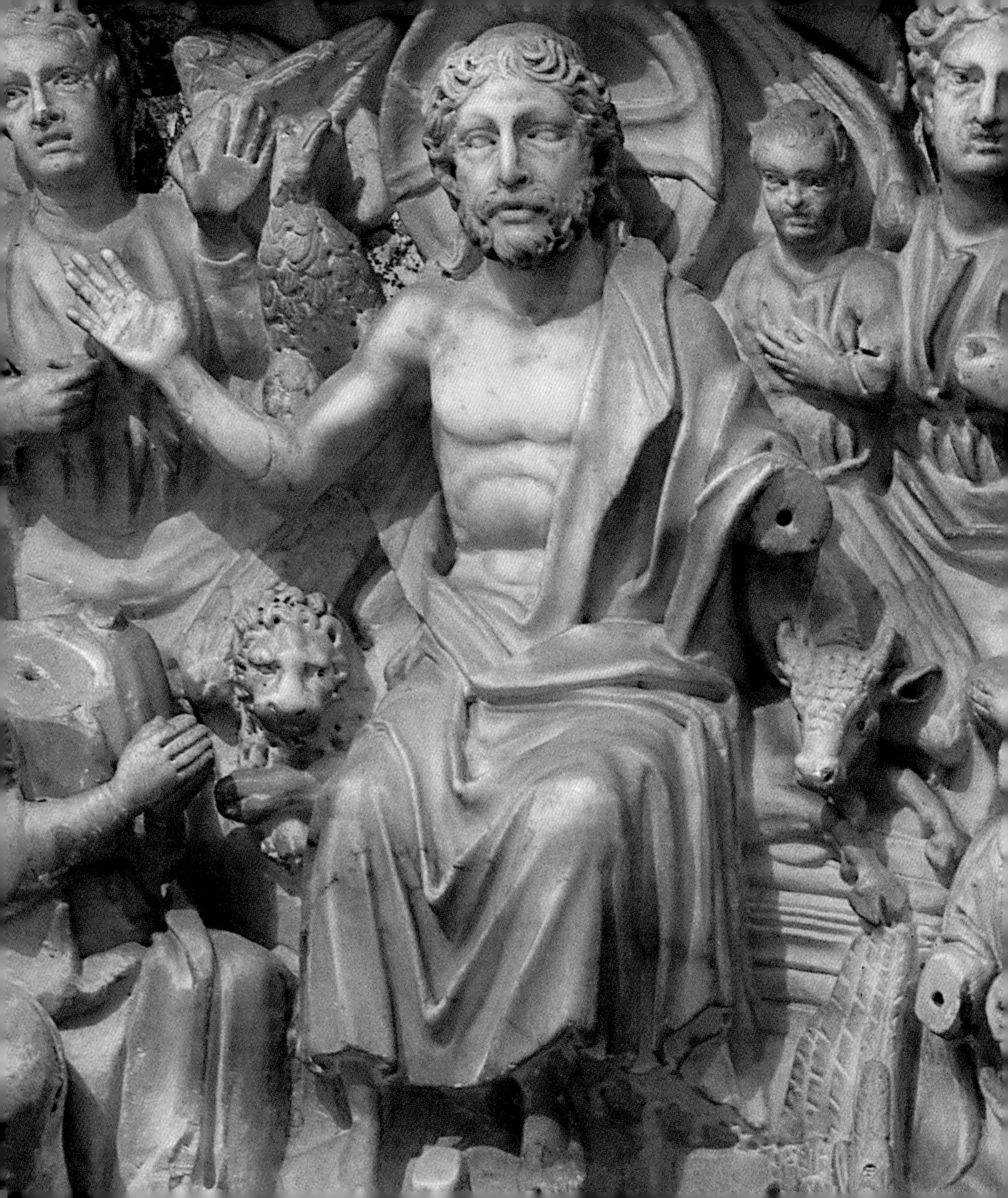

Regional Characteristics of Gothic Sculpture

In the last chapter we traced the development of Gothic sculpture from portal sculpture to free-standing works. Now it is time to deal with an overview of art works from the different regions of Europe. The regional styles in this choice of examples from Italy, France, the "German Lands," England, Spain and Portugal may seem more different than they actually are as we have only chosen the most special and outstanding works. The selection stretches from marble relief works of 13th-century Italy, to 14th-century royal burial sites on the Iberian Peninsula, all the way to northern woodcarvings of the early 16th century.

Niccolò Pisano,
Portrayal of the Last Judgment, relief plaque from the pulpit in Pisa Baptistery,
marble,
c. 1260

We will start by differentiating between plastic art and sculpture: by sculpture, we mean the result of the subtractive method, i.e. the taking away of material, such as in the chiseling of stone or woodwork. By plastic art, on the other hand, we refer to an additive process. Cast bronze is mostly based on an additively produced template of malleable material such as wax. Occasionally the term plastic is used to cover all three-dimensional mobile art objects. And to com-

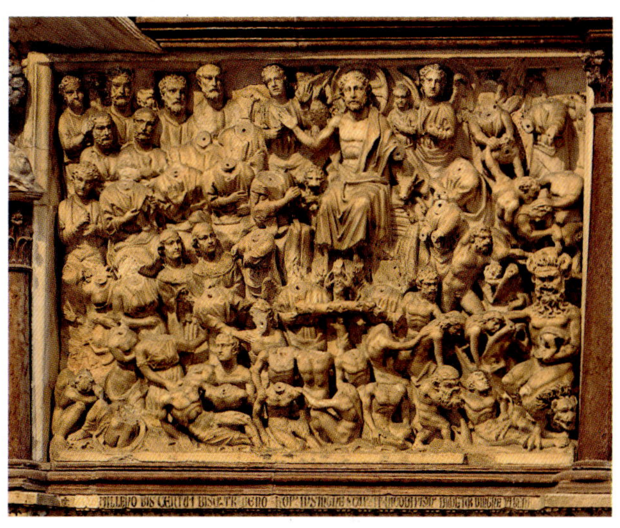

pletely confuse things: the Middle Ages also had an additive process with stone: decoratively cast bricks used to adorn building (see p. 68). The Gothic works we will deal with here, apart from Andrea Pisano's bronze door (pp. 148, 149), are actual sculptures in the above sense.

Italian Sculptures

The stone reliefs in the pulpit, depicting scenes from the life of Christ, emphasized the preacher's sermon, which was given from the eagle-shaped lectern.

We will begin our tour of the sculpture workshops of Europe in Italy. Whereas in France sculpture was restricted to portal figures for the longest time, in Italy the sculptors were already looking for new contexts in the early 13th century. One reason for this, as we have already mentioned, is the varied development in Italian church architecture that benefited murals on interior walls, and inlays or other non-figural decorations on outer walls. However, the early Italian sculptors didn't always create fully three-dimensional figures either, but also relief works or half-relief figures which were placed on pulpits and fountains, or used to decorate buildings.

The most outstanding Italian artist of the Duecento was **Niccolò Pisano** (*c.* 1205–1280). The first work definitively attributable to him, by means of a written document, is also one of his masterworks: the pulpit in the **Pisa Baptistery** (pp. 144, 145, 147), begun in 1259. The stone-carved pictorial works were intended to support the preacher who spoke from the eagle-shaped lectern. The pulpit rests on six columns that are finished off with small capitals; these are connected to one another with cloverleaf-shaped arches. In the spandrels we find small statues portraying the Evangelists, the Old Testament prophets and the virtues. A seventh column supports the pulpit in the middle. On the orator's level there are five sides – the sixth is the entrance to the pulpit – filled with rectangular reliefs showing scenes from the life of Jesus, from the Annunciation to the Crucifixion. One not only notices that these reliefs contain an abundance

Niccolò Pisano,
pulpit of Pisa Baptistery,
marble,
c. 1260

of figures and acts but also that the figures, in total, produce geometrically balanced structures of light and shadow. Are there any models for this? Without a doubt Pisano had Roman sarcophagi in mind. Italy's unbroken bond to its past allowed such age-old styles to influence, centuries later, artists of the Middle Ages. Naturally, the pictorial themes and solutions from the Middle Ages are mostly new. The multi-figured portrayal of the Last Judgment (pp. 144, 145) shows Christ the Judge sitting slightly displaced from the middle. His right hand greets and blesses the virtuous, the missing left hand was lowered, and condemned the sinners whose naked bodies roll in front of demons with sharp featured, grimacing faces and bird's feet. When it came to portraying the horrors of hell and purgatory and the agony of being supervised by bizarre monster figures, the Italian sculptors, mosaic makers and painters of the Middle Ages were unbeaten.

Even the early Christians posed the question of whether an unchristened person should be allowed to enter a church. Depending on how the clergy answered the question, this meant that, alongside baptismal fonts inside the church proper, sometimes fonts were needed in an

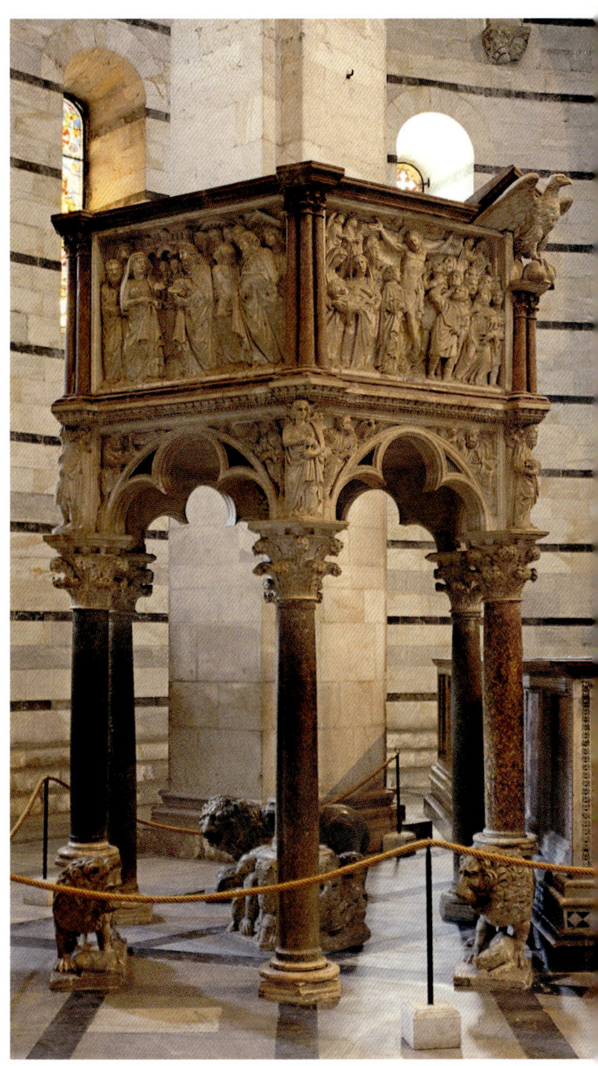

annexed baptistery. These were then built with varying elaborateness, depending on the time and the region. A famous early Christian example, from the 5th century, can be found in Ravenna. The medieval city states of Florence and Siena also afforded monumental baptisteries next to their cathedrals; most of them are round, with a baptismal font in the center. The entrances to the baptisteries were granted special meaning, as they also served as advertizing panels for the unchristened. Nevertheless, there is only one example of a Gothic baptistery door with elaborate figural design: originally designed for the east portal but moved during the Renaissance to the south portal, it is the bronze door of the Florence Baptistery, by **Andrea Pisano** (between 1270/90–*c.* 1348), a relative of Niccolò Pisano. Andrea Pisano was a goldsmith by trade; after Giotto di Bondone's death in 1337, he succeeded as the head of construction of the bell tower, the campanile in Florence (see p. 43). Around 1330 he was contracted to construct the bronze doors of the Florence Baptistery. The theme he chose is hardly surprising, given the purpose of the building: scenes from the life of John the Baptist. The twenty-eight reliefs on the south side are each framed with quatrefoils. With clear forms and low relief they depict groups of figures whose bodies and clothes still display signs of gilded copper. The door wings were cast in one piece, the reliefs and other ornamentation were added later. The baptism scene shows John the Baptist on the right side and an angel on the left. Two trees frame the area where the events occur. In the middle stands Christ: John the Baptist pours water from a shallow bowl over his head. The style of portrayal stems from a Byzantine formula of book illumination and mosaic. Pisano solves the problem of where to place Jesus in the river in the same way as his models: ribbon-like waves flow around the lower part of the body, while John the Baptist and the angel stand, slightly raised, on the rocks.

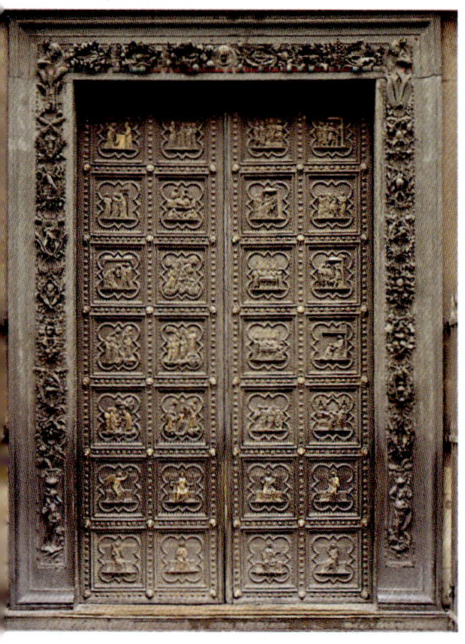

Andrea Pisano,
doors of Florence Baptistery,
bronze and gild,
1330–1336

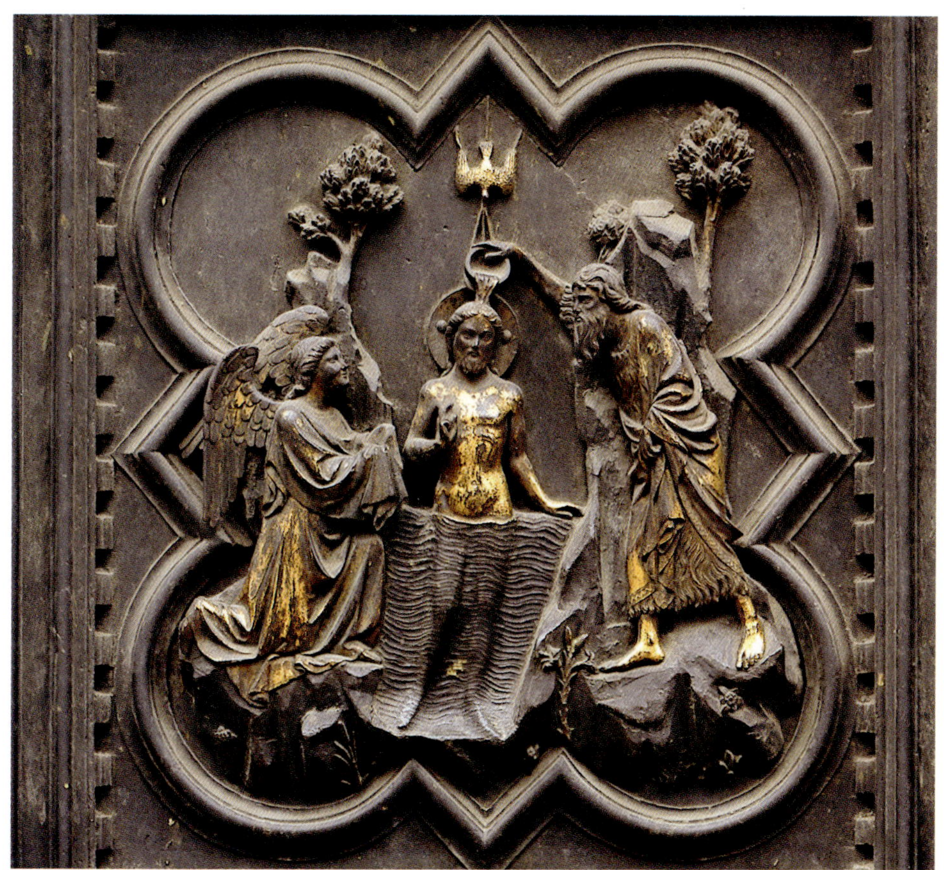

We can follow the development of figural ornamentation with a Venetian work from approximately one hundred years later. **Filippo Calendario** (died 1355) was responsible for the building and the sculptures of the monumental Doge's Palace in the heart of Venice. There, among other groups of

Andrea Pisano,
Christ's Christening,
detail from the doors of Florence Baptistery, bronze and gild,
1330–1336

figures, in one of the corners of the building, the theme of the Fall of Man is broached. The Tree of Paradise, a fig tree, is placed in the middle. Why a fig tree? In the Old Testament the botanical name of the tree was never stated. Because of this, artists from the Middle Ages to modern times switched between figs, oranges and quince-like fruits; in later times these were replaced with apples in the north. Basically, the artist chose the most enticing fruit of his land. Here, it is a fig tree through which the snake winds his way. To his side stand Adam and Eve – they are not facing one another but drawing the beholder into the event by their gestures. Judging by these gestures, the world's first couple are in disagreement about their proportion of the blame for Original Sin. While Adam, like Eve, is clutching at the fruit, at the same time he makes a defensive gesture with his right; Eve meanwhile points accusingly at him. In the way that they mutually blame one another and in their communicative involvement of a third party we can see marital habits that Adam and Eve took from the Garden of Eden and handed down to their progeny. The creeping tendrils of the fig tree that cover their nakedness intimate that Adam and Eve, as well as the viewer are in a state of original sin.

Filippo Calendario,
The Fall of Man,
architectural sculpture on the Doge's Palace, Venice,
1340–1355

Northern Sculpture

We can argue as to whether artistic characters such as Tilman Riemenschneider and Veit Stoss, who were contemporaries of the Italian Renaissance artists Michelangelo and Raphael, still count as Gothic. North of the Alps, the development of sculpture and painting which we consider to be Gothic was sometimes delayed by more than a century. In their expression and their conception of anatomy and space, the wooden carvings of the above named were untouched by the Renaissance, in spite of the innovation and diversity of improvements they display. When comparing the famous altars of the 16th century with the triumphal crucifix of an unknown 13th-century carver, you can see the stylistic similarities continuing over the three hundred years of the Gothic period in central Europe.

In early Christian churches rood screens often separated the choir with the altar from the seats of the laity. In Byzantine tradition this developed into the *iconostasis,* a wall decorated with icons between the presbytery – where the consecration of bread and wine took place – and the congregation. The widespread central European alternative of the Middle Ages was the wooden rood screen: this separated the area for priests and monks from the rest of the church. At the same time, this walk-in construction served as a lectern for the priests. Later the pulpit replaced the rood screen in this function. The arch over the rood screen, which separated the choir from the transept and nave, was called a rood, or triumphal arch. We need to know this in order to under-

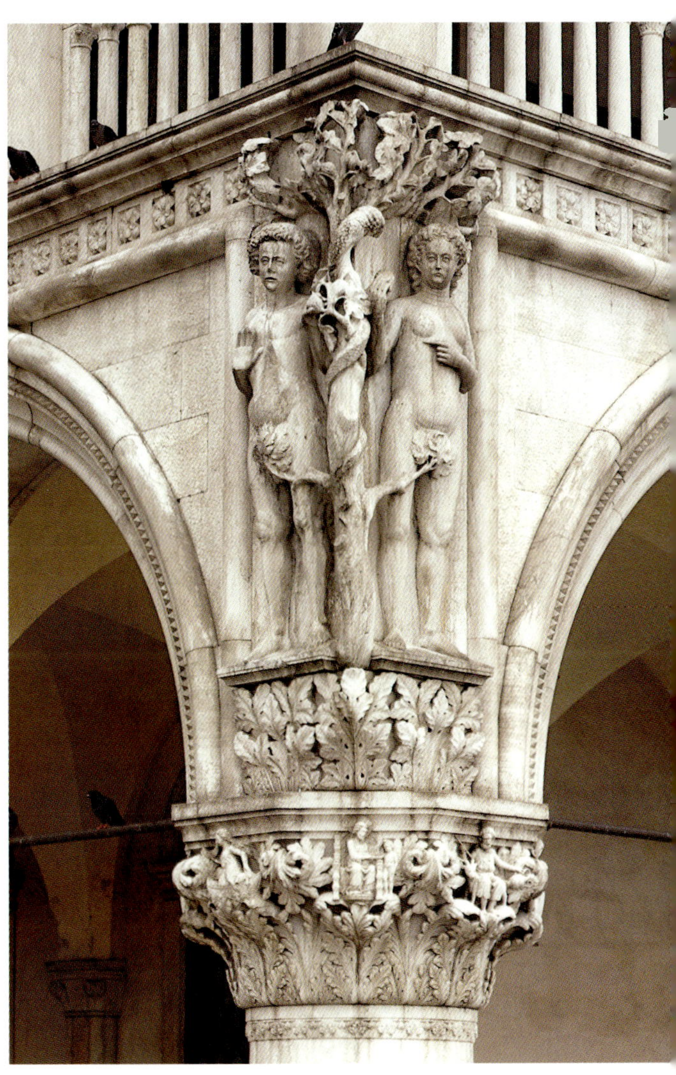

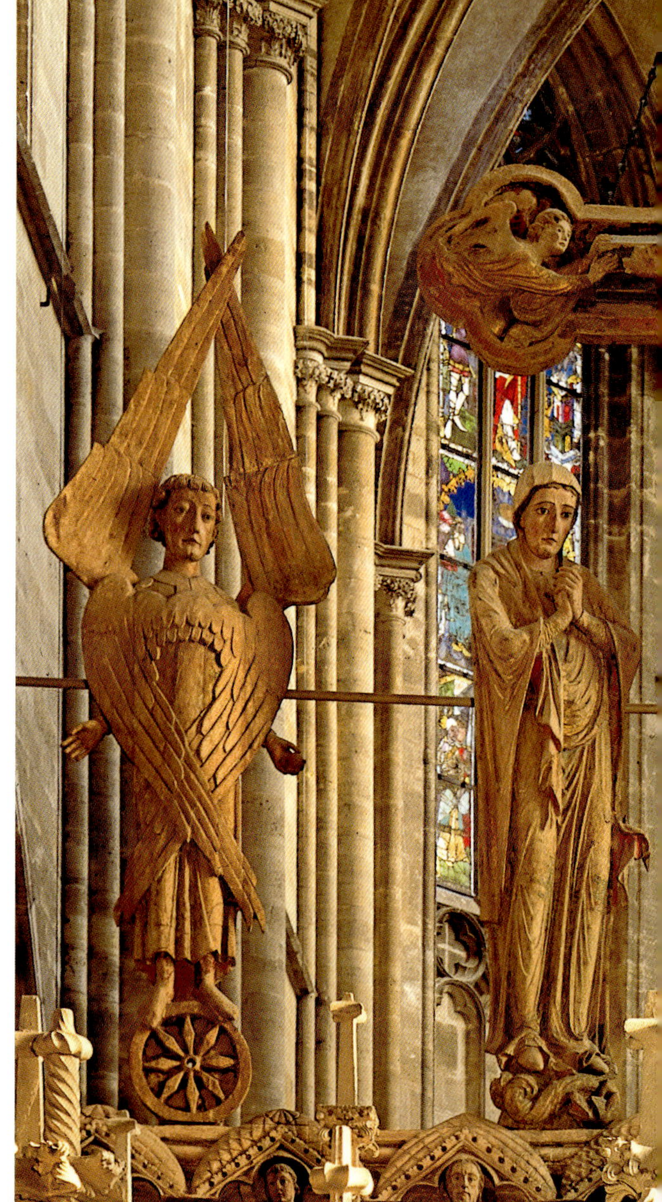

Triumphal Crucifix Group,
oak, linden, spruce,
height 515 cm
c. 1210,
Halberstatdt Cathedral

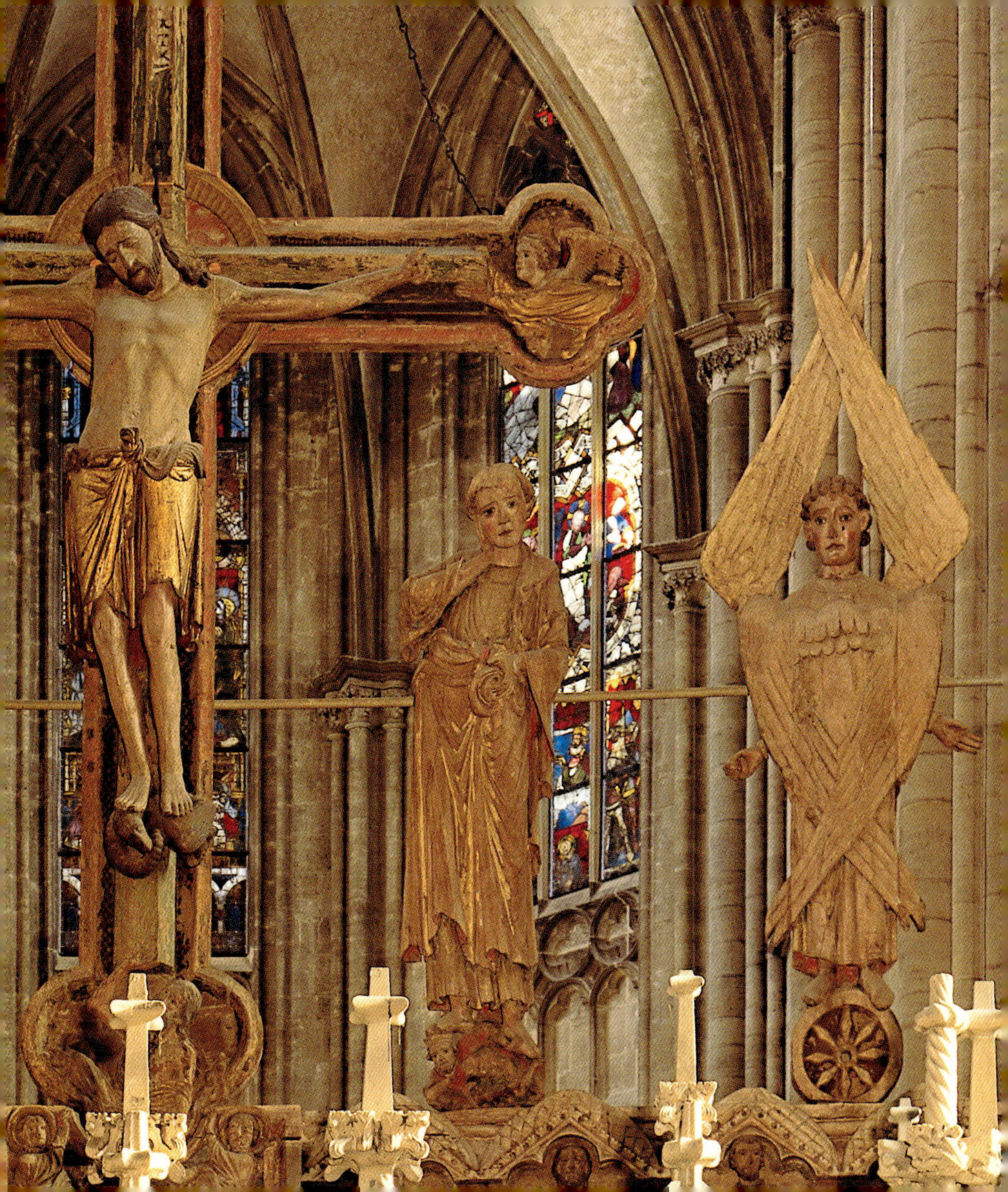

stand why the great wooden crosses that were mounted onto the rood screens in the Gothic period were called triumphal crucifixes. In **Halberstadt Cathedral** one can see a very early and artistically prominent **triumphal crucifix** (pp. 152, 153) from around 1220. How did the sculptors manage to give the portrayal of the Crucifixion the look of triumph, which Christian interpretation professed? His hanging head depicts Christ as dead. His mourning mother Mary and St. John surround him. The moment of the apparent great defeat, the death of the Redeemer, the precondition for triumph – which is Christ the Judge – is achieved through the reference in the detail: the dead Christ is not only *not* wearing a painful crown of thorns and has no scars, but as well as hanging on the cross he is also, at the same time, standing on a dragon – the symbol of the overcoming of death. This graphic representation of more than five meters height is the ultimate spatial realization of the pictorial examples. And so, the triumphal cross is placed – like a picture – to be viewed from one side only. It can only be viewed from the nave and not, as usually is the case with three-dimensional sculpture, from various viewpoints.

The portrayal in the main wing of the altar creates the connection between the precious relic and the highpoint of the Mass: the consecration.

The veneration of relics began only a few centuries after Christ's death, and with that began the relic trade. From the slivers of wood, supposedly from Christ's crucifix, many crosses were made. For us, the veneration of relics – a form of popular piety that is found in many religions – may seem a transparent historical forgery, but for the "offenders" it was, mostly, purely a reconstruction of history. A very special relic, namely a drop of the Redeemer's blood, belonged to **Rothenburg ob der Tauber.** In the early years of the 16th century, **Tilman Riemenschneider** (*c.* 1460–1531) created an altar for this relic: the Holy Blood Altar in St. James's Church (pp. 155, 156, 157). The drop, originally a drop of wine from Jesus' chalice used at the Last Supper that was transformed into blood as a result of the consecration, can be found inside

Tilman Riemenschneider
Holy Blood Altar,
St. Jacob's Church,
Rothenburg ob der Tauber,
linden wood, height 9 m,
1499–1504

a rock crystal in the center of the pinnacle decoration. The portrayal of the Last Supper in the main wing of the altar creates the connection between the relic – the drop of Christ's blood – and the high point of the church service: the consecration of bread and wine into body and blood of Christ. But Riemenschneider has put a new accent to the thematic emphasis of this Last Supper scene: the main figure in the middle of the event is Judas, the traitor. His payment, the purse full of silver, is held in his left hand. Thus, Riemenschneider is making the question of Jesus' betrayal the central theme. Without a doubt this is to challenge believers to examine the strength of their own faith. But not only is the pictorial scheme unusual, the artist also breaks away from the original altar format, especially with the extremely tall and slender pinnacle decoration. Over and above all that, the main wing of the altar is surprisingly done in openwork: the windows in

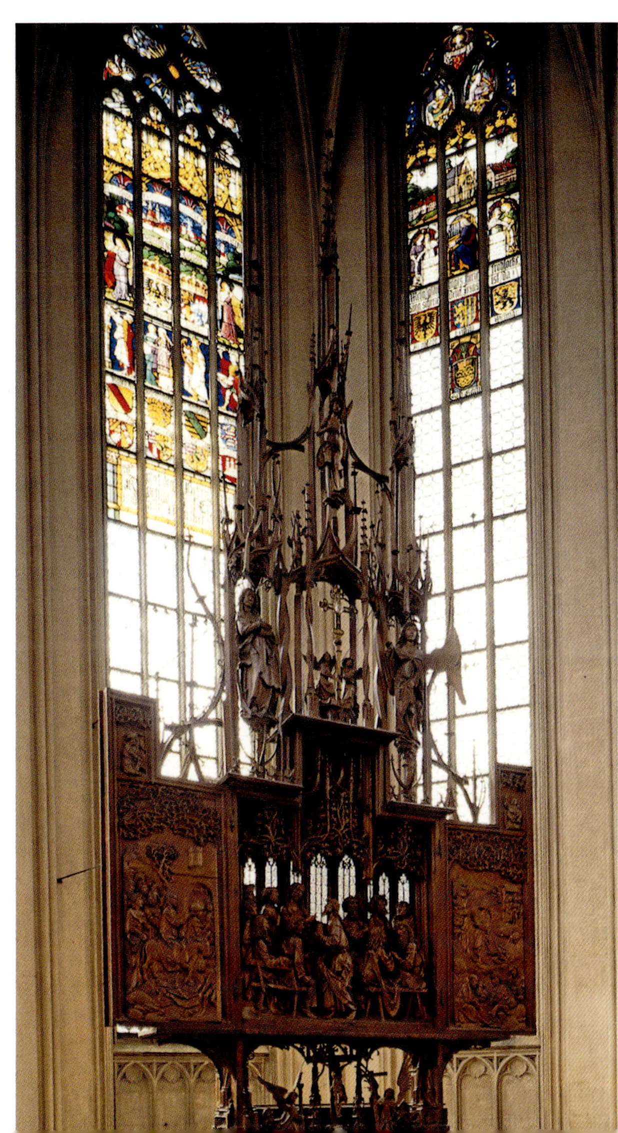

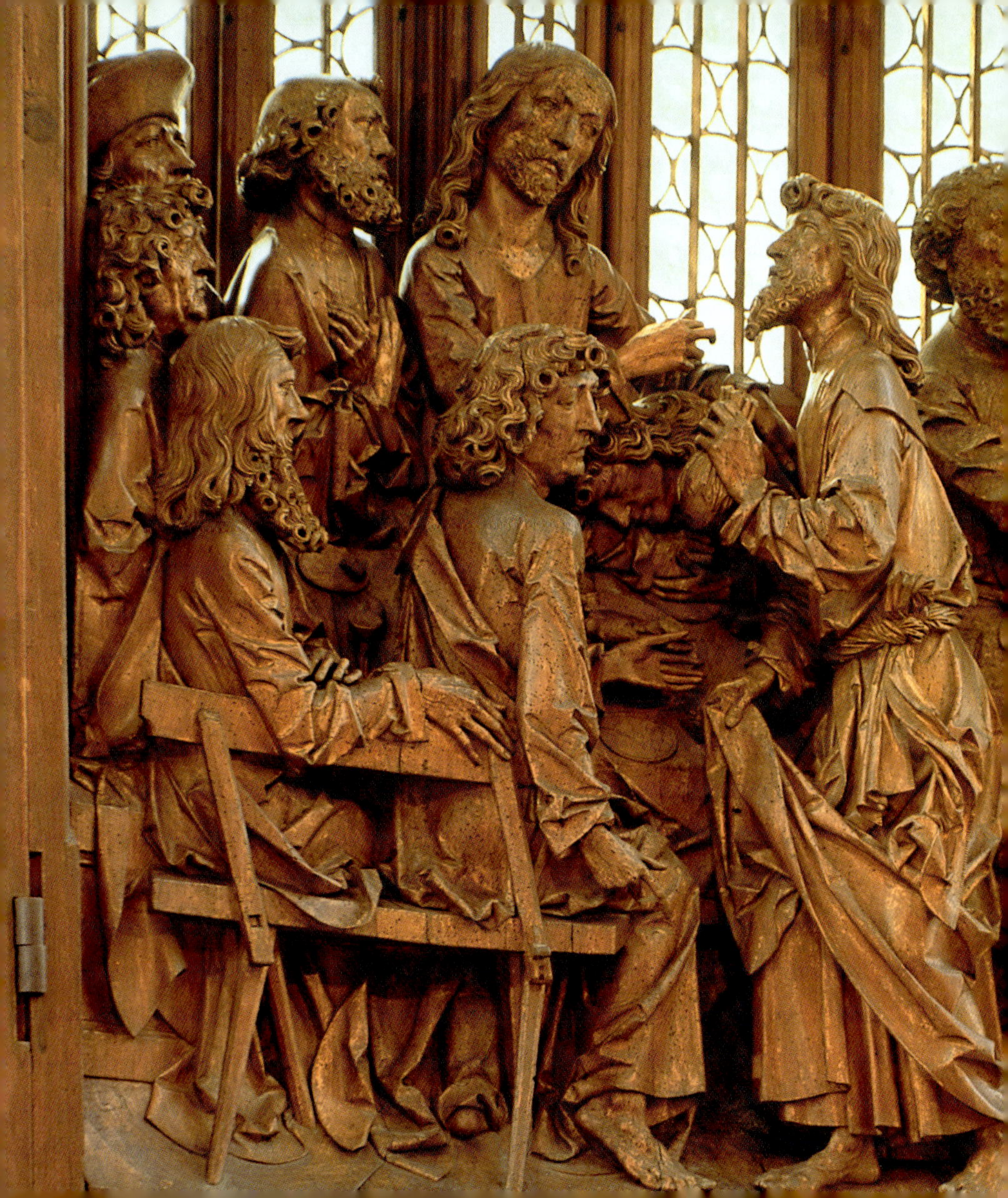

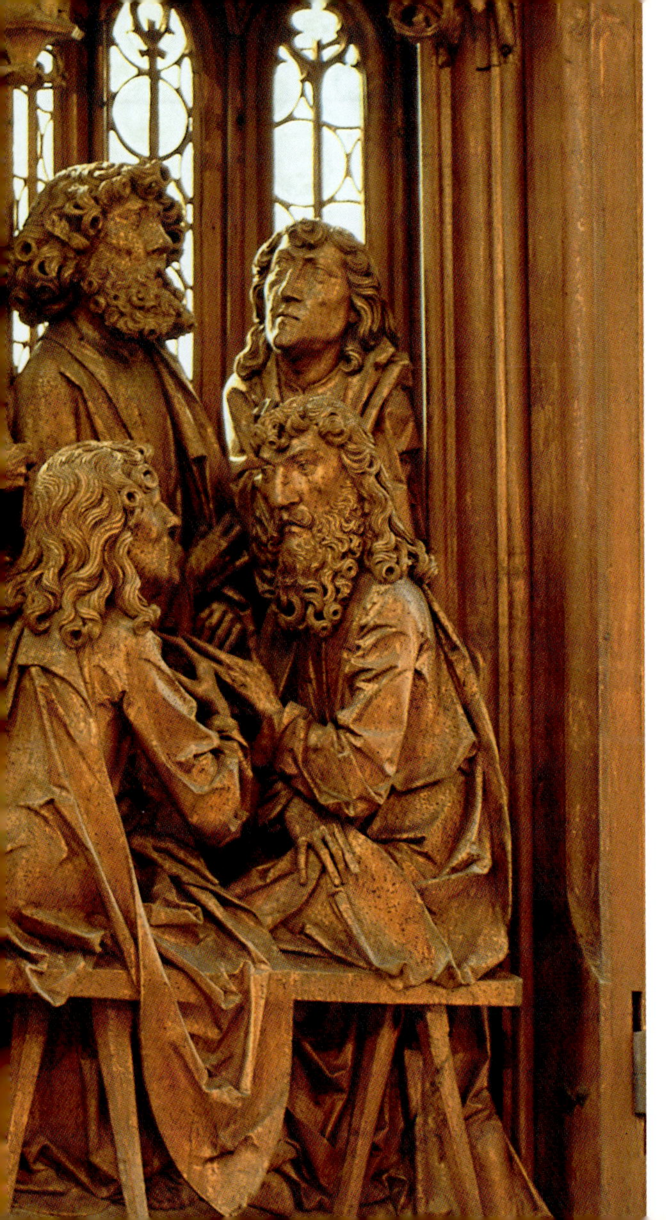

The vivid surfaces make painting superfluous. Only the eyes of Riemenschneider's sculptures were discreetly colored.

Tilman Riemenschneider
Last Supper,
middle section of the Holy Blood Altar,
St. James's Church,
Rothenburg ob der Tauber,
linden wood,
1499–1504

the background of the central Last Supper scene are actual translucent wooden carvings. The Last Supper scene changes, depending on the light in the chancel. Riemenschneider's workshop in Würzburg is most famous for a new form of wood carving: instead of painting and gilding the statues, here they were left bare, showing the pattern and original color of the wood. With that Riemenschneider was the first wood sculptor who allowed the finished material itself to become the theme – though not in the sense that he neglected the surface: first of all his sculptures were so perfectly carved that the play of light and shadow on the surface made color superfluous. Secondly, the wood is finished with a dark varnish, quasi monotone, and so is not untreated. And

Veit Stoss,
Apostles supporting the praying Mary,
detail from the Marian Altar,
St. Mary's Basilica, Cracow,
colored wood,
1477–1489

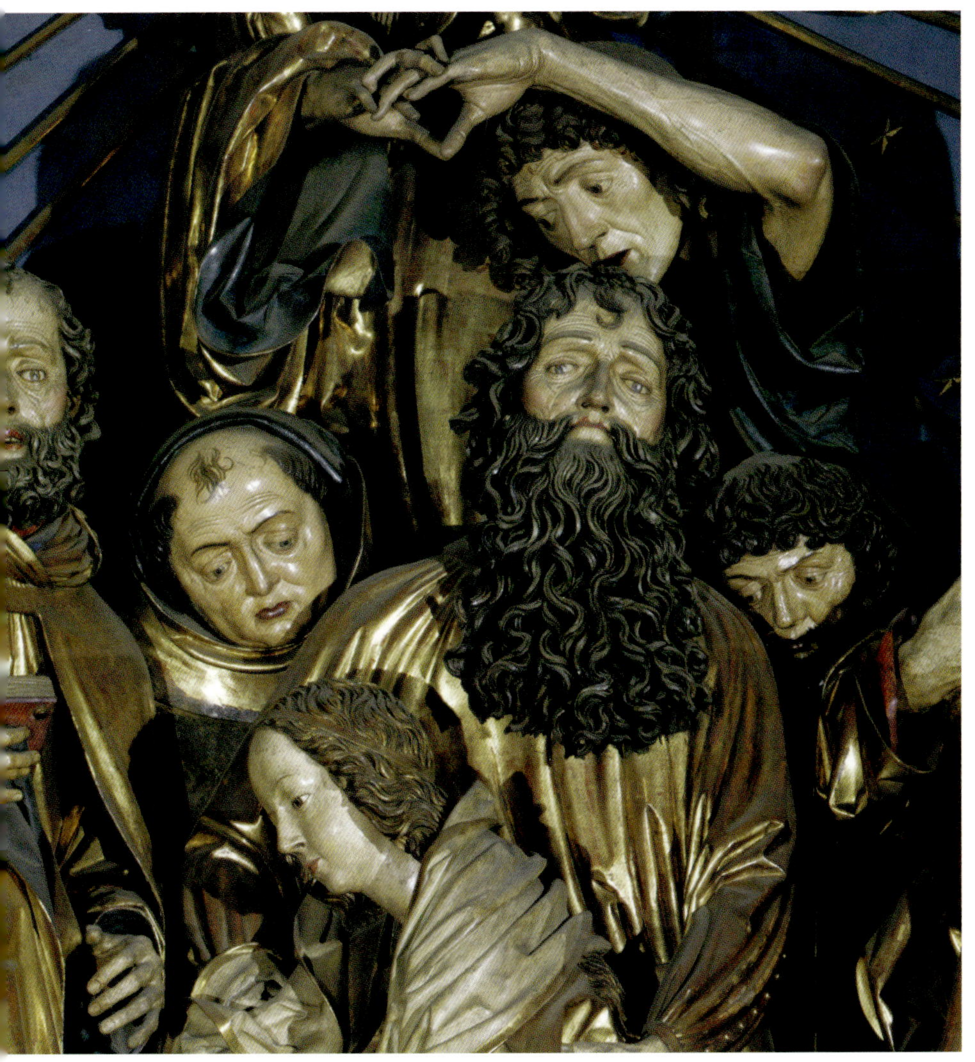

Veit Stoss,
Marian Altar,
St. Mary's Basilica, Cracow,
colored wood, height 10.68 m,
1477–1489

thirdly, Riemenschneider did paint his figures discreetly in particular areas, namely the eyes and the eyebrows. There is also some red on the relief on the right wing of the altar that shows Christ praying at the Mount of Olives. Using this device and practically without any other use of color, he places the real theme of the altar and the uniqueness of the church back in the foreground: the relic of the drop of Christ's blood.

The high altar in St. Mary's Basilica, Cracow, by **Veit Stoss** (*c.* 1447/48–1533), gives a completely different impression. Sumptuous painting and gilding decorate the 14-meter-high Gothic winged altar (pp. 158, 159, 161). This, the first named work of the artist, is also his greatest: his move from Nuremberg to Cracow is attested in archives from the year 1477. In this year he started a contract that included the coordination of the decorative artists who painted and gilded the carved wood, other assistants, as well as his own carving. Not only the size, but also the portrayals, marks this Marian altar as an exceptional work. The considerably larger than life figures on the main wing deal with the theme of the Death of Mary. But it is not the traditional scene of a group of mourners around the bed of the dying Mary. Rather, here we see moments from before and after:

Tilman Riemenschneider

(*c.* 1460–1531)

Born in Heiligenstadt in Thuringia between **1459** and 1462.

1470's Apprenticeship as sculptor and woodcarver in the southwest of the "German Lands," possibly in Ulm and Strasbourg.

1483 As a painter's assistant he joined the Saint Luke's Guild of painters, sculptors and glass artists. The town became the center of his work.

1485 Through his marriage to Anna Schmidt, a craftsman's widow, he reached the level of master in his trade.

From **1504** A member of council in Würzburg.

1520–1524 Mayor of Würzburg.

1525 The people of Würzburg are defeated in the Peasants' War. As a member of council, the victors held Riemenschneider jointly responsible for the revolt; he was taken prisoner and tortured. After his release most of his fortune was confiscated and he received no more contracts.

1531 Death of Riemenschneider. His works fell into obscurity. He was only rediscovered in the 19th century.

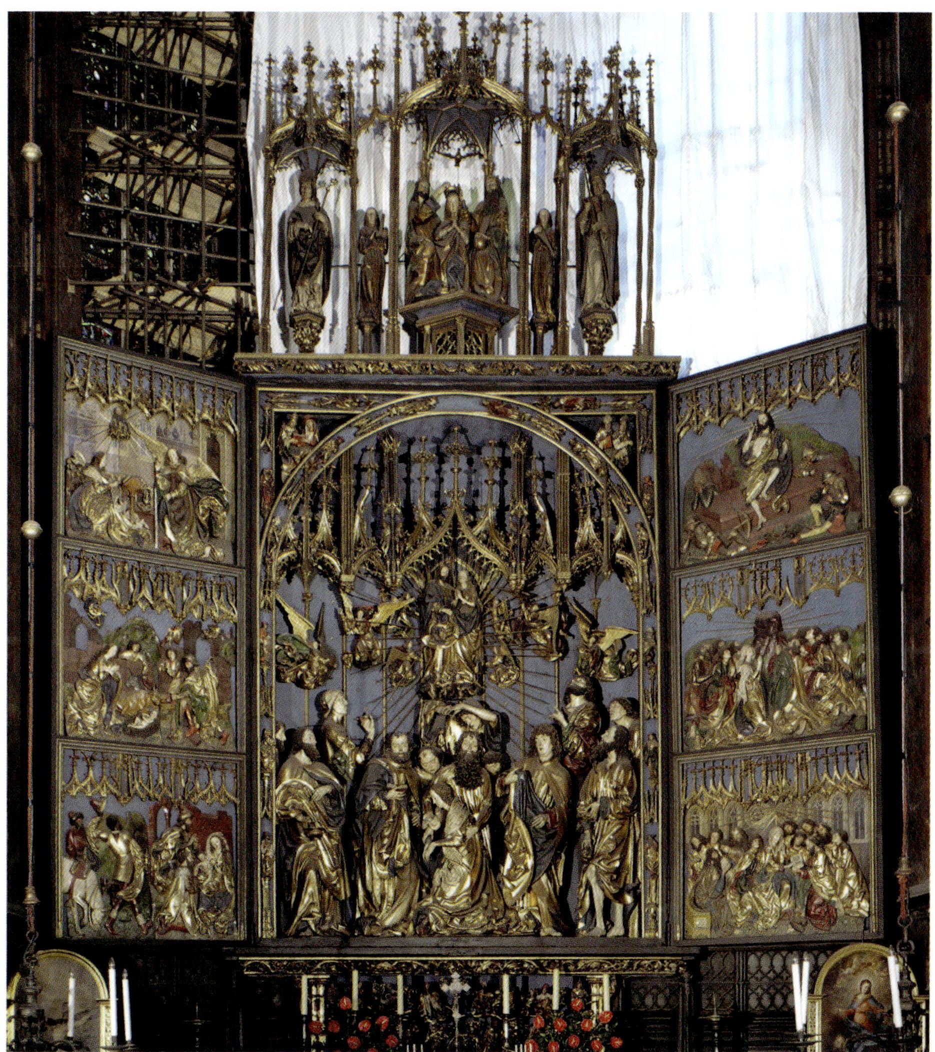

Veit Stoss

(c. 1447/48–1533)

Born *c.* **1447/48** most probably in Horb am Neckar.

From **1473** He resided for the first time in Nuremberg.

1477–1596 he resided in Cracow. Important works in Cracow: High Altar in St. Mary's Basilica, tomb of Kazimir IV, Altar of St. Stanislaus.

1496 Stoss returned to Nuremberg. Important works in Nuremberg: the Crowning of the Madonna, Madonna statue in the Church of Our Lady, Angel's Greeting in St. Lawrence's Church.

1503 Charged with falsification of documents. As punishment he was branded in the face with a glowing hot iron, lost his citizenship for a while and was only allowed to leave Nuremberg with special permission. Because of this he fled to Münnerstadt in Lower Franconia.

1506 He was taken prisoner again. Emperor Maximilian I interceded for him and wanted him pardoned, the free city of Nuremberg refused in spite of this intervention.

1512 Stoss was involved in the planning of Kaiser Maximilian's tomb in Innsbruck.

1533 Death of Stoss in Nuremberg.

in the foreground we see a frail Mary who is supported while praying. Above this scene we see her again, now she is beside her son Jesus as they ascend into heaven, surrounded by radiant haloes. Once again we see her, high up in the crest, at her coronation. Again, on the side wing reliefs, Mary is the theme on the festal side, whereas those visible on the workday side show scenes from Jesus' life. With all the naturalism in the detail, the gestures and the subject matter, this altar seems dreamlike, like a vision. The way in which the attendees in the lower zone switch their attention between Mary who is praying among them, and the real event: the Assumption into heaven of the weightless Mary, is unsurpassed. With all the gilding and with the strong use of color – the background remains in blue monochrome – Stoss uses opposites: his figures are stepping forward and backward, some are in the shade while others are clearly seen, there is a stark play of light and dark. With this, he chose a completely different strategy to Riemenschneider with his uncovered wooden sculptures. Yet, both of these accomplished artists manage to create altars that quickly develop their main theme, but which, at the same time, are so complexly portrayed that every visit to the church will offer up a new facet, or meaning, or stimulation.

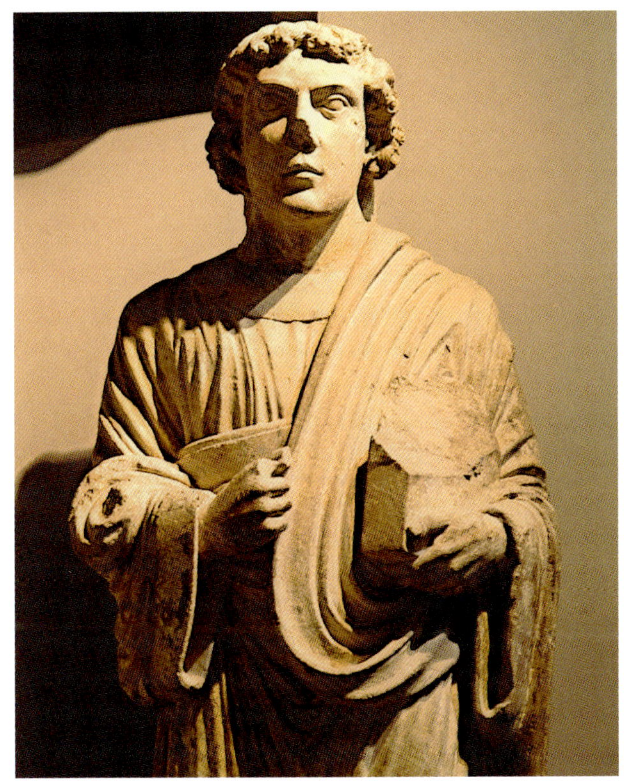

St. John,
St. Mary's Abbey, York
sandstone,
c. 1200–1210
Yorkshire Museum

Sculpture from England and Wales

The remaining sculpture works from the Gothic period in England and Wales are mainly facade sculptures from church buildings as well as sarcophagi. Excavations inside St. Mary's Abbey in York (see pp. 65, 66, 67) brought twelve life-size statues to light. The original placement of these figures is unknown, nor do we know how or why they were buried. Maybe their burial is somehow connected to a renovation of

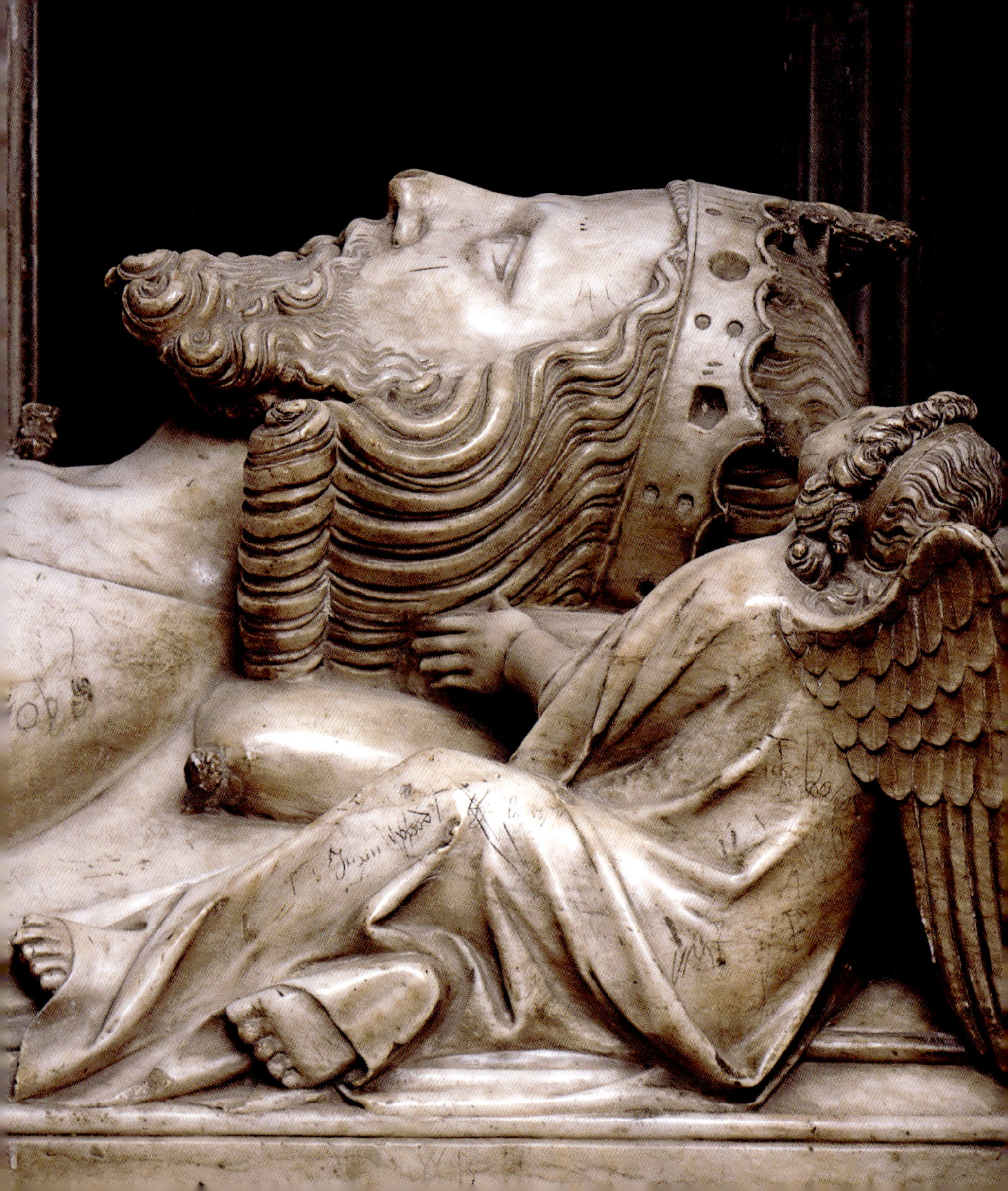

the church. Christians are not the only ones known to have used the burial of artwork with a religious context as a suitable way of dealing with sacred objects that were no longer required. The statues are fully three-dimensional but on their backs they have column shafts. This indicates that they were probably originally integrated into the architectural facade. Among them is the **sandstone figure of St. John** (p. 163), from around 1200, which stands today in the Yorkshire Museum. What is remarkable about this sculpture is its relatedness to Late Classical portraiture: especially the successful head form, the lifelike cheeks in spite of their flatness and the anatomically correct placement of the jaw area within the mouth. Bundles of curls surround the face and fall over the low forehead. And, just as in Classical likenesses, St. John and the other discovered Apostle figures were painted; this would have increased their vibrancy. but even if we assume there was an unbroken tradition of workshops from the Late Classical diocesan town of York via the Anglo-Saxon period, when York became the capital city of Northumbria, up to the beginning of the Gothic period, we are still left in the dark as to which work ultimately exerted this classical influence.

The next example of English sculpture, from over 125 years later, brings us into the High Gothic period. The **tomb of King Edward II,** situated in Gloucester Cathedral, shows the king lying in the middle of an elaborately carved marble baldachin that assimilates decorative elements of Gothic architecture. Even though it doesn't look like it: the person depicted here did not die a natural death. The unhappy reign of Edward II (1284–1327) – who was born in Caernarfon Castle (see p. 102, 103) – ended with his murder. Consequently, there are many different legends regarding the ultimate cause of his death. His second wife, Isabella of France, and her lover, Mortimer, deposed him. After his official abdication, in the following year, his sheer existence seemed too dangerous. The general contempt for his political and military

Tomb of Edward II
Gloucester Cathedral,
various types of marble,
c. 1300–1335

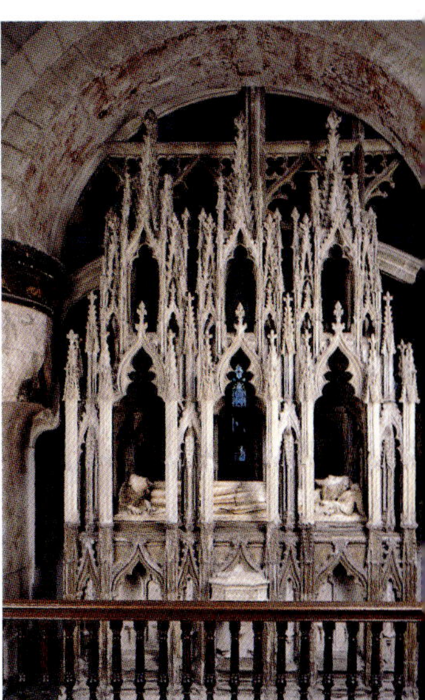

incompetence is not obvious from his tomb, which was erected a few years after his death. The elegant burial place in general, but also the delicately chiseled facial features, the carefully combed luxuriant hair, the crowned head and the lion at his feet all come together to give an ideal portrayal of a King of England and Wales.

Spanish Sculpture

With the unification of the Spanish kingdoms, in the 15th century, there began a new series of extravagant royal burial sites that would be considered more Renaissance in style. In the centuries before, contracts for sepulchral sculpture were rare and more moderate. As a result, 13th and 14th-century sculptures from the areas of Castile and León, and Catalonia were mainly in the form of portal sculptures or simple burial sites. Not only did local artists work there but artists from abroad were also recruited.

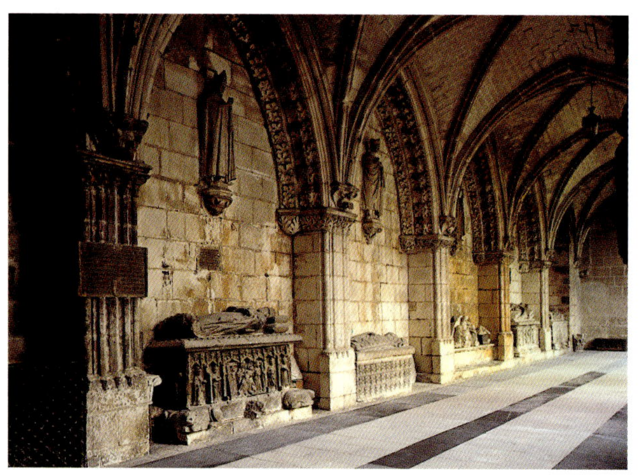

Cloister of Burgos Cathedral, 1265–1270

In the **north wing of the cloister in Burgos Cathedral,** standing on protruding cornices, are the royal couple **Ferdinand III** and **Elisabeth of Hohenstaufen, called Beatriz** in Spain. The couple are facing one another; in composition and expression it resembles countless other Gothic effigies of rulers (see Emperor Otto I and his wife Adelheid in the Meissen Cathedral p. 132). The sculptures date from between 1265 and 1270, which was well after the death of those depicted. As King Ferdinand III of Castile and heir to the royal title of León, Ferdinand III (1199–1252) united both kingdoms to create the united reign of Castile and León in 1230. The area, to which Asturias and Galicia also belong, later provided the basis for the Spanish kingdom. Ferdinand III was a remorseless persecutor of the Moors, as well a committed ruler and a benefactor of the university and many Christian buildings. He married Beatriz in the Romanesque church in Burgos in the year 1219. The sculptures are in memory of the patron of the new Gothic structure, the foundation stone of which was laid in 1221. Other wall areas on the upper floor of the two-storied cloister of Burgos Cathedral (p. 166) also contain with royal and Episcopal statues and crests. Since the 14th century, when burial was first allowed within the cloister, sarcophagi also ornamented the cloister corridors.

Ferdinand III and Elisabeth of Hohenstaufen,
Cloister of Burgos Cathedral, painted limestone, 1265–1270

Between 1327 and 1339 Italian sculptors made the **marble sarcophagus** in which the remains of **St. Eulalia** are kept in the crypt of Barcelona Cathedral. The tomb, which stands on gilded Corinthian columns, is decorated with secenes from the life of the locally venerated saint. On a

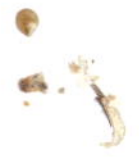

blue background, her biography is depicted up to her death. Eulalia, a young Christian girl, was martyred in the late 3rd century. In Méridá, in southwest Spain, they also venerate a young Christian saint of the same name who met the same fate. It may be the case here, as has happened with other venerated relics, that they are one and the same person, integrated into local history. The reliefs on the sarcophagus are surprisingly naïve; the figures appear strangely unreal and incorporeal. The lid of the sarcophagus is done in a completely different style: at the head and foot are two angels; in the middle is a Madonna and Child, raised and fully three-dimensional. The angels, with gilded wings, hold elegant candlesticks away from their bodies; Mary displays the typical Gothic swing of the hips that bends her body into an S-form. It is presumed that several workshops shared work on this commission.

Eulalia, a young Christian of the Late Classical period, died a martyr's death. Her remains were honorably interred in this tomb in the late Middle Ages.

Portuguese Sculpture

The Gothic period of architecture and sculpture started later in Portugal. It is mainly funerary monuments that remain. The successor of Master Pere of Aragón, the prominent Portuguese artist of this era, was an unknown artist who created the grand **sarcophagus of King Peter I,** between the years 1360 and 1367. This elaborate monument, which rests on the bodies of lions with human faces, stands in the Abbey of Santa Maria, Alcobaça (pp. 170, 171), next to that of his lover, Inês de Castro, who was once his wife's lady-in-waiting. Three of the four delicately carved sides – done in Gothic tracery that looks like ebony – show scenes from St. Bartholomew's life. At the head of the sarcophagus we find the symbol of the Wheel of Life: the twelve outer scenes depict the life of Peter ascending in a circle, the first six cover his childhood to his coronation, in the upper middle he sits as king on his throne, the following six scenes show the murder of his lover Inês and how he avenged himself on her murderers. The repeated use of the Wheel of Life, which not only gives us a disassociated glance at our own life but also reminds us of the inevitability of death, is tailored here in pictures to the king's own formative experience.

Sarcophagus of St. Eulalia,
Crypt of Barcelona Cathedral,
marble,
c. 1327–1339

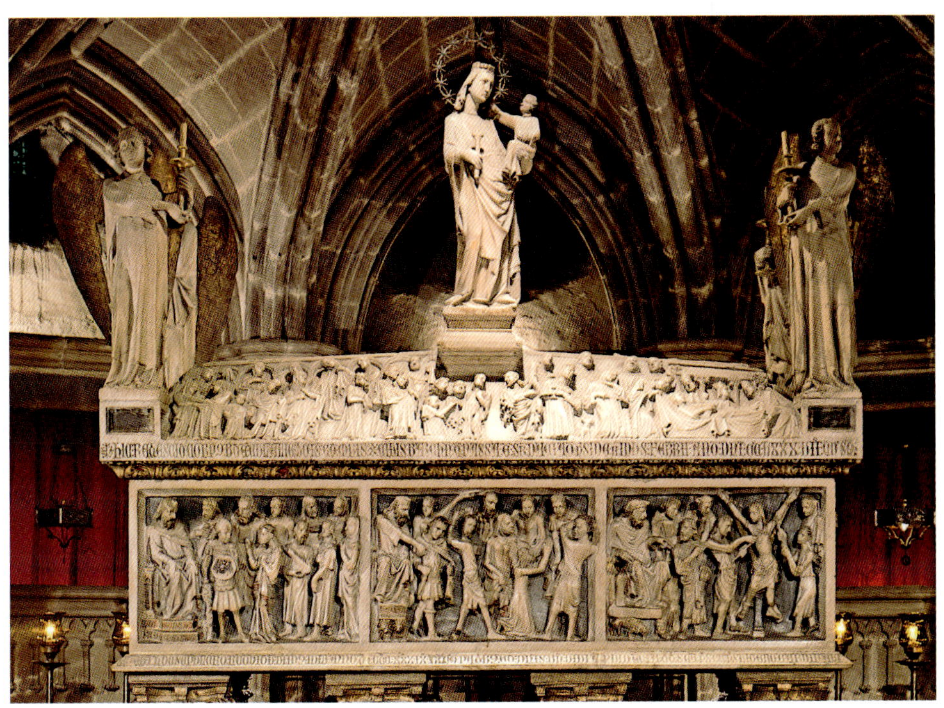

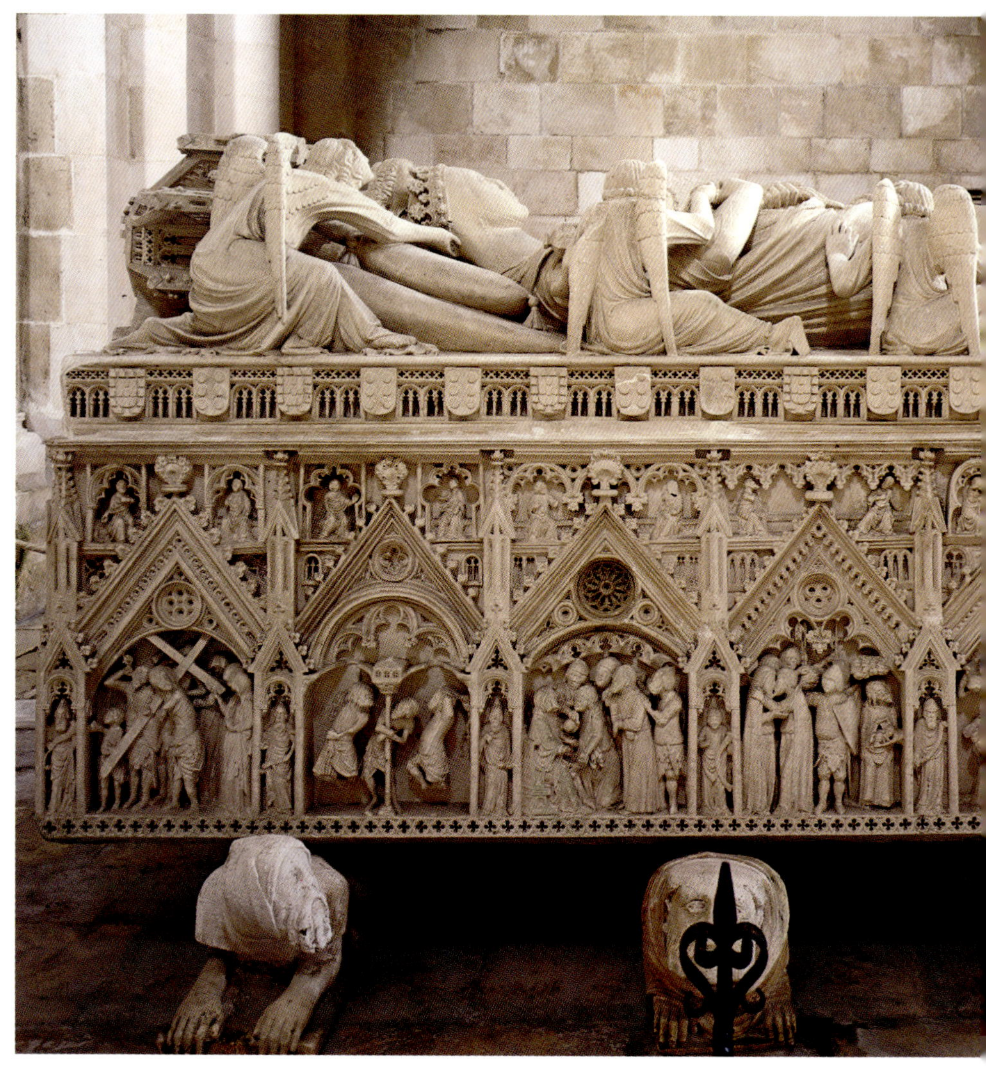

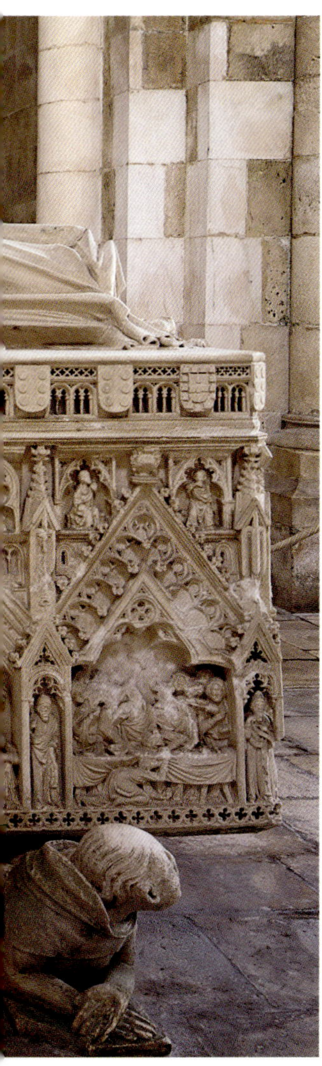

Sarcophagus of King Peter I,
Abbey of Santa Maria, Alcobaça,
marble,
1360s

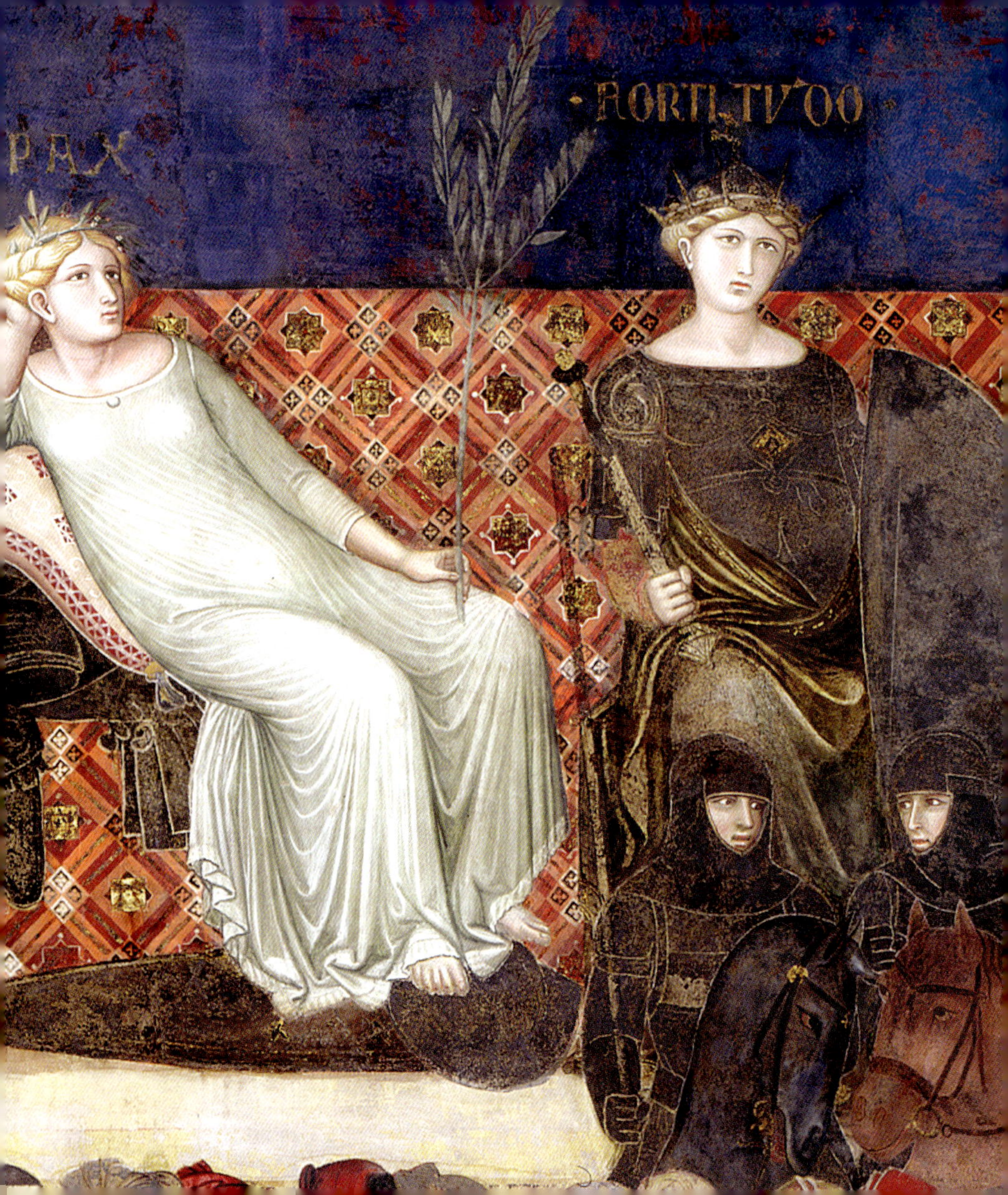
PAX

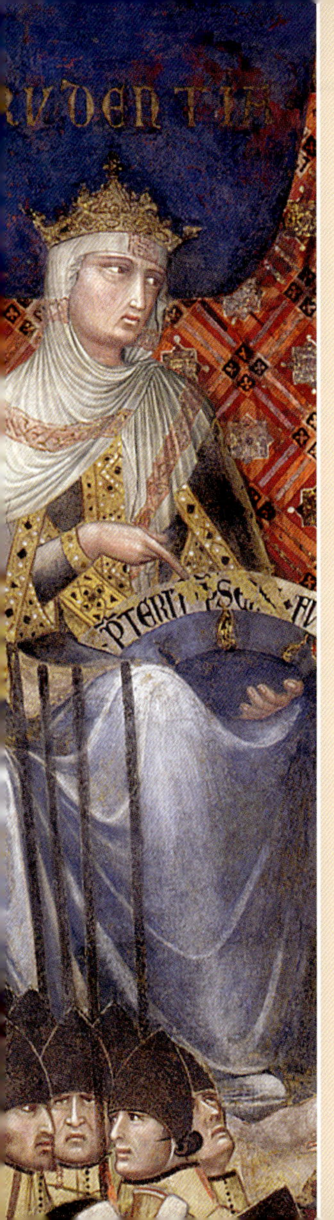

Gothic Painting

This sofa, fitted with exquisite fabrics, looks very inviting. If only the lady dressed in white would move over a bit, with her delicate blanket and foot warmer. Then one could partake in the courtly elegance and magnificence, and be surrounded by graceful creatures with slender wrists, wearing precious robes, and resting on expensive furniture. Gothic painters liked to display the beauty of their figures, playing with the perception of light and shade, fabric and surface, color and proportion, gaze and movements. The contours of the bodies are modeled by soft light, the effect of space is created by overlapping and foreshortening. But beauty serves a higher cause. The scope is to make the heavenly spheres tangible through earthly means. The lady in white, who seems so relaxed, is Pax, the allegory of peace. Just to be on the safe side, she is supporting herself on armor and by her feet lie shield and traveling hat.

Ambrogio Lorenzetti,
Allegory of Peace, Fortitude and
Prudence, detail of the fresco
from pp. 186/87

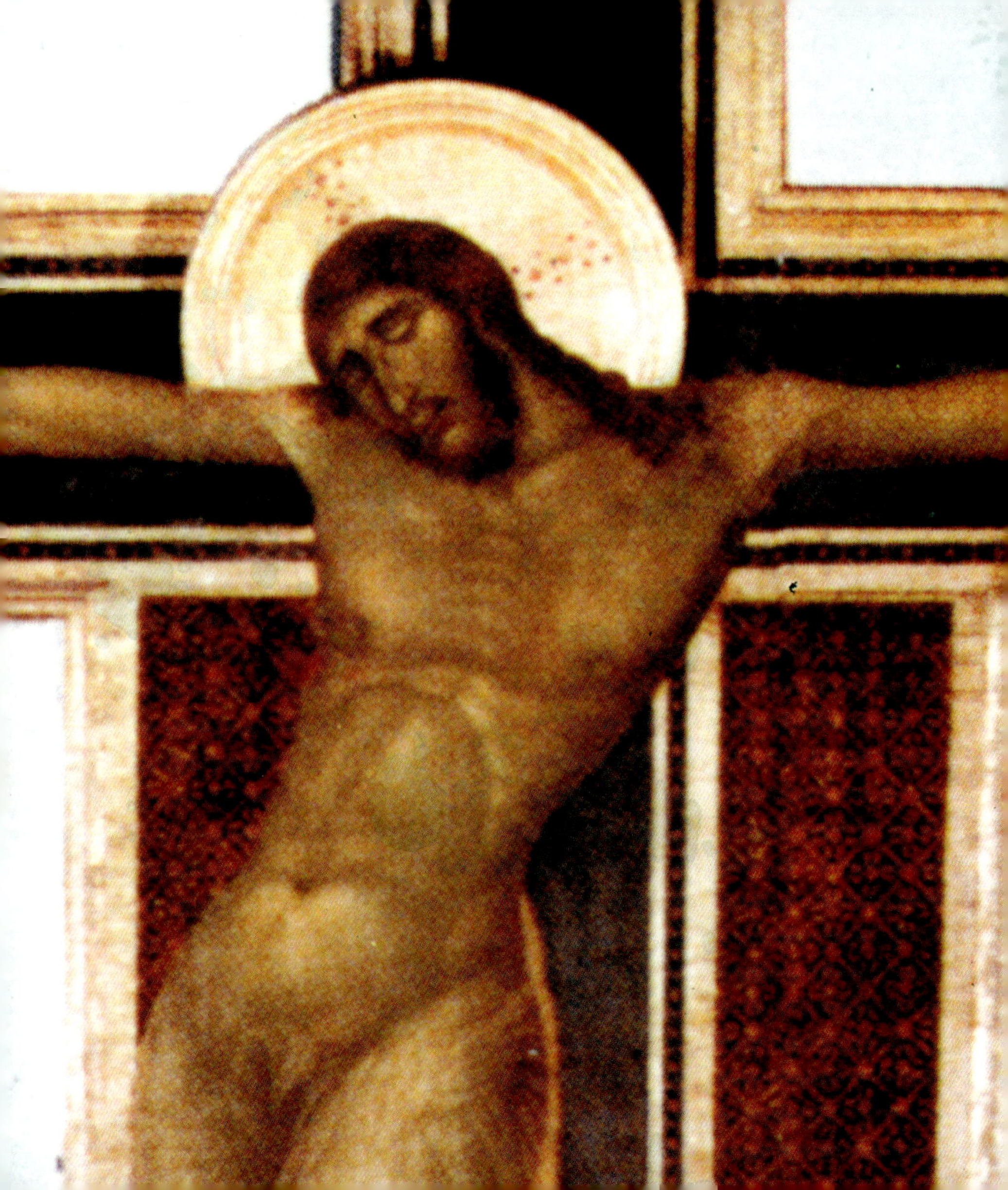

Wall and Panel Painting in Italy

As with architecture and sculpture, when defining the term "Gothic painting", the question arises as to when this period took shape and when it ended. One problem relates to the differing rates of development in the varying countries. In Italy, painting was already emancipating itself from Romanesque and Byzantine traditions in the 13th century, the Duecento. As much as 100 years later, northern European painting too found its own expressiveness, though the vocabulary of form still owed a lot to earlier traditions. The various strands converge in the decades around 1400, in a style termed International Gothic. Thereafter, the painters of Italy rushed forward to develop what nowadays is known as the Renaissance style, while in France, Germany and the Netherlands Gothic painting reached its peak only towards the mid-15th century.

Various reasons have been named to account for these diverging developments: the political situation in the respective regions, the different social structures and resulting variety of clients. Italy in the decades around 1300 had to struggle with a variety of crises and battles. The pope fought the emperor, the popish Guelphs the Ghibellines, who supported the emperor, the emerging middle class tried to gain ground against the nobility. The plague that erupted in 1348 caused millions of deaths. And yet, the arts flourished in the 14th century. Several new buildings were erected in cities like Florence, Siena, Rome and Venice, and vernacular literature witnessed the outstanding works of the *Tre Corone,* the three crowns of literature: Dante's *Divine Comedy,* Petrarch's *Sonnets* and Boccaccio's *Decamerone.*

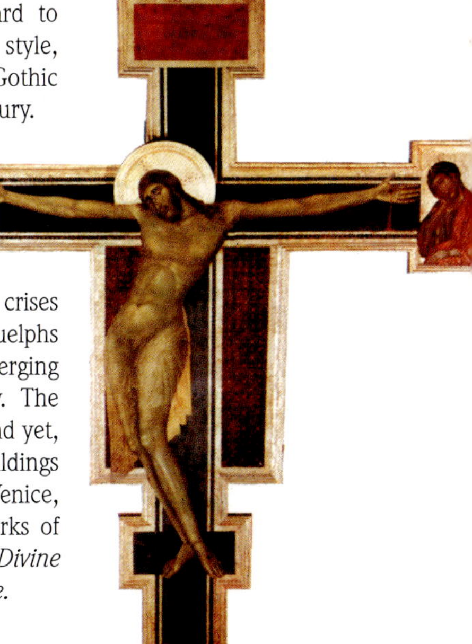

Cenni di Pepo called Cimabue, Crucifix, *c.* 1275, tempera on wood, 448 × 390 cm, Museo dell'Opera di Santa Croce, Florence

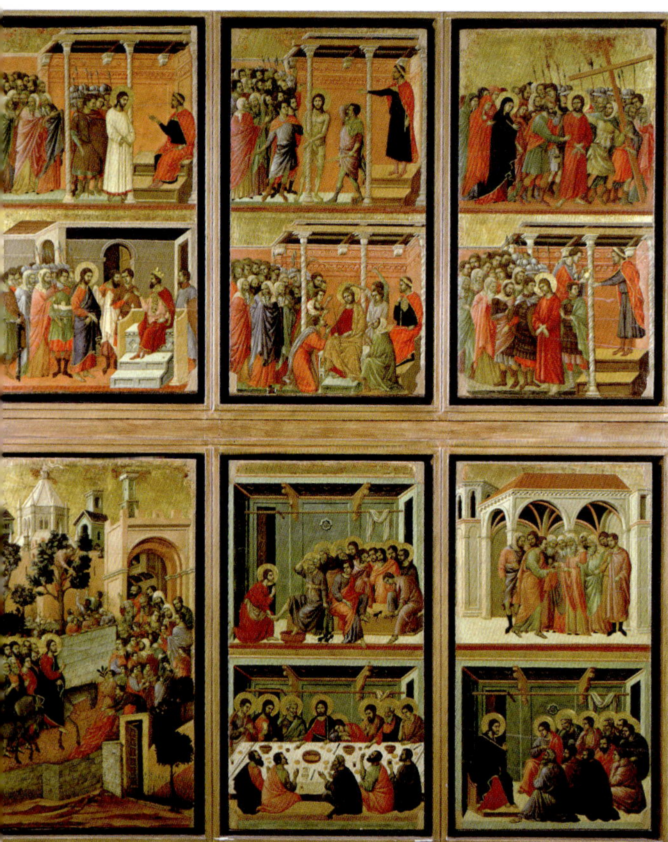

One might also say that Italian painting was supported by the fact that the region lagged behind in another artistic field: architecture. Unlike developments in France, in Italy the massive walls were not opened up to introduce larger windows. This left a lot of space for wall paintings. Frescoes were usually conceived as narrative cycles; they were intended to instruct, remind and edify the congregation, as is specified in the statutes of the painters' guilds and the commission contracts drafted by the Church. Since only the educated upper class was able to read, a painting was understood to be a vital contribution to the spoken word. The painters and their workshops would use their numerous commissions to experiment with various binding agents and additives. Practically every artist who did murals also painted panels, especially for altars. In this way, knowledge of the painting techniques for various supports (plaster and wood) helped development in the various media.

Duccio di Buoninsegna, altarpiece, left part of rear side, *c.* 1310, tempera on wood, 370 × 450 cm, Museo dell'Opera del Duomo, Siena

Yet another technique can be seen in the tessellated apse of Pisa Cathedral – the only work that can undoubtedly be ascribed to **Cenni di Pepo, known as Cimabue** (*c.* 1240–*c.* 1302). A total of six murals and panel paintings are ascribed to the Florentine artist, who participated in the decoration of the Upper and Lower Basilicas of San Francesco in Assisi. In around 1275, he created the great Crucifix, one of his late works, which once hung above the rood screen of Santa Croce in Florence (pp. 174 and 175). In spite of the vocabulary of form, which is evidently influenced by medieval tradition, a new approach to the crucified Christ can be identified: He is no longer just a religious symbol, but also a dying human.

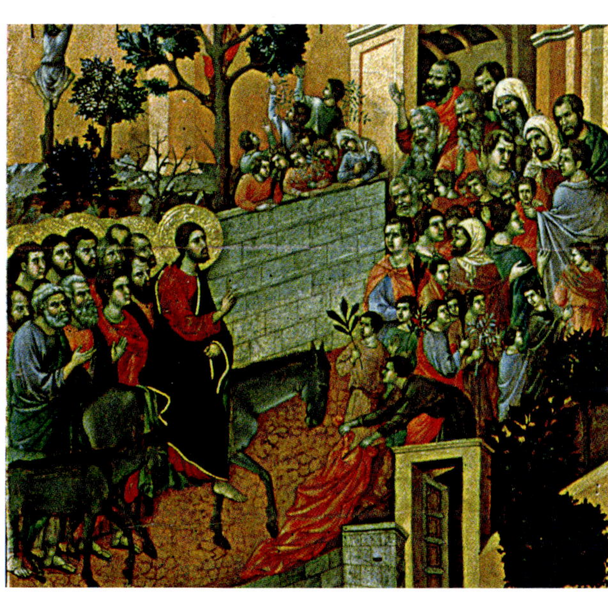

Alongside Cimabue from Florence, the most outstanding artist was the slightly younger **Duccio di Buoninsegna** from Siena (*c.* 1255–1319). Unlike Cimabue, he owes much to the influence of Byzantine painting, as can be seen from his altar retable for Siena Cathedral, painted in around 1310. The front shows a multi-figured depiction of the Maestà, visible for the congregation, whereas the other side, facing the clergy, shows twenty-six episodes from the Passion of Christ (pp. 176 and 177). The scene to the bottom left, which the viewer beholds from a bird's-eye perspective, shows the arrival of Jesus in Jerusalem (p. 177). He comes from the left, riding a donkey and surrounded by his disciples. To the right stands the group of welcomers, holding palm fronds and other twigs in their

Duccio di Buoninsegna,
Entry into Jerusalem, detail from the rear side of the altarpiece from p. 176

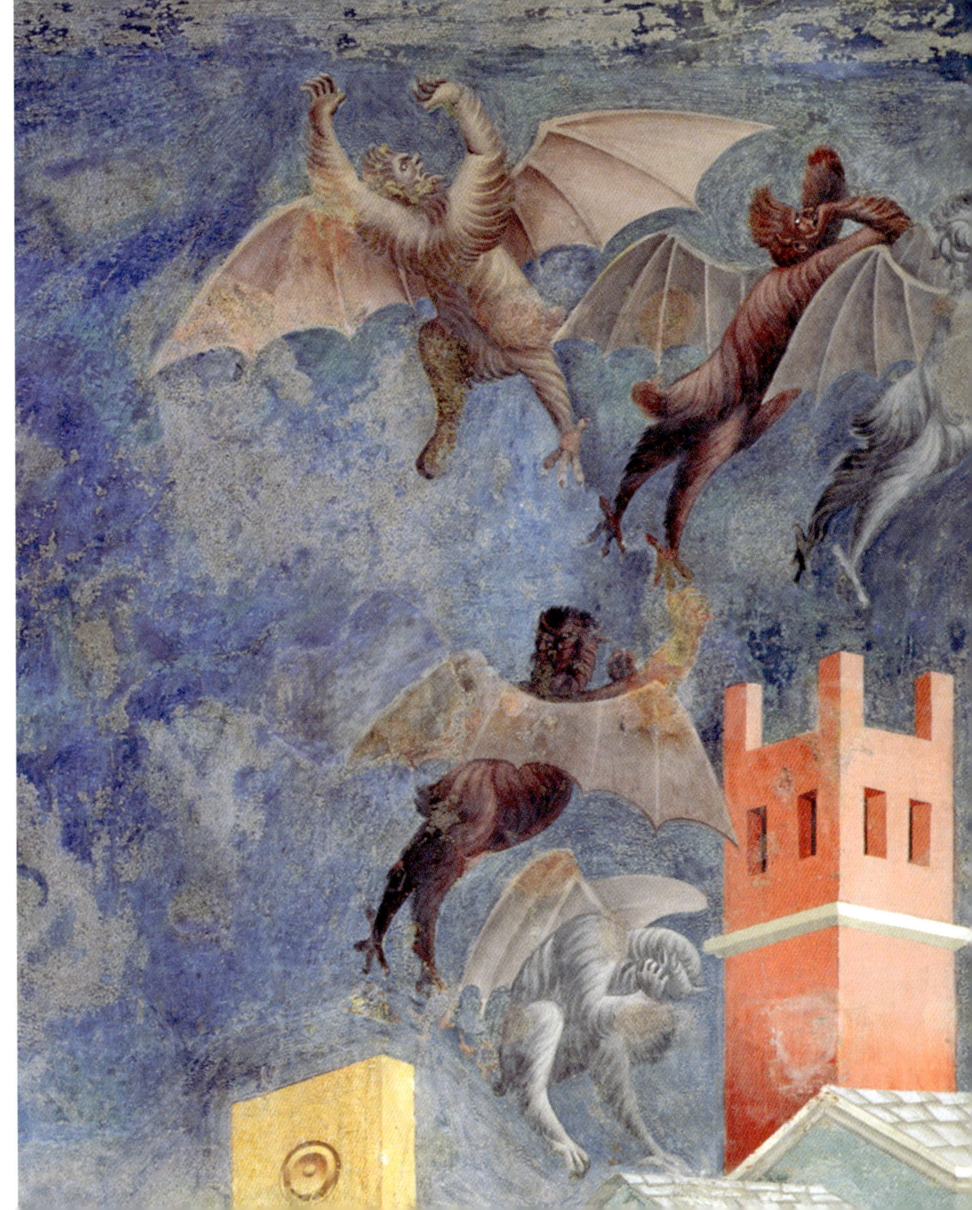

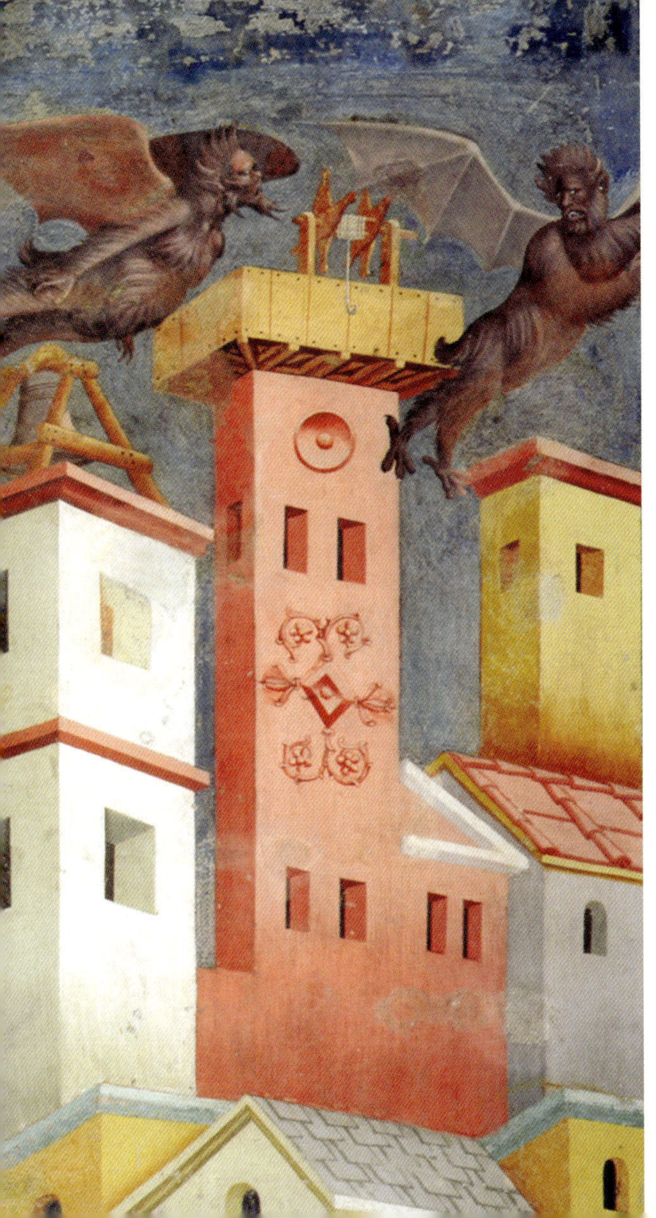

The demons are fleeing from the city: these are ferocious-looking, bearded creatures overgrown with fur, complete with bat's wings and clawed feet.

Giotto di Bondone,
Fleeing Demons,
detail of the fresco from p. 181

St Francis of Assisi (1181/82–1226)

1181 or **1182** Born in Assisi as Giovanni Francesco Bernardone, the son of a cloth merchant.

1202 Takes part in the war against neighboring Perugia.

1202–1204 Is taken prisoner in Perugia but released when his father pays a ransom.

1205 On his way to a campaign in Puglia he returns and determines to renounce further worldly service for the sake of religious service.

1205 or **1206** Makes a pilgrimage to Rome.

1206 Dissociates himself from his father, with whom he had quarreled about payments for the restoration of churches, amongst other things. Begins to live as a hermit outside of Assisi.

1208 Establishes an order and initiates the Imitatio Christi, the imitation of the life of Christ.

1209 Francis of Assisi and his twelve (!) closest disciples travel to Rome to seek permission of Pope Innocent III to found an order within the Catholic Church.

1212 or **1215** The Catholic Church permits the foundation of the Order of the Friars Minor. Franciscan priories are established in Italy and abroad.

1219 Takes part in a crusade. St Francis travels to Egypt in order to convert Sultan Melek-el-Kamel to Christianity.

1220 Francis steps back as head of the order. He is nearly blind and weak from fasting.

1224 According to legend, Francis received the stigmata, scars in accordance with the wounds Christ received during the crucifixion.

1226 Francis of Assisi dies in one of the chapels he had restored, the Portiuncula Chapel south of Assisi.

1228 Pope Gregory IX pronounces him a saint. Construction of San Francesco in Assisi begins.

1230 The relics of St Francis are brought to the sepulcher in the Lower Basilica of San Francesco.

hands. One of them is spreading out a red drape for the arriving group. Two figures have climbed onto trees and are throwing twigs into the crowd. A remarkable feature is the differing size of the figures. The ones further in the background are not depicted smaller; on the contrary, some of them have clearly larger heads than the figures in the foreground. And yet, by cunningly staggering the groups of people and the various parts of buildings, the artist manages to convey a sense of space and depth.

One of Cimabue's pupils was **Giotto di Bondone** (*c.* 1267–1337, further details see p. 232), who was also active in Assisi in the mid-1290s. Among his works is the extensive cycle of twenty-eight scenes of the life of St. Francis, in the Upper Church of San Francesco. St. Francis is seen praying, bidding goodbye to his father, living as a hermit in the surrounding countryside of Assisi, and preaching to the birds. One of the scenes depicts a miracle: the expulsion of the devils in Arezzo (pp. 178, 179, 181). To the left, there is a soaring Gothic church, against a blue background, and in front of it, St. Francis, making a sign of blessing with his hands. To the right can be seen the fortified city of Arezzo. The houses are adorned with ornamentation, oriels and dynastic towers, the profuse high buildings overlapping each other, even more than is the case in the actual Tuscan city of Arezzo. Demons can be seen fleeing: grisly-looking, bearded creatures with bats' wings and clawed feet, their entire bodies covered in fur. The one closest to St. Francis is holding his ears from the pain caused by the exorcizing words which the saint is uttering.

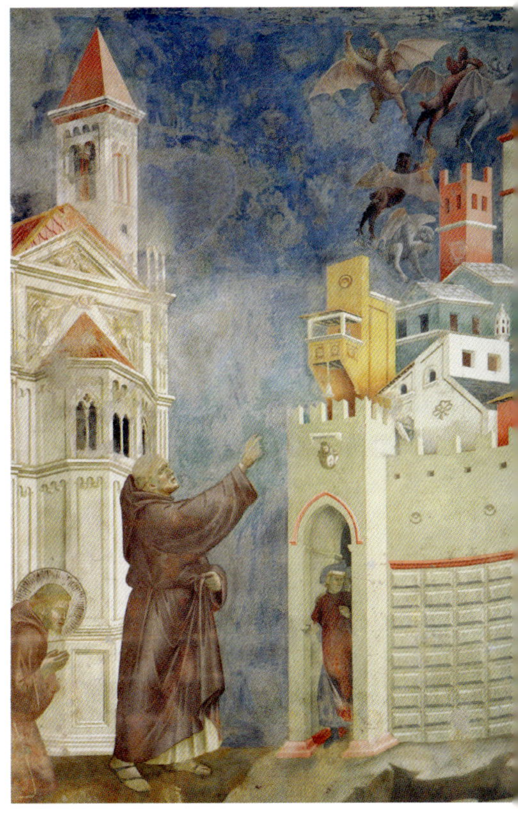

Giotto di Bondone,
Expulsion of the Devils in Arezzo, St. Francis cycle, *c.* 1295, fresco, nave of the Upper Basilica of San Francesco, Assisi

Simone Martini (1284–1344) is generally seen as the successor of Duccio di Buoninsegna, but the painter from Siena was also inspired by the innovative ideas of Giotto. He wove them into his own works, as can be seen in the spatial arrangement of the fresco cycle of the legend of St Martin, in the Lower Basilica of San Francesco. After all, these works were created only a few feet from Giotto's paintings. In around 1315, Martini created the Maestà wall painting for the Sala del Mappamondo on the second floor of the *Palazzo Pubblico,* the town hall of Siena (pp. 182, 183, 185). It is not only the first documented work of the great Sienese painter but also one of the oldest wall paintings to have survived in Siena. The staggered arrangement of the figures and the foreshortening of the baldachin give the effect of space. The saints have gathered to honor the enthroned Madonna and Child. Some of them are

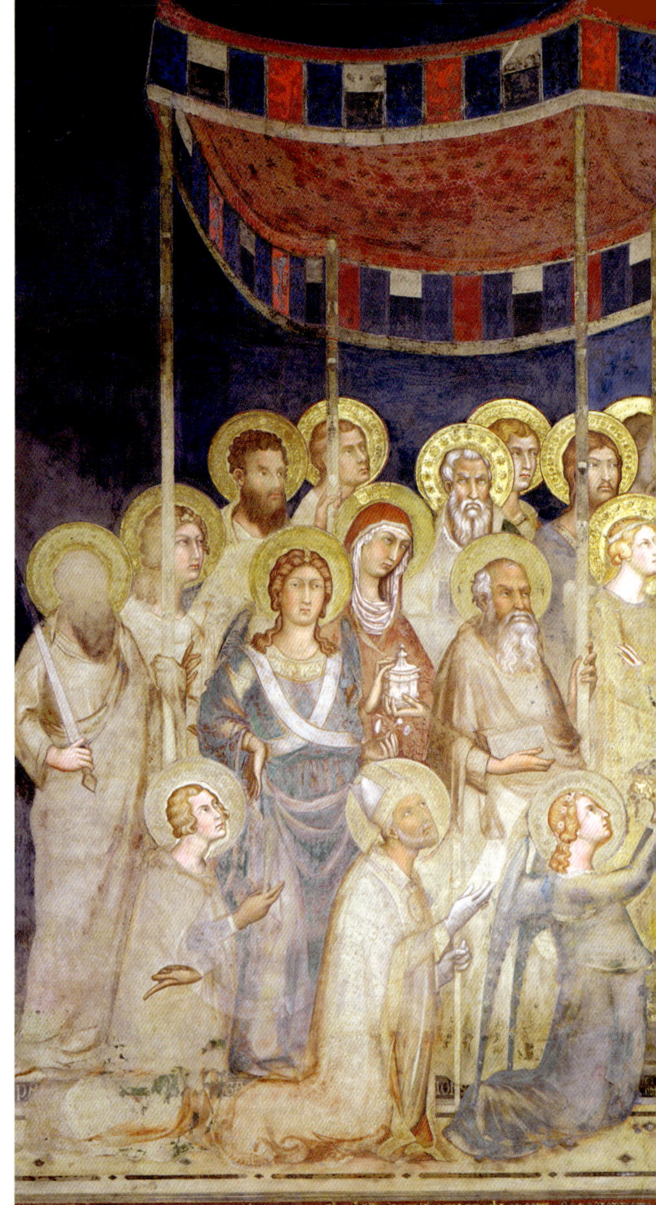

Simone Martini,
Maestà,
fresco, 763 × 970 cm,
Palazzo Pubblico, Siena

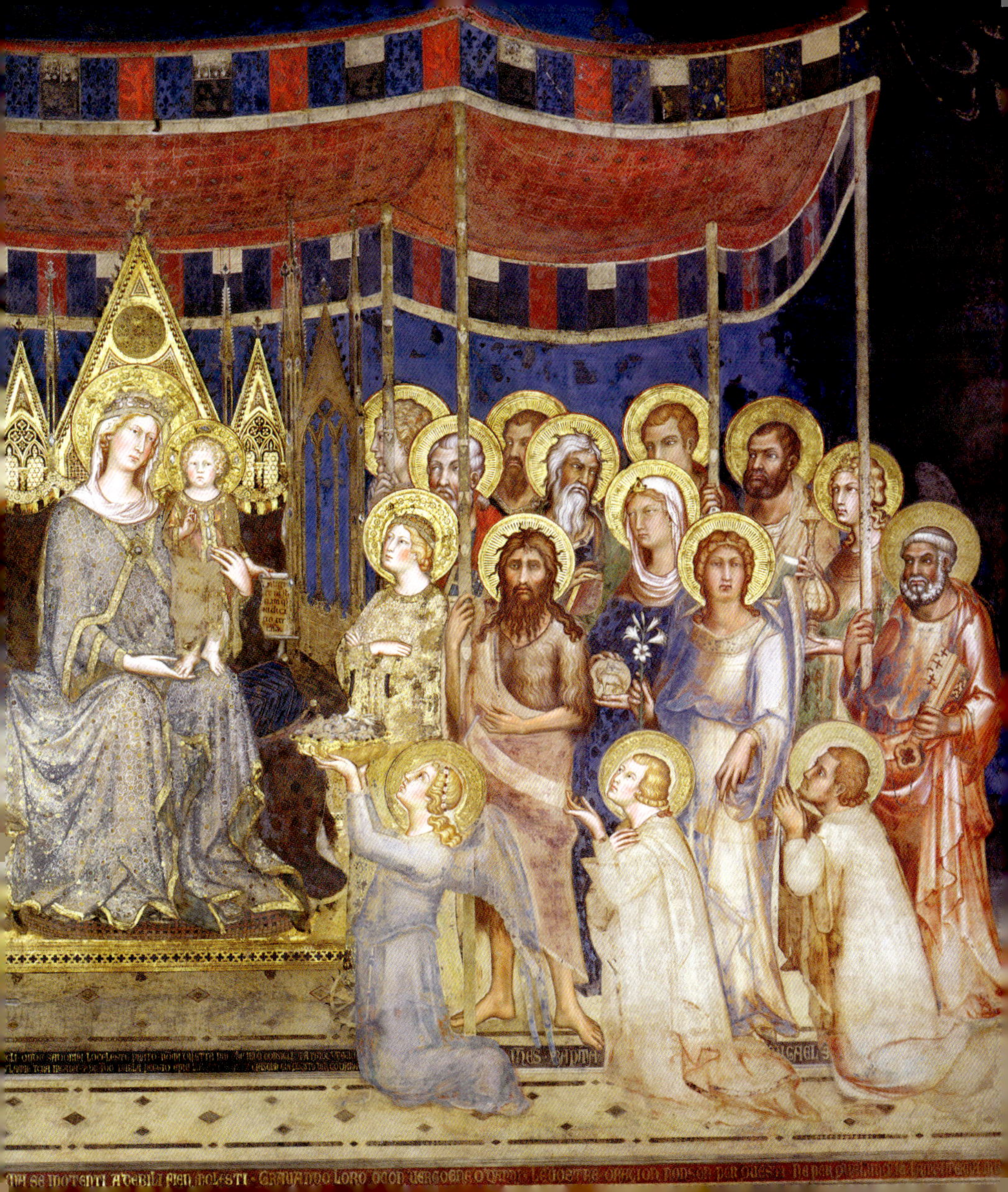

looking out of the picture towards the beholder, who is thus integrated into the scene. The haloes deserve special attention: some of them were imprinted into the moist mortar, in the style of a relief. Thus, the most immaterial part of the depiction is given an express sense of materiality. Martini developed a wide range of ideas to make his pictures more true to life. For instance, he used colored glass, relief pieces and metal plates; even paper. The opened scroll which the Christ Child is holding is a pasted piece of paper, written on with real ink. Restoration works have brought to light that the figures in the center had been revised. The second version is of much lighter tonality; the heads now are smaller, which lends the figures even more grace.

More than painting: the artist also included colored glass, metal plates and paper. The reliefs of the haloes were pressed into the moist mortar.

Another representative of the Sienese school is **Ambrogio Lorenzetti** (*c.* 1290–*c.* 1348). His masterpiece was the decoration of the Sala della Pace (Hall of Peace) in the Palazzo Pubblico of Siena, where Simone Martini painted his Maestà. Lorenzetti's frescoes in this great hall, measuring 14 by 8 meters, are allegories of the preconditions and results of Good and Bad Government, respectively. Good Government (pp. 186, 187) first of all requires Justice, who is represented to the left, sitting in a red robe with gold embroidery. In the scale pans to her sides are Distributiva and Comutativa. The first one treats every person according to their merits: one is beheaded, another receives a little crown. Comutativa lends two merchants cups to weigh and measure out their goods, thus setting the rules for barter trade. The entire group is watched over by Sagacity. Underneath, Harmony sits enthroned, she holds a ribbon – symbol of connectivity – which passes through numerous hands, until it finally reaches the main figure on the right: the commune of Siena. It is personified by a bearded man wearing precious robes and holding the insignia of rule. To his right sit Peace, Fortitude and Prudence (pp. 172, 173). Pax is holding an oil branch, Fortitudo is armed, and Prudentia points at a sun dial

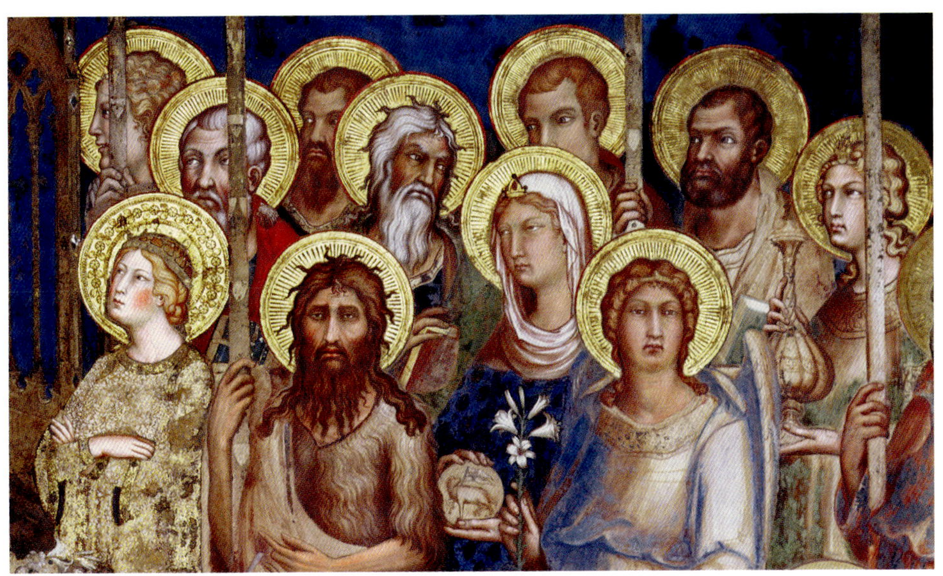

Simone Martini,
Entourage of the Enthroned Madonna, detail of the fresco from pp. 182, 183

which is inscribed with the words past, present, and future: true prudence only interferes into the present after having accrued knowledge of the past and considered plans for the future. There are three more allegories to the left of the commune: Magnanimity, Temperance and Justice once more (*Magnanimitas, Temperantia* and *Iustitia*). Above her hover her three advisors Faith *(Fides)*, Charity *(Caritas)* and Hope *(Spes)*. In the lower zone of the painting and on the side walls, the citizens of Siena are engaged in everyday life. Ambrogio Lorenzetti here gives us a beautifully nuanced kaleidoscope of civic hustle and bustle, including fish stalls on the market, agriculture outside the city gates, music and dance.

The elder brother of Ambrogio Lorenzetti, **Pietro Lorenzetti** (*c.* 1300–*c.* 1348), has been ascribed a fresco in the

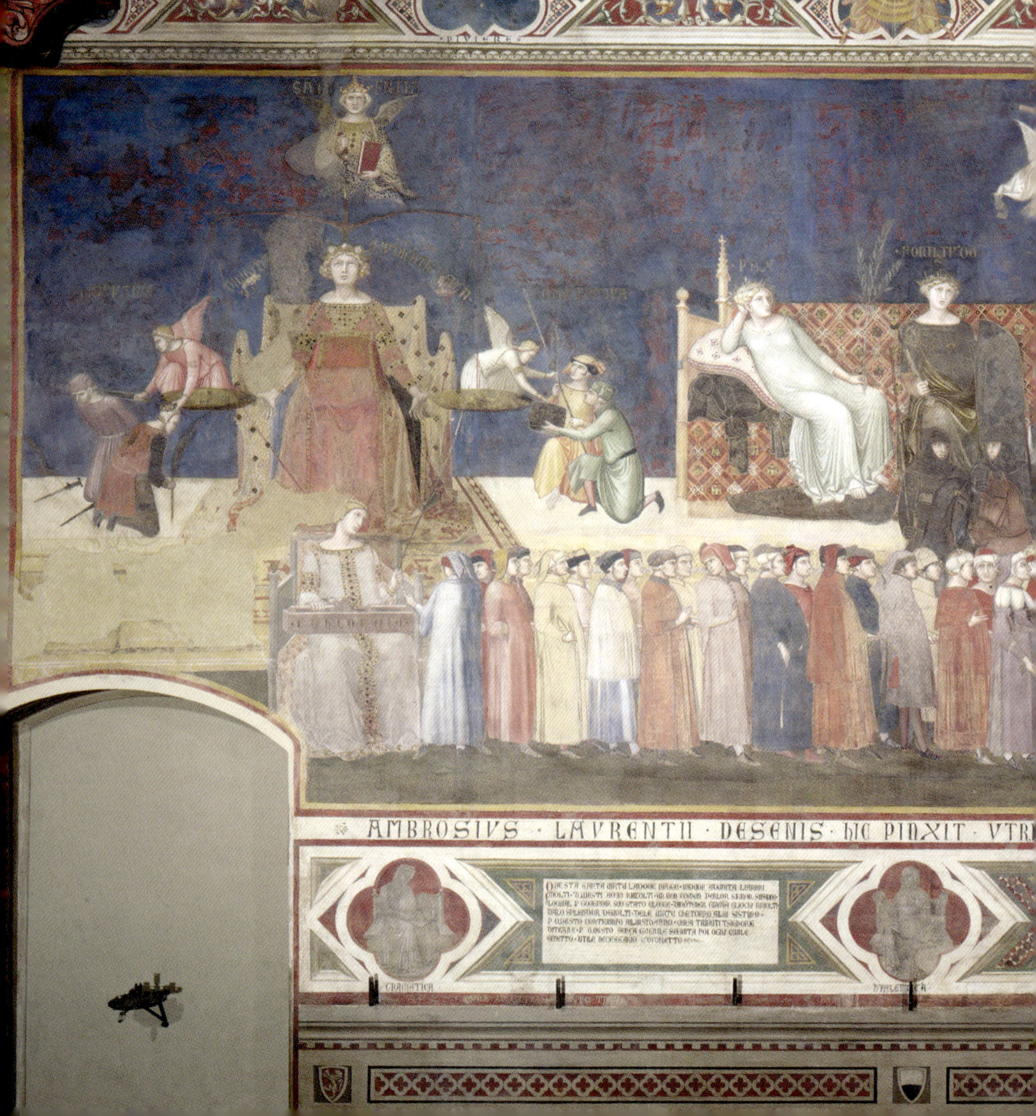
AMBROSIVS · LAVRENTII · DESENIS · HIC PINXIT · VTR

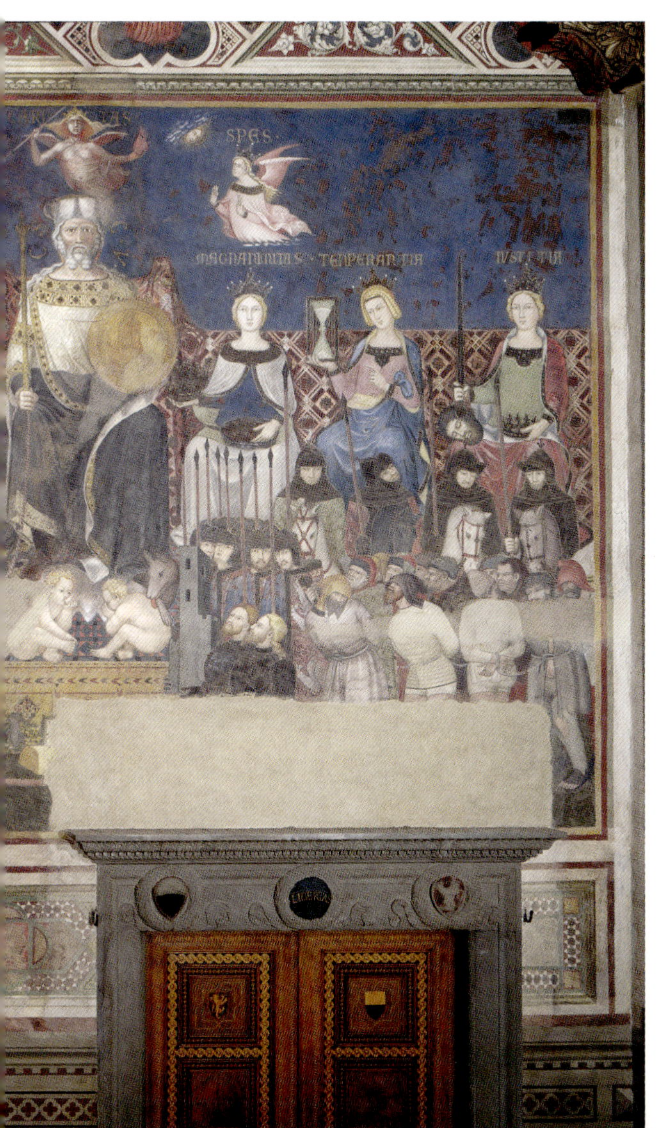

The ideal advisors of a good civic government: Peace, Fortitude, Prudence, Magnanimity, Temperance and Justice support the commune of Siena.

Ambrogio Lorenzetti,
Good Government,
c. 1340, fresco,
Palazzo Pubblico, Siena

Lower Basilica of San Francesco in Assisi. It depicts the Last Supper. Jesus and his disciples have gathered one last time to sup together. His favorite disciple, John, is sitting close by him, grieving. Compared to Ambrogio, this fresco by Pietro Lorenzetti, which dates from around 1340, is in a more earthy style with figures that are highly naïve, recalling the style of illuminations. But here, too, the new fascination for three-dimensionality can be felt: the space has been vaulted in perspective: the ceiling is seen from below, while table and floor are seen from above. In the adjoining room, the dog is helping with the washing up – a masterly work of foreshortening. But this beautiful little incident should not be judged from a point of view of hygiene. Rather, it is an allegory: by licking the plates clean with abandon the dog symbolizes unrelenting faith in the son of God. His antagonist is a fat cat, sitting next to him, with the facial features of the devil.

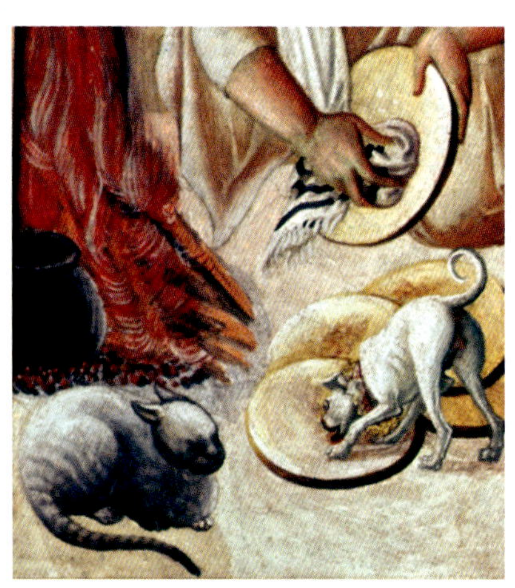

Pietro Lorenzetti,
dog and cat,
detail of the fresco from p. 189

Our series of Italian Gothic painters will be concluded with **Andrea da Firenze** (1343–*c.* 1378) and his frescoes in Santa Maria Novella in Florence. In around 1365, he painted the walls of the so-called Spanish Chapel. Andrea da Firenze, also known as Andrea di Bonaiuto, was not an overly famous artist – the more astonishing is the fact that he was commissioned to design an entire pictorial scheme for this important space in the Dominican friary. The fresco, which is painted onto the east wall (pp. 190, 191) is understood to be an allegory of the Church. But to this day the meaning of many of the figures has not been decoded. It is presumably the pictorial interpretation of the profession of faith of St. Thomas Aquinas, a Dominican philosopher of the 13th century. One very convincing interpretation assumes that the picture shows, from the bottom right to the top left, the way of penance. On this way, the four bad reasons for lack of willingness to do penance have to be passed, which are represented as a group of four seated figures: wrong despair is playing the violin, resigned; wrong hope is holding a falcon, vain; wrong pity of having to renounce worldly goods is too elegantly dressed and is holding a small lap dog as an accessory; wrong shame to the far right is hiding in the garb of a penitent instead of moving. The right way, on the other hand, leads via the confessional, in the center of the fresco, and then up through heaven's gate, depicted in the top left. All of these different events, all of these allegories, have been combined into one pictorial space. Although all of the single groups as such are harmonious, the overall effect is collage-like. Basically, the artist simply intended to answer one of the rules of Gothic art: every element within the painting is both an allusion and a conclusive part of the composition.

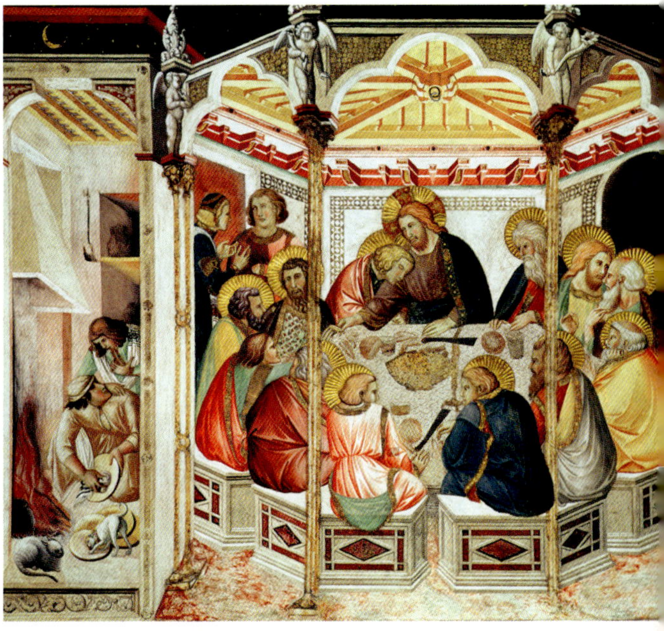

Pietro Lorenzetti,
The Last Supper,
c. 1340, fresco,
Lower Basilica of San Francesco,
Assisi

Following double spread:
Andrea da Firenze,
Allegory of Church,
East wall of the Spanish Chapel,
c. 1365, fresco,
Santa Maria Novella, Florence

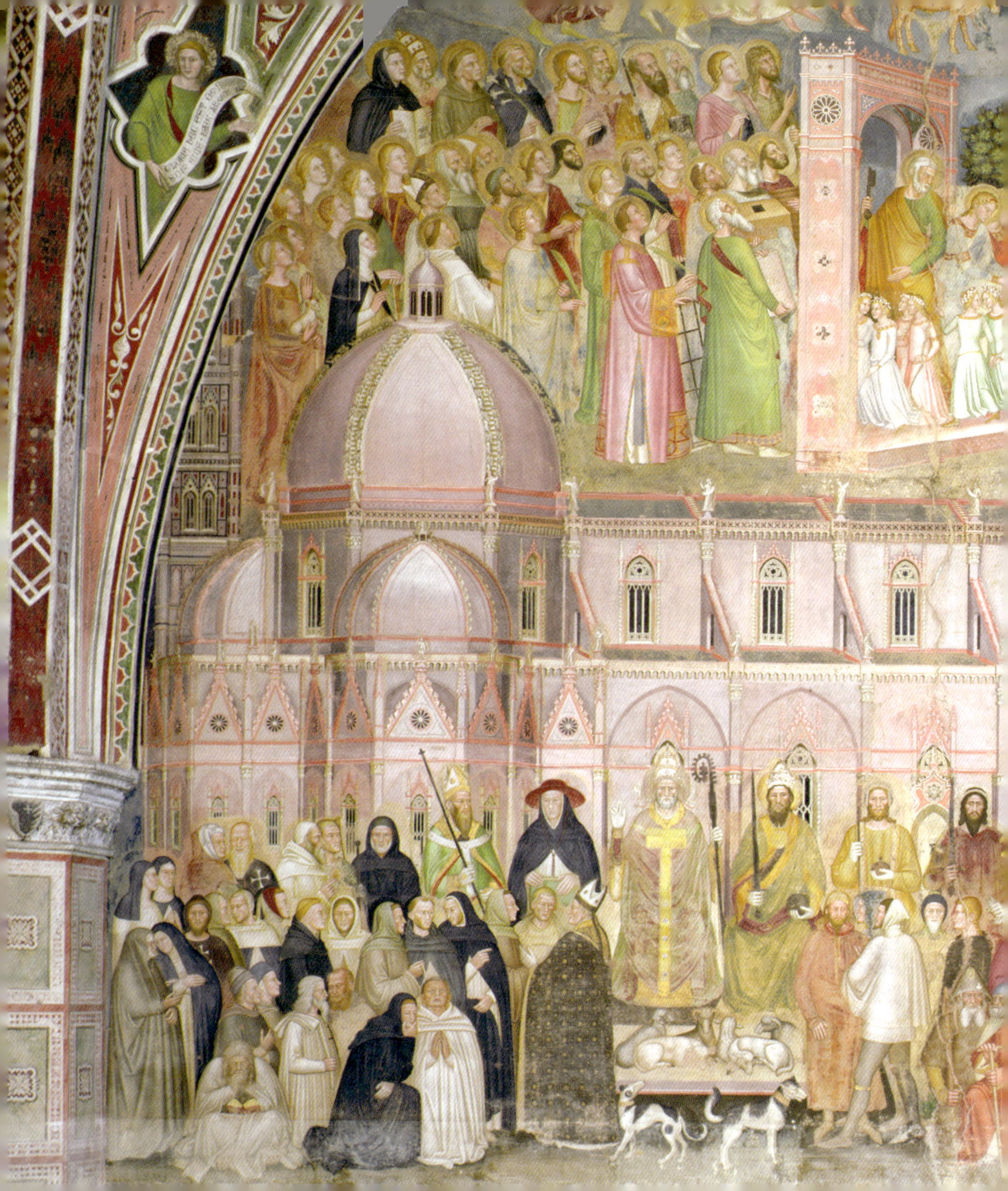

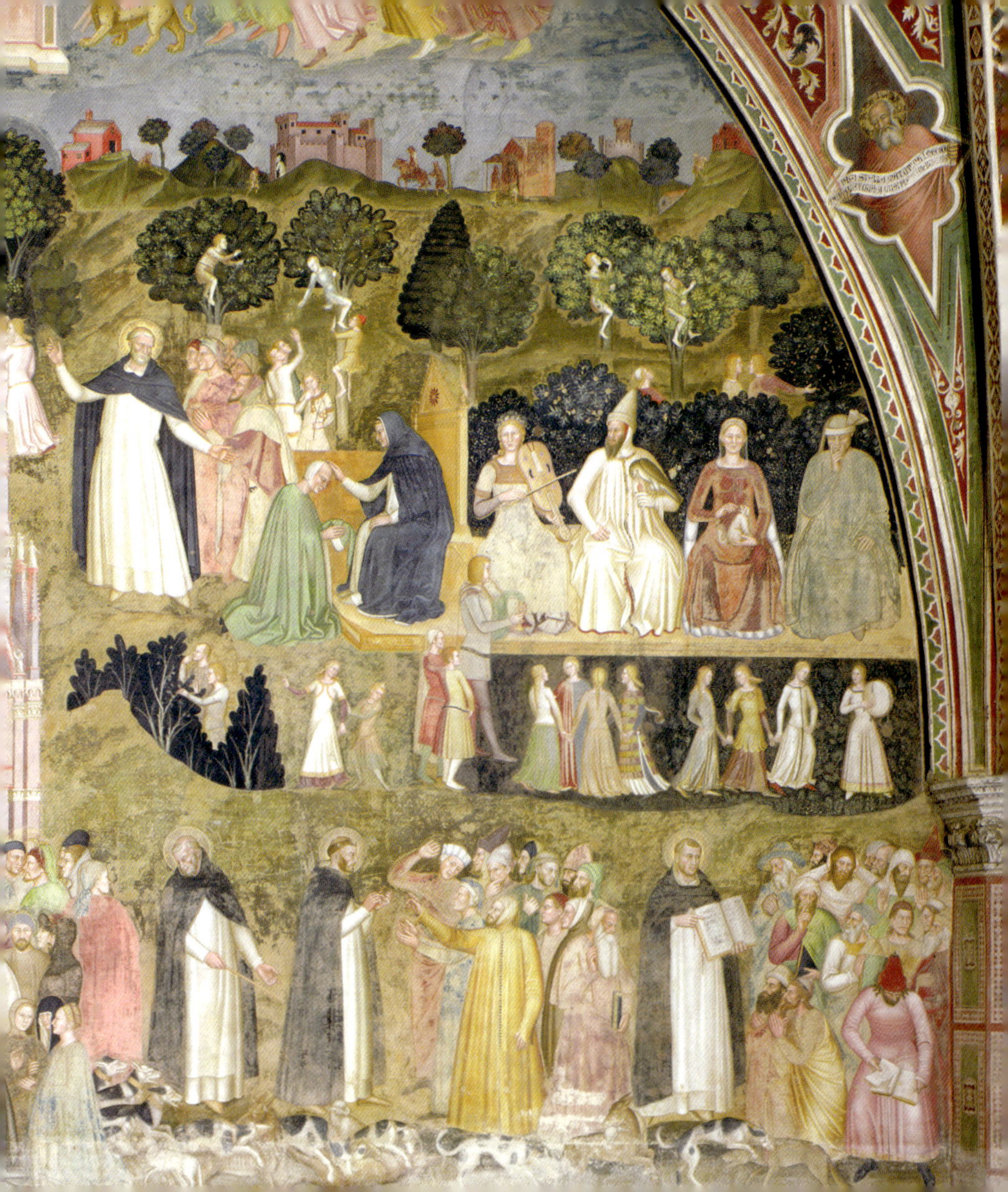

From the Darkling Wood to the Celestial Rose – Dante Alighieri and *The Divine Comedy*

Dante Alighieri,
fresco by Giotto di Bondone,
c. 1335,
Bargello, Florence

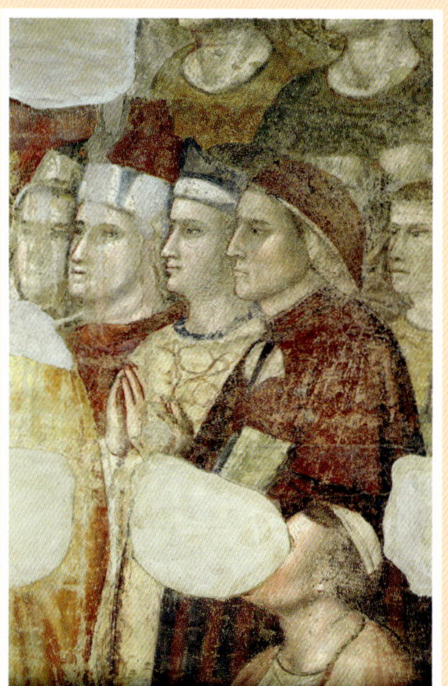

In the years 1373/74, the writer Giovanni Boccaccio (1313–1375) was asked by the city state of Florence to give daily introductory lectures on *La Commedia* by Dante Alighieri, which since Boccaccio's time has become known as *La Divina Commedia, The Divine Comedy*. This didactic project was in fact extraordinary because the poet Dante Alighieri (1265–1321), who was to be honored with these lectures, had been forced into exile from his hometown of Florence only seventy years previously, due to political conflicts, and had been sentenced to death in his absence. For nearly twenty years, until his death, the poet had hoped to be able to return home, but in vain. Only by pure coincidence had his first notes for the *Divine Comedy* survived the author's flight and the subsequent looting of his possessions. Dante completed the manuscript while living in exile. "Thereby shalt thou make proof what bitter fare / is bread of others, and how hard a road / the going up and down another's stair." (Paradiso, XVII, 58 ff.) The disappointment of the exiled Florentine also shows in the might with which he criticizes both the honoraries of his hometown as well as the papacy in the *Divine Comedy*. The political influence exerted by the popes on the Republic of Florence lay at the heart of this conflict, which had momentous consequences for the poet. News about Dante's life and the development of the *Divine Comedy* are known to us through his own notes, through events that he alluded to in his work, as well as through an essay by Boccaccio, written in approximately 1360, roughly forty years after Dante's death.

Before being banished, Dante held several civic posts and wrote poetry as well as prose texts and philosophical treatises. His masterwork, however, was *The Divine Comedy,* the most famous and probably most thorough depiction of a midlife crisis in world literature: "Midlife the path of life that men pursue / I found me in a darkling wood astray / for the direct way had been lost to view." These are the introductory verses of the oeuvre composed in Italian vernacular and consisting of 100 cantos (canti) and a total of 14 230 verses. It is a truly Gothic work in the way we interpret Gothic art, in as much as the ingenious descriptions can be read both as a narration and as an allegory. Three wild beasts threaten Dante in the Darkling Wood: a lynx, metaphor of luxuriousness; a lion, symbol of pride; and a she-wolf, standing for avarice. Dante can only be saved through the support of the classical Roman poet Virgil, who symbolizes reason, a quality closely related to the Golden Age of Antiquity. Together, the two poets start on their journey through the nine circles of Hell *(inferno)* and the seven terraces of Purgatory *(purgatorio).* Finally, Dante meets his first love Beatrice in Paradise *(paradiso)*

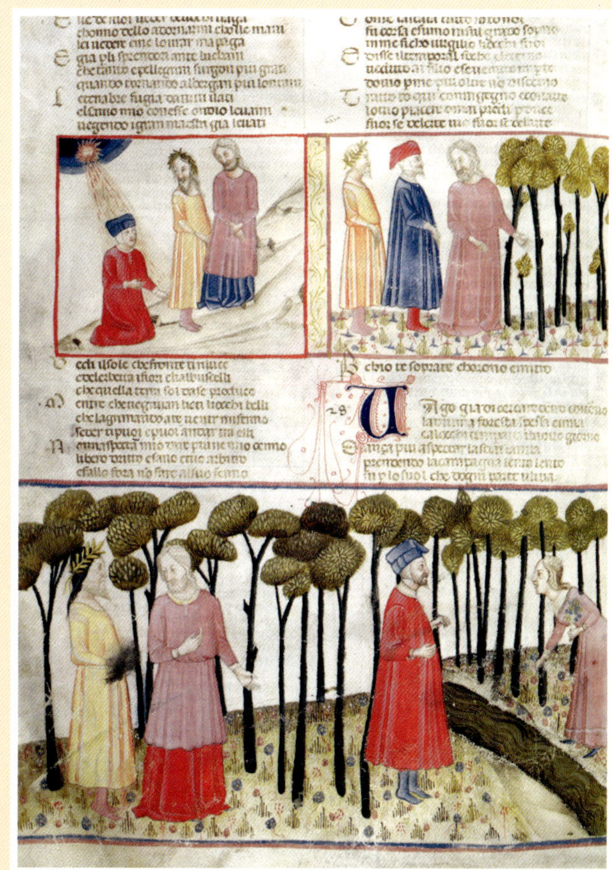

Book illustration of the *Divine Comedy,*
14th century, Biblioteca Marciana, Venice

– biographical facts and fiction here amalgamated – and it is she who leads him through the nine spheres of paradise to the Empyrean celestial rose composed of light.

Domenico di Michelino,
Purgatory, detail of the fresco from p. 195

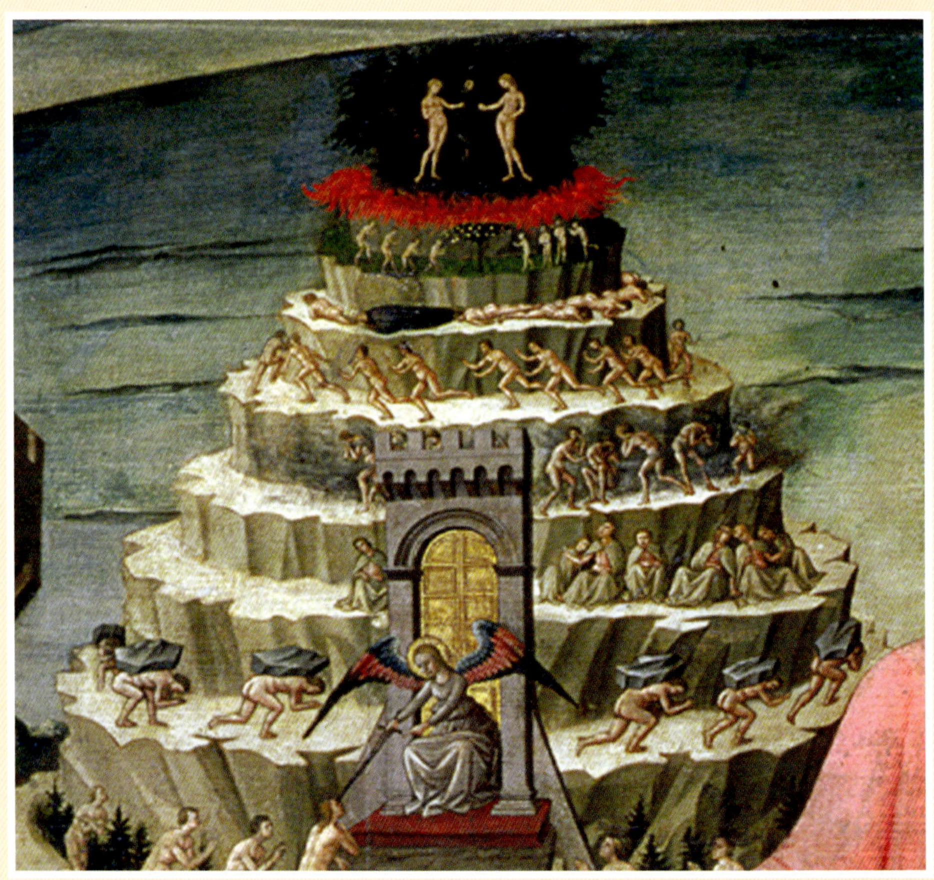

The Divine Comedy quickly became popular. The work which stands at the very beginning of Italian vernacular literature was also to become one of Dante's major works. Soon there were illustrated copies. Our example from a **14th-century manuscript** (p. 193) shows Dante taking leave of his guide Virgil – the hero, his mind fortified, will hence walk on with another guide. Here, too, Dante finds himself in a wood, but this time it is the Garden of Eden. He reaches Lethe River, drinks from the waters and forgets all past sins. Only then is he prepared for the following lessons, which Beatrice imparts him, on the nature of the world, of angels and of God the Father.

There is one passage in *Purgatory* which holds a special fascination for art lovers. In passing, Dante occupies himself with the narrative power of the reliefs which he sees there, worked in marble. He is astonished by the ability of the depictions to suggest scents, expressions of the figures, even entire dialogues of the depicted persons. In fact, the naturalistic depiction to him seems more real than reality itself. These thoughts allow us an insight into what was important to Gothic viewers when looking at a work of art. Here, as well as in other descriptions, the figures and their gestures are pointed out, the illusionist effect of their vividness is stressed. What does not seem to be important are topics such as space, the effect of depth and perspective; topics which we, knowing how art further developed, take much more into consideration.

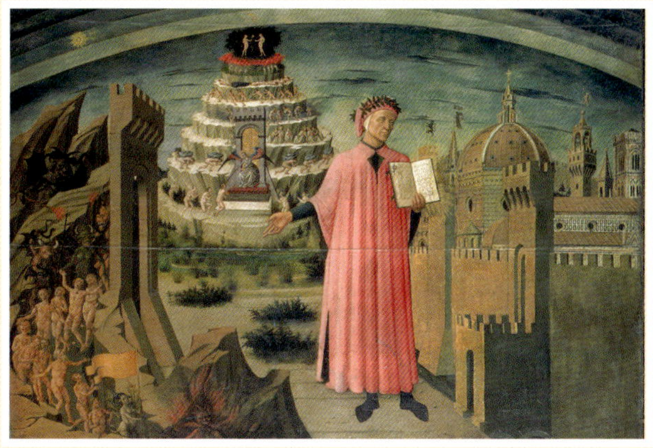

Domenico di Michelino,
Dante and the *Divine Comedy,*
1465, fresco,
Cathedral, Florence

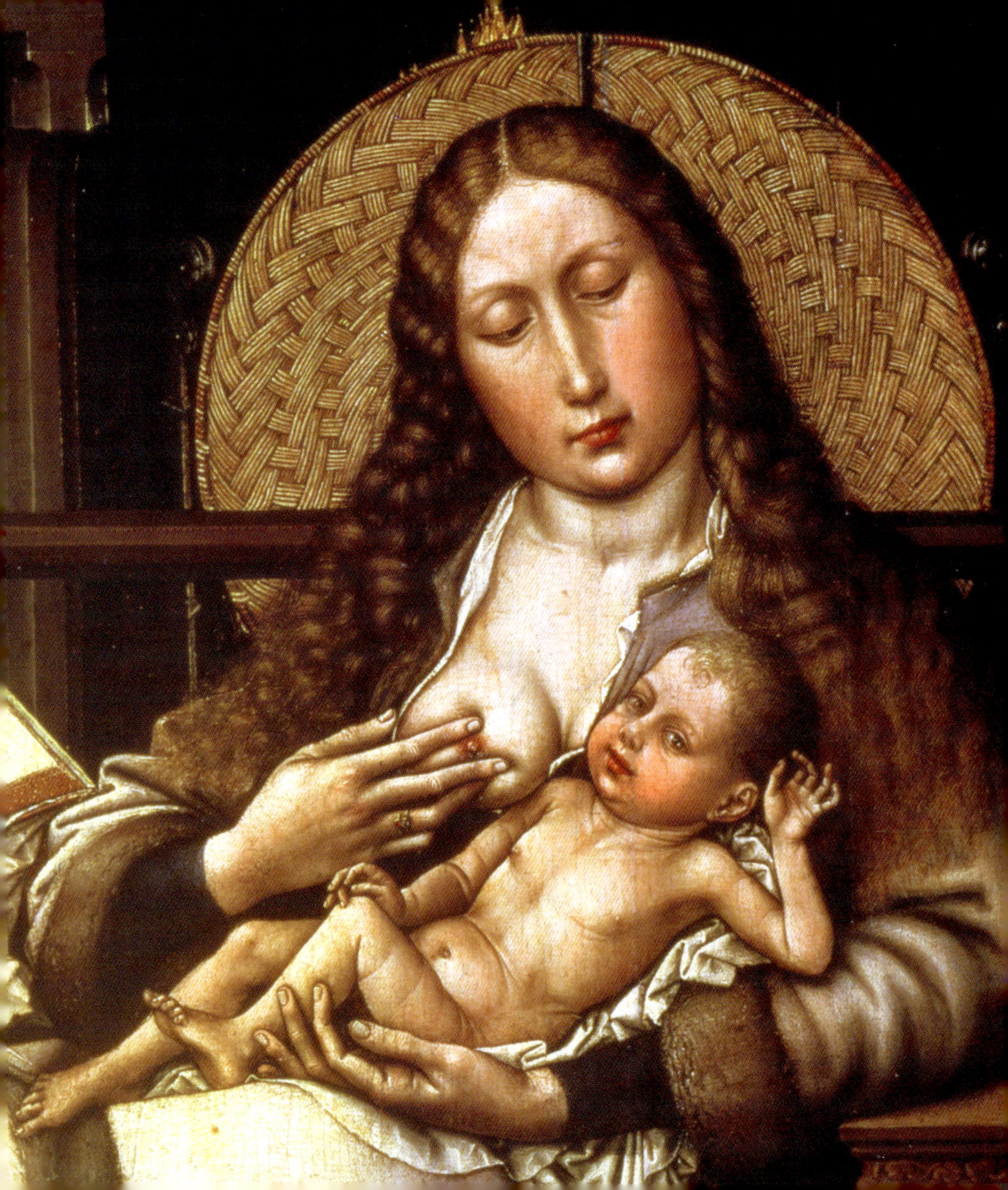

Painting North of the Alps

Whereas in Italy painting was already beginning to detach itself from the vocabulary of form of the Romanesque and Byzantine style in the late Duecento, in France, the German lands and the Netherlands, a new style did not evolve until the 14th century. The change can be seen in panel paintings, where, in the 15th century, a new technical device was introduced: oil painting. Whereas Italian painters gave proof of their new compositional consciousness by predominantly focusing on the depiction of space and physicality, the artists north of the Alps focused on draftsmanship to illustrate the change in the perception of the world. However, this new approach to a naturalistic, true-to-life depiction of humans, objects and landscapes still remained in a religious context even in northern European painting.

To modern viewers it may seem strange that a halo can at the same time serve as the screen of a fireplace. However, in around 1425 the Master of Flémalle – presumably to be identified with **Robert Campin** (*c.* 1375–1444) – painted a *Madonna lactans,* a Virgin nursing the Christ Child, placed in such a context. This was surely not an act of disrespect on the artist's part, even though Robert Campin's life may not have exactly corresponded to the Church doctrines. Documents from the archives have proven that Campin, who was born in Tournai on the Schelde River, a city at the time belonging to the French crown lands, was even banished for a year because of adultery. What can be detected, though, is a new interest in showing the material world both in a naturalistic way and yet imbued with spirituality. This new approach is comparable to the development of painting in 14th-century Italy. Both the composition and many details of the picturesque scene shown

Robert Campin,
Madonna of the Firescreen,
c. 1425, oil on panel,
63 × 49 cm, National Gallery,
London

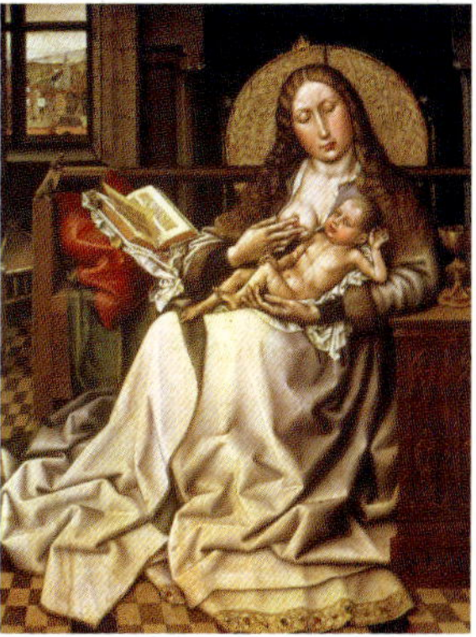

Jan van Eyck,
Arnolfini Marriage, 1434,
oil on wood,
82 × 60 cm without the lost frame,
National Gallery, London

here are full of religious allusions. Even though one of the wood panels to the right has been replaced at a later date – maybe due to restoration works – it can be presumed that the motifs of the painting have remained intact. Mary is sitting on a low wooden bench; together with a chalice, the Christ Child and an open book, she forms an even triangular composition. The Christ Child is supported by the Virgin, the book rests on a cushion; Mary's exquisite garment is arranged in many folds. Contemporary viewers would immediately have recognized the painting as an allusion to the Virgin Mary as *sedes sapientiae* (seat of wisdom). The two carved lions on the upper edge of the arm rest of the bench, beneath the window, are an allusion to King Solomon of the Old Testament, thus transforming this rather middle-class seat into a royal throne. The window proffers a view of a city dominated by a Gothic church. Both Mary and the church are painted in similar colors, white and blue, which identify them as mediators between heaven and earth. But in spite of all these religious connotations, the scene retains its intimate atmosphere. The Child has left off drinking and is turning

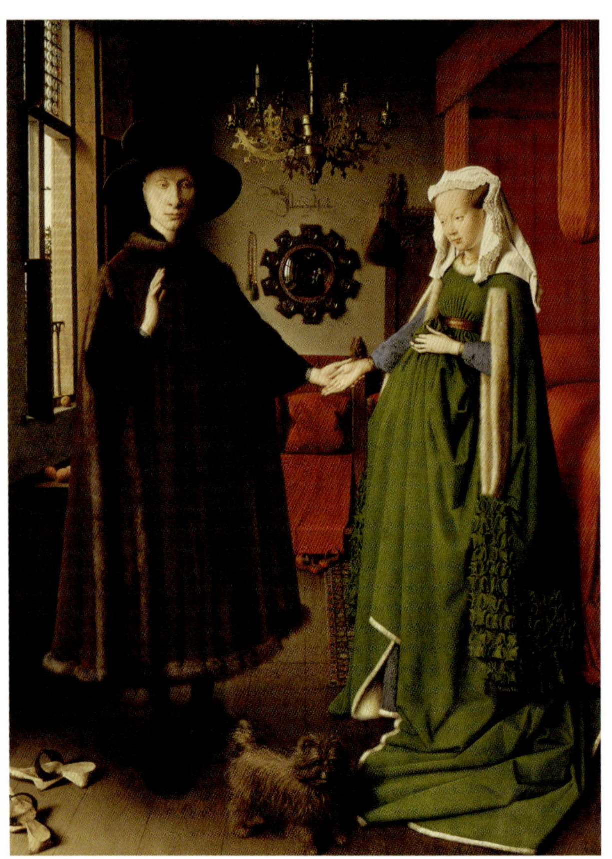

towards the viewer; His gaze is alert and innocent, the mouth is slightly open, there is a baby's dimple in his chin. The vivid expression of the Christ Child is conveyed through the means of very fine, sharp lines, a manifestation of the brilliant drawing abilities of the artist.

If the rich religious context of Robert Campin's Madonna seems far-fetched, then a true challenge comes in the person of **Jan van Eyck** (*c.* 1390–1441). His works are the highlights of Gothic art: he brought the technique of oil-based painting to perfection, excelled in atmospheric density and compositional skill. But what's more, his works abound in allusions and are exceedingly complex. The so-called *Arnolfini Marriage* may serve as an example. It is not even certain whose marriage is actually portrayed. But let us first describe the painting: it shows an indoor space, a man and a woman have joined hands. He is wearing a fur coat and a high hat, his right hand is lifted as if ready to declare on oath. She is wearing an exquisite dress, girdled relatively high; underneath it, her belly is protruding. This might mean that she was pregnant or that the two are planning to start a family. But there is an essential detail in the picture which the contemporary viewer would have recognized immediately: the bridegroom is offering the lady his left hand. This is the symbol of a morganatic marriage between two people of differing social rank, also called left-handed marriage. The partner of lower social rank would have no claim to titles, rights or entailed property. This means that the painting cannot possibly depict the marriage of Giovanni Arnolfini and Giovanna Cenami. Both came from rich merchant families and had the same social rank. In other words, we do not know who is por-

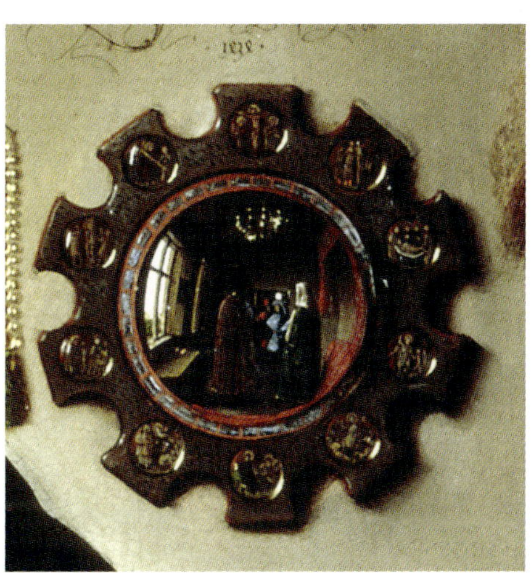

Jan van Eyck,
mirror, detail of the painting from p. 198

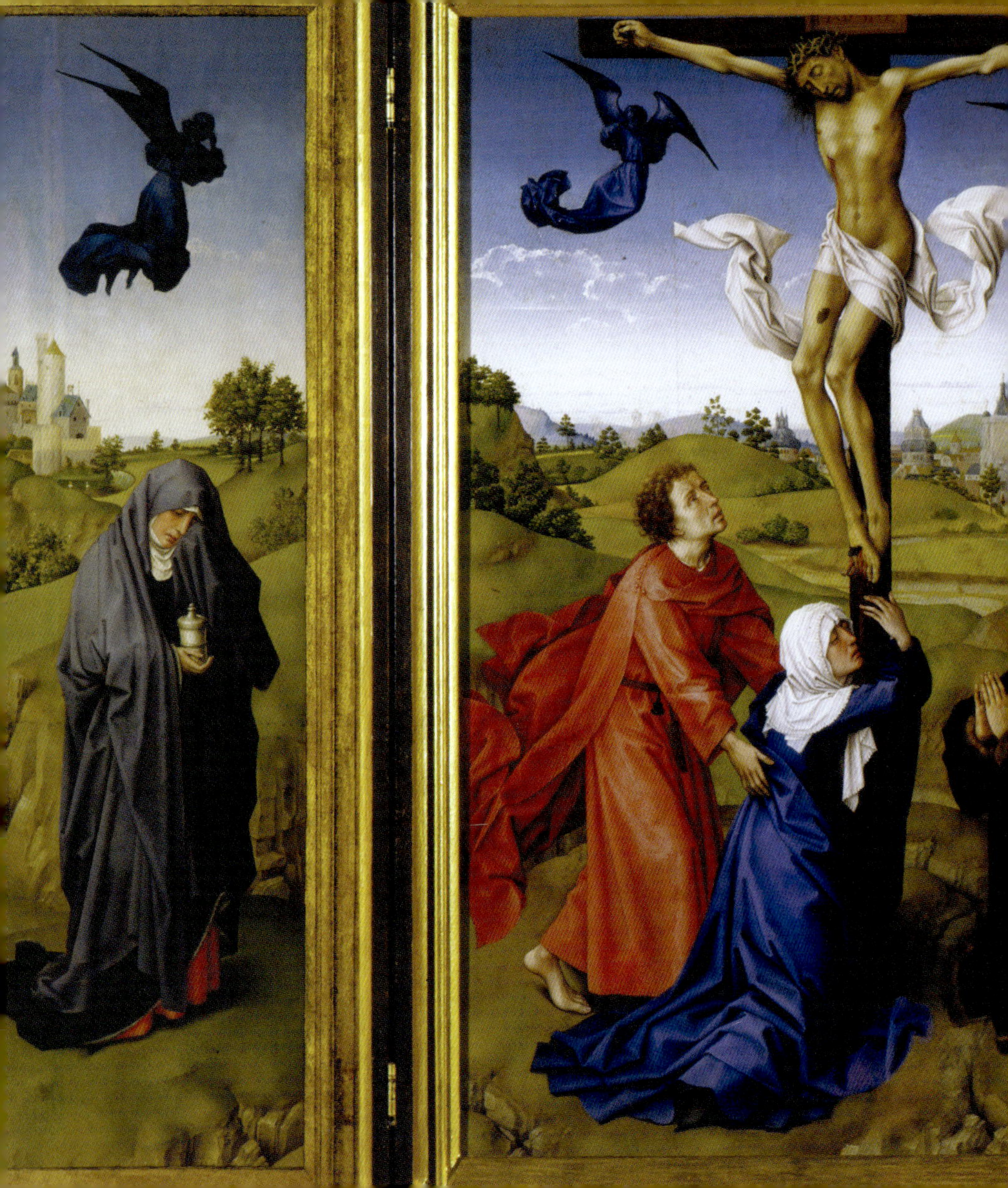

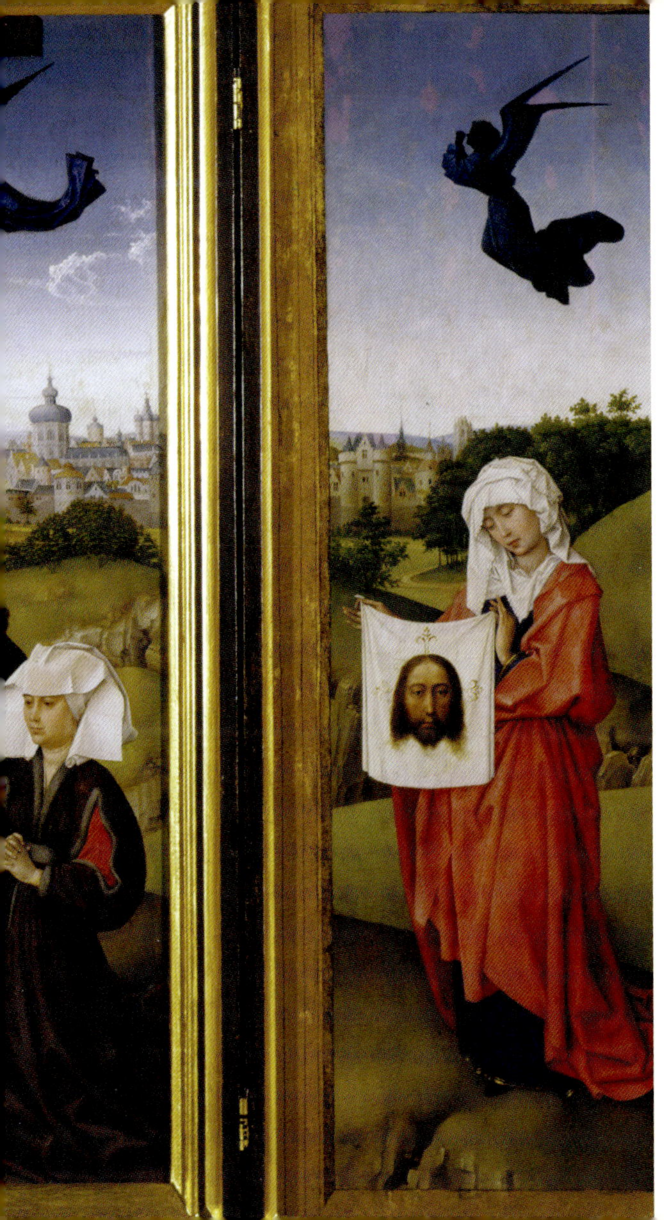

The upper part of the cross does not appear in the painting. This trick gives the effect of the dying Christ floating upward, away from the other figures, the landscape and the city.

Rogier van der Weyden,
Crucifixion Triptych, *c.* 1444,
oil on wood,
main panel 96 × 69 cm, side panels 101 × 35 cm each,
Kunsthistorisches Museum,
Vienna

trayed here. However, there are a few indicators to make us believe that van Eyck was not just the painter, but more familiar with the couple. Van Eyck's signature has been placed above the mirror, in a central position, thus dominating the pictorial reality. Also, instead of the usual *"fecit"* (painted by), the artist signed with a *"fuit hic"* (was here). This has led to the thesis that van Eyck might have been a friend of the bride and groom, and maybe even involved as witness. It would explain why he should introduce himself so overtly into the topic of the picture. On the other hand, he even plays with his absence because the mirror, decorated with a fine frame showing scenes from the Passion, does not show the reflection of a painter (p. 199). Instead, two more, unidentifiable, figures can be discerned in the doorway. Van Eyck is experimenting with the convex mirror whose curvature makes the room seem smaller than it actually is. Might one of the two figures actually be the artist himself? This complex painting leaves more questions than answers, because it is so rich in allusions. Underneath the mirror, there is a chair. The finial on the chair consists of a carving of St Margaret, the patron saint of pregnant women and childbirth. The dog at the lady's feet is a symbol of fidelity. In connection with the rosary, the broom can be understood as a symbol of the Christian law of prayer and work *(ora et labora)*. The patten clogs to the left of the picture, seemingly cast aside, not only underline the intimacy of the atmosphere, but also are arranged in a position reminiscent of the open female thighs during sexual inter-

Rogier van der Weyden,
view of the city,
detail of the triptych from
pp. 200, 201

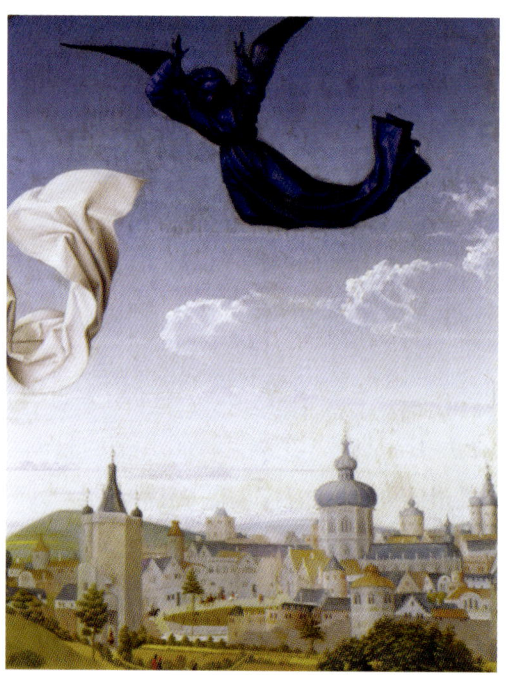

course. Is this just the lecherous imagination of an art historian? Van Eyck should never be underestimated. He consciously animates the viewer to find associations, maybe even to invent them, by artfully imbuing the work with a wide range of symbols and allusions.

Rogier van der Weyden (*c.* 1399–1464), who was also born in Tournai, was a pupil of Robert Campin. His *Crucifixion* triptych from around 1444 (pp. 200, 201) introduces an exciting new way of approaching the earthly and the heavenly spheres. At first sight, the donor figures are completely integrated into the scene; the saints are even lacking their haloes. The entire space, including the side panels, is a harmonious unity. Does this mean that there are no more differences between the spheres of Heaven and Earth? No. The artist simply develops them differently. For example, the cross is so high, or rather, the viewer's perspective is so close to the scene, that the upper part of the cross is beyond the edge of the picture and out of sight. The resulting impression is that of the dying Christ floating away from the other figures, the landscape and the town in the background. This town is meant to be Jerusalem. It is a mixture of a late medieval European city and an oriental one, with the typical bulbous spires (p. 202). To the left, we see the grieving John the Apostle and the Virgin Mary. To the right, the donors are seen kneeling; they are dressed in typical 15th-century middle-class robes. A cleft in the ground separates them from the other figures. There is also a difference in the choice of colors: the saints are dressed in red or

Rogier van der Weyden,
St Veronica with the sudarium, detail of the triptych from pp. 200, 201

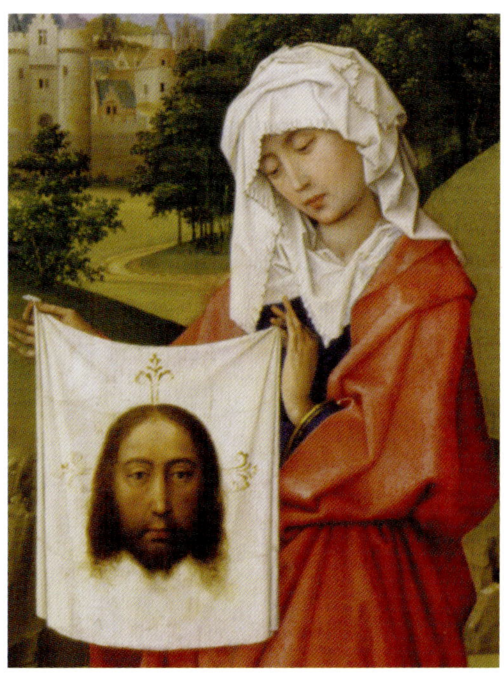

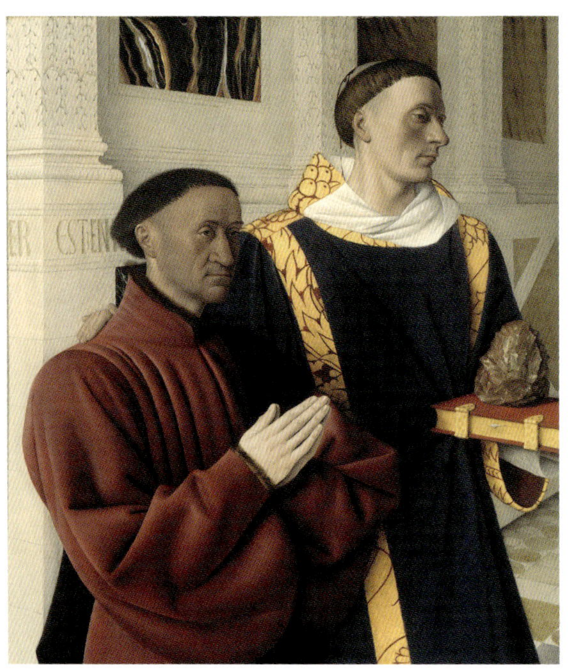

Jean Fouquet,
Étienne de Chevalier and St Stephen, left panel of the so-called Melun Diptych, *c.* 1450, oil on wood, 93 × 85 cm, Gemäldegalerie, Berlin

blue whereas the donors are depicted in subdued colors. The left side panel shows Mary Magdalene, who witnessed the Resurrection; the right side panel shows St. Veronica holding the sudarium (p. 203). The name Veronica comes from the Greek and means "Bearer of Victory". According to the New Testament, however, there was a woman who accompanied Christ to Calvary offering Him a towel to wipe off the blood and tears during the Passion. Her name was Veronica. Legend has it that Christ's imprint was left on that cloth. And so, a new etymology was devised for her name, consisting of the Latin term *vera* (true) and the Greek term *eikon* (image). During the Middle Ages, a cloth was found which was held to be St Veronica's sudarium. It quickly became both an important relic as well as an image of the likeness of Christ. In this painting, Veronica holds up a sudarium with the portrait of the Saviour; the specific iconography had been established in the 6th century.

In contrast to the *Crucifixion Triptych,* the so-called *Melun Diptych* (pp. 204, 205) shows a distinctive separation between the heavenly and the worldly spheres. It was commissioned by Étienne de Chevalier, treasurer at the French court, and was mounted above the tomb of his wife in the Church of Notre-Dame in Melun, as a devotional picture. The work was painted in around 1450 by **Jean Fouquet** (*c.* 1420–*c.* 1480), an illuminator and panel painter. The frame has not survived, but it was supposedly decorated with enamel medallions depicting scenes from the life of St. Stephen. The right-hand panel depicts the Virgin and Child, whereas the donor and his interceptor, St. Stephen, are on the left panel. As a symbol of his martyrdom, the saint is holding a book with a stone on it. But this is not just any stone or flint indicating that he was stoned to death; it is a huge, uncut gemstone. The precious stone is more appropriate for the stylish surrounding: the kneeling donor Étienne de Chevalier is wearing expensive robes, and the surrounding space, a marble-clad, luminous room, conveys a courtly ambience. The right-hand panel, on the other hand, is dominated by the colors blue, red and white. This seemingly innovative technique was actually influenced by manuscript illumination, where it was normal to restrict the color palette to a small range. The Virgin Mary with her bare breast corresponds yet again to the iconography of the *Madonna lactans.* The circular form of the breast has often been an object of derision. In fact, however, there are several geometric shapes used in this painting. The figure of Mary, for example, is arranged in a pyramidal composition. Even though this solution reflects a rather more cubist than organic (three-dimensional) approach to the depiction of a body, this, together with the red and blue angels that look as if they were varnished, heightens the magical atmosphere. Undoubtedly,

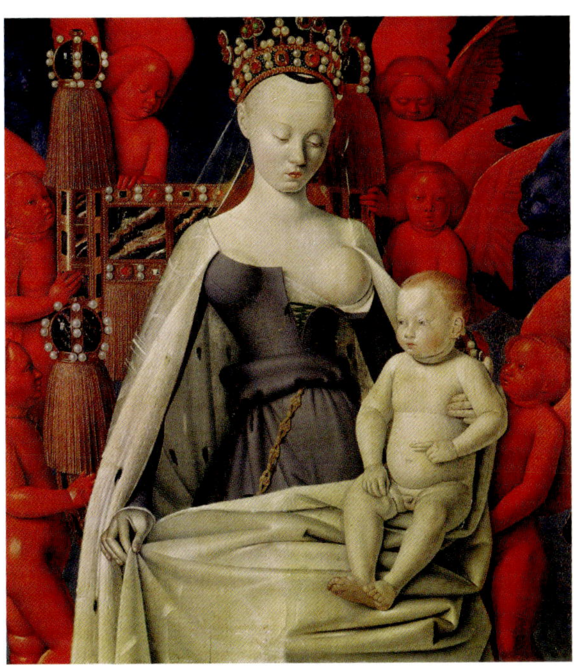

Jean Fouquet,
The Virgin and Child, right panel of the so-called Melun Diptych, *c.* 1450, oil on wood, 94 × 85 cm, Koninklijk Museum voor Schone Kunsten, Antwerp

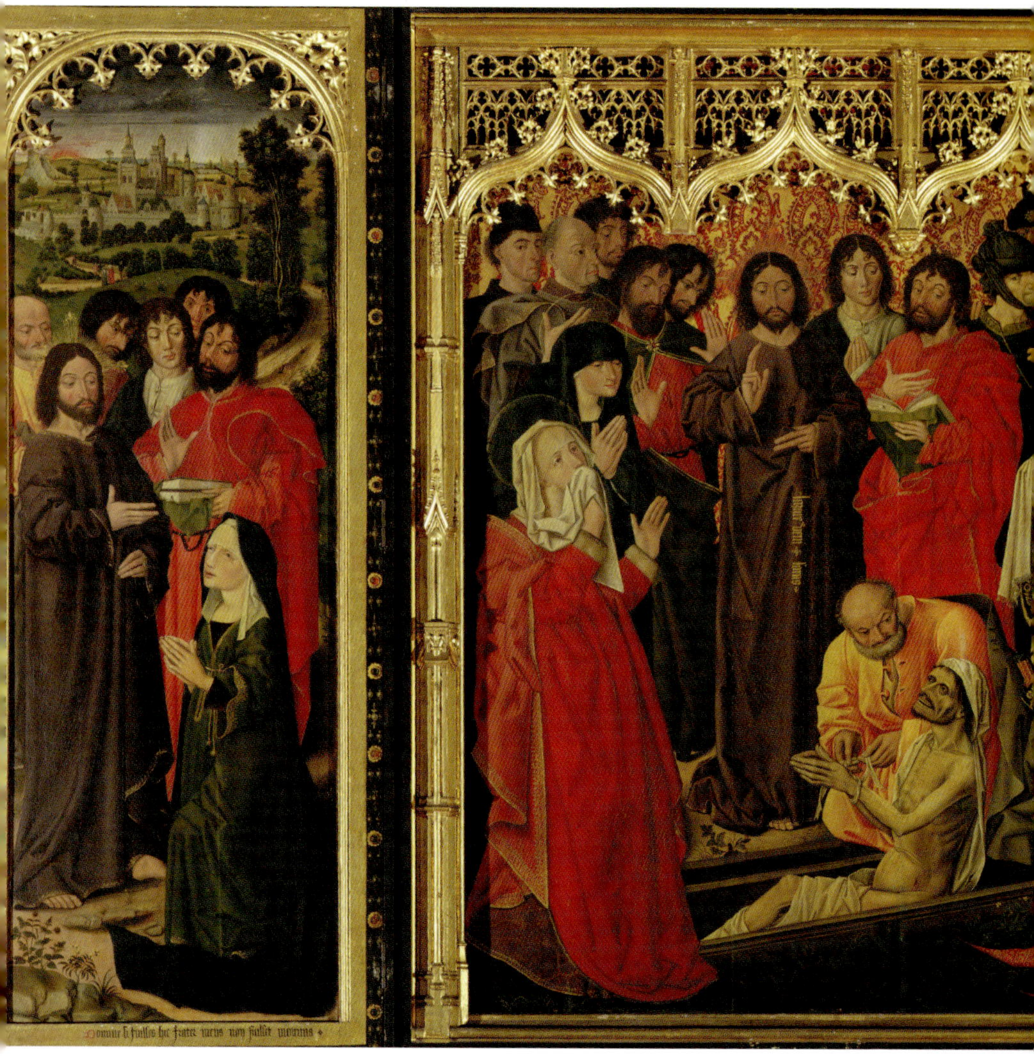
Domine si fuisses hic frater meus non fuisset mortuus

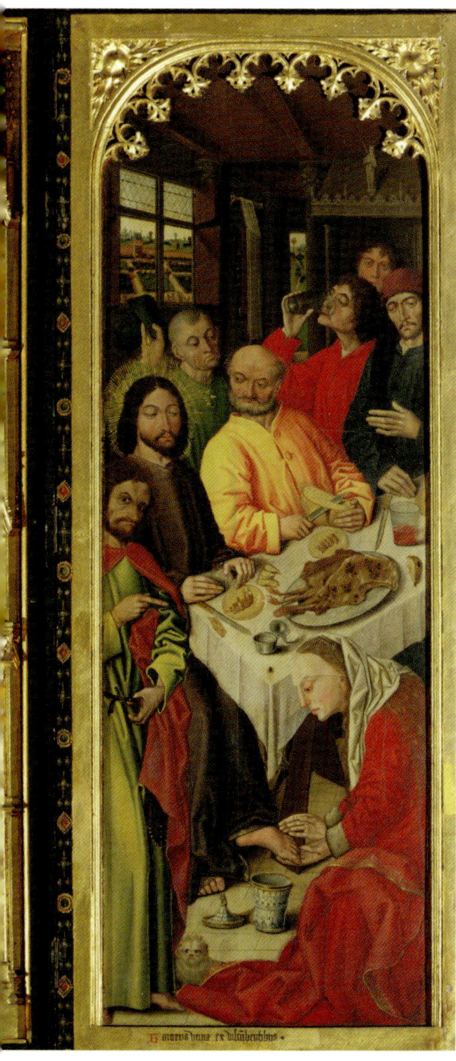

Étienne de Chevalier and the Virgin belong to two separate spheres. Both the pictorial space and the color scales are entirely different. It is the small Christ Child who connects the two spheres by pointing his finger at the donor, on the other panel of the Diptych.

Amongst the deeds of Jesus Christ depicted in art are His miraculous healings, never exemplified more perfectly than in the raising of the dead. In around 1461, **Nicolas Froment** (*c.* 1435–*c.* 1485) dedicated himself to this topic and painted the Lazarus Triptych. According to the Gospel of John in the New Testament, Lazarus was brought back to life by Jesus. In the center panel we see the deceased, bony and clad in loose folds of cloth, sitting up in his coffin. Christ, his hand raised in blessing, is surrounded by amazed onlookers. In 1467, Froment, who came from the Languedoc, moved to Avignon. He was the head of a very successful workshop that not only painted panels, but also created murals, devised coats of arms and designed glass paintings. Last but not

Nicolas Froment,
Lazarus Triptych, 1461,
oil on wood,
175 × 134 cm (center panel),
175 × 66 cm (side panels),
Uffizi, Florence

least, he also designed stage sets, which explains the theatrical atmosphere of the triptych. One aspect to underline this is the fact that the total of thirty figures do not engage in a spatial union with the landscapes painted in the background. What's more, they seem to be play acting, as can be seen in the right-hand panel: Jesus has been paying a visit to a Pharisee; a prostitute is washing His feet with her tears, then wiping them with her hair. The host to the front left is theatrically looking out of the picture, his taut lips expressing his disapproval. Christ said to him, "Her sins, which are many, are forgiven; for she loved much : but to whom little is forgiven, the same loveth little." (Luke 7, 36f.)

No stable, no crib, no Joseph: Stephan Lochner mixes the iconography of the Magi, the patron saints of Cologne, with that of the Enthroned Madonna.

Stephan Lochner (1400/1410–1451) was presumably born in Meersburg on Lake Constance. A document from the archives of Cologne proves that he bought a house there in 1442. It is known that he served twice as member of the city council of Cologne and that he died at the age of approximately fifty, possibly a victim of the plague. It was he who painted the altarpiece of the city patrons of Cologne, originally intended for the council chapel and now in Cologne Cathedral. The topic for the painting, created in around 1445, came naturally, since the city's entire pride was the relics of the Magi, which had been brought to Cologne in the twelfth century. Even the city's coat of arms, with the three crowns, alludes to these presumed three kings of the orient. A further intention was to honor the local saints, Gereon and Ursula, who were depicted on the insides of the side wings. When folded up, as was the case on usual working days, this altarpiece shows the Annunciation. The inside center panel shows the *Adoration of the Magi.* Mary is enthroned on a seat, the Christ Child on her lap is lifting a hand in blessing. No stable, no crib, no Joseph can be seen. This is due to the fact that the depiction is connected with the painting type referred to as Maestà, a representation showing the enthroned Madonna and Child surrounded by saints or angels, but usually not including

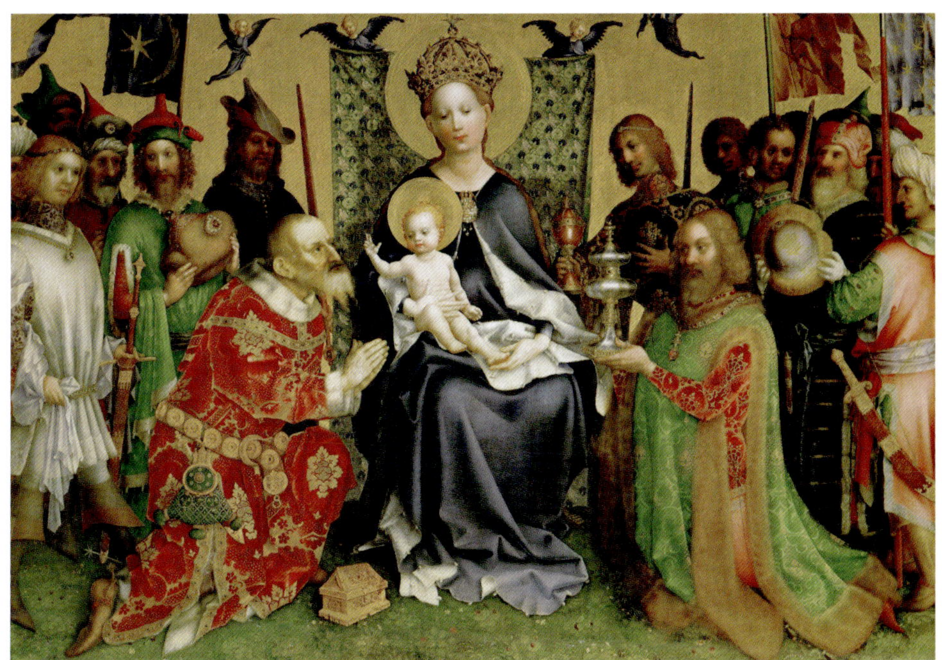

the Magi. Lochner alludes to the motifs and stylistic features of the International style of Gothic art by introducing luxurious garments and depicting the Magi with soft facial features. Traditional aspects of decorative devotional art are here combined with strong naturalistic elements.

Stephan Lochner,
Altar of the Patron Saints of Cologne, center panel,
painting on wood and (in part) canvas,
238 × 263 cm,
Cathedral of St. Peter and Mary, Cologne

Konrad Witz (1400–1446), too, imbued his painting with old-fashioned piety. It is assumed that this representative of the Late Gothic school of the Upper Rhine area was born in Rottweil and died in Basle. Time and again, Witz sought inspiration in stories of the saints, such as the *Legenda aurea,* a collection compiled by Jacobus de Voragine in the 13th century. One of the stories deals with the giant Christopher, who is

The magic atmosphere of this waterside landscape with its gigantic rocks is underlined by a pictorial trick: the rocks further in the background have the same sharp contour, but are lighter in color than the ones in the fore-ground.

searching for the greatest king on Earth and finally makes his living by carrying loads across a river. One night, a small boy demands to be carried across the river. It is Jesus Christ, and while carrying him, Christopher feels the weight of the whole world on his shoulders. Konrad Witz places this scene in his painting of St Christopher from around 1435 in a riverscape dominated by soaring rocks. The figure of the giant is bent forward to show the weight he is bearing in spite of the Christ Child being so small. The astonished expression of St Christo-pher is charming; it illustrates that he is realizing that some-thing quite unheard of is happening to him.

Chronologically, **Hans Memling** (*c.* 1433–1494) is the last representative of central European Gothic painting. His panel painting showing Scenes from the Passion (pp. 212, 213, 214, 215) is barely 1 × 1.5 meters and was painted in around 1480. A comparison with the fresco by Andrea da Firenze (pp. 190, 191), which was done roughly 100 years earlier, illus-trates once more the parallel development of Gothic painting, even though north of the Alps it evolved decades later than it did in Italy. But we can also make out some clear differences, not only in the technique, but also in the manner of expres-sion. Memling transforms the wide landscape with its many figures into an enclosed pictorial space. The depictions function both in detail and in the work's entirety. The beholder sees a city from a bird's-eye perspective unfolding before him like a stage set: Jerusalem, depicted as a medieval fortified city embellished with oriental-style towers, turrets and domes. The rising sun to the top right explains the extreme use of shade. The scene showing the Last Supper, to the left, can thus justly be depicted as taking place in the dark and lit by candles. This kind of depiction is referred to as a simultaneous representa-tion, because several – in this case, twenty-three – situations which actually took place in chronological order are depicted simultaneously. Read in a zigzag line from top left to bottom left, we see the Entry into Jerusalem, the Expulsion of the

Money-Lenders from the Temple, the Last Supper, the Prayer on the Mount of Olives, and the Seizing of Jesus. From the bottom right to the top right, equally in a zigzag line, we see the Carrying of the Cross, the Resurrection and the Risen Christ Appearing at Emmaus. The center of the painting is dominated by the palace (pp. 214, 215). In here, Christ is mocked, flagellated, brought before the people, and condemned. The cross is being carpentered in the palace courtyard. The painting abounds in a variety of details, each of which serves as a specific allusion. Close to the scene depicting the Last Supper, there is a cock sitting in a window. "Before a cock crows, you will deny Me three times," Jesus said to Peter during the supper. And finally, the scene depicting Christ's meeting with Pontius Pilate inside the palace is framed by sculptures in the facade alluding to the Judgment of Solomon. However, Pilate's decision will not be so wise as that of Solomon.

Konrad Witz,
St Christopher, 1435,
tempera on wood,
102 × 81 cm,
Kunstmuseum, Basle

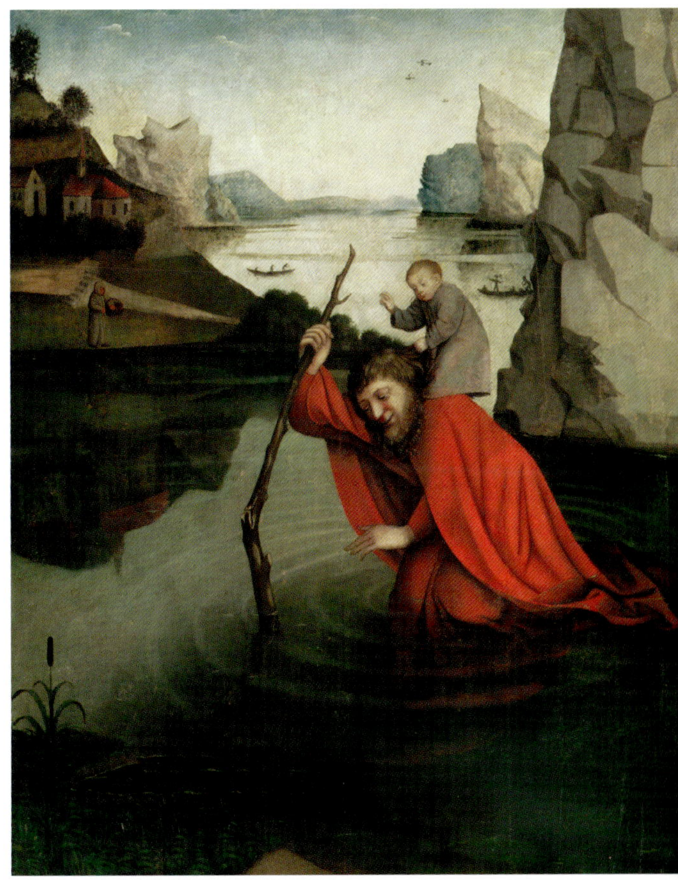

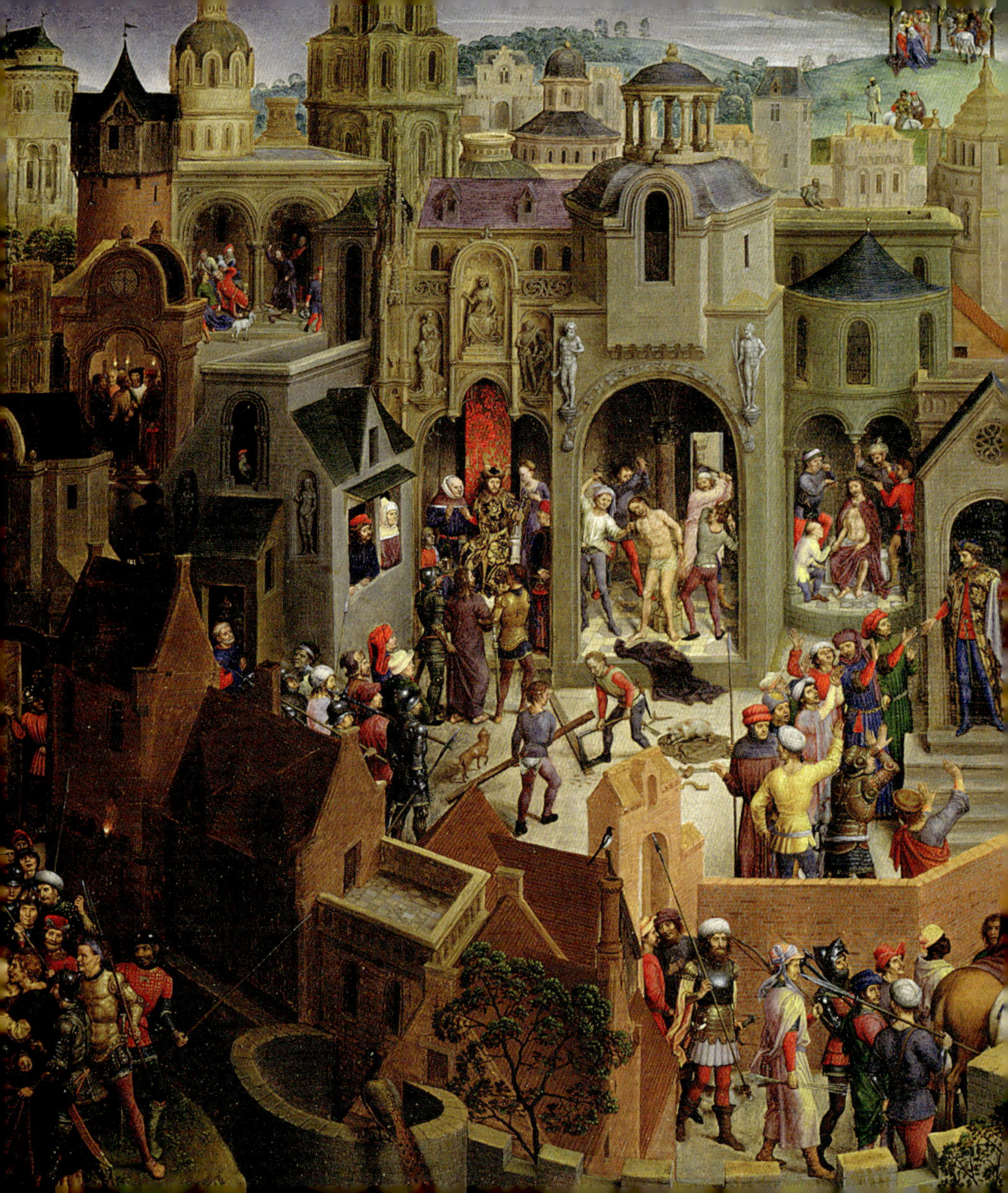

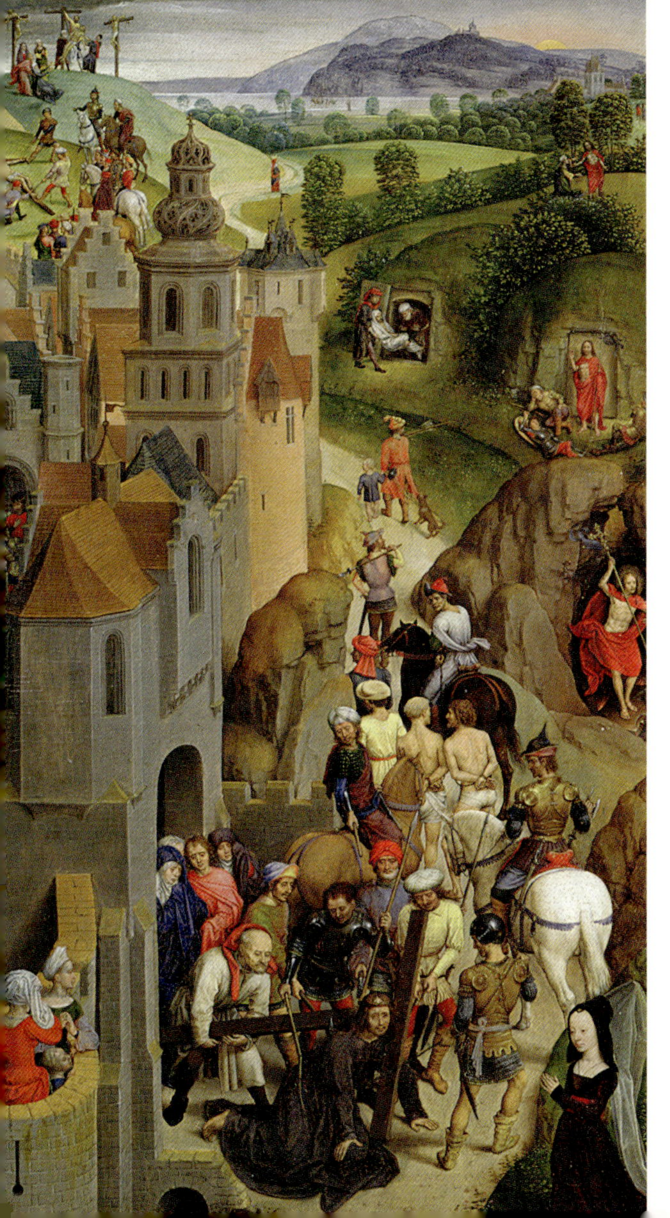

Hans Memling,
The Passion of Christ, *c.* 1480,
oil on wood, 57 × 92 cm,
Galleria Sabauda, Turin

Following double spread:
Hans Memling,
The Flagellation, the Crown of Thorns, the Making of the Cross; details of the Passion of Christ from pp. 212, 213

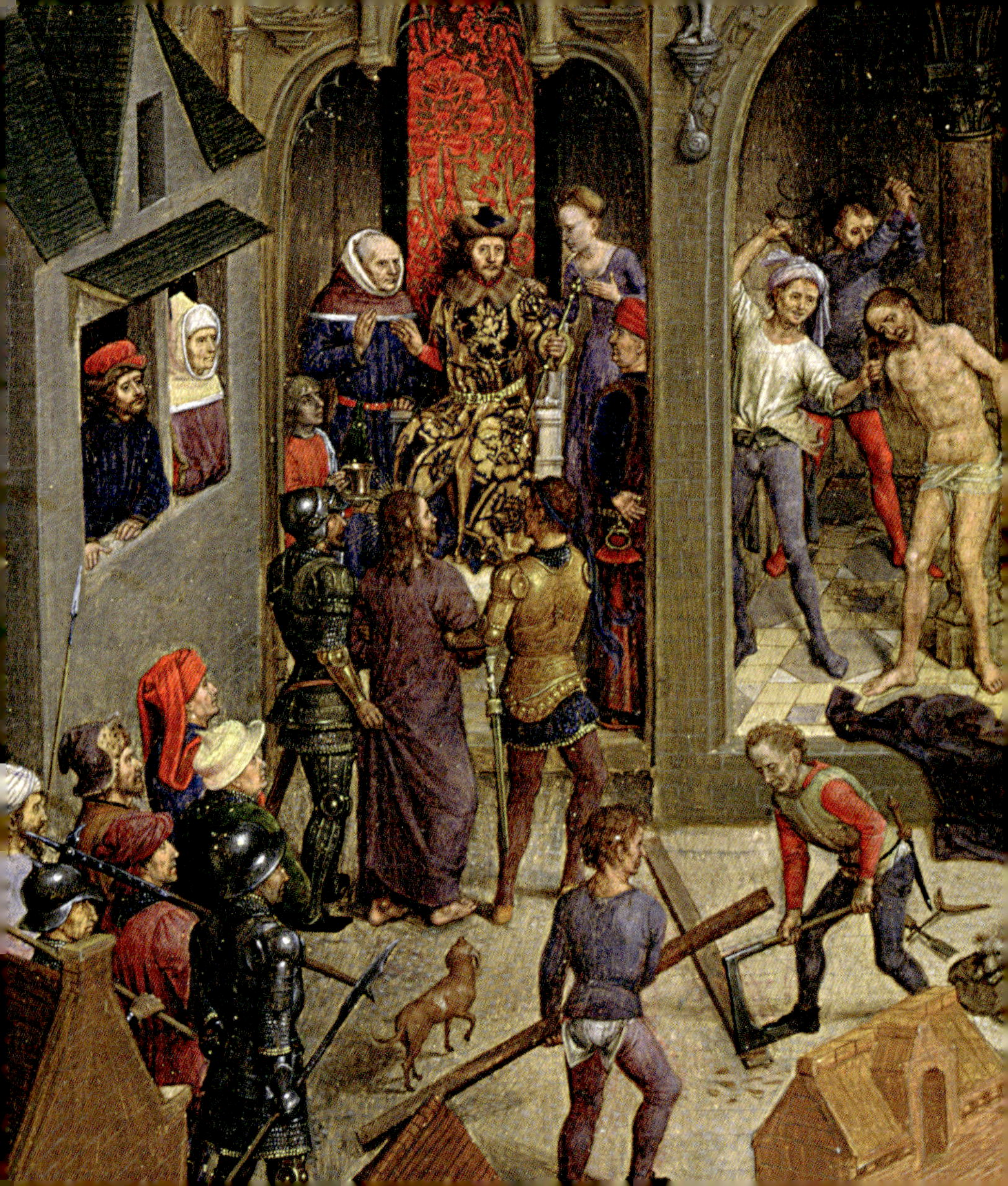

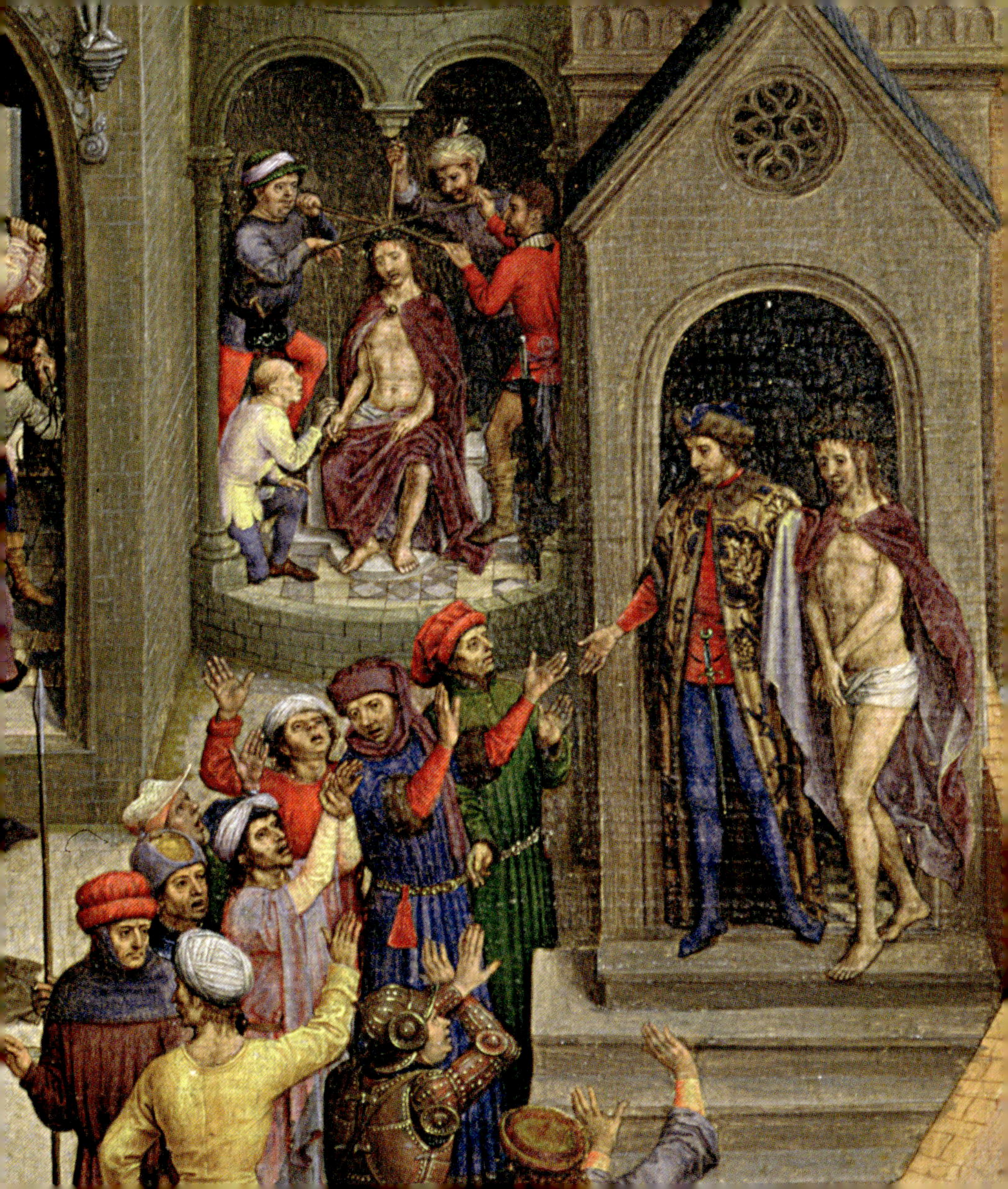

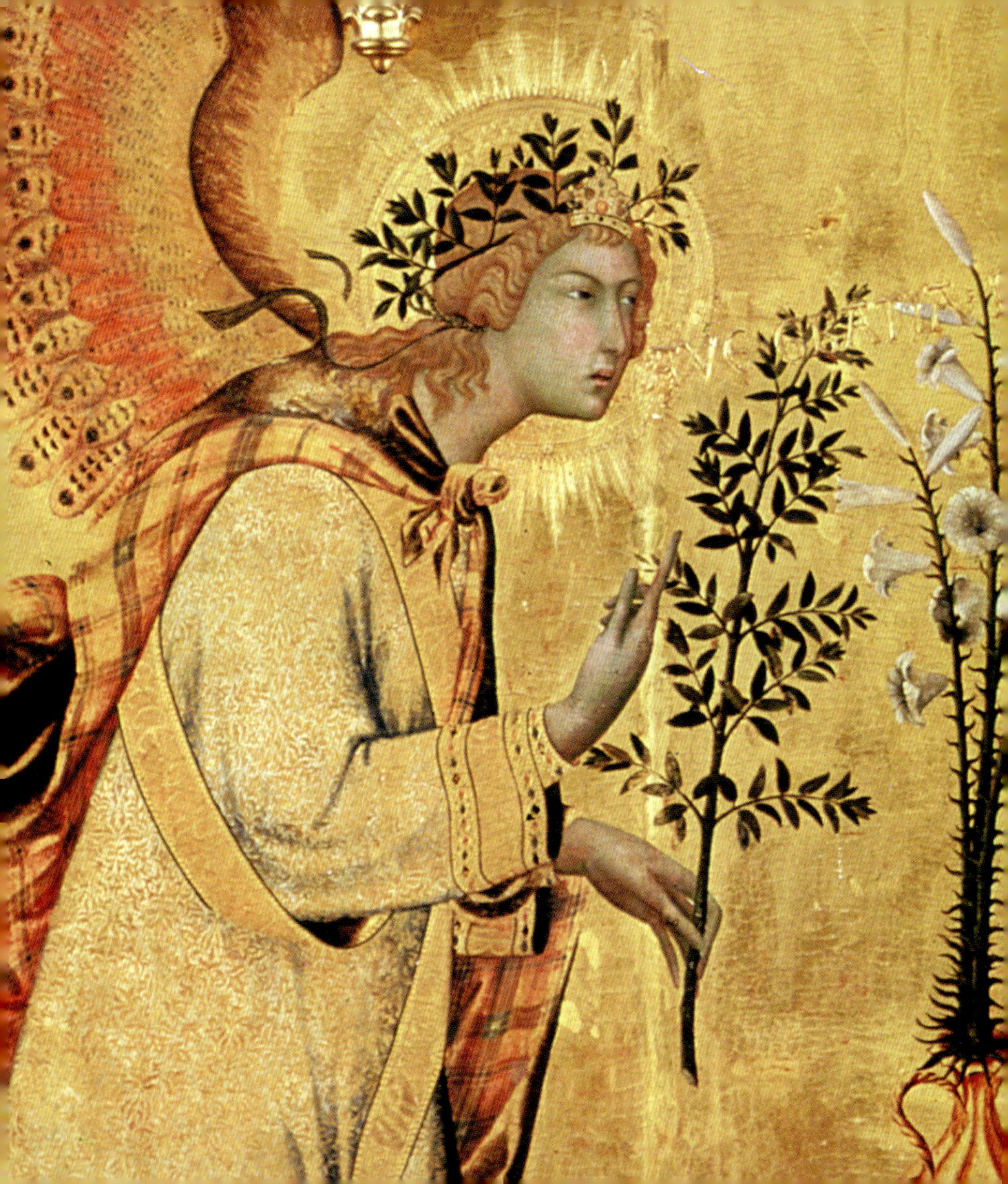

The Blessed Virgin and Child – Gothic Painters and their Style

An artist's style and interest can best be determined by analyzing and comparing painting with a similar topic. What does style actually mean? The term comes from the Greek and originally meant a writing tool. In a figurative sense, it means the way someone paints. This way, this personal "handwriting", can best be seen when comparing artists who handled the same topic, or the same motif. A stylistic comparison helps, in retrospect, to determine certain characteristics of which the artist himself might not even have been conscious. This feature is especially apparent when analyzing fakes. If, for example, a clever painter of the 19th century has created a painting, faking it to be a much older work of art, this fake might mislead people for several decades. But after a while the inevitable style of the forger's own times shine through, because style can only be influenced so much. Style is influenced by viewing patterns of a certain era, a certain surrounding, of individual models and every person's unique view of the world. Every painter has his

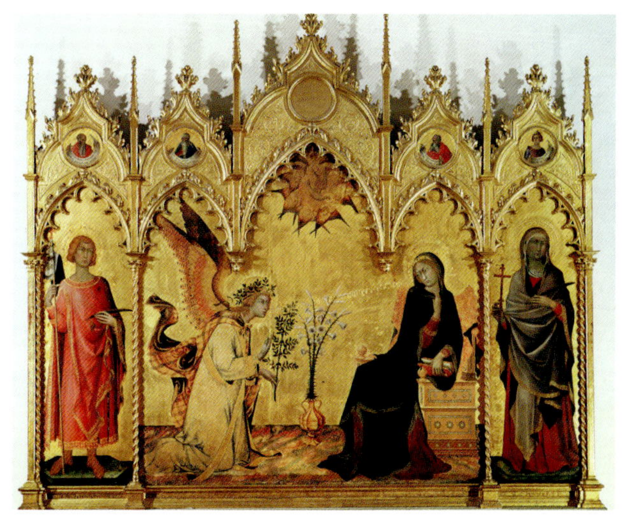

Simone Martini,
Annunciation Altarpiece,
1333,
tempera on wood,
263 × 305 cm,
Uffizi, Florence

own style, just like every person has their own distinctive handwriting. If the style of two artists seems similar, this does not mean that they have the same style, but that we are not trained well enough to realize the differences. But style is not the only thing that we can detect when comparing pictures with the same topic: an artist's specific interests show equally well. What did he add, which elements did he ignore, what did he invent or combine? The following chapter is devoted to two narrative motifs: the first will analyze Annunciations created within a period of 100 years. Subsequently, we will focus on the "Enthroned Madonna" paintings of artists from one generation.

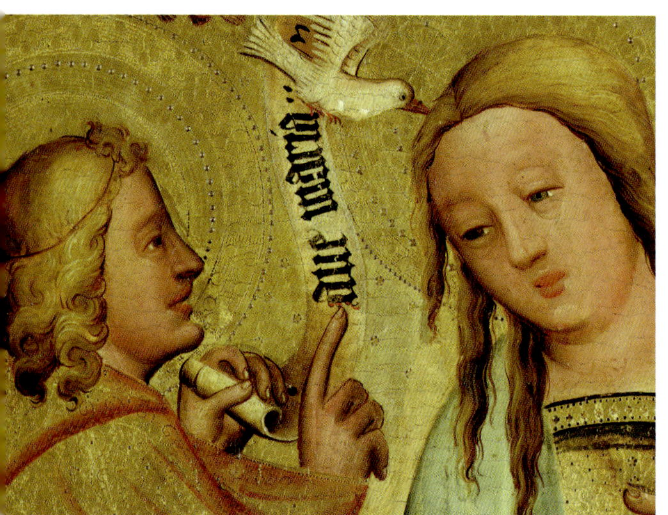

Master Bertram of Minden,
Archangel Gabriel and the Virgin Mary,
detail of the Annunciation from p. 219

Archangel Gabriel and the Virgin – Five Annunciations

More than a thousand paintings have survived from the Gothic period dealing with the Annunciation, the scene where Archangel Gabriel visits Mary. Accordingly, the topic is especially appropriate for comparing paintings from a period of over 100 years. The five examples presented here are altarpieces, done in tempera or oil on wood. We are going to analyze how the depictions relate to the story as it is told in the Bible and interpreted in later writings, and what kind of pictorial solutions the artists came up with. The Annunciation is described in the New Testament, Luke I, 28–31: "And the angel came in unto her, and said, Hail, thou that art highly favored, the Lord is with thee." Mary reacts frightened and confused, but the angel speaks on: “Fear not, Mary, for thou hast found favor with God. And, behold, thou shalt conceive in thy womb, and bring forth a son, and shalt call his name Jesus. He shall be great, and shall be called the Son of the Highest.” The future Mother of God asks the angel a few more questions and then agrees: “Behold the handmaid of the Lord.”

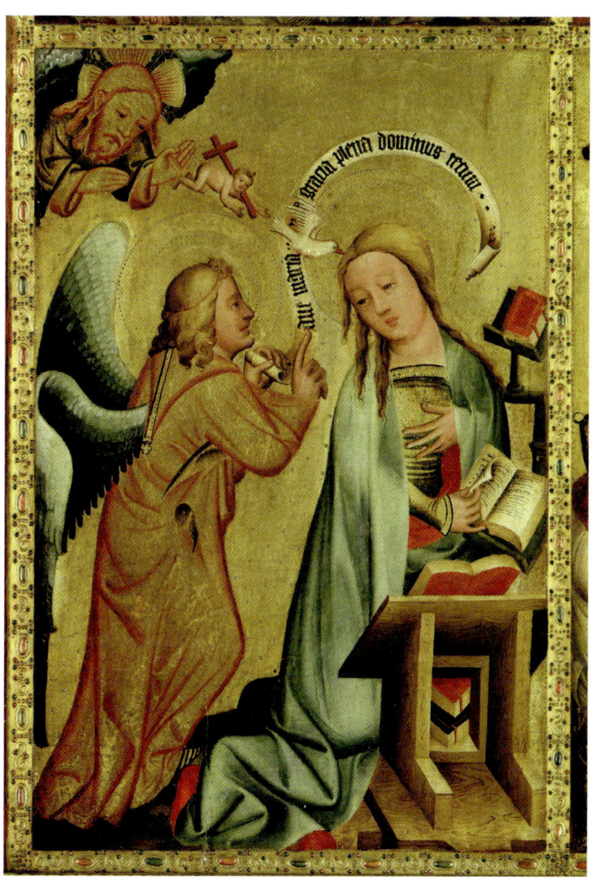

Master Bertram of Minden,
Annunciation scene from the Grabow Altarpiece, *c.* 1383, painting on wood, 277 × 726 cm (entire altar), Kunsthalle, Hamburg

Where did this encounter take place? In the Bible, it merely says that the angel came “in unto” Mary. This leads to the supposition that the scene took place indoors. But how this space was to have looked was entirely up to the artist’s imagination. And so the encounter between Mary and the angel is at times depicted in a middle-class living space, or in a courtly great hall, or even in a sacred space. The pictorial representation was not only based on the Bible source, but on later interpretations as well. These included the Apocrypha; the annotations by the Cistercian St Bernard of Clairvaux; the version told in the *Legenda aurea* by Dominican Jakobus de Voragine; and the *Vita rhythmica* by Walther of Rheinau. The idea that Mary might have been interrupted by the angel while reading or praying led to a multitude of representations in art showing the Blessed Virgin with a prayer book in her hands, at a lectern, kneeling on a prayer bench, or in the act of writing. All of these furnishings allowed the artist to show off his talent, but the objects are equally understood as Christian symbols. The Madonna lily (lat. *Lilium candidum* for bright white) and the depiction of glasses, for example, were symbols of Mary's virginity. On the other hand, the representation of everyday objects, clothes and private spaces also helped to make the beholder realize that this divine incident actually happened.

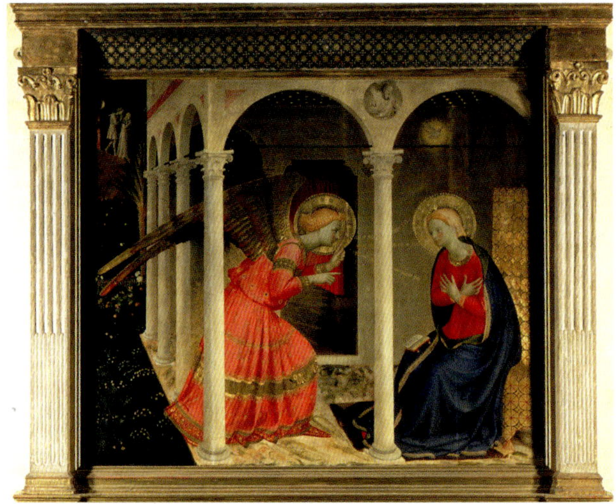

Fra Angelico,
Annunciation Altarpiece,
c. 1430, tempera on wood,
175 × 180 cm,
Diocesan museum, Cortona

The Annunciation altar panel from the St. Ansano Chapel in Siena Cathedral dates from 1333 (pp. 216, 217) and is the work of **Simone Martini** (1284–1344). Surviving documents prove that Martini painted it together with his brother-in-law, Lippo Memmi. However, it remains unclear which parts should be ascribed to Memmi. The solemn and remote looking figures with their elegant poses and elongated limbs are typical of the style of Simone Martini. He has also given special attention to the various textures of the surfaces, from the marble floor to the metal receptacle, and from the Madonna lilies to the luxuriously trimmed gowns. The Archangel Gabriel and the Blessed Virgin are flanked by two saints. In the gables above, there are four small tondi depicting the heads of prophets. In the large center spandrel of the frame, which is made up of pointed arches, a choir of cherubim is grouped around the Dove, symbol of the Holy Spirit. The main picture shows the angel kneeling before Mary, who is seated. His words of greeting are painted onto the gilded background: *"Ave gratia plena dominus tecum"* ("Hail, thou that art highly favored, the Lord is with thee"). The Virgin looks frightened, she is shrinking back. With her right hand, she is securely clutching her cloak while with her left hand she is marking the page of her prayer book, which she had been studying. There are more quotations from Luke on Gabriel's stole and on his sleeve, as for example *"Ne timeas"* ("Fear not"). In other words, the artist is here depicting the moment when the angel arrives and Mary is taken by surprise. This is further underlined by the angel's cloak, which is billowing behind him, as if he had only just stopped his flight. Simone Martini uses written text passages to refer to the ensuing plot of the Biblical story.

Our next piece, a German Annunciation from fifty years later, is still very much indebted to the medieval pictorial schemes. The so-called Grabow Altarpiece from around 1383 (pp. 218, 219) was made by **Master Bertram of Minden** (1340–*c.* 1414) and was originally used for the high altar of St. Peter's in Hamburg. It came to Grabow in the 18th century – a stroke of luck, since St. Peter's was severely damaged during the Hamburg fire of 1842. With the inner wings folded in and the outer wings folded out, the altarpiece displays a total of twenty-four individual scenes. The center of the second row

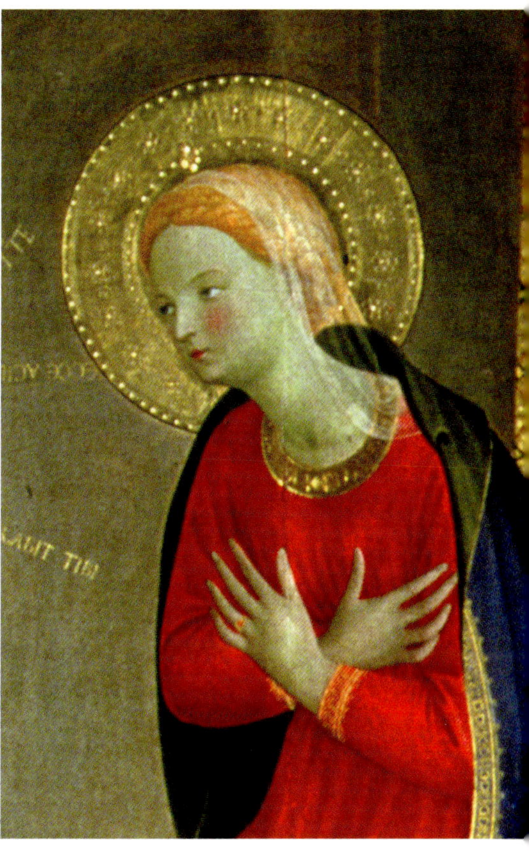

Fra Angelico,
Virgin Mary,
detail of the Annunciation from p. 220

shows the Annunciation, the Nativity and the Adoration. The Annunciation is painted on a gilt background. Only a wooden lectern reminds us of the spatial context; there are no other pointers. The drapery is characterized by angular folds, the faces are very flat. All of these aspects remind one rather of medieval manuscript illuminations, but Master Bertram also strove to introduce some variations. For example, the angel is shown in profile, whereas Mary, her head lowered, is shown in three-quarter view. The angel's words are recorded in a banderole, starting in Gabriel's left hand and unwinding to form Mary's halo. This banderole is the only one in all the many scenic paintings of the altarpiece. The fact that the angel's words, as documented in the Bible, are quoted in several Annunciation scenes allows the assumption that the Word of God, voiced in this situation, was held to be exceedingly important. The artists did not dare to simply convey the event through their medium, the picture.

Jan van Eyck,
Archangel Gabriel,
detail of the Annunciation from p. 223

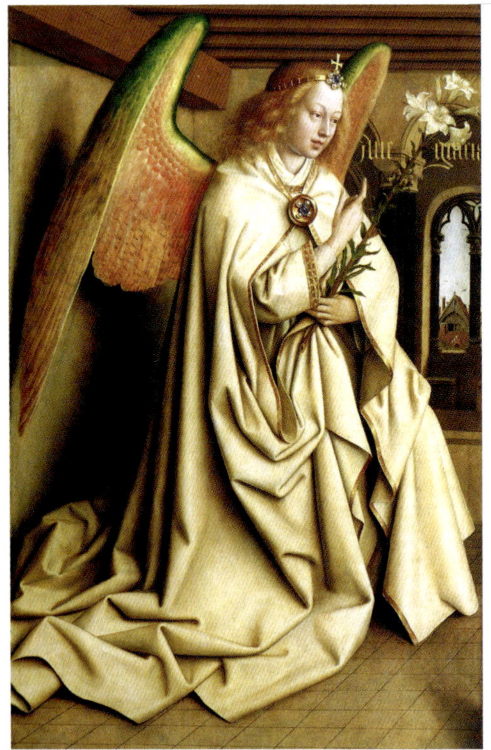

In around 1430, **Fra Angelico** (*c.* 1395–1455) painted an exemplary work of the Italian Late Gothic: the altarpiece for Cortona (pp. 220, 221). The main panel shows the Annunciation, the five paintings of the predella also show scenes from the life of Mary, amongst others her Betrothal and her Burial. Two more versions exist of the Annunciation with the same pictorial arrangement; one is in San Giovanni Valdarno close to Arezzo, the other is now in the Museo del Prado in Madrid. Both of these originate from the school of Fra Angelico; some art historians even ascribe them to the artist himself. This means that the clients were highly satisfied with the pictorial solution presented by Fra Angelico. His style is characterized by the soft faces of the figures and the vividly colored robes. The interior spaces are usually left rather sober, thereby offering a calm background for the various, ornamentally designed zones. What is most remarkable is the way Fra Angelico creates the effect of depth by overlapping various pictorial planes and painting receding rows of columns. However, he does not create the effect of space purely for art's sake: Fra Angelico separates the realms of Mary and Gabriel by placing a column between them; this is to underline the two different spheres, the celestial and the earthly. In the background, there is a small depiction of the Expulsion of Adam and Eve from the Garden of Eden. This has symbolic value, since the Fall and the consequences this entailed, as described in the Old Testament, ultimately led to Salvation, in the New Testament. Jesus Christ is born to deliver mankind from sin. Fra Angelico intertwined the plots of Old Testament Expulsion and New Testament Annunciation to indicate that the latter event stands beyond all temporality. As the name indicates, Fra Angelico was not just a painter, but a friar as well. He joined the Dominican Order although he came from a wealthy family that did not need to send their progeny into a monastery. The small pictures on the socles of the flanking pilasters indi-

Jan van Eyck,
Annunciation scene from the Ghent Altarpiece, *c.* 1430, oil on wood, 375 × 260 cm (with wings closed), St. Bavo Cathedral, Ghent

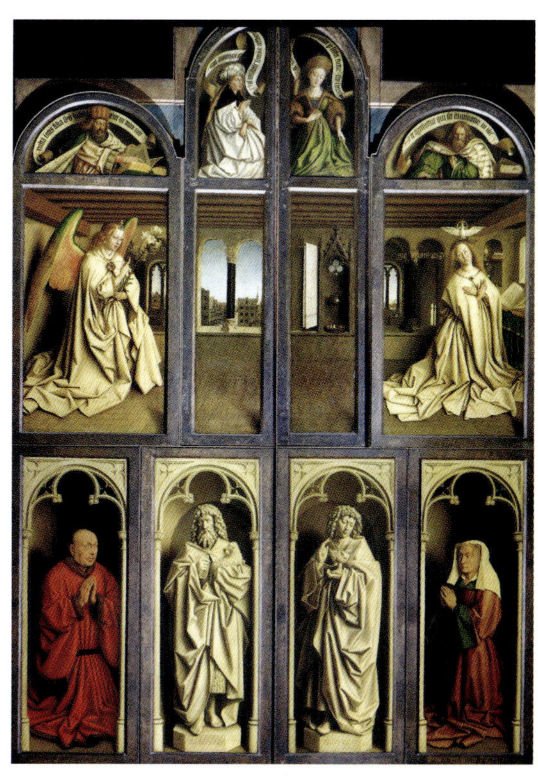

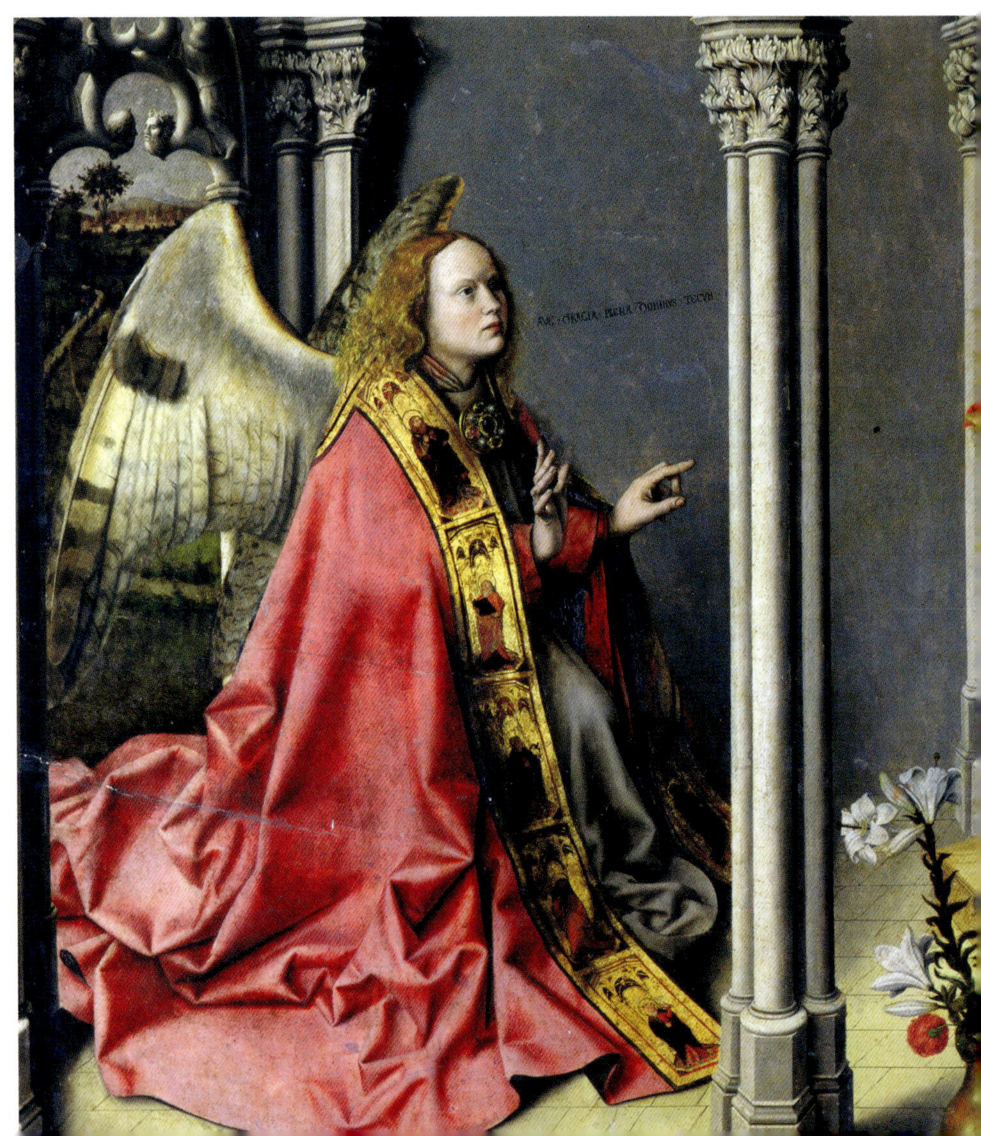

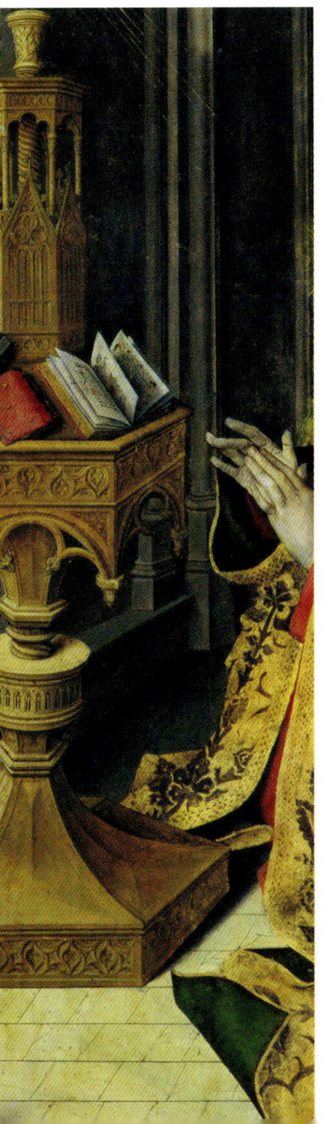

cate that this altarpiece was intended for use in a Dominican priory: they illustrate two scenes from the life of St. Dominic.

According to a dedication added later, the Ghent Altarpiece (pp. 222, 223) stems from before 1432. The dedication states that the panel was started by the elder of the two alleged brothers van Eyck, Hubert van Eyck. After his death, so it is said, Jan van Eyck completed the work. However, owing to stylistic analysis and a close study of documents in the archives, recent research has put forward the assumption that it is the sole work of **Jan van Eyck** (*c.* 1390–1441). The altar was already highly renowned in the late 15th century. There are so many correlations and allusions that every decade a new interpretation is presented by art historians. The *Annunciation* is placed in the center of the outside wings. Here, too, the written letters of the Biblical source hold an important place, but the artist is presenting a number of variations: the angel's salute rings from his mouth toward Mary. Her acquiescence, voiced through her *"Ecce ancilla domini"* ("Behold the handmaid of the Lord"), habitually marks the end of the scene. Here, however, it is depicted upside down – maybe because

Aix Annunciation,
Archangel Gabriel,
detail of the Annunciation from
p. 227

Who is the master responsible for this Annunciation? The list of possible artists is long; and our tools of comparative observation are not fine enough to make a final decision.

her answer addresses the Holy Spirit, who hovers close above her head, in the form of a dove. The overall representational space, divided into four panels, shows the two protagonists on the outer panels; there are only two slender panels in the center. Of these, the left-hand panel affords a view of a Flemish-style city seen through two round arches – a rather prominent spot within the composition. In other words, the *Annunciation* is set in 15th-century Ghent. On the right-hand center panel, we can discern a niche with a wash bowl, a jug and a cloth. This motif, as well as the glass vessel by the window just behind Mary, which is highlighted by rays of sunlight, is an allusion to Mary's virginity. The angel is far too large for the room with the low wooden ceiling (p. 222). Is this a mistake on the artist's side? Not so. Rather, van Eyck is making the divinity of the visitor visible to us. This effect is all the stronger because all the other details have been painstakingly given a naturalistic likeness. The detailed Madonna lily, for instance, could have been taken from a botanical reference book. Even the characteristic long stalk of this plant has been marked. Also, van Eyck has amused himself by playing with the wooden frame of the various panel parts. These, in a way, separate the scene, but by painting the shadows onto the scene where the *Annunciation* takes place, the beholder has the impression that the real wooden frames actually are a part of the depicted scene.

The **Aix Annunciation** (pp. 224, 225, 227), painted by an unknown master, brings our first survey of paintings with the same topic to an end. It was commissioned in around 1445 by the cloth merchant Pietro Corpivi. The altarpiece from Aix-en-Provence unites stylistic influences and pictorial solutions of various periods and regions. The influence of the Italian school can be seen in the treatment of the light, and the architectural construction with receding rows of columns. But there are also traces of the Netherlandish style, for instance the sharp contours of the figures, and the love for narration and detail, which shows especially in the depiction of objects. The artist manages to weave all these influences into one unique style. The figures remain in their position as if they were frozen, and look past each other in solemn detachment.

Aix Annunciation,
c. 1445, 155 × 176 cm,
oil on wood,
Ste. Madeleine,
Aix-en-Provence

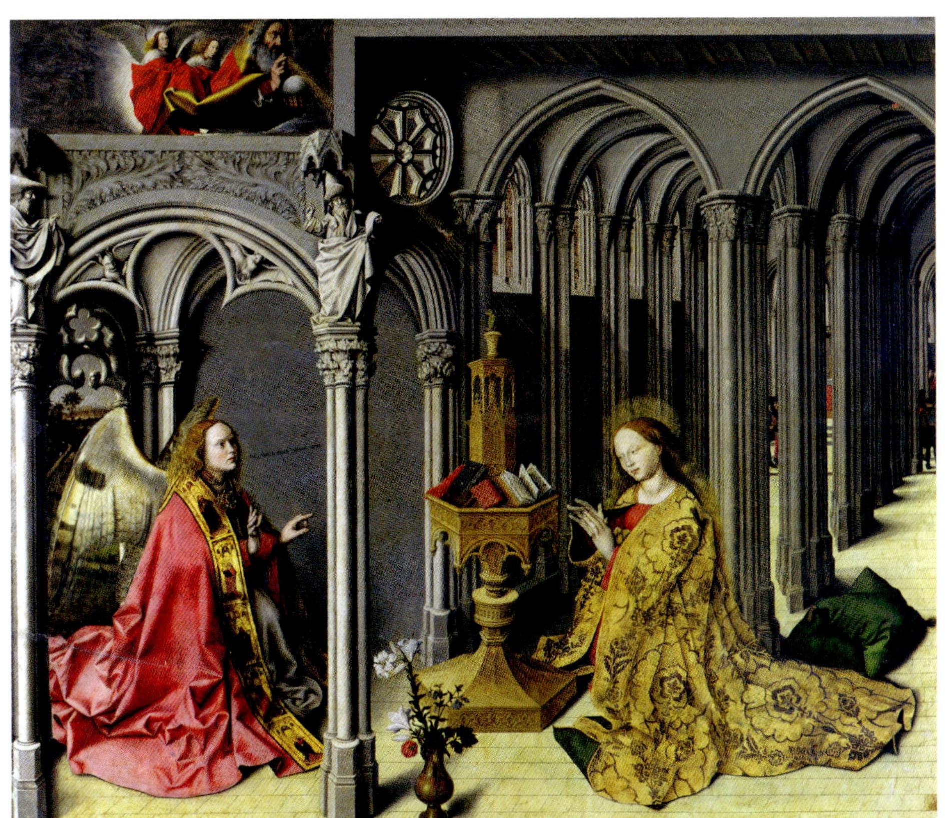

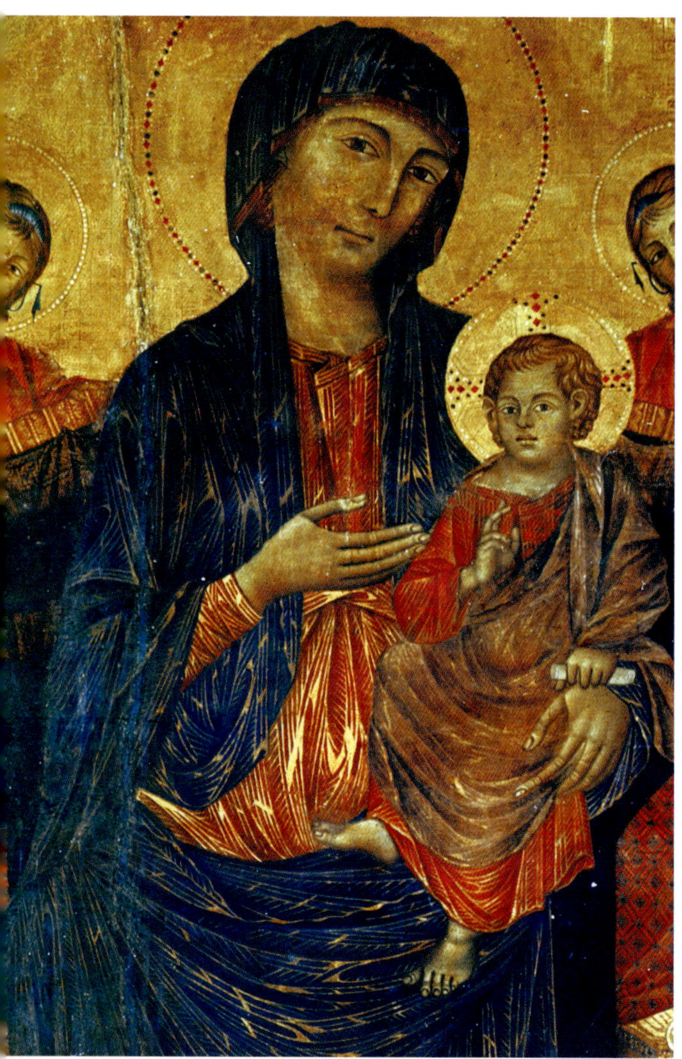

Trying to Define the Origins of Gothic Painting

As with the Annunciation scenes above, we will now analyze three depictions of the “Enthroned Madonna”, focusing on the style and personal interest of each artist. However, this time we are limiting ourselves to the artists of one single generation. All of the masters mentioned here knew each other and worked in the same places. What are we trying to prove by looking at three so similar paintings with a comparable composition, made by three artists who possibly influenced one another? We are investigating the pulse of time at around 1300, when Gothic painting was first documented in Italy, and we can watch how, within a very short period of time, the preconditions for the visual arts changed, fundamentally and relentlessly. Nowadays, the three altarpieces depicting a Maestà, by Cenni di Pepo, called Cimabue, Duccio di Buoninsegna and Giotto di Bondone, are united in Room II of the Uffizi in Florence – an ingenious idea for museum education. As a matter of fact, these three masterpieces count among the earliest works in the collection, but they were acquired rather late. The three Maestàs only came into the museum in the late 18th century, when church institutions were experiencing a decrease in strength and a new interest developed for "Primitive Art". The current form of presentation was only realized in the 20th century. All three works show the Mother of God enthroned, holding the Christ Child on her lap. She is surrounded by a host of angels. The pictorial motif of the Enthroned Madonna with angels and saints was only introduced in the 13th century. In other words, compared to other topics, it was rather young. Nor can its iconography refer to sources in the Bible, where the only prophetic scheme is that of Christ as Ruler of the World; a pictorial scheme that occurs frequently in Early Christian mosaics in apsides. Maybe the apocryphal texts in the 4th-century *Vulgate* by St. Jerome inspired the artists to portray the Virgin Mary as Ruler of the World. The fact remains that before this pictorial motif became popular in the Late Middle Ages, there was a blooming of the Marian cult, which soon also found its poetic expression in the fast spreading Marian poetry.

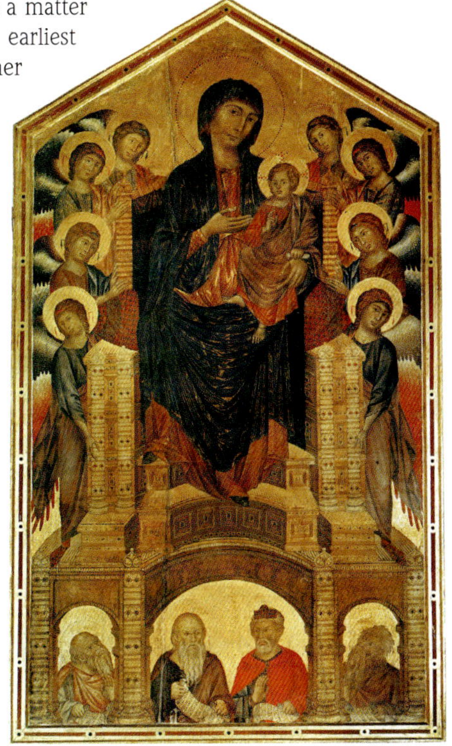

Cenni di Pepo, called Cimabue,
Maestà, *c.* 1285,
tempera on wood,
385 × 223 cm,
Uffizi, Florence

In around 1285, **Cimabue** (*c.* 1240–*c.* 1302), a painter and mosaicist from Florence, created a Maestà that was used for several centuries as an altar panel for Santa Trinità in Florence. This painting marks the final moment in the Romanesque, Carolingian, and medieval conception of art. The sheer monumentality of the panel knows no precursors. In the center, we see the Mother of God enthroned, the background is gilded. Her hand is pointing toward the Ruler of the World. The Christ Child is on her lap, making a sign of blessing. To

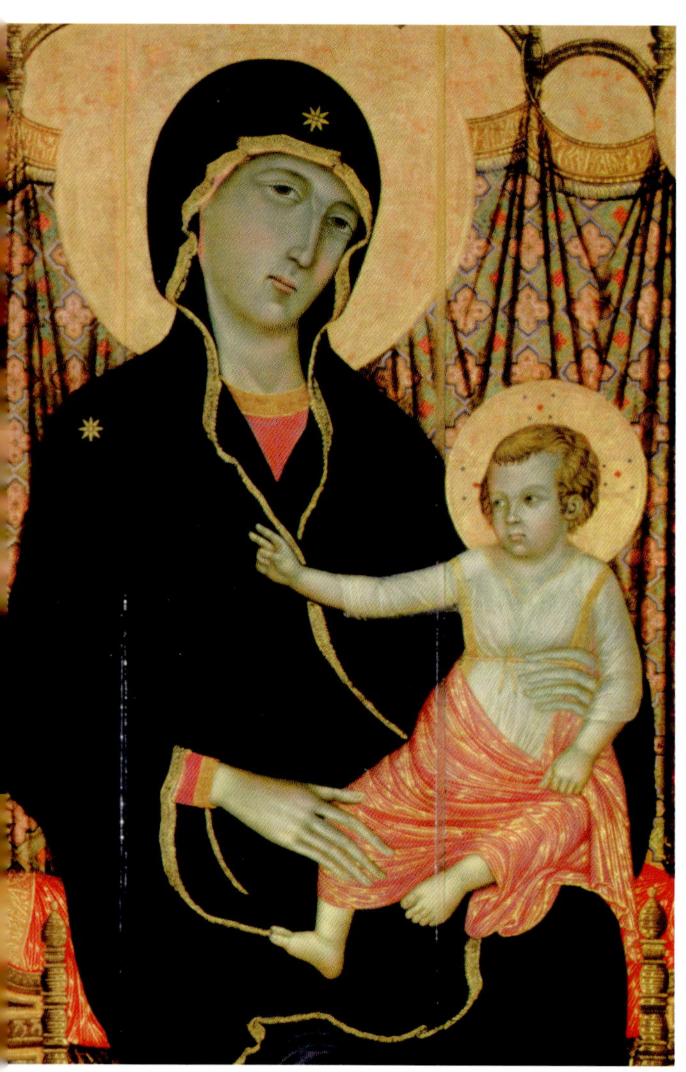

the left and right of the Virgin are four angels each, their bodies overlapping, but their faces can clearly be seen. Some of the angels look out of the picture, integrating the devoted beholder into the event. Underneath the throne there are four bearded men, known from the Old Testament: Abraham, David, Jeremiah and Isaiah: each can be discerned through the banderoles. The panel's atmosphere is exceedingly solemn. The way the artist depicts the clothes with their rather schematized folds and the overall rigid composition are much indebted to tradition. Their faces, however, make us realize that something new is evolving: the varying facial features of every angel turn them into individual beings; the angels' faces are no longer merely a means to represent a religious message.

Also in the year 1285, **Duccio di Buoninsegna** (*c.* 1255–1319) painted the so-called *Rucellai Madonna* (pp. 230, 231), named after the donors of a chapel in the Dominican church of Santa Maria Novella in Florence. Judging by its formal characteristics, it closely resembles the panel described above and has in fact also been ascribed to Cimabue. This is another proof of the fact that it is not only highly difficult to ascribe a painting to a certain artist, but that even regional ascriptions can sometimes be faulty. Duccio di Buoninsegna came from Siena, while Cimabue was a Florentine. It might be that Duccio as a youngster was inspired by the early works of Cimabue, who in turn appreciated the style of Duccio. Duccio was mainly inspired by works from Eastern Europe, those painted in the Byzantine style. Byzantine icon painting is known for the angular folds in the draperies as well as for the asymmetrical facial features. The latter goes back to the religious background of Byzantine art: icon painters did not try to develop their own signature style. Rather, they tried to copy the pattern as faithfully as possible. This idea is based on the conception of every painting simply being a copy of the original, the initial Holy Face. In other words, an artist would have destroyed the charismatic aura of his work, had he tried to bring his own ideas into the composition. The interesting aspect here is that Duccio was not part of this long-standing tradition – rather, the imitation of the Byzantine style evolved after renewed contact with the vocabulary of form typical of the East. Duccio di Buoninsegna used this vocabulary without being indebted to it in the strict religious sense. The poses of the gracefully kneeling angels reveal Duccio's artistic freedom to introduce some of his own observations into the composition.

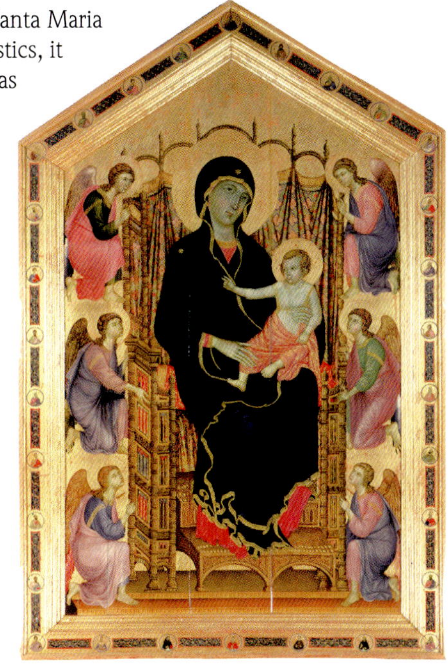

Duccio di Buoninsegna,
Maestà, *c.* 1285,
tempera on wood,
450 × 290 cm,
Uffizi, Florence

Giotto di Bondone (*c.* 1267–1337) also painted a Maestà panel. It was created in around 1310 for the altar of the Ognissanti church in Florence. At first glance, it doesn't

Giotto di Bondone,
Maestà, *c.* 1310,
tempera on wood,
325 × 204 cm,
Uffizi, Florence

seem to differ much from its predecessors. But on closer observation, there are numerous details here that point to a pioneering new interpretation of the motif of the Enthroned Madonna. The throne, for example, is done in openwork and decorated with Gothic gables. In other words, it is also a piece of carved architecture, a superb structure. In the works by Cimabue and Duccio, the throne was simply a large piece of furniture. Giotto's Mary is lager than life, deep folds show in the heavy fabric, which would initially have been blue and nowadays is a shade of green. Giotto is exceedingly mindful of the axis of symmetry: the grouping of the entourage on both sides of the Madonna and Child is identical, but at the same time, he makes the figures tangible, locates them within the space. The angels show inner tension; the ones kneeling are turning their palms outward. The artist has put special attention on the representation of the facades, such as the marble panes or the richly decorated garments. The slightly translucent garment of the Christ Child allows a glimpse of His arm. This effect makes the whole scene more plausible, more "believe-able", so to say. The narrative composition also features some innovations: now, the angels are bringing objects – flowers in a vase, a crown, a chased

Giotto di Bondone (*c.* 1267–1337)

c. **1267** Born in Florence or Vespignano, north of Florence, to a blacksmith.

Up to *c.* **1290** Assumed to have been apprentice of Cimabue.

c. **1295** Works on the frescos in San Francesco, Assisi.

Presumably **1298–1301** Active in Rome.

c. **1304–1306** Active in Padua.

Post-**1320** Returns to Florence, where he owns a house. He frequently came here in the previous years.

1334 Master builder for Florence Cathedral.

1337 Dies in Florence.

Giotto's biography was written in the **15th century** by Lorenzo Ghiberti and in the **16th century** by Giorgio Vasari. Both mix facts and fiction to create the story of a unique artist. For instance, there is one anecdote that tells how Cimabue once met the young Giotto. He was shepherding and drawing ants on a stone in an astonishingly naturalistic way. Another variation on this theme has Giotto, who, as an apprentice in Cimabue's workshop, painted a fly onto a picture. Cimabue tried to chase it away, then realized his mistake and acknowledged the immense artistic talent of his pupil.

receptacle. This means that, unlike with the Maestà by Cimabue, the beholder is not integrated into the painting; rather, the figures are obeying a logic immanent within the painting. This work is no longer simply a devotional object; it is also an art object. This new approach, this trying to depict, to represent an object, can be defined as the beginning of modern-day painting. It would take less than a century for art with its new interest in worldly appearances to lead to a disengagement from purely sacred topics. There is one detail here which makes this change palpable: The haloes are not only larger than in the previous paintings, they have become physical, because now they conceal parts of the heads. This form of overlapping intensifies the effect of spatiality. But, what's more, the nimbus becomes an earthly fabric. This might be the shortest description of what characterizes modern painting. In his *Cicerone* (1855), Jacob Burckhardt, the renowned art historian, once wrote that for Giotto, causalities were higher and more spiritual

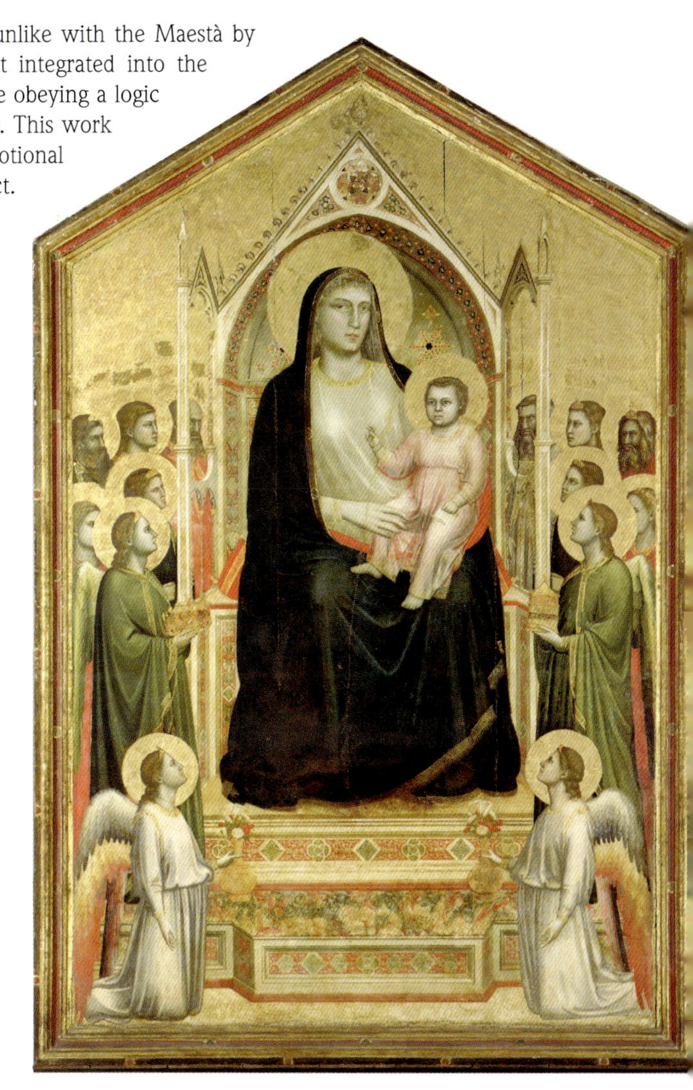

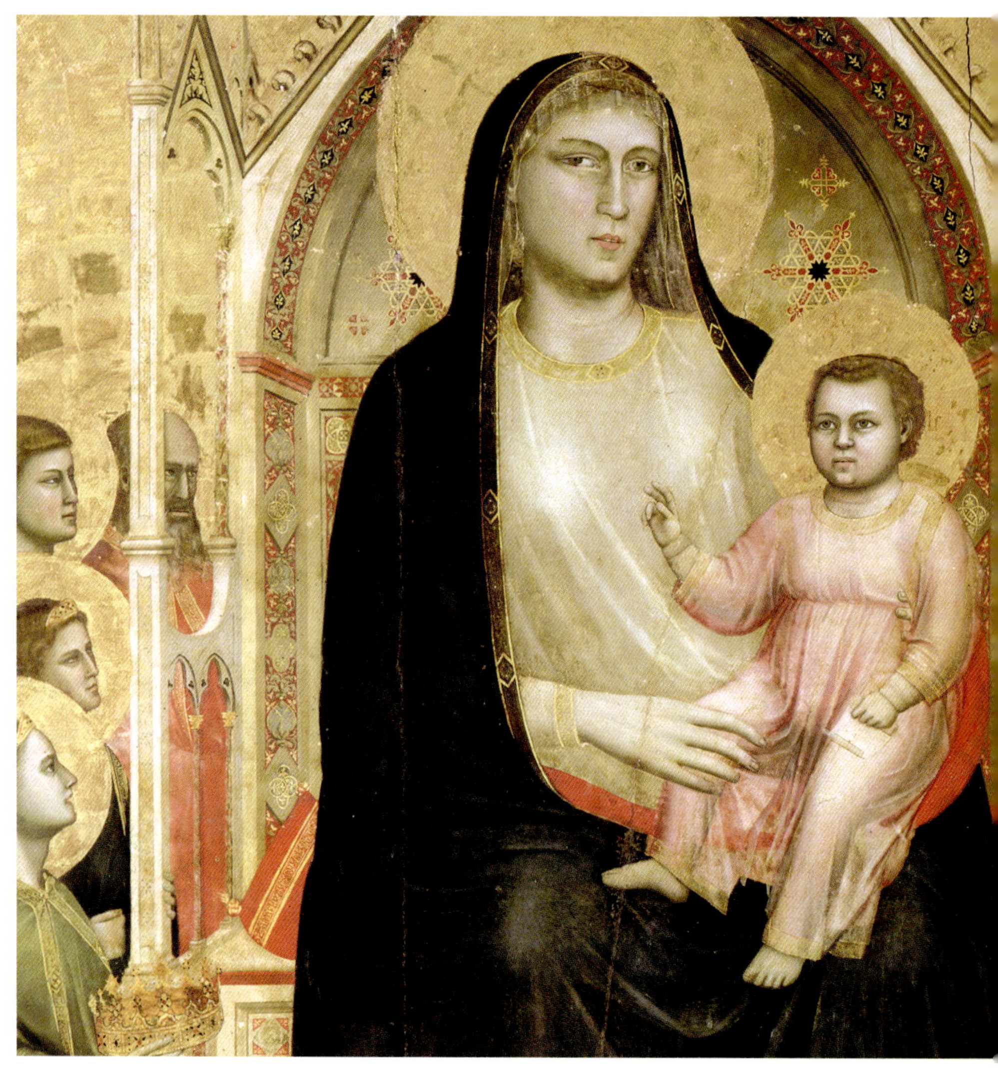

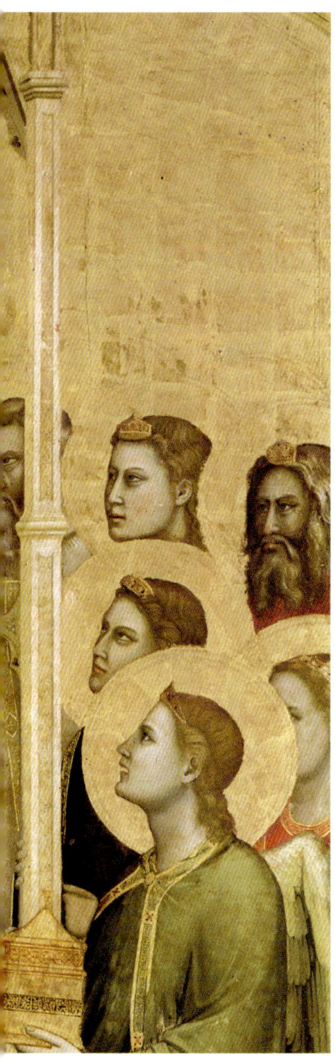

than for many of the greatest artists that came after him. This is exactly what astonishes us when looking at Giotto's Maestà. No other later artist could ignore Giotto's achievements. Be it Simone Martini (see pp. 182, 183), Pietro Lorenzetti or Lippo Memmi – none of them could paint an Enthroned Madonna by simply following the medieval formulas set by Cimabue or the Byzantine influence introduced by Duccio di Buoninsegna. In fact, they had to stand comparison with Giotto and his revolutionary way of introducing reality into painting. This is why the three paintings demonstrate in an exemplary way the transition from the 13th to the 14th century, and equally, the transition from the Middle Ages to modern times. The passage leads from transcendence to materiality, from metaphor to plausibility, from belief to questioning. There is no direct stylistic line of development that leads to this masterpiece. Rather, Giotto's view of the world and his innovations in painting were indebted to two stylistic influences. But after Giotto, nothing could ever be the same as before.

Giotto di Bondone,
Virgin and Child, detail of the Maestà from p. 233

Merchants and Craftsmen – Urban Culture in the Middle Ages

Freiburg im Breisgau,
the medieval fortification as it shows in today's urban layout

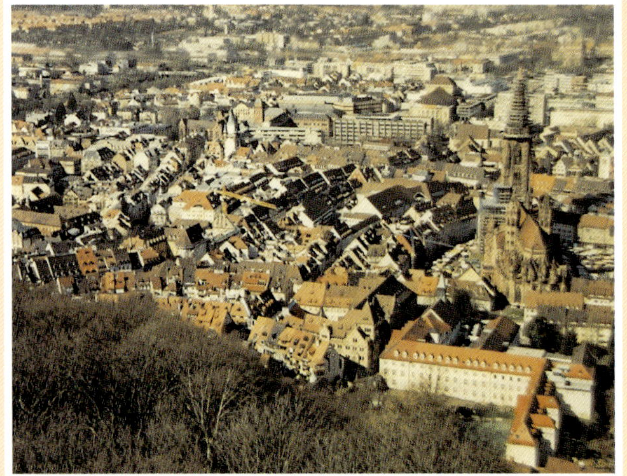

Generally, buildings get much older than their builders. And so, later inhabitants would profit by their predecessors' manpower. But there were factors that made restructuring of the former buildings necessary, such as wars or other catastrophes. **Freiburg im Breisgau** in southern Germany for example grew continuously from the Middle Ages, adding one circle to another, turning the surrounding villages into suburbs. Even when the city was badly damaged during the Second World War rebuilding had to conform to the existing structures and so the medieval layout of the city can be detected in spite of the modern buildings of today. The old fortifications show in the course of the roads, between the Martinstor and Schwabentor city gates. Directly outside of these are the Gerberau (tanners' mead) and the Fischerau (fishers' mead). The street names allude to the original trades: both needed running water, both were rather smelly, which explains why they were situated outside the city walls. The distribution of different trades among different districts, the establishment of guilds as organizations to promote common interests and provide mutual security, the rigid regulation of trade, the high building density, the necessary sewerage arrangements, and the fact that large sections of the population were not engaged in agriculture: all this was the result of a process of accommodation between rulers, the Church, the nobility, the burghers, and the peasants of the Middle Ages.

The public attention which town life enjoyed in the Middle Ages is also illustrated by the emergence of a new genre: the veduta, a painted or drawn illustration of a town. A typical example of the Renaissance is the so-called *Nuremburg Chronicles (Schedelsche Weltchronik)* from 1493. Written in Latin by Hartmann Schedel (1440–1514), it shows the seven ages of world history, from the Creation to the End of the World and the Last Judgment. The sixth chapter, representing the present day at the time, is especially detailed. Its vedutas illustrate the early interest in urban life; in the way towns looked and how they were organized.

Nuremberg Chronicles,
illustration of Florence,
first published 1493,
printed book

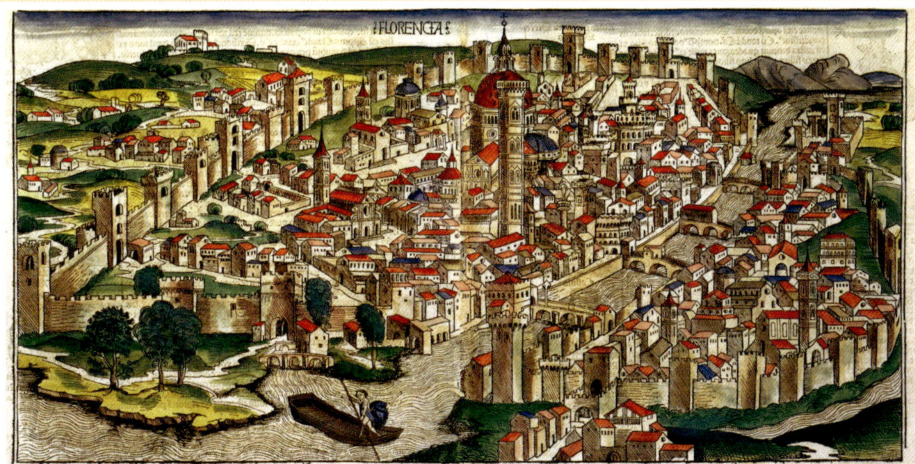

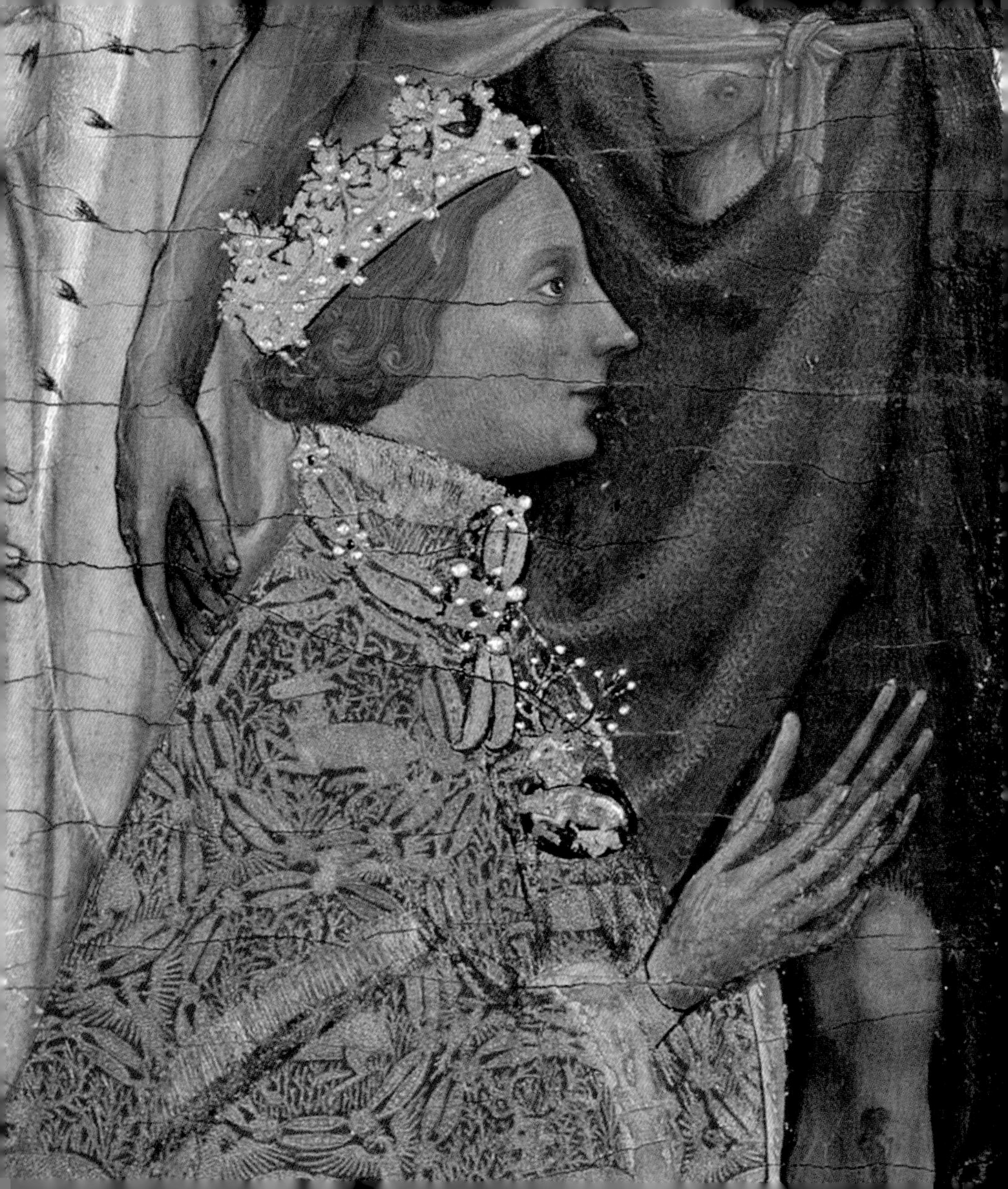

Painting at the Dawn of the 15th Century

Gothic painting underwent a decisive change in the decades before and after 1400. The expression changed; the style became visibly more delicate and softer. The change was not restricted to panel painting, either: it can also be seen in other genres such as manuscript illuminations, and some works of sculpture also reflect the new vocabulary of form. It is a development that surfaced in the various regions of Europe and can be studied from Paris to Prague and London to Naples, from courtly centers of culture to the remotest monasteries. Indeed, for a while the overall taste in art became so unanimous that art historians at times find it difficult to define a given artist's, miniaturist's or sculptor's nationality. At the same time, though, the various artistic genres have enough individual facets to prevent them being directly comparable. And even within one medium, similarities boil down to the use of descriptive terms, simply marking one as more beautiful, soft, delicate, natural than the other. In art history, there are three stylistic terms to define the Gothic art of the early 15th century. Each of these labels starts from another analytical point of view, such as the genre or material. International Gothic (or

Master of the Wilton Diptych,
Wilton Diptych
(detail opposite page:
Richard II),
c. 1395–1399,
tempera on wood (oak),
each wing 46 × 29 cm,
National Gallery, London

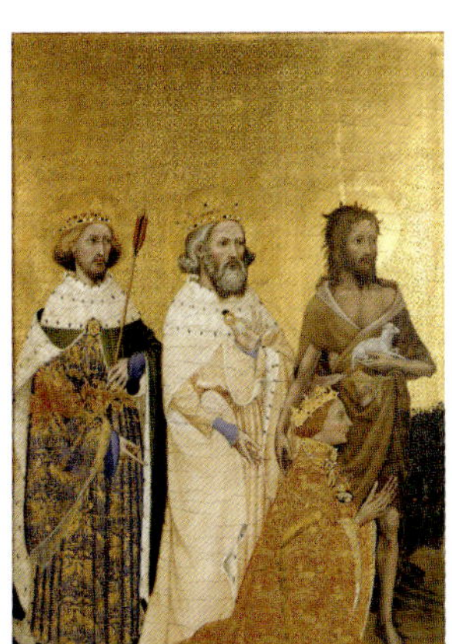

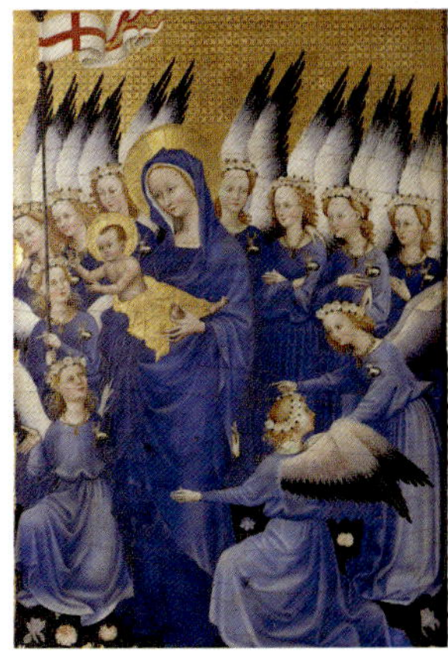

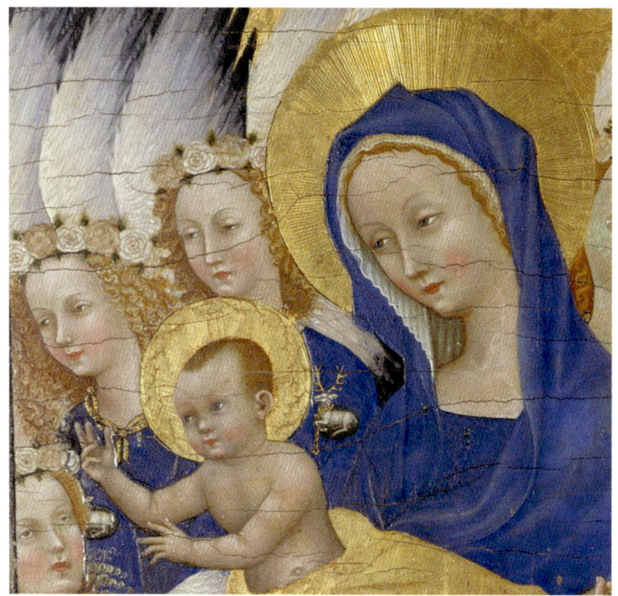

International Style) illustrates our inability to define regional differences in the painting of the decades around 1400.

The term *Beautiful Madonnas* is used for a series of wood and stone sculptures from around 1380 onward, whereas Soft Style (or Courtly Style) defines paintings and manuscript illuminations, reflecting in its name the new elegance and sweet expressions in miniatures. We will now present a few characteristic examples of each of these three scientific approaches.

Master of the Wilton Diptych,
Virgin and Child,
detail of the diptych from
p. 239

A Style that Knows no Borders: International Gothic

King Richard II of England is kneeling before the Virgin and Child. He is accompanied by his intercessor, John the Baptist, and by two former kings of England, St Edward the Confessor and St Edmund. Mary is surrounded by eleven angels – this is what we see on the interior panels of the **Wilton Diptych** (pp. 238, 239, 240, 241). The portable altarpiece consists of two panels joined by two hinges so that it could be opened like a huge book. On the outside, it is painted with the king's coat of arms and a stag on a flowering meadow. The outstanding masterpiece takes its name from its one-time owners, the Earls of Pembroke, who kept the work in Wilton house, Wiltshire. The altarpiece was used for private devotion by King Richard II (reigned 1377–1399) and

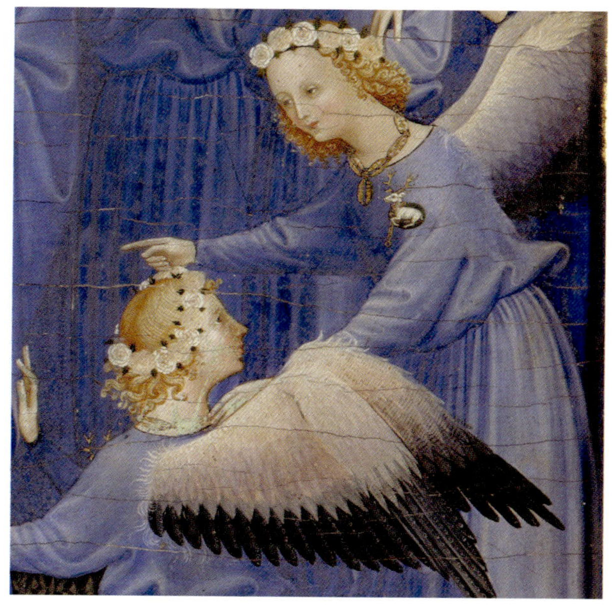

Master of the Wilton Diptych,
Angel,
detail of the diptych from
p. 239

it is presumed that it was painted during the last five years of his reign, i.e. between 1395 and 1399. We know neither the name nor the origins of the artist.

English art historians presume he was an Englishman while some French researchers suspect he came from France. In other words, this is a perfect example for the International Style. Artists had been active beyond national borders even several generations before – think of the Sienese painter Simone Martini, who was called to the papal palace at Avignon in the 1330s. But it wasn't until the late 13th century that the pan-European activities of the artists also led to a mutual, international style. It is characterized by extremely delicate facial features; graceful, elongated fingers; richly decorated draperies with flowing folds; and an overall lyrical, idyllic atmosphere. If we look more closely at the various motifs of this particular painting (executed on gilded oak), we will detect a wide range of allusions. Richard II was born on 6 January 1367. The left interior panel relates to this, because it shows the Three Magi adoring the Virgin. Next to her is John the Baptist. The halo of the Christ Child also refers to the Testament: it is embossed and decorated with a crown of thorns and three nails, thus pointing towards the Passion of Christ. But the painting also abounds in secular references: Richard wears a medal on his robe with the depiction of a hart; indeed, his entire cloak is covered with richly embroidered golden harts, the emblem of the king. Looking more closely at the angels, we can observe that they too wear a symbol on their shoulders, a white hart in a green oval frame. And although Richard is kneeling before the Mother of God, a sign of submission, she and her host of angels, are, in a way, also submitting to the English king: their robes, which look as if they had been made by the same appointed tailor, sport the royal emblem; the entire group has assembled under the English St George's banner, the red cross on a white ground. This undoubtedly is an idiosyncratic melange of pious devotion and heraldry! There is another little detail, a discreet word pun, to underline the fact that this altarpiece was indeed used for private devotion by the English monarch: the name "England" originally derived from the West Germanic tribe, the Angles. Legend has it that in the 6th century, Pope Gregory the Great was inspired to send missionaries to England by the sight of two blond boys in the Roman slave-market. On being told they were Angles, he said: "Not Angles, but angels" *("non Angli sed angeli").* In the Wilton Diptych, above the mast of the banner, art historians have recently found a miniature globe – one centimeter in size – depicting the island: England – land of angels.

Some researchers have even suggested the existence of a traveling "Master of the Beautiful Madonna" to explain to fast and cosmopolitan change in style.

A Piece of Nature: the Beautiful Madonnas

From the 1380s, Madonna figures made of stone or wood were created in various places throughout Europe. Their distinguishing feature is a lack of that rigidity and heaviness typical of earlier Madonna sculptures. Instead, their faces are clear-cut with a high, elegantly formed forehead, fine lips and an indulgent, loving gaze. To this day, there remain a lot of questions about the transnational development of this style. The fact that all of a sudden these noble Mothers of God were erected both in remote little abbey chapels and large

Madonna of Toporc,
c. 1420, lime wood,
140 cm, Magyar Nemzeti Galéria,
Budapest

churches cannot be explained by courtly rivalry and widely traveling artists. There is even one thesis suggesting the existence of a Master of the Beautiful Madonnas, who on his travels is to have convinced the local workshops of his style. Indeed, it is more probable that artists were inspired to work in this new, common style by gifts of works that were sent around as well as by artists traveling to fulfill special commissions and to further their own knowledge. It is less reasonable to think that one single person would have had an impact on the entire European art production of the late 14th century, without his name having survived. Neither will the so-called **Madonna of Toporc** have been carved and colored after a major model. It is rather to be presumed that it was created around 1420 by a local artist active in what today is Slovakia, someone who since his childhood might have been impressed by the Beautiful Madonnas typical of Silesia and Bohemia.

The **Krumau Madonna** (p. 240), made of limestone, is even more famous. It was made in around 1400 in the area of Český Krumlov in Bohemia (now Krumlov in Czechia) and possibly intended for a chapel in the Franciscan or Cistercian abbeys close by. In 1913, it was acquired by the Kunsthistorisches Museum in Vienna. The Christ Child's left arm, right hand and left leg have been lost. The Madonna's crown and the tip of her hood were chiseled away and there are only poor remains of the original coloration. But we recognize that the polished stone, or parts of it, such as the Madonna's hair, was originally gilded. What is most impressive here is the modeling of the figure. For example, the Virgin's fingers virtually leave a mark on the soft skin of the Christ Child. If you are wondering what this Mother and Child

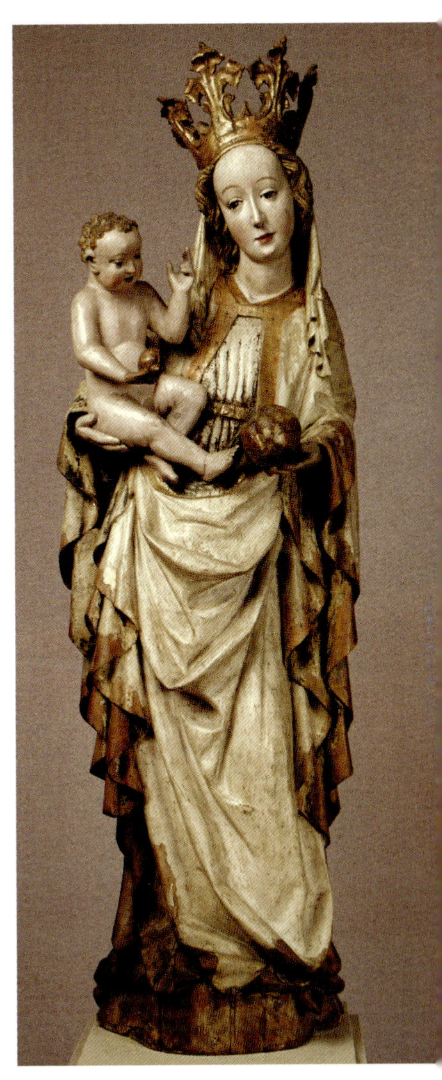

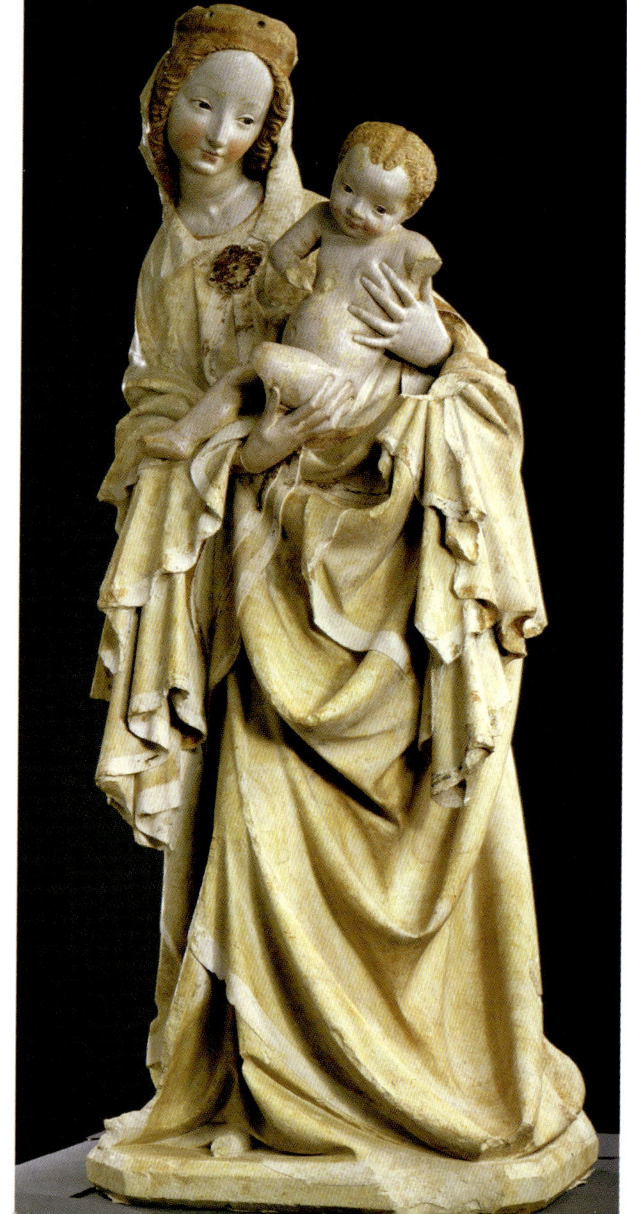

Krumau Madonna,
c. 1400, limestone,
112 cm, Kunsthistorisches
Museum, Vienna

sculpture would have looked like in its original state and coloration, browse back to the Wilton Diptych (pp. 239, 240). There is an astonishing similarity between the sculpture from Bohemia and the painted Virgin and Child facing the English king. In both cases, the slender and dainty Mary is holding the Christ Child in front of the flowing folds of her drapery; she is leaning back slightly in order to counterbalance His weight, lovingly inclining her head toward Him. The Child is stretching His arms forward, curious and adventurous. The same narrative solution was realized by two artists living hundreds of miles apart: a sculptor and a painter.

The similarities between wood sculptures and paintings in the years around 1400 are astonishing. Here, in both examples, the slender and graceful Mary is leaning slightly back to balance the weight of the Christ Child.

Beauty Rules the World: the Soft Style

The term Soft Style is predominantly used for describing the manuscript illuminations of the decades around 1400, but it is at times also used for panel painting. The problematic aspect of this term is that it is not precise enough. Furthermore, it does not take account of the tendency towards more drastic representations, which also define the art of the time, such as depictions of death, and of sick or dying people. Dainty and graceful portraits only cover one side of the coin and are restricted to certain topics. This means that the term can be used fittingly to define a particular movement, but not the overall stylistic phase of the period. The synonymous definition "Courtly Style" is equally debatable; it is too vague and of little use. A courtly style, influenced by the clients and with a certain pictorial solution, undoubtedly existed both before and after the period in question here. What's more, the term "Courtly Style" has even been used to define Gothic art in general. In other words, it only makes things more confusing if we use this term to define the art produced during the late 13th and early 14th centuries. An exemplary piece of Soft Style miniature painting is this late 14th-century manuscript page by **André Beauneveu** (*c.* 1335–*c.* 1402) (p. 247). Micah, the Old Testament prophet, is sitting on a

André Beauneveu,
Prophet Micah,
1390s,
manuscript illumination,
Bibliothèque nationale, Paris

throne, his left hand holding an unfolded scroll. This is not at all an unusual way to illustrate the beginning of a chapter. But around the actual depiction, twines and curling fantasy creatures are interwoven with the letters, dissolving the boundaries between script and picture. This book was not made to be read quickly; its intention is to make the well-known mysterious. And yet, due to the carefully chosen color combination and the well-considered proportions, the work remains playful and pleasant for the reader/beholder.

The *Adoration Altarpiece* by **Gentile da Fabriano** (*c.* 1370–1427) combines the various stylistic features that define the new style of around 1400 (pp. 248, 249). Gentile da Fabriano had traveled widely in Italy, had met artists from Italy and from north of the Alps, had been an apprentice to miniaturists and had also worked as a wood sculptor. Then, in around 1423, he was commissioned by Florentine merchant Palla Strozzi to paint an altar panel for the family chapel of Santa Trinità. There is a crowd in front of the stable which the Holy Family shares with ox and donkey. A dog in the front right-hand corner is nearly crushed by the horses; he is just making his escape. The Three Magi have stepped forward from the host of people. The youngest one, the third, is having his spurs taken off by a servant. The second is just going down on his knees while the first of the Magi, the oldest, is receiving the Christ Child's blessing. The whole scene is illuminated like a stage set. In spite of the darkness, the variety of colors shows to advantage and create a peaceful and festive atmosphere. The amount of golden clothes and the golden harnesses of the horses is remarkable. In fact, the painter's pay will have been much lower than the costs the client had to put up with for the pigments. This, our latest example of the art of around 1400, quite clearly shows the overall atmosphere which reigned in the works of art at the time. Gentile da Fabriano uses all the technical finesses possible at the time: staggering to create an effect of space;

Following double spread:
Gentile da Fabriano,
Adoration,
c. 1423, tempera on wood,
173 × 220 cm,
Uffizi, Florence

careful lighting; a variety of surfaces and materials; lifelike bodies. But even though here and in other contemporary works the figures look exceedingly gentle and dainty, they still appear more earthly than those of other Gothic works of art, created before or after this period.

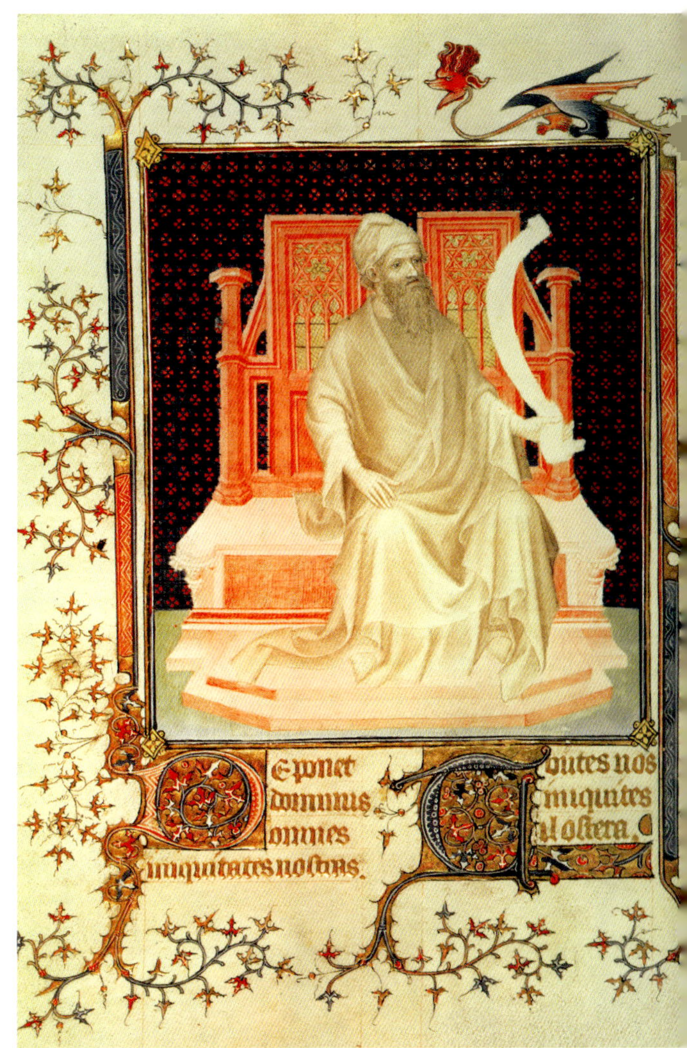

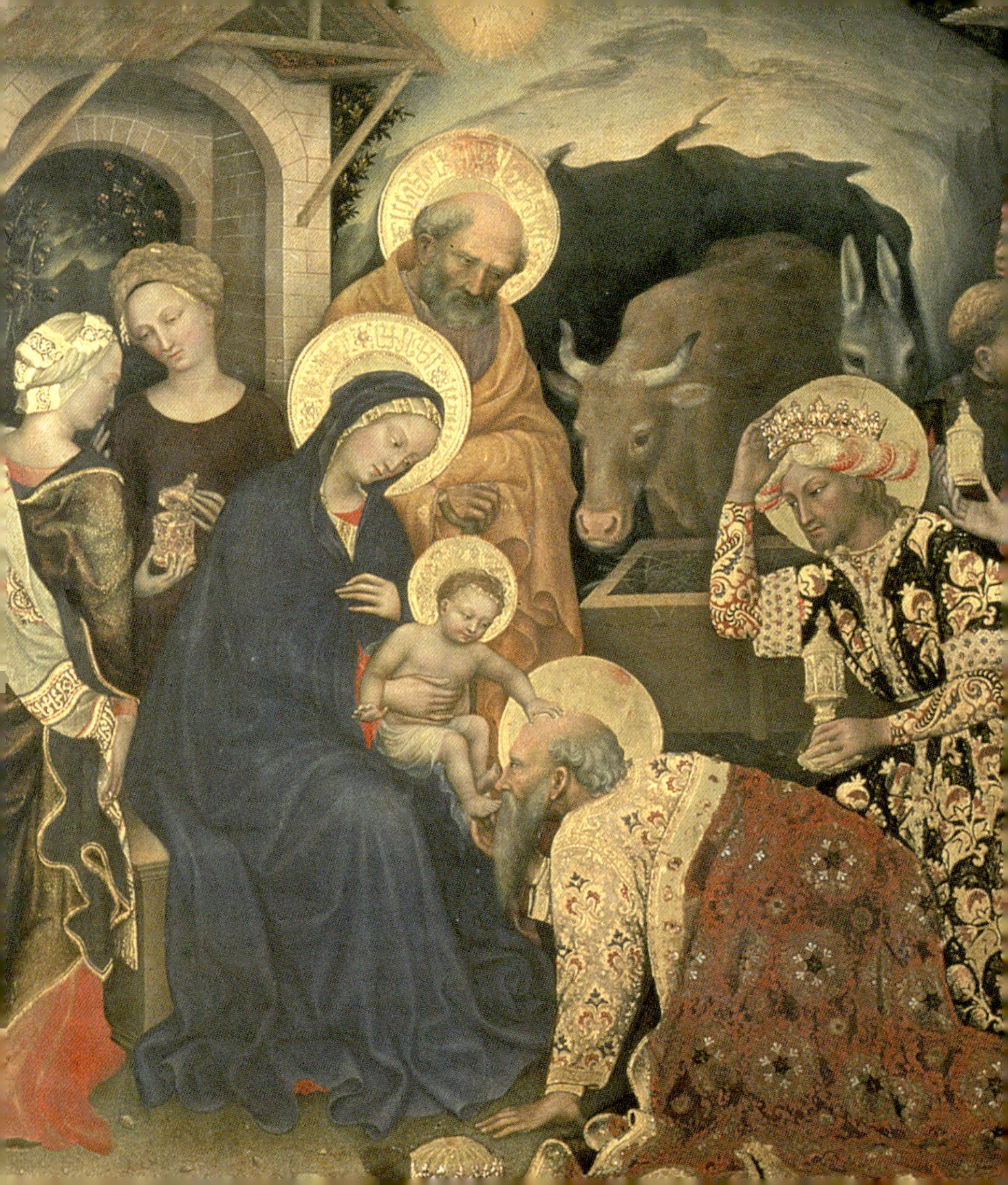

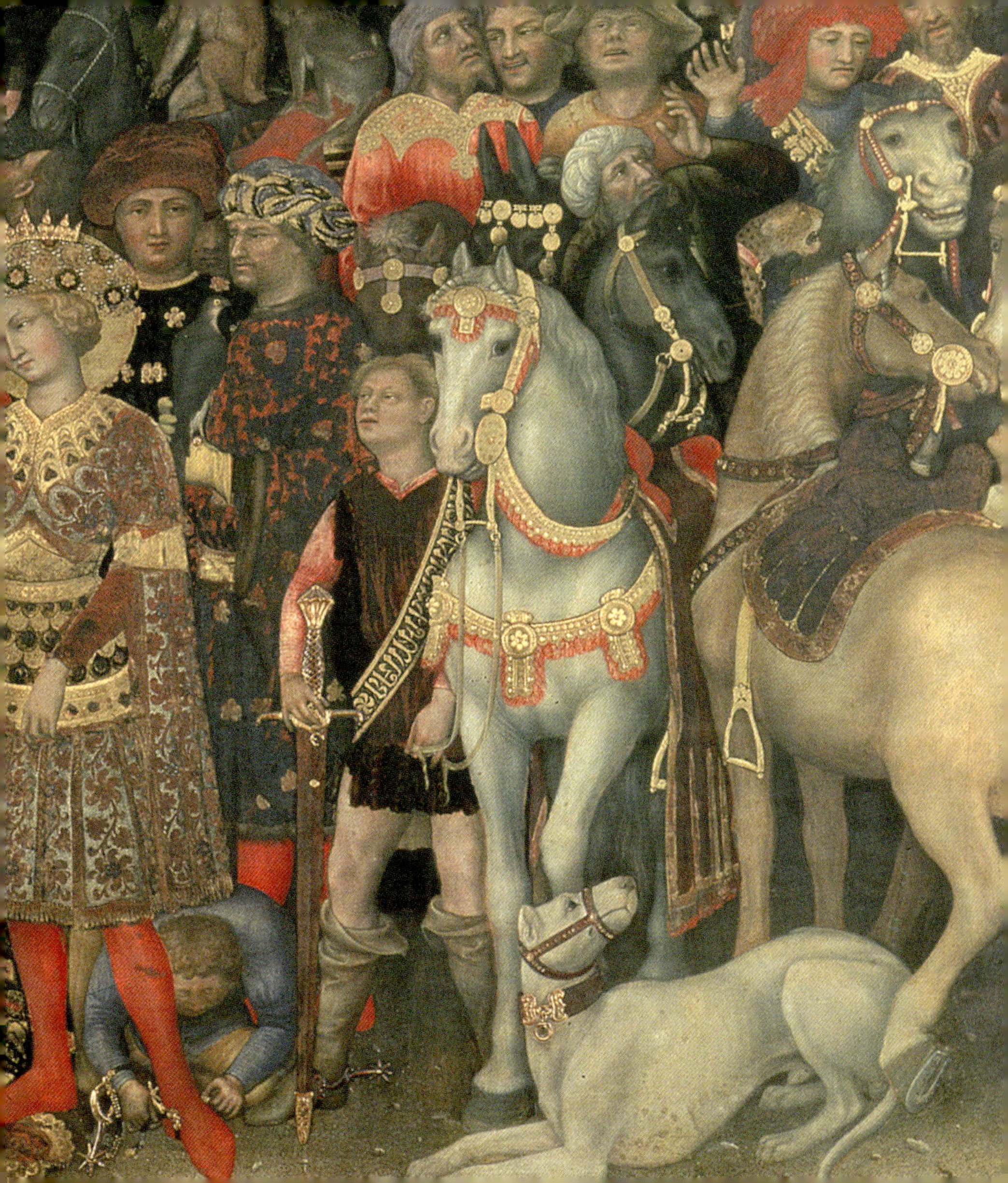

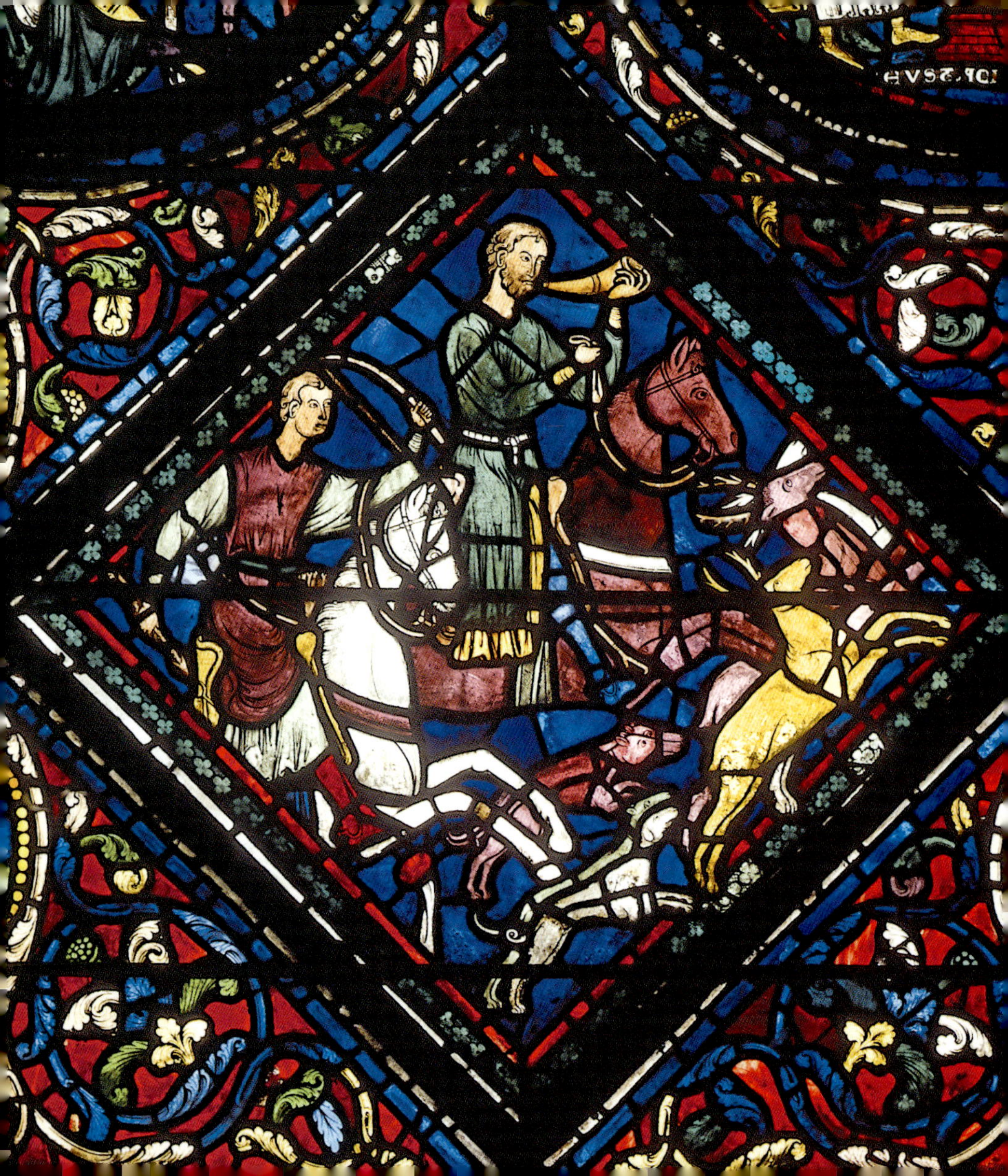

Stained Glass

Glass is the most solid of all fluid materials. When we take a closer look at Gothic glass windows, we will recognize that over the years they have changed their form, becoming thinner at the top and thicker at the bottom. Furthermore, this highly sensitive building material is constantly exposed to the climate, as well as being endangered by war and neglect. Finally, even if a window has survived external threats, it might at the end be at the mercy of the clergy and churchgoers, and the changing trends in fashion. As a consequence, only very few stained glass works have survived as an ensemble in their original context. Stained-glass has often been underestimated from an artistic point of view, although it often played a vital role, coming to full blossom in Early Gothic art. Though the technique of producing window glass had been known since Antiquity, until the end of the Romanesque period window openings had been relatively small. The new engineering techniques of building in the Gothic period allowed a drastic reduction of solid walls in church spaces. Instead, facades could now be opened up and allowed the insertion of large windows. The high spaces were suddenly flooded with the light of the sun's rays, beaming through the stained-glass windows. A new conception and aesthetic of space was created which was still religiously motivated, representing the light of Heaven. Furthermore, narrative scenes on the windows took on the didactic function which until then had been fulfilled by the wall paintings: showing deeds of the saints and events from the Bible. Every single component of the

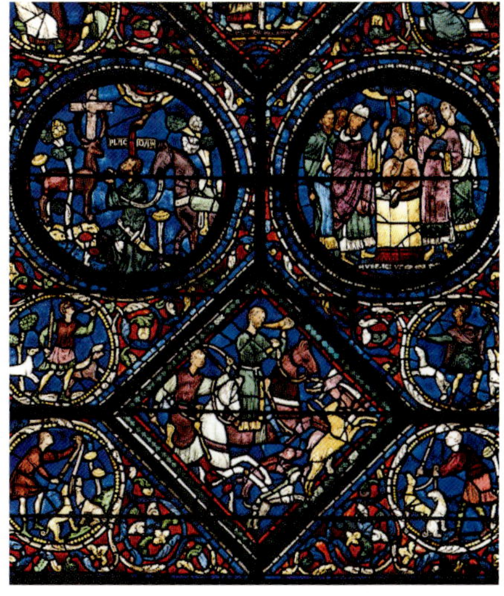

St Eustace window
(detail opposite page:
St Eustace and the hunting party),
c. 1200– 1210,
glass painting,
Notre-Dame Cathedral, Chartres

Prophet Isaiah,
detail of the eastern choir window,
c. 1301–1304,
glass painting,
St. Peter's Cathedral, Exeter

designed window was painted beforehand onto wood panels, in original size, which also served to indicate the network of lead frames holding together the single glass panes. Then, the size and form of the glass pieces could be determined. The pieces were produced in various colors and painted with a mixture of finely ground lead and ground glass, which was burned into the glass pane. From a technical point of view, the approach was the opposite of that of wall or panel painting, because here dark was added onto light. In glass painting, the lighter areas came into being by leaving spaces blank. From around 1300 onward, artists used silver stain, a yellowish color made of silver and stibine and dissolved in water. This was applied to the reverse of the glass pane to highlight certain parts of the stained glass, allowing for modulation and a greater lifelikeness of the paintings. The various glass panes were assembled with lead rods and the joints soldered together and then mounted in the window embrasures. The individual components of a stained window always retained the dark lead frame, a fact that makes them difficult to read when standing too close. However, when viewed from the normal distance of a churchgoer, deciphering the mounted window would pose no problems, since the human eye concentrates on the lighter panes, virtually ignoring the dark frames.

The **St Eustace window** in the north transept of Chartres Cathedral (pp. 250, 251) dates from 1200 to 1210 and shows scenes from the life of the martyr St Eustace. The lower one of a total of five rhomboid presentations, mounted one above the other, shows St Eustace going on a hunt. The saint's real name was Placidus; he only adopted the Greek name of Eustace when he was christened. The *Legenda aurea,* a collection of histories of the saints, tells how Placidus spotted an especially beautiful stag and followed him deep into the forest. Suddenly he saw a shining cross between the animal's antlers. This experience made him convert to the Christian faith. To the left, above the hunting party, there is a tondo showing Placidus and

Following double spread:
Southern rose window (left)
detail of the window from p. 256
Northern rose (right)
detail of the window from p. 257

the stag while on the top right we see the bishop of Rome christening St Eustace. Further towards the top, the paintings tell of the saint's life and death. The various scenes are beautifully arranged and framed by ornate foliage. Small flanking tondi show secondary scenes which are intended to further explain the main events. In the hunting scene, for example, this is a depiction of beaters with hounds. The predominating colors are blue and red, embellished with accents of green, purple, yellow and white. The window is structured by the ornamental arrangement of the pictorial scenes and the dense lead framework.

The further development of stained-glass painting is illustrated by the eastern **choir window of St Peter's in Exeter,** built roughly 100 years later, at the beginning of the 14th century. Our detail shows the Old Testament Prophet Isaiah. His right hand is pointing towards the unrolled script in his left. There are columns to both of his sides. His feet, placed on a checkered floor, give the effect of space, as if the window were not a flat plane but instead consisted of protruding and receding parts. The background is in one solid color, which confers an atmosphere of peace and harmony.

But let us return once more to Chartres. One of the innovative features of Gothic architecture is the large rose

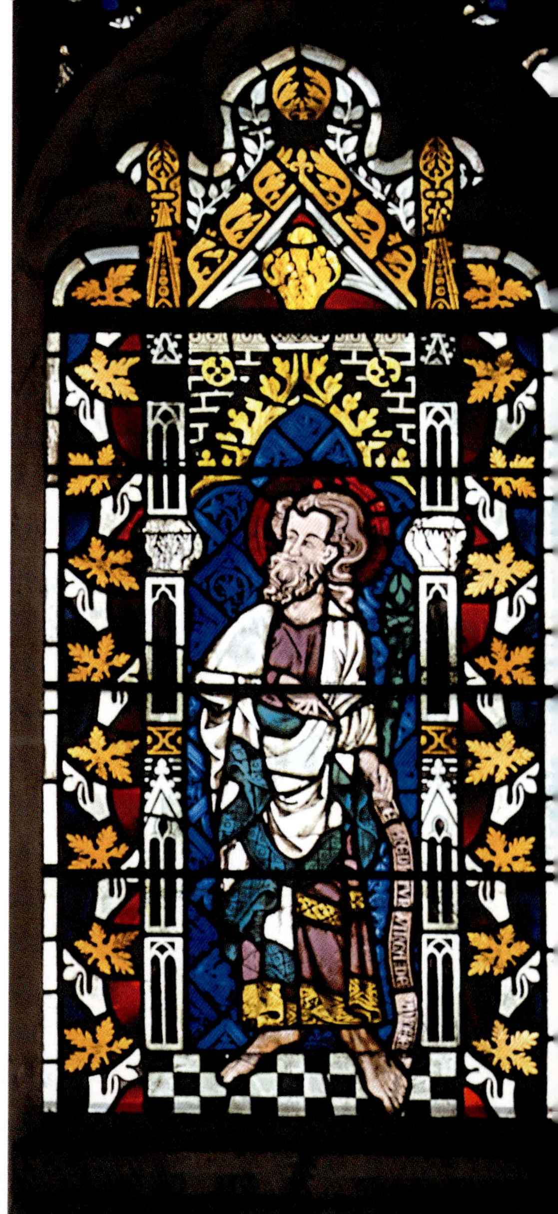

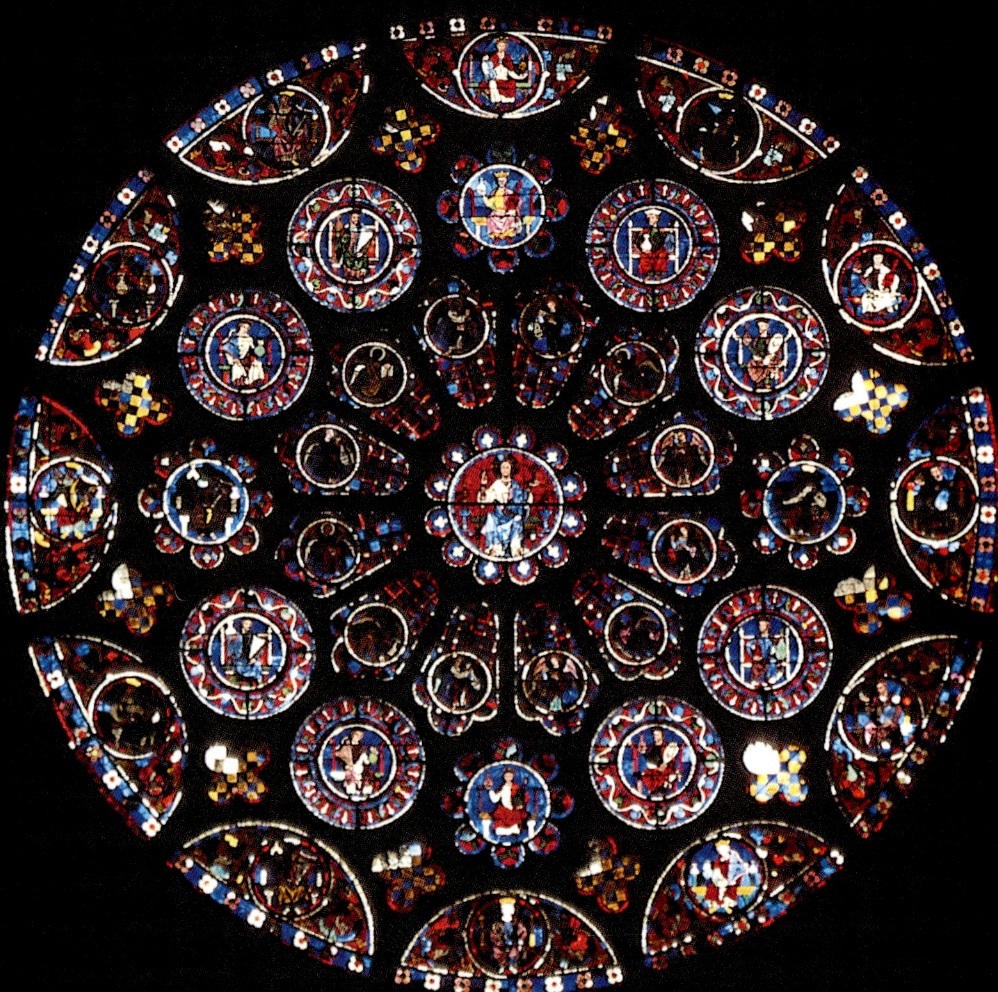

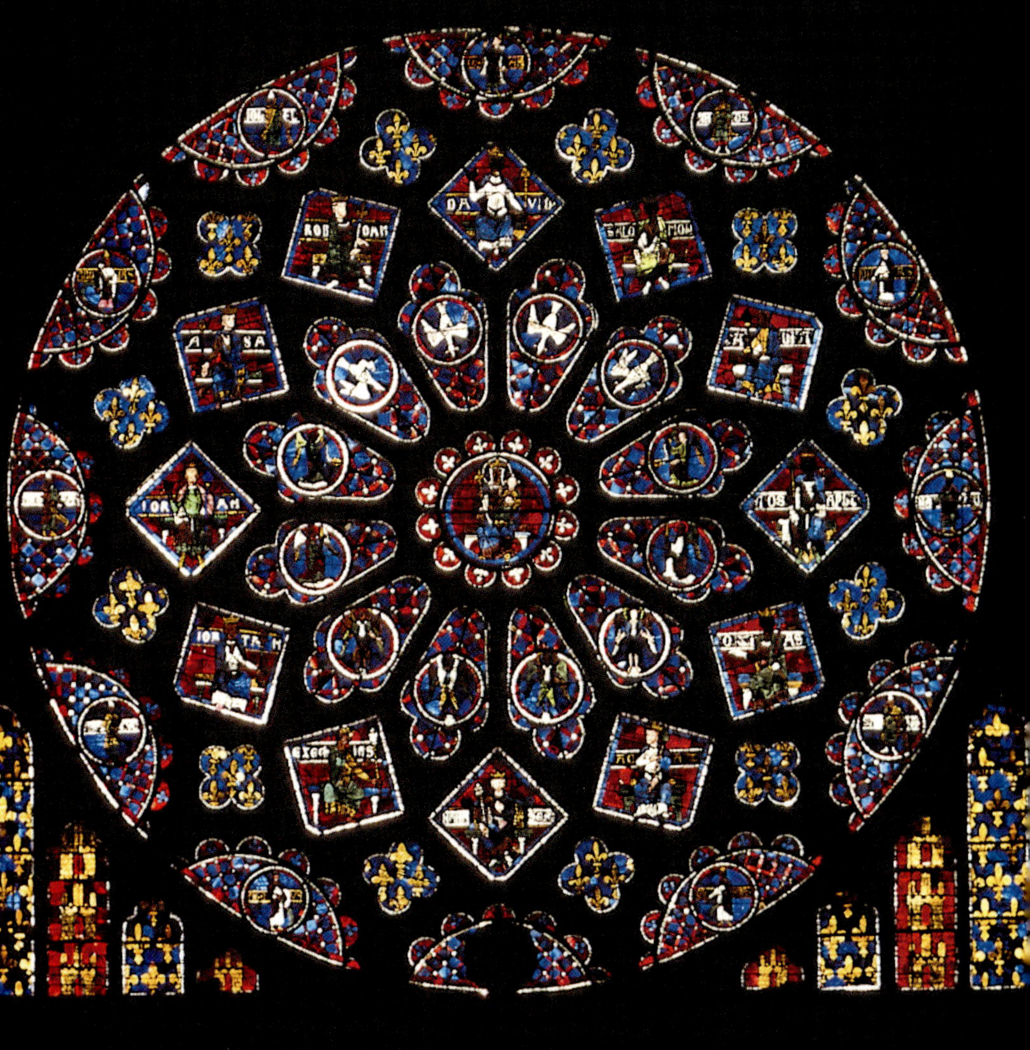
DA VID
ROB OAM
SALO MON
A SA

Southern window,
1220–1230,
glass painting,
Notre-Dame Cathedral, Chartres

windows in the facades, usually on the west front or on the ends of the transepts. The eastern end of a church was usually reserved for the apse. The immense **rose windows in the transept of Chartres Cathedral** date from the 1220s and are part of the original overall architectural design. The southern rose window (pp. 254, 256) is made up of several circular structures. In its center there is Christ Enthroned as Ruler of the World. A wreath of twelve tondi surrounds him, depicting, in the corners, the symbols of the Four Apostles – lion, bull, eagle and man – as well as eight angels with censers. The two outer rings consist of twelve medallions showing the twenty-four elders playing music, which St John mentions in the Apocalypse. Underneath the rose window are five lancet windows showing the Virgin and Child surrounded on each side by two prophets of the Old Testament: Jeremiah, Isaiah, Ezekiel and Daniel. But they are not alone: on their shoulders, they each carry one of the New Testament evangelists, Luke, Matthew, John and Mark. The astonishingly physical and concrete aspect of one "shouldering" the other strongly connects the New with the Old Testament. The same symbolic content can also be found in the window of the north facade (pp. 255, 257). In the center we see Mary Enthroned with the Christ Child. She is surrounded by circles of angels and doves representing the

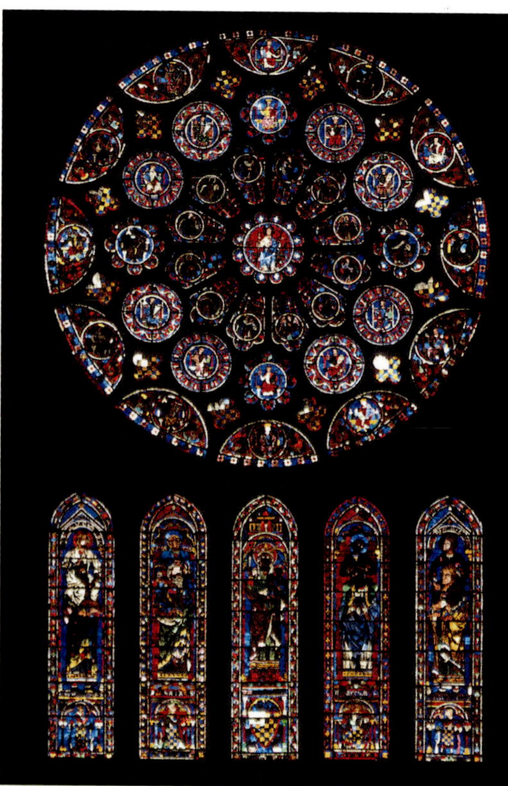

Holy Spirit, as well as by prophets and kings from the Old Testament. However, the ornamental layout of this rose window is slightly changed; for example, extra little windows have been added between the rose and the lancet windows. All in all, the artists working at Chartres Cathedral adopted the medieval theory of beauty by displaying variation and uniformity – superficially contradictory elements – as a harmonious entity.

Northern window,
1220–1230,
glass painting,
Notre-Dame Cathedral, Chartres

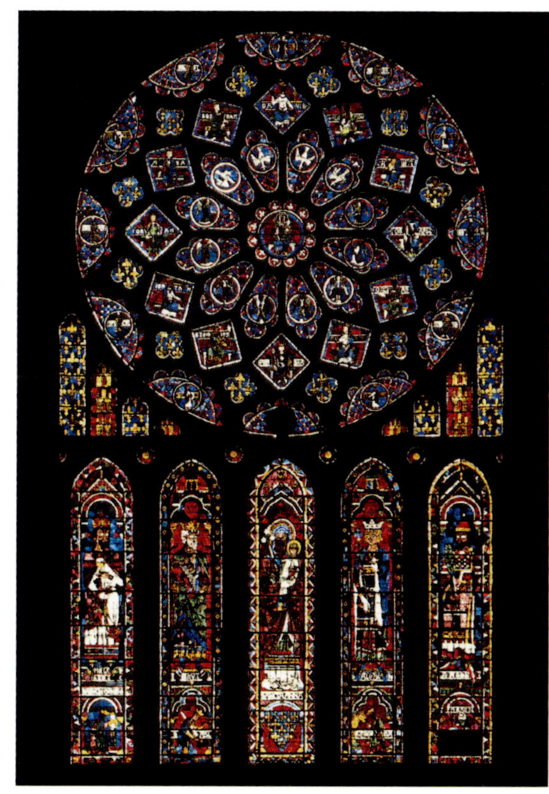

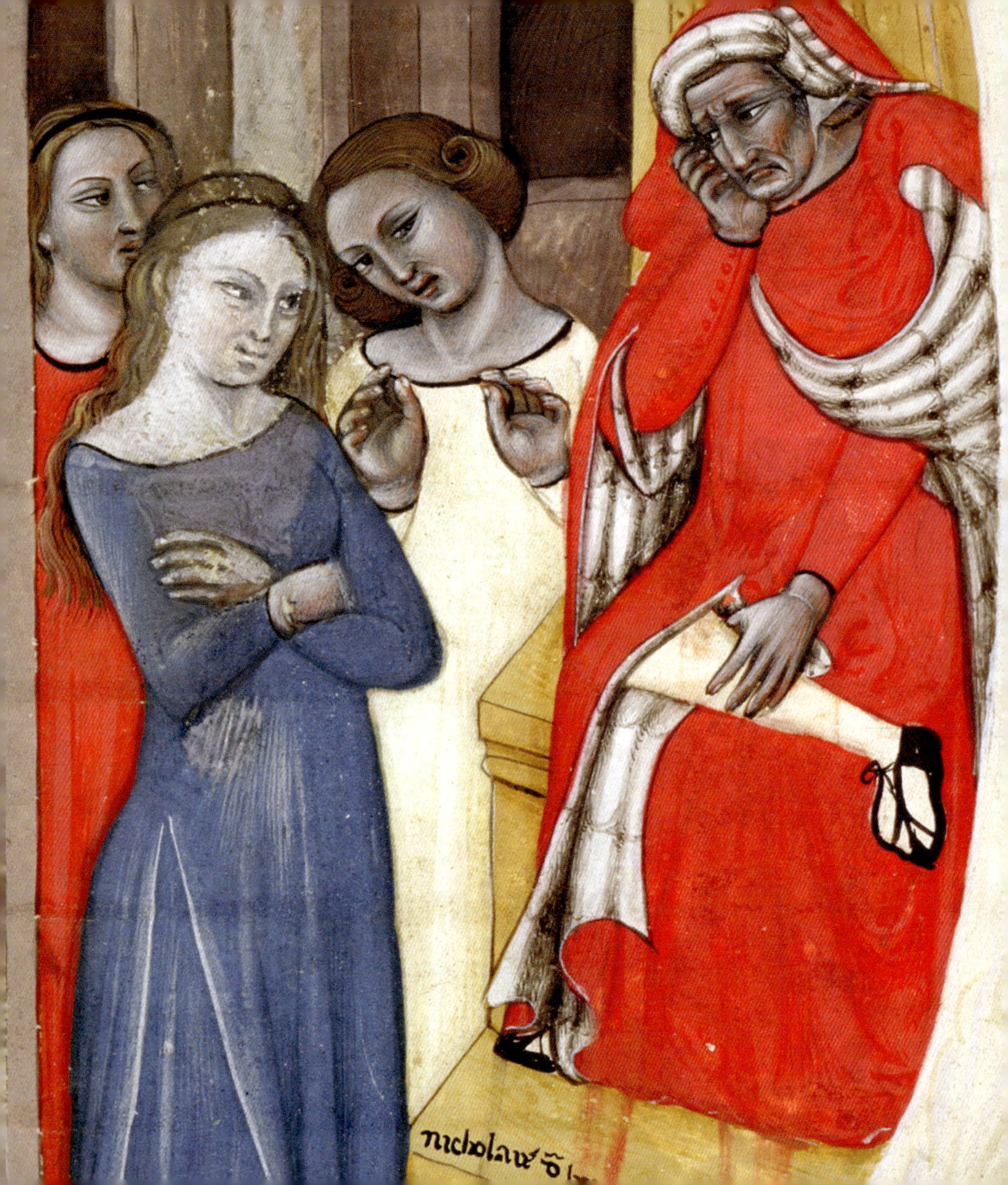
nicholaus

Manuscript Illumination

Whereas a modern-day beholder will immediately appreciate the uniqueness of works of art such as panel or glass paintings, our perception of books has changed fundamentally since the invention of the letterpress in the 15th century. In order to fully appreciate Gothic manuscript illuminations, we first of all need to be aware of the originality of every single work. Indeed, we know that manuscript illuminations featured many more variations than other art forms. From the very outset, books had always been collectors' items. Sheltered from light by the book covers, the only enemies of the paintings and letters are mould and fire. If we consider the wide range of surviving works from religious Psalter to secular songbook, we are led to presume that probably many more secular panel paintings were produced than we now know of. But it might simply be that illuminations covered a different spectrum of commissions. After all, it is a medium in its own right, with a much more private and personal approach than monumental panel painting. In most cases, we do not know the names of the artists. Though some documents have survived listing names, these do not suffice to envisage an individual artistic personality. Initially, all books were copied in the monastery scriptoriums, but since the 13th century texts and copies were also produced at universities. Furthermore, noblemen began to commission luxurious Bible editions and prayer books. This situation prepared the field for the invention and huge success of the let-

Niccolò di Giacomo da Bologna,
initial letter with a representation of St Nicholas (detail opposite: the worrying father), *c.* 1395,
manuscript illumination,
Fitzwilliam Museum, Cambridge

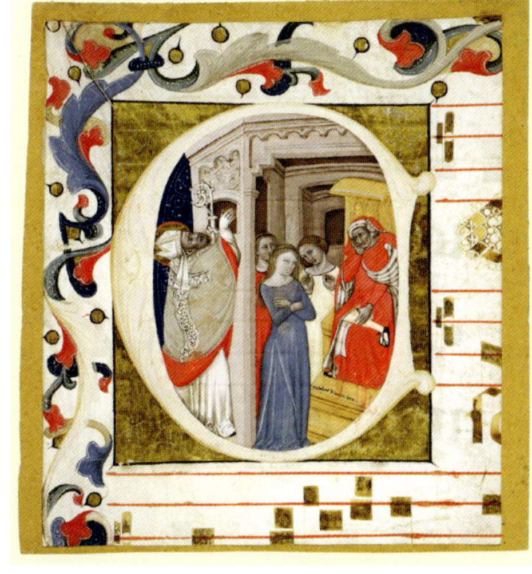

Jacquemart de Hesdin,
Adoration of the Magi from *Les Petites Heures du Duc de Berry,* *c.* 1385, manuscript illumination, Bibliothèque nationale, Paris

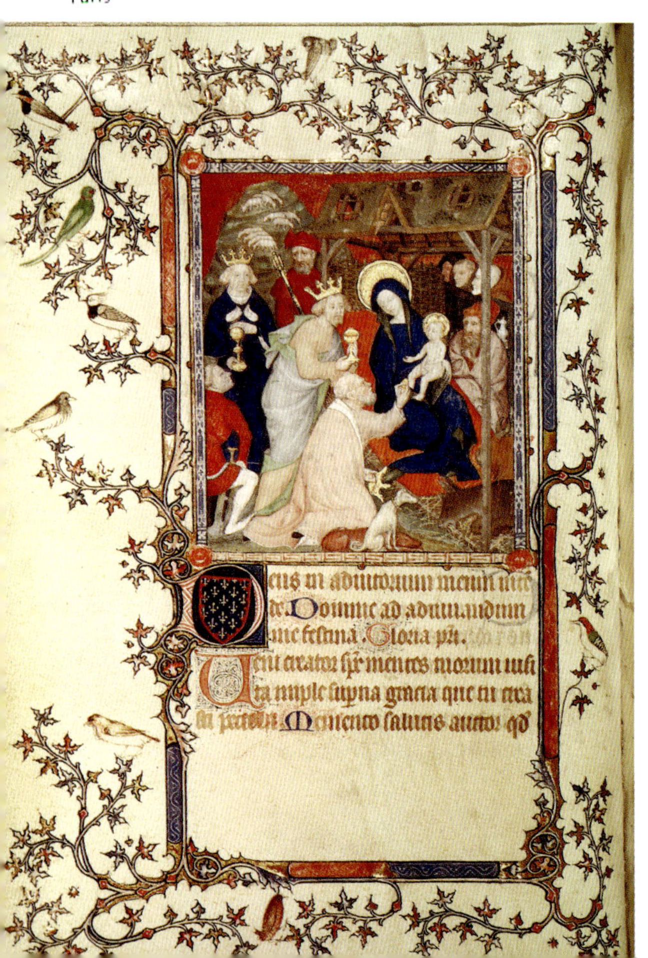

terpress, the commercial, serial production of books. Professional workshops developed where specialists worked on the various aspects of the commissions. From project co-ordinator to apprentice, from painting the main works to designing the initials and creating the framework, every artist had his individual task. In the course of time, the workshops would prepare works or components in advance. A miniature designed for a manuscript did not have to be painted in one location only; spaces were left empty to be then filled in by another artist, who sometimes lived in another region, maybe even another country. We have the example of an edition of Giovanni Boccaccio's *Decamerone,* a copy of which came to France fifty years after Boccaccio had written it in Italy. It was illuminated in France in the early 15th century. Often, miniaturists would travel from one European court to another, settling down and working there for a few years only. Renowned panel painters such as Jean Fouquet (p. 24) and Gentile da Fabriano (see pp. 248, 249) also got involved with manuscript production. This entailed that the style of illuminations evolved in a parallel line to that of panel painting. Here, too, the figures showed more movement and elegant poses and gestures, the artists used light and shade to modulate the bodies, and gave the folds of the draperies an elegant flow. Stained-glass painters and their predilection for red and blue colors had an equal impact on miniaturists. Another characteristic feature of Gothic manuscript illumination is the introduction of architectural elements as a means of structuring the pictorial scenes.

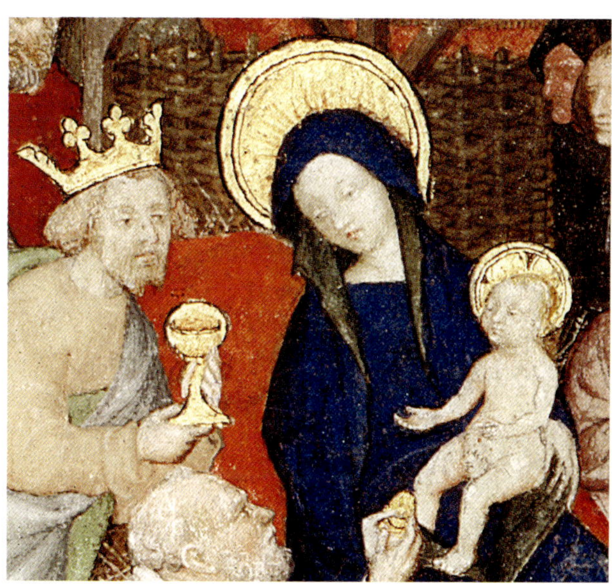

Adoration of the Magi, detail from the manuscript illumination of p. 260

For a comparatively long time, manuscript illuminations in Italy remained in the tradition of the Byzantine style. Only in the mid-14th century did a new style evolve in Milan and Pavia: the illuminations of medieval chivalric novels were heavily indebted to the French style. In Florence, miniaturists were influenced by the style of Giotto and Ambrogio Lorenzetti. Artists in Bologna, which at the time was a very important university city, mostly composed works on the history of law, as well as copying and illustrating works by the classics. **Niccolò di Giacomo da Bologna** (*c.* 1335–*c.* 1403) was the most remarkable artist active in Bologna. On an extremely confined space, this historicizing initial of an anthem (pp. 258, 259) from around 1395 shows the quintessential scene of the story of a 4th-century saint. It tells of the man who, due to his poverty, saw himself constrained to force his daughters into prostitution, as he could not afford a dowry. Luckily, St Nicholas, the Bishop of Myra in

Asia Minor, helped by offering money without asking any services in recompense. He is just stretching out by the window balustrade in order to throw down his bag full of dowry money; below him is the worried-looking family.

The most important centers of Gothic manuscript illumination developed in Central and northern Europe, in England, in the "German Lands," the Netherlands, and most of all in France. Since the late 13th century, Paris had evolved into the center of book illumination. The city's tax registers from around 1300 listed more than a dozen illumination workshops. These worked on commission from the university libraries as well as for members of the aristocracy. Duke Jean de Berry (1340–1416), a younger brother of King Charles V of France, was a great patron of the manuscript artists of the early 15th century. He was an art collector best-known for his commissions of luxurious breviaries. Jean de Berry summoned various illuminators from all over Europe to work in his castles, in Mehun-sur-Yèvre, Bourges and Poitiers. Amongst these was **Jacquemart de Hesdin** (*c.* 1350–*c.* 1410) from Flanders, who worked for the duke from 1384 to 1409. It is he who painted the *Adoration* (pp. 260, 261) from the book of hours, the *Petites Heures du Duc de Berry.* Books of hours derived their name from the fact that they *fe*atured prayers to be read at certain hours of the day. This abundantly illustrated book of hours was created between 1372 and 1390; all in all, five painters were involved in its illustration. De Hesdin here

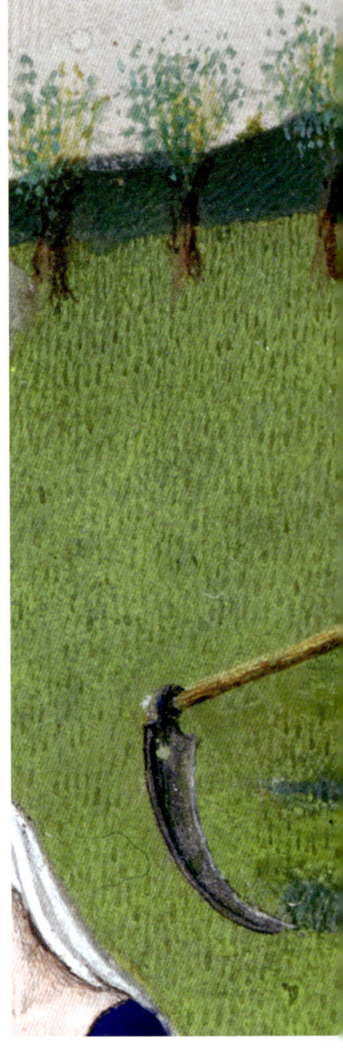

Limbourg brothers,
Reapers,
detail of the month from p. 264

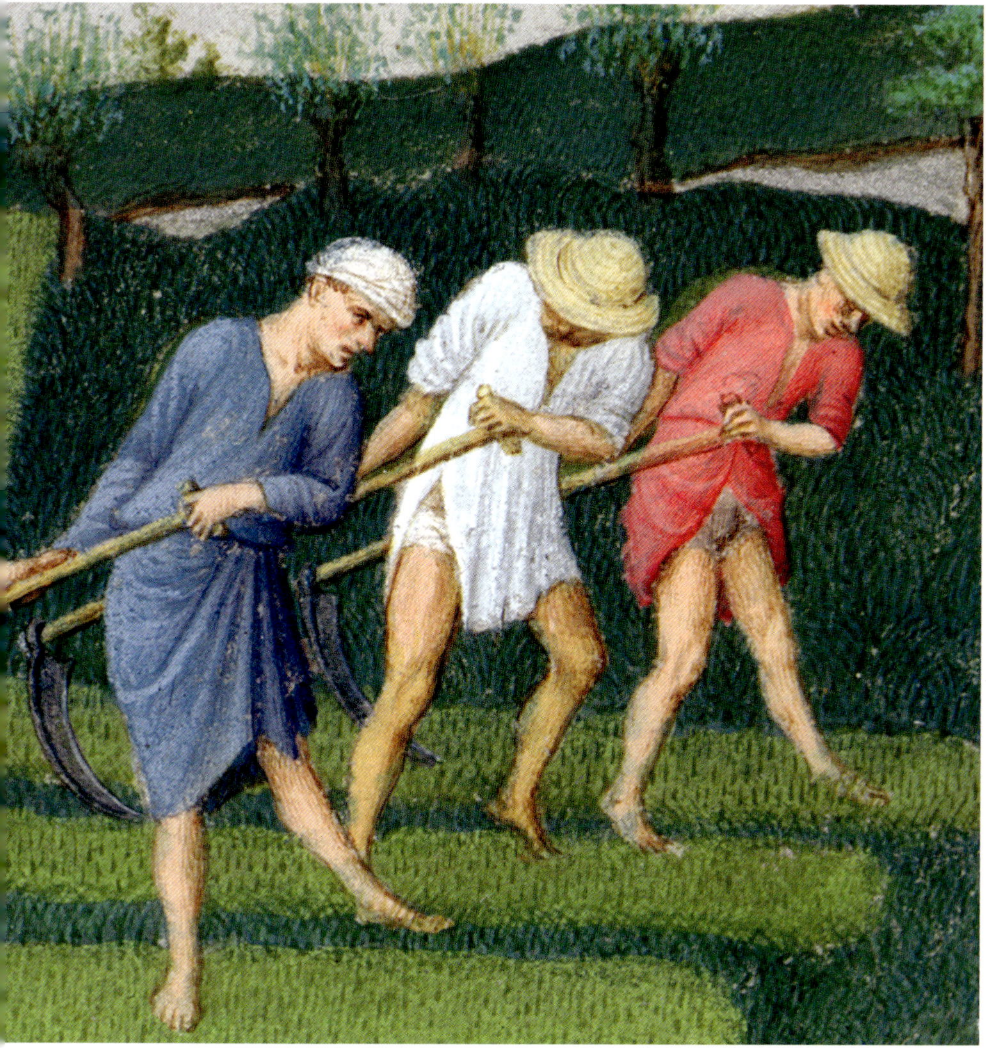

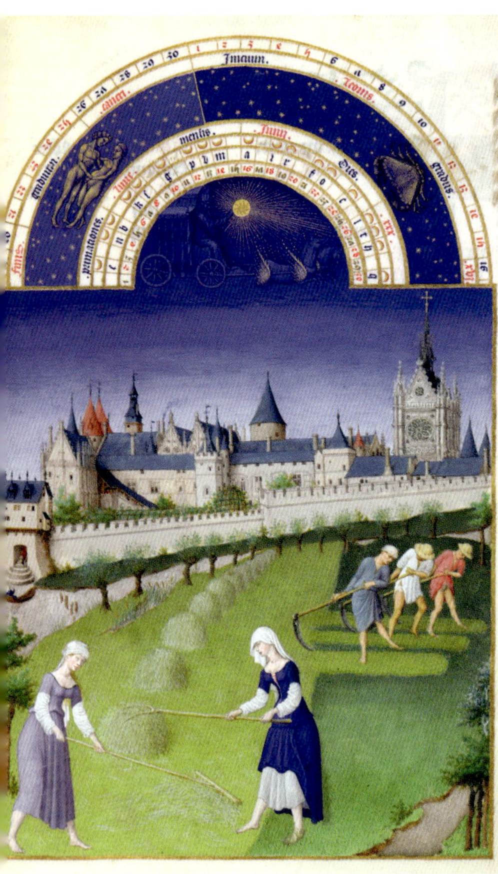

Limbourg brothers,
Month of June, from *Les Très Riches Heures du Duc de Berry,*
c. 1415,
Musée Condé, Chantilly

stands out as one of the foremost painters of the beginning Soft Style. The pictures and texts are decorated by a frame of finely nuanced twigs and foliage populated by songbirds.

The three **Limbourg brothers** also worked for the Duke Jean de Berry. Herman, Paul and Johan (born 1385, 1386/87 and 1388, all of them died 1416) were miniaturists from the Netherlands. They had also been apprenticed as heraldic painters and goldsmiths. They had already traveled widely in Central Europe before being offered a contract by Philip the Bold in February 1402. The Duke of Burgundy – a brother of Jean de Berry and Charles V – gave them a four-year contract and commissioned them to illuminate a Bible for him. But Philip the Bold died in 1404, before completion of the work. So the Limbourg brothers continued to work for Jean de Berry. Their first commission was the completion of a book of hours. The result was so satisfactory that the duke commissioned them with more books of hours. One of these is the famous *Très Belles Heures de Notre-Dame.* The prayer to the angels (pp. 265, 266, 267) illustrates the amazing artistry of the brothers: with their unique approach, text, painting and decoration are combined to create a harmonious overall impression. The principal painting is always placed in the top two thirds of the page. Below, there is some text with an initial letter the length of the entire text block. Underneath the text there is room for yet another figurative representation. The *Très Riches Heures du Duc de Berry,* which was commissioned subsequently, is renowned as the undisputed highlight of the genre, even though the artists could not complete it. In 1416, Duke Jean de Berry as well as the three Limbourg brothers died of the plague. The book changed hands several times and was only completed by other artists in the late 15th century. The picture representing the month of June (pp. 262, 263, 264) from this book of hours shows, in an idealized way, the agricultural chores of that month: reaping and gathering hay. Three farm laborers are reaping the grass while two maids are gathering it and building haystacks. The Limbourg brothers turned the laborious work into a light-footed dance by showing a harmonious unity of movements. The landscape panoramas are simplified and very ornamental; the thoroughly planned color scheme, as exemplified by the three shades of grass, heightens the overall effect. In the background, some buildings of the *Île de la Cité* in Paris can be detected, such as the *Palais de la Cité* (see p. 87) with the Sainte-Chapelle (see pp. 140, 141). In the top semicircle of every calendar sheet, there are astronomic indications – some drawn in advance, some added subsequently – informing about the phases of the moon, and giving the symbols of the respective signs of the zodiac.

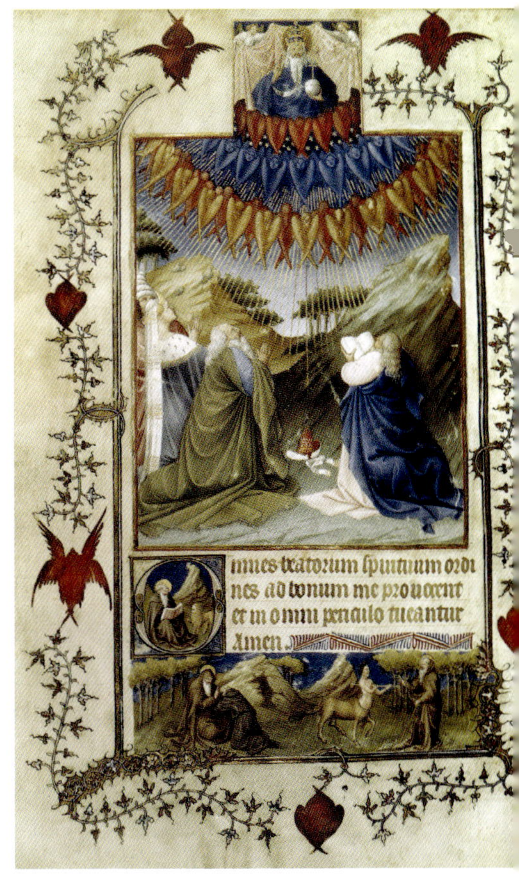

Limbourg brothers,
Prayer to God the Father, from *Les Très Belles Heures de Notre-Dame,* *c.* 1410, manuscript illumination, Bibliothèque nationale, Paris

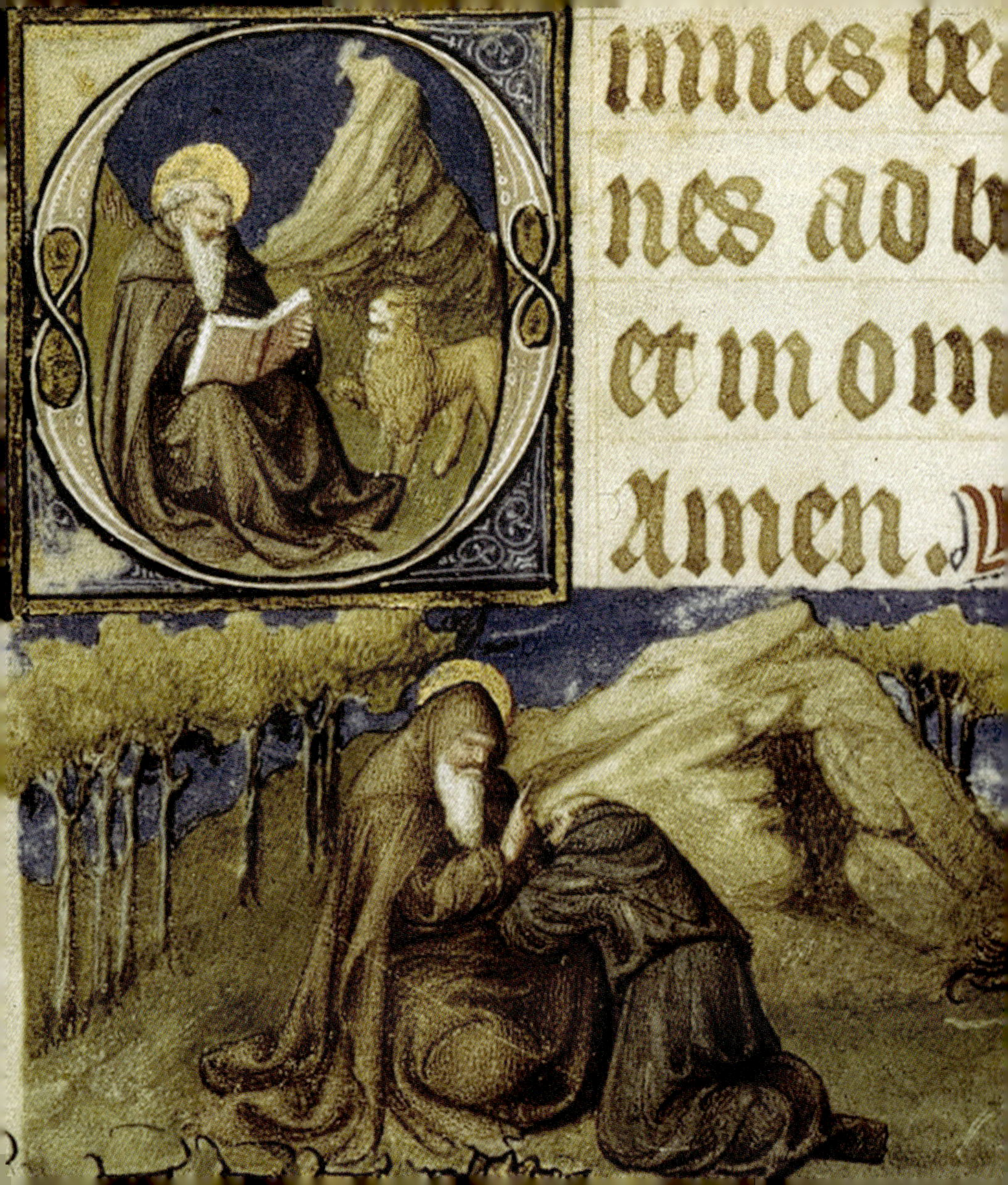
mnes be
nes ad b
et in mon
Amen.

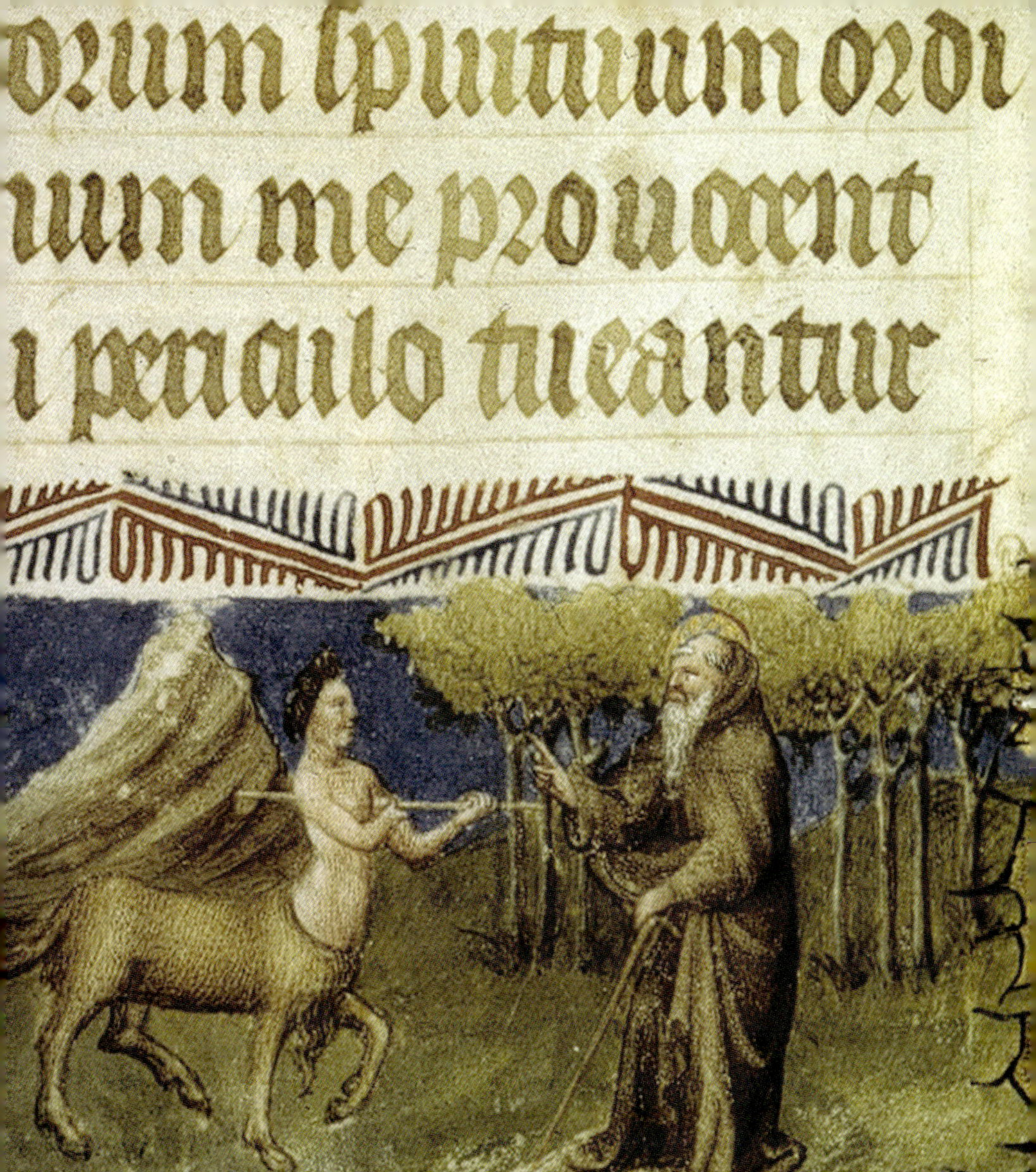

Of Minstrels, Maidens, and Married Ladies – Courtly Love Poetry in the Middle Ages

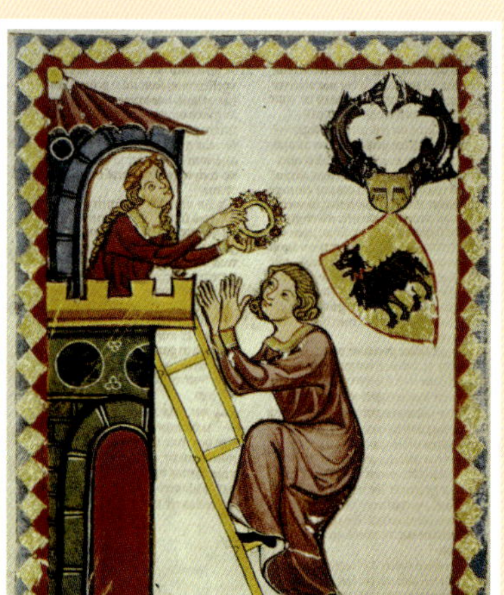

Codex Manesse,
Count Kraft III of Toggenburg, 1315–1340, manuscript illumination, university library, Heidelberg

"Mir ist von ir geschehen, / daz ich disen sumer allen meiden muoz / vaste under diu ougen sehen. / Lîhte wirt mir eine, sô ist mir sorgen buoz." – "Through her it happened to me / that this summer I have to look deep into the eyes / of every maiden. / Maybe one will hear me, / then I will be relieved of my troubles." It took German poet Walther von der Vogelweide (*c.* 1170–*c.* 1230) a mere four lines to turn an unhappy love affair around and convert it into a charming love offer for the remaining ladies. The songs and verses composed by medieval minstrels could be anything from heartbreaking to facetious, and from thoughtful to ambiguously direct. What was the aim of minstrels? In their verses, they make us believe that all they wish to attain is their chosen lady's attention, a smile or a wreath. The *Codex Manesse,* an illuminated manuscript from between 1315 and 1340, shows us the poet **Count Kraft III of Toggenburg** standing on a ladder. Above, from her chamber's window, the lady to whom he dedicates his songs is passing him a wreath. On the right-hand side is the count's coat of arms. The *Codex Manesse* is an outstanding collection, a kind of medieval songbook, presenting the works of a total of 140 poets. It is today kept in the university library of Heidelberg and was presumably commissioned by the Swiss Manesse family of Zurich; hence the name.

Walther von der Vogelweide is also included in the manuscript. He was born in around 1170 and from 1190 on served several dukes, earls and kings. In around 1220 he was given a fiefdom by Emperor Frederick II. From now on, he was a freeman and finally able to settle down. He expresses his gratitude in the following verses: "Ich hân mîn lêhen, al die werlt! Ich hân mîn lêhen, / nû enfürhte ich niht den hornunc an die zêhen" ("I have my fiefdom, all the world! I have my fiefdom, now I need not fear a February's bitter cold") Walther was an exceedingly prolific poet; approximately eighty songs and 100 proverbs of his have survived: courtly love songs, derisory chants, religious poems and self-reflexive works. The stylized portrait of him in the *Codex Manesse* shows him sitting down in a position which he also describes in one of his songs: legs crossed, he is sitting on a stone, his left hand supporting his head. Many an article has been written about this posture. It was deemed to be an expression of a melancholy state of mind; melancholia being understood in medical terms as a metabolic disease which nowadays can be treated but in the olden days was accepted as a "sacred sickness" typically afflicting artists. Another interpretation follows the topic of the poem in which he describes the very position, the first three stanzas of which treat general questions about an ideal lifestyle. The determining values of the time, honor, property and faith, are confronted with the political situation. In other words, Walther's point of view is that of a visionary or judge. There are plenty of picto-

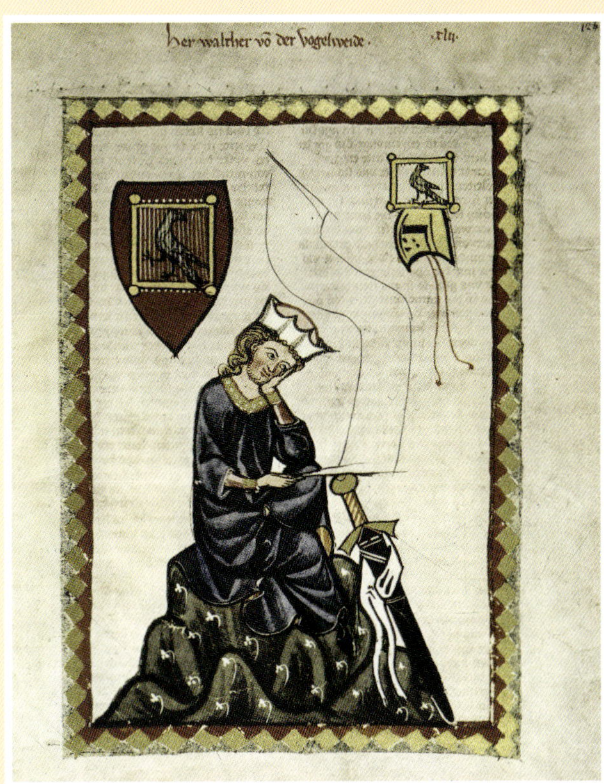

Codex Manesse,
Walther von der Vogelweide, 1315–1340, manuscript illumination, university library, Heidelberg

The Gotha Lovers show their deep love for one another. We should not commit the mistake of setting more store by the ambiguous text than by the picture.

rial elements that support both the interpretation suggesting melancholia as well as the one about the visionary and judge.

The visible tokens of affection introduced by the minstrels, such as a wreath of flowers or a rose, kept their validity for a very long time. One example is a painting from around 1480, documenting a betrothal: the so-called **Gotha Lovers.** The picture shows a young girl fastening a golden ribbon on a young man's scarf – a common feature of courtly love habits. Neither the painter nor the two protagonists are known. Art historians refer to the painter as the *Master of the Housebook*. He might be Erhard Reuwich, a painter from Utrecht in the Netherlands, who was active in Mainz and the Middle Rhine region from 1486 to 1500. The name *Master of the Housebook* derives from a remaining house book done for the aristocratic Waldburg-Wolfegg family. But in which context are the traditions of courtly love shown in the painting of the Gotha Lovers? There is an inscription, written on two banderoles. The girl's banderole reads: "Sye hat uch nyt gantz veracht, dye uch das schnürlin hat gemacht." ("She who made this ribbon for you does not think too meanly of you.") And the youth's banderole reads: "Unjustly she did it, while I let her enjoy it." The meaning of this dialogue remains doubtful. The modest declaration of love voiced by the maiden is less hard to understand, she gives him a golden ribbon as a token of her affection. But the young man's riposte is a riddle, as it seems to be containing some kind of patronizingly formulated reproach. Some historians have suggested that theirs might have been an unequal relationship, a marriage between two different social classes. But who would commission a magnificent panel painting over one meter high with the portrait of the lovers, only to embarrass the lady on it? This would only be a satisfactory explanation if the social differences were extremely high, as an official document of affection for the woman, so to speak. This is why it has been suggested that the painting could be a present commissioned by Phillip I of Hanau-Münzenberg (1449–1500) for his lower-class lover Margarete Weisskirchner – maybe he was planning one of his extended voyages and wished to leave this painting as a warranty for his lady love, who remained at home? An argument that speaks against this thesis is the fact that Margarete is not mentioned in Phillip's last will. It may be that we do not understand the quotes of the unknown couple properly because they relate to certain facts or rituals that have not survived. Maybe there is just as much between the lines of what he says. It could, for example, be merely flirtatious and mean: "She gave me this ribbon, though it was an unnecessary present, and I let her enjoy giving it to me." Finally, if we take a closer look at the painting and ignore the written words, what we see is profound affection on both sides. And we should know by now that the clear message in a painting is doubtless to be preferred to an ambiguous text.

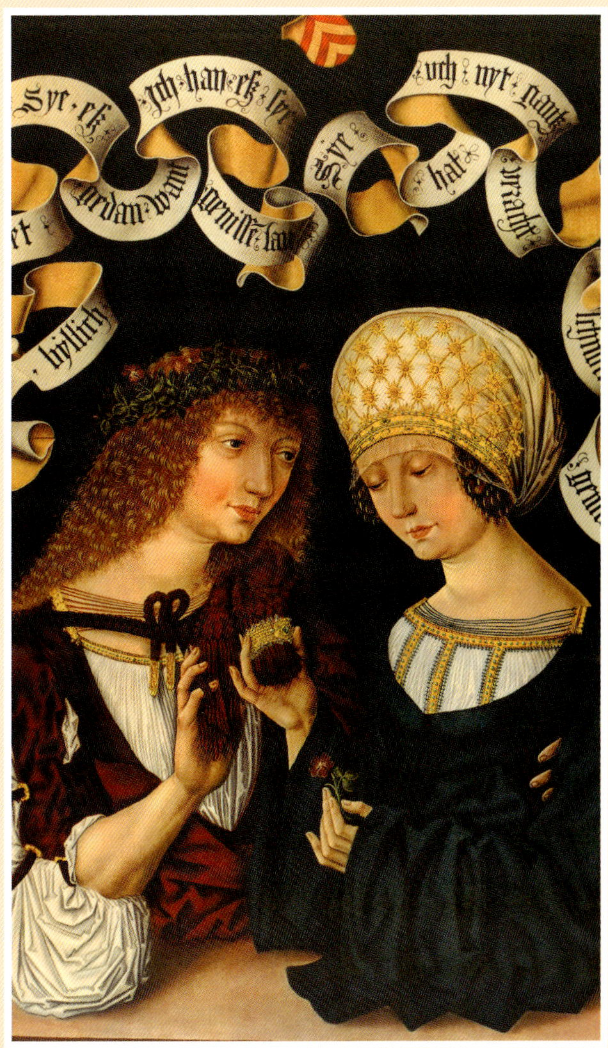

Master of the Housebook,
Gotha Lovers,
c. 1480, oil on lime wood,
114 × 80 cm,
palace museum, Gotha

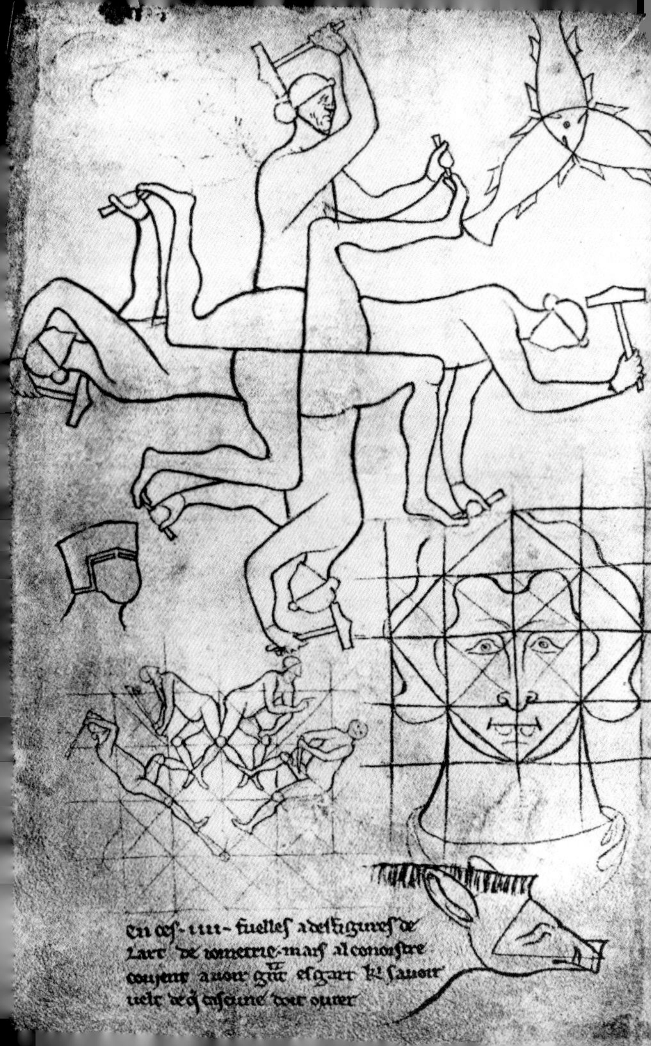
En ces ·iiii· fuelles a des figures de
lart de iometrie · mais al conoistre
covient avoir grant esgart ki savoir
velt de qoi cascune doit ovrer

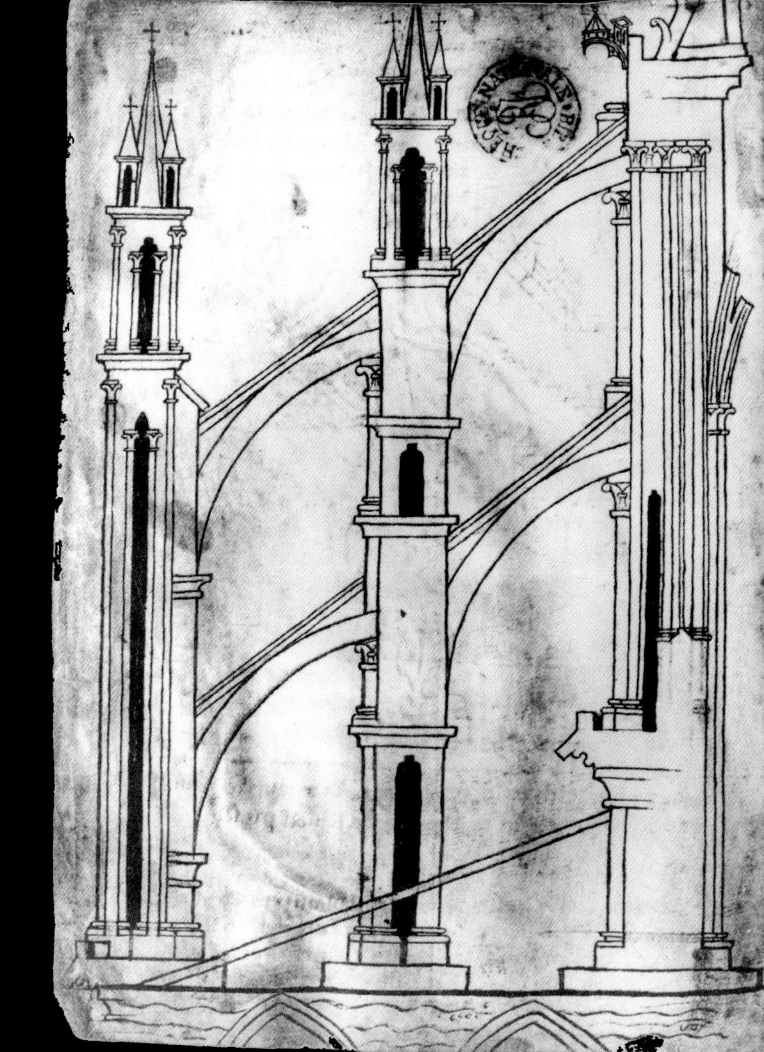

Glossary

Abbey church: see Collegiate Church.

Apocalypse: The end of the world as described by John the Evangelist in the New Testament. Christ returns to earth to judge over good and evil, separating the blessed from the damned.

Apocryphal Gospels: Texts written about Jesus Christ and the lives of the saints that are not included in the New Testament.

Apse: Semicircular or polygonal space placed at the eastern end of a church, behind the choir.

Arcade: Arch supported by a shaft or column.

Archivolt: A moulding, often staggered, in a round or pointed arch. In Gothic portals, it is often decorated with figural ornamentation.

Baldachin: A canopy sheltering an important person or sacred object or place; inspired by the tent-like canopies from the Arabian world.

Baptistery: Chapel for christenings, usually a separate building.

Basilica: A colonnaded hall where the nave vault is higher than that of the aisles. This structure originated in Roman architecture and was adapted for church buildings.

Beautiful Madonna: A specific style of representing the Virgin Mary, which coincides with the periods of the Soft Style and International Gothic, in around 1400. It refers to the especially soft, dainty representation of the Mother and Christ Child.

Campanile: The bell-tower of Italian churches, often detached from the main building.

Capital: Separate element crowning a column or pillar and leading on to the vaulting.

Chapter: Assembly of the clergy of a collegiate church, or of a cathedral.

Choir: The part of a church between the nave and the altar, formerly reserved for the clergy.

Clerestory: A row of windows in the upper part of the nave wall.

Clergy: Generic term referring to the body of all people ordained in the Christian Church.

Cloisters: A covered walk or arcade in the inner courtyard of a church or monastery.

Collegiate church: Church of a Christian community that is not administered by a bishop. Often, these were monastic communities supported by donations.

Crest: Late Gothic altar crowning made of extremely filigree and abundant tracery elements.

Crocket: A Gothic architectural ornament in the form of an unfurling leaf; crowning gables, finials and other structural elements.

Crossing tower: A church tower erected directly above the crossing, the part where nave and transepts intersect.

Crossing: The part of the church where nave and transepts intersect.

Crucifix: Modeled or painted depiction showing Christ on the Cross.

Crypt: Underground vault of a church, often used as burial place and for church services.

Diocese: Administrative unit of the church administered by a bishop, also referred to as bishopric.

Diptych: Originally, this was a writing board made of two wood panels and coated with wax. In the Middle Ages, devotional and panel paintings consisting of two wings.

Duecento: Italian term for the 13th century. From the 13th century on, Italian centuries are termed after the second cipher of a century.

Dwarf Gallery: Low arcade just underneath the roof, usually found on the exterior of the apse.

Early English: Early form of English Gothic architecture from the late twelfth to the second half of 13th centuries. In contrast to French Early Gothic, where the cathedrals were seamlessly integrated into the urban context, English churches introduced the Cathedral Close, a free space surrounding the cathedral.

Embossing: Ornamental technique for metal works. Decorations are chased, stamped or carved into the metal.

Encrustation: Decorative element in low relief made of colored stones or wood chips.

Finial: An ornament of crosswise applied flower buds crowning architectural elements such as pinnacles or gables.

Flamboyant Style: (French "flamboyer," to flame) In window tracery, a flame-shaped, flowing ornament typical of French Late Gothic.

Gallery: Architectural component of the High Gothic period; upper storey over the aisle, open to the interior space, used as a corridor.

Gothic Gable: Gable-formed architectural element mounted as decoration above the portals and windows of Gothic cathedrals and often ornamented with crockets and finials.

Gothic Revival: 18th- and 19th-century adoptions of Gothic art placed in a new, modern context of architecture and painting.

Hall church: Building type that differs from the basilica in that nave and aisles have the same height.

Heresy: A variant of the Christian creed deviating from the official doctrine; heretics were persecuted.

Icon painting: Depictions of saints in Byzantine art which follow a strict scheme. The painting is understood as a likeness of the saint/cult object and as such is equally an object of veneration. Icons are still commonly seen in orthodox churches.

Illumination: Illustrated manuscript including the design of the written words and the ornamental features.

Imitatio Christi: (Latin) Imitation of the way of life practiced by Christ.

Inquisition: Church tribunal to control the true faith. Especially in the 13th to 15th centuries, the prosecutions led by the Inquisition were much feared and often led to the death of the alleged heretics.

International Gothic: Art style of around 1400 which appeared simultaneously in various regions throughout Europe.

Lancet window: A slender, pointed window typical of Gothic architecture. The form is reminiscent of the blade of a sword.

Layman: Non-ordained member of the Christian Church, thus not member of the clergy.

Loggia: Hall or protruding balcony, often supported by arcades.

Maestà: (Italian) Depiction of the Virgin and Child Enthroned.

Manueline style: Typical, richly decorated style of Late Gothic architecture in Portugal.

Martyr: A person who is tortured or killed because of his religious belief.

Miniature: Designation for the paintings in illustrated manuscripts.

Mudéjar style: Decorative style influenced by Moorish architecture; predominant in Spain from the 13th to the 16th centuries.

Nave: Usually the main space in a church running from west to east, sometimes including aisles which are separated from the main body with columns or piers. A basilica consists of a higher nave and lower aisles at each side.

Nimbus: Halo.

Order: The community of a monastery, nunnery or abbey living by the rules and regulations set down by the founder of the order.

Panel: Rectangular piece of wood, painted for use as decoration.

Passion: The suffering and death of Jesus, from his seizure to Crucifixion.

Patron Saint: A saint to whom a given church is dedicated, whose patron he or she thus becomes.

Perpendicular Style: Typical feature of the English Late Gothic with a strong emphasis on verticality, sporting mullioned windows and fan-shaped vaults.

Pier: A free-standing column supporting a vault.

Pilaster: A pier with capital and base, built into or applied onto a wall, and slightly projecting from it.

Pinnacle: Slender, turret-shaped ornament mounted on the exterior of Gothic buildings, for example to crown flying buttresses.

Plateresque Style: Spanish architectural style of the 16th century typically with exuberant ornamentation.

Predella: The lower part or plinth of a Gothic altar shrine or altar panel.

Presbytery: The part of the church reserved for the clergy, where the high altar stands.

Quatrefoil: Architectural decoration, part of the Gothic tracery consisting of four lobes that is used for ornamentation of windows and walls.

Quattrocento: Italian term referring to the 15th century (see Duecento).

Relic: The bodily remains of saints, or objects touched by the saints or in some way closely related to them, venerated by the believers.

Retable: Carved or painted panel situated behind or on the altar, depicting saints or showing scenes from the life of Christ.

Ribs: Supporting element of Gothic architecture. Ribs protrude from the capitals and spread, for example to form cross vaults, fan or stellar vaults.

Rood screen: Altar screen running across the chancel arch to separate the choir and nave areas during mass; often abundantly decorated with sculptures.

Rose window: Large, circular window, decorated with tracery and stained glass, usually on the western facade or transept fronts of a Gothic church.

Sarcophagus: A stone coffin, often richly decorated.

Shaft: Architectural support of the Gothic period, often in the form of clustered columns (attached shafts), passing through the various stories of the building to support the vaults.

Shrine: Receptacle to store various holy objects such as relics.

Soft Style: Movement in the Gothic art of the late 14th and early 15th centuries, characterized by the flowing folds of the draperies and the soft, elegant lines.

Stigmata: The wound marks left on Christ's hands and feet by the Crucifixion.

Stole: Part of a priest's vestment: a scarf or shawl covering both shoulders.

Thrust: The weight of the vault produced an outward thrust on the supporting walls and could be managed by various engineering techniques such as flying buttresses.

Tondo: Circular painting or relief sculpture, often with figurative decoration.

Tracery: Ornamental stonework element of Gothic windows and walls. The various tracery components consist of harmoniously aligned geometric proportions. Trefoil and quatrefoil are typical examples of tracery patterns.

Transept: The part of the church building that runs from south to north and intersects with the nave at the crosssing. When the transept extends beyond the sides of the nave, a cross-shaped ground plan is the result.

Trecento: Italian denomination referring to the 14th century (see Duecento).

Trefoil: Architectural ornamentation consisting of three lobes, often part of the window tracery or used to decorate solid walls.

Triforium: A narrow corridor between the arcade of the nave and the clerestory in the interior of a Gothic cathedral. Later, this developed into a purely ornamental component.

Triptych: Painting consisting of a main central panel and two side wings. The wings are often hinged, so that the triptych can be folded.

Tympanum: The circular or triangular area situated between the entrance of a building front and the upper end, such as a roof or gable. In Gothic architecture, the tympanum is often a semicircular arch above the horizontal bar of a lintel, decorated with figural sculptures.

Veduta: A detailed and topographically correct painting or drawing of a landscape or town.

Vulgate: Latin translation of the Bible, prepared mainly by Church Father St Jerome in the 4th century.

Further Reading

A

Gerd Althoff et al. (ed.), Menschen im Schatten der Kathedrale, Darmstadt (1998)

Mary Apelt, English-German Dictionary: Art History – Archaeology, Berlin 1987.

Rosario Assunto, Die Theorie des Schönen im Mittelalter, Cologne (1963)

B

Armand Baeriswyl, Stadt, Vorstadt und Stadterweiterung im Mittelalter, Basel (2003)

Herbert Beck (ed.), Kunst um 1400 am Mittelrhein, Frankfurt am Main (1976)

Thomas Bein, Walther von der Vogelweide, Stuttgart (1997)

Luciano Bellosi (ed.), Simone Martini. Atti del Convegno 1985, Florence (1988)

Hans Belting et al. (ed.), Malerei und Stadtkultur in der Dantezeit, Munich 1989

Luciano Berti et al., Die Uffizien Florenz (Museen der Welt), Munich (1993)

Jan Bialostocki, Spätmittelalter und beginnende Neuzeit (Propyläen Kunstgeschichte), Berlin (1990)

Günther Binding, Was ist Gotik? Eine Analyse der gotischen Kirchen in Frankreich, England und Deutschland 1140–1350, Darmstadt (2000)

Günther Binding, Als die Kathedralen in den Himmel wuchsen, Darmstadt (2006)

Giovanni di Boccaccio, Das Leben Dantes, Frankfurt am Main (1987)

Albert Boeckler, Deutsche Buchmalerei der Gotik, Königstein im Taunus (1959)

Walter Bombe, Stephan Lochner, Berlin (1937)

Till-Holger Borchert (ed.), Jan van Eyck und seine Zeit, Stuttgart (2002)

Barbara Borngässer et al. (ed.), Grabkunst und Sepulkralkultur in Spanien und Portugal, Madrid (2006)

Alaxandra Buchanan, Gothic Glories, Norwich 2005.

Martin Büchsel, Die Skulptur des Querhauses der Kathedrale von Chartres, Berlin (1995)

Martin Büchsel, Die Geburt der Gotik. Abt Sugers Konzept für die Abteikirche Saint-Denis, Freiburg (1997)

C

Liana Castelfranchi Vegas, Die Kunst des Mittelalters, Solothurn und Düsseldorf (1995)

Enrico Castelnuovo, Ambrogio Lorenzetti. Il buon Governo, Milan (1995)

Lucie Chamson, Nicolas Froment et l'école avignonaise au XVe siècle, Paris (1931)

Julien Chapuis, Tilman Riemenschneider, New Haven/London (1999)

Albert Châtellet, Robert Campin. Le Maître de Flémalle, Antwerp (1996)

Giulietta Chelazzi Dini, Sienesische Malerei, Cologne (1997)

Dario Cimorelli (ed.), Duccio. Siena fra tradizione bizantina e mondo gotico, Siena (2003)

Karl Heinz Clasen, Der Meister der Schönen Madonnen, Berlin (1973)

Trewin Copplestone, The Macmillan Art Informer, London 1983.

D

Dante Alighieri, The Divine Comedy (translated by Melville B. Anderson), London (1921)

Heinrich Decker, Gotik in Italien, Vienna (1964)

Odile Delenda, Rogier van der Weyden, Stuttgart and Zurich (1988)

Patrick Demouy, Reims – Die Kathedrale, Regensburg (2001)

Deutsche Stiftung für Denkmalschutz (ed.), Die Hanse. Macht des Handels (Wege zur Backsteingotik Bd. 1), Bonn (2002)

Deutsche Stiftung für Denkmalschutz (ed.), Die Sprache der Steine. Schmuckformen der Backsteingotik (Wege zur Backsteingotik Bd. 3), Bonn (2002)

Elisabeth Dhanens, Hubertus und Jan van Eyck, Königstein im Taunus (1980)

Margarete Dieck, Die Spanische Kapelle in Florenz, Frankfurt am Main (1997)

Alexander Dorner, Meister Bertram von Minden, Berlin (n. y.)

Georges Duby, Die Zeit der Kathedralen. Kunst und Gesellschaft 980–1420, Frankfurt am Main (1980)

Rob Dückers, Pieter Roelofs, Die Brüder van Limburg, Stuttgart (2005)

E

Johann Konrad Eberlein, Christine Jakobi-Mirwald, Grundlagen der mittelalterlichen Kunst, Berlin (1996)

Andrea Emiliani (ed.), Capire l'Italia: I Musei, Milan (1980)

Alain Erlande-Brandenburg, Gotische Kunst, Freiburg (1984)

F

Uta Feldges-Henning, Werkstatt und Nachfolge des Konrad Witz, Basel (1968)

Johanna Flemming, Dom und Domschatz zu Halberstadt, Vienna/Cologne (1974)

Francesca Flores d'Arcais, Giotto, Munich (1995)

Bernd Fuhrmann, Die Stadt im Mittelalter, Stuttgart (2006)

G

Erich H. Gombrich, The Story of Art, London 1995 (1950).

Dillian Gordon, Making and Meaning: The Wilton Diptych, London (1993)

Dillian Gordon et al., The regal image of Richard II. and the Wilton Diptych, n. p. (1997)

Louis Grodecki, Architektur der Gotik, Stuttgart (1976)

H

Hans R. Hahnloser, Villard de Honnecourt, Graz (1972)

Ronald Halfen, Chartres, Stuttgart and Berlin (2007)

Leonhard Helten, Mittelalterliches Maßwerk. Entstehung – Syntax – Topologie, Berlin (2006)

Volker Herzner, Jan van Eyck und der Genter Altar, Worms (1995)
Daniel Hess, Das Gothaer Liebespaar, Frankfurt am Main (1996)
Theodor Hetzer, Giotto. Grundlegung der neuzeitlichen Kunst, Mittenwald (1981)
Erwin Hintze, Der Einfluss der Mystiker auf die ältere Kölner Malerschule, Breslau (1901)

J

Hubert Janitschek, Die Kunstlehre Dante's und Giotto's Kunst, Leipzig (1892)
Werner Jüttner, Ein Beitrag zur Geschichte der Bauhütte und des Bauwesens im Mittelalter, Cologne (1935)

K

Iris Kalden-Rosenfeld, Tilman Riemenschneider, Königstein im Taunus (2001)
Gottfried Kiesow, Wege zur Backsteingotik. Eine Einführung, Bonn (2003)
Dieter Kimpel, Paris. Führer durch die Baugeschichte, Munich (1982)
Dieter Kimpel, Dieter und Robert Suckale, Die gotische Architektur in Frankreich
1130–1270, Munich (1985)
Eberhard König, Das liebentbrannte Herz. Der Wiener Codex und der Maler Barthélemy d'Eyck, Graz (1996)
Hans Koepf, Plastik und Malerei der Gotik (Schwäbische Kunstgeschichte Bd. 3), Konstanz/Stuttgart (1963)
Günter Kowa, Architektur der Englischen Gotik, Cologne (1990)
Bernd Kratz, »Unbyllich hat sye es gedan«. Die Inschrift des »Gothaer-Liebspaar«-Gemäldes, Zeitschrift für Kunstgeschichte 63 (2000), 120ff.
Gert Kreytenberg, Andrea Pisano, Munich (1984)
Brigitte Kurmann-Schwarz, Peter Kurmann, Chartres – Die Kathedrale, Regensburg (2001)

L

Hugo Lange, Chaucer und das Wilton-Diptychon, Nachrichten von der Gesellschaft der Wissenschaften zu Göttingen Fachgruppe 4: Aus der Neueren Philologie und Literaturgeschichte, Berlin (1934), 31ff.
Jean-Michel Leniaud, Françoise Perrot, La Sainte-Chapelle, Paris (2007)
Edward Lucie-Smith, The Thames and Hudson Dictionary of Art Terms, London 1984.
Sven Lüken, Die Verkündigung an Maria im 15. und frühen 16. Jahrhundert, Göttingen (2000)

M

Andrew Martindale, Simon Martini, Oxford (1988)
Mathilde Meg-Koehler, Die Bilder des Konrad Witz und ihre Quellen, Basel (1947)
Wolfgang Müller (ed.), Freiburg im Mittelalter, Bühl (1970)

N

Bernd Nicolai, Gotik (Kunst-Epochen vol. 4), Stuttgart (2007)
Norbert Nussbaum, Deutsche Kirchenbaukunst der Gotik. Entwicklung und Bauformen, Cologne (1985)

O

Uwe A. Oster (ed.), Die großen Kathedralen. Gotische Baukunst in Europa, Darmstadt (2003)

P

Otto Pächt, Van Eyck. Der Begründer der altniederländischen Malerei, Munich (1989)

Erwin Panofsky, Gotische Architektur und Scholastik. Zur Analogie von Kunst, Philosophie und Theologie im Mittelalter, Cologne (1989)

Joachim Poeschke, Wandmalerei der Giottozeit in Italien 1280–1400, Munich (2003)

John Pope-Hennessy, Fra Angelico, n. p. (1974)

R

Roland Recht, Straßburg und sein Münster, Strasbourg (1994)

Stefanie Renner, Die Darstellung der Verkündigung an Maria in der florentinischen Malerei, Bonn (1996)

Karl Richter (ed.), Johann Wolfgang von Goethe, Sämtliche Werke, vol 1.2, Munich (1987)

Helmut Philipp Riedl, Das Maestà-Bild in der Sieneser Malerei des Trecento, Tübingen (1991)

S

Dany Sandron, Amiens – La cathédrale, Paris (2004)

Willibald Sauerländer, Das gotische Figurenportal in Frankreich, Eigendruck, Munich (1953)

Claude Schaefer, Jean Fouquet. An der Schwelle zur Renaissance, Dresden/Basel (1994)

Werner Schäfke, Mittelalterliche Backsteinarchitektur. Von Lübeck bis Marienburg, Cologne (1995)

Georg Schmidt, Konrad Witz, Königstein im Taunus (n. y.)

Manfred Günter Scholz, Walther von der Vogelweide, Stuttgart (1999)

Georg Schwaiger, Mönchtum, Orden, Klöster, Munich (1993)

Helga Sciurie, Friedrich Möbius, Der Naumburger Westchor, Worms (1989)

Otto von Simson, Das Mittelalter II (Propyläen Kunstgeschichte), Berlin (1990)

Geneviève Souchal et al., Die Malerei der Gotik, Gütersloh (1965)

John T. Spike, Fra Angelico, Munich (1997)

Michael Stuhr, Der Krakauer Marienaltar von Veit Stoss, Leipzig (1992)

T

Dagmar R. Täube, Monochrome Gemalte Plastik, Essen (1991)

Johannes Taubert, Farbige Skulpturen, Munich (1978)

Dagmar Thoss, Französische Gotik und Renaissance in Meisterwerken der Buchmalerei, Graz (1978)

Felix Thürlemann, Robert Campin, Munich (2002)

Rolf Toman (ed.), Gotik. Architektur, Skulptur, Malerei, n. p. (2004)

Rolf Toman (ed.), Orden und Klöster. 2000 Jahre christliche Kunst und Kultur, n. p. (2007)

U

Ernst Ullmann, Gotik. Deutsche Baukunst 1200–1520, Leipzig (1994)

Wolfgang Ulrich, Uta von Naumburg, Berlin (1998)

Universität des Saarlandes (ed.), Hartmann Schedels Weltchronik, Saarbrücken (1995)

V

Benoît VanDenBossche, Straßburg – Das Münster, Regensburg (2001)

Egon Verheyen, Der Bamberger Dom, Königstein im Taunus (1962)

August Vezin, Dante, Dülmen (1949)

Carlo Volpe, Pietro Lorenzetti, Milan (1989)

Dirk de Vos, Hans Memling. Das Gesamtwerk, Stuttgart/Zurich (1994)

Dirk de Vos, Rogier van der Weyden. Das Gesamtwerk, Munich (1999)

W

Renate Wagner-Rieger, Die italienische Baukunst zu Beginn der Gotik, 1. Teil Oberitalien, Graz/Cologne (1956)

Ingo F. Walther (ed.), Codex Manesse, Frankfurt am Main (1988)

Horst Wenzel, Frauendienst und Gottesdienst, Berlin (1974)

John White, Duccio. Tuscan art and the medieval workshop, London (1979)

John White, Art and Architecture in Italy 1250–1400, New Haven/London (1993)

Stadt Wien (ed.), Prag um 1400, Vienna (1990)

Z

Frank Günther Zender, Katalog der Altkölner Malerei, Cologne (1990)

Index of Places

Index of Names

Picture Credits

Publisher's Information

Thanks to Melanie Eichhorn for suggestion of and research for the text boxes; to Sigrid Hünewinkel and Irene Klasen for helping on the glossary; and to Felicitas Pohl and Anne Williams for their support in photograph research.

Original title: *Gotik*
ISBN 978-3-8331-4935-1
Project management: Lucas Lüdemann
Authors: Clemens Schmidlin (pp. 6–9; 11; 24–27; 78–81; 111–279), Caroline Eva Gerner (pp. 12–23; 28–77; 82–109)
Editor: Christina Kuhn
Graphics editor: Hubert Hepfinger
Layout: Buchmacher Bär
Cover: Simone Sticker and rincón medien gmbh, köln

Translated by Dr. Lizzie Gilbert
Edited by ce redaktionsbüro für digitales publizieren
Typeset by ce redaktionsbüro für digitales publizieren
Project coordination for the English edition by Kristina Scherer

ISBN 978-3-8331-4936-8

Printed in China

10 9 8 7 6 5 4 3 2 1
X IX VIII VII VI V IV III II I

www.ullmann-publishing.com